RICHARD BURTON

very close up

RICHARD BURTON

very close up

by

JOHN COTTRELL *and*

FERGUS CASHIN

PRENTICE-HALL, INC.
Englewood Cliffs, New Jersey

Richard Burton, Very Close Up by John Cottrell and Fergus Cashin
Copyright © 1971 by John Cottrell and Fergus Cashin
Published in England 1971 by Arthur Barker Limited (*Richard Burton, A Biography*)
First American Edition published by Prentice-Hall, Inc., 1972
Printed in the United States of America

Library of Congress Cataloging in Publication Data
Cottrell, John.
    Richard Burton, very close up.
    First published in London in 1971 under title:
Richard Burton: a biography.
    1. Burton, Richard, 1925–   I. Title.
PN2598.B795C6 1972 791.43′028′0924 [B] 70–38619
ISBN 0-13-780908-5

Acknowledgments

For making this biography possible we are indebted, above all, to Mr. Richard Burton, and then especially to his many relatives, friends and acquaintances who gave up their time for interviews. To all of them, whether their contribution be great or small, our sincere thanks. They know who they are and the ensuing pages will identify them.

Specific thanks are separately due to those whose assistance went beyond single interviews; to Mr. Graham Jenkins for invaluable advice and guidance; to Mrs. Elizabeth Burton and Mr. and Mrs. Archie Howard-Ady for their hospitality; to Professor Nevill Coghill for painstaking correspondence; to Mrs. Hilda Owen, Mrs. Elizabeth Smith, Mrs. Gwynneth Cullin and Mr. Trevor George for personal photographs; to Mr. Charles Hockin and Mr. Colin Nelson for generous help in Taibach.

We are grateful also to Mr. Burton and the *Sunday Times* (London) for permission to reproduce his article, "The Magic of Meredith Jones" (June 17, 1956); to *The Observer* (London) for permission to reproduce lengthy extracts from theater reviews by Mr. Kenneth Tynan; to William Morrow & Co., Inc., for permission to quote from *Scratch an Actor* (1969) by Sheilah Graham.

Contents

I: *Richie Jenkins*   *1*

Pontrhydyfen   *3*
Taibach   *13*
Meredith Jones   *24*
Jenkins the Co-op   *40*
Philip Burton   *47*

II: *Richard Burton*   *65*

The Druid's Rest   *67*
Oxford   *78*
The RAF   *85*
The London Years   *94*
Stratford   *114*
Hollywood   *124*
The Prince of Players   *141*
The Bobby-Soxers' Idol   *158*
"I Need Never Work Again"   *169*
King on Broadway   *178*

III: *Richard and Elizabeth*   *191*

Elizabeth   *193*
Scandal in Rome   *212*
The V.I.P.s   *226*
The Night of the Long Sausages   *240*
The Night of the Iguana   *255*
Hamlet   *263*
Winning Streak   *285*
The Taming of the Shrew   *300*
Boom Time   *314*
The Court Without a Country   *330*
Burton—The Man and the Myth   *345*
Burton the Actor   *364*
St. David's Day   *378*

RICHARD BURTON

very close up

1
Richie Jenkins

Pontrhydyfen

Pontrhydyfen, like the backward spelling of Dylan Thomas's village of Llareggub, really has sweet nothing to commend it. Lying on twin hills bestriding the narrow Afan Valley of South Wales, it is the middle of nowhere with crossroads leading to everywhere—south and west to industrial towns, north and east to remote beauty spots. There is nothing to make the visitor linger, except perhaps a certain vague scenic charm in summer, and even then the great mass of Foel Fynyddau mountain blots out the sun in early evening and forever denies a view over the valley to the sea of Swansea Bay.

In the wet gloom of winter, the scene is a macabre child's drawing of Switzerland, with the Alps black-tipped and desolate and leaking coal-juice into the gutters. Yet it is more attractive than it was. The hills have shed their mourning, and by courtesy of the Forestry Commission have put on a bright new frock of brown and green. Free-wandering sheep, black-bellied like the undersoil, nibble around the hem; otherwise there is no movement on the slopes of fir trees, grass, fern, and gorse. No shunting of coal wagons, no clanking of colliery wheels, no boot-shuffle of helmeted miners with black faces and red cherry lips and eyes like half-sucked gobstoppers. A few miners remain, but for them the coal-face, by bus and subterranean tunnels, is fifteen miles or more away. It is a graveyard of coal, and the birthplace of Richard Burton.

Quiet it is. Nothing is heard except the blue Thomas Brothers bus as in bottom gear it grunts and groans over the brow of a hill, heading for Neath, four miles to the west. A passenger on the bus had said, "You should see a wall plaque on the house where Richard Burton the actor was born. But if it's not there, not to worry, boy, because it's always being whipped. Anyway, you'll see a *For Sale* there, and it will be there forever at the bloody price they're asking. Duw! Three thousand eight hundred! Off their bloody rockers they are. Not worth half the price."

The plaque had indeed been stolen from outside No. 2, Dan-y-bont, a dilapidated, four-bedroomed, semi-detached—the second of two isolated box-houses. The sale sign, like the dwelling, looked tired in its dull paint. A front window was smashed; fencing was flattened to the ground. But as the man on the bus said, "A nice position. A bit of flooding perhaps, but tucked up all comfy like in a sort of dip below Pontrhydyfen proper." Close by, overhead, a high and narrow four-arch bridge that was once an aqueduct connects the two halves of the village. On one side, where the bus had gone, stands the only pub, the Miner's Arms, and beyond it a few tiny shops. On the other is the chapel and the school where Richard never went. In between the Afan River splits the valley, rushing silently by at the foot of the sloping back-garden patch of Dan-y-bont.

Across the road and a little way up the hillside, Mrs. J. E. Jones opens the door to her old stone cottage and says, "Will you have a cuppa tea? Just wet it this moment. Saw you looking at the house. Ooo! You hear the price they're asking?" She chats sweetly, offering Welsh cakes and salty butter. The sitting room is straight off the street and has a grate full of coal and hob with a singing kettle, coconut matting on polished linoleum, and on the sideboard a ticktock clock and oval photographs of Kitchener moustaches and watch chains.

"Now I tell you, Richie used to play on that very mat as a baby. And when his mother would bring him over here she would sit on that very chair. Oh, a lovely woman! A lovely family the Jenkins! That was their name, of course. Oh yes, very happy. And such a handsome woman, the mother. Edith her name. Barmaid in Cwmavon when Richie's father met her. Couldn't have been sixteen. A lot younger than her husband, but a good bit taller. Sweet man, only five foot and a bit was Dic, but full of beans and a terror for his beer. No harm in him, though. Very easy going, you know. Now Mrs. Jenkins was quite different. Happylike, if you follow my meaning, but dignified. Not strict, but kept the children tidy and proper. And she had her share of heartbreaks, believe me. When they first married and lived back there in Station Road—that row of cottages they have pulled down to make way for the flats—she lost two babies and then had another eleven. They moved across there to Dan-y-bont when Richard was born. He was the twelfth and weighed twelve pounds—a real whopper! Then about a year later Mrs. Jenkins couldn't believe she was having another baby. She said to me, sitting right there in that chair, 'God Almighty, another mouth to feed!' That baby, Graham it was, done for her. I think it was club money they buried her on."

As local wits say, the village cemetery beside the stone church on the hilltop is the dead center of Pontrhydyfen. Those who never traveled beyond a rugby match lie buried there under Welsh inscriptions alongside their babies who never burped beyond the bottle. "Also a child, eight months . . . also a child, no age," reads an old man waiting for a stonemason to carve his name. His face is pitted with the blue scars of the mines and he remembers Dic Jenkins and all his friends, now under the ground forever. He has no interest in Richard Burton the filmstar. "Every stone here, boyo, tells the history of this village. Hardship and bloody starvation. There's few buggers here, I'll tell you, who didn't die through coal one way or another. Dug their own graves—everyone."

On the day of winds and showers that Richard Walter Jenkins Jr. was born, no one could reasonably suppose that he would not go the same way. It was a time of blackest despair, a time without future. There was tomorrow, of course—Wednesday, November 11, 1925. Everyone was aware of that date. They were polishing their medals and dusting their banners in readiness, and on that Armistice Day they would do their traditional duty to the dead: put on their Sunday-best for parades and services, fill the valleys with hymns of praise, and at the eleventh hour stand with heads bowed in two minutes of silent homage to the three-quarters of a million fallen in the Great War. But after the Remembrance— what? Only empty bellies and empty lives. They remembered, but who, they asked, remembered them? Eighty-four thousand miners in South Wales unemployed. The coal-owners paying lower wages than before the war, over a decade ago, and it was getting worse. Within half a year, a million miners would be wantonly locked out. They called the ensuing General Strike the most disastrous single labor dispute in British history, but those nine days of national paralysis in May were only a fleabite of discomfort to the mining martyrs of South Wales. Having been offered ludicrously reduced wages for increased working hours, they alone stayed out, proud and defiant for six more months of mass unemployment and near starvation, and in the region that already had the highest mortality rate in all Britain.

Tuberculosis was the great killer of the twenties and thirties, and malnutrition was its powerful ally. When there was work to be had, the miners faced the additional hazards of loathsome industrial disease and underground disasters that set off some pithead alarm almost every day. But the Jenkins of Pontrhydyfen were and are a tough, durable, and resourceful breed, and against all statistical probability, the seven boys born to Dic and Edith between 1901 and 1927 survived. They grew tall like their mother, rugged and strong like their father, and the first five went down the mines like their ancestors before them. Of the six daughters, two died in infancy and another in middle-age. Today, only one of the family still lives in the village—Mrs. Hilda Owen, a mother of four. Near the school, at No. 4 Penhydd Street, she has a dark-bricked house with three windows and a communal slate roof that runs the length of the terrace. Here every house has the same squat chimney pots, every front parlor has its discreet net curtains, and their porch steps, worn down by decades of elbow grease, shine all the way to the churchyard below. The old villagers can never forget the appalling poverty of the twenties and thirties. But Hilda, then in her childhood, looks back on those years only with glowing affection.

"I was eight when Richard was born and I can only remember the happy times—like the summers that always seemed long, and like it was all mountains and seaside, and as though the mines were there but unnoticed. We were poor, but we never thought so because it was just the same for everyone. All my memories of the family are happy, and while we were a lot of children, we were not really all that many. Why, there was a family up the road with twenty-one children, another with eighteen. And we were lucky, because unlike a lot of families, there were no deaths down the mine or children dying. Mind you, I had two sisters none of us remembers, who were only two when they died. Both were named Margaret, and they would have been the oldest.

"What's the family now? Well, starting with Tom, he's the oldest and has one girl. Then there's Ciss (Cecilia) who has two girls, and Ivor who has no children. Will, living in Scotland, has two children. David, now a Police Inspector in Swansea, has got one. Then comes Verdun (named after the World War I battle) with two, and myself with four. I've got the biggest family of the lot. After me there is my sister Katherine in London, with three children, and my youngest sister Edith, who had three children and is now dead. Finally, of course, there is Richard with his daughters Kate and Jessica, and then the very last and youngest, Graham, who has two sons.

"We had nicknames for everybody. For example, Will is 'The Soldier' because he joined the army when there was no work. And Ivor I call 'King Farouk.' He's the boss, and always has been. Ever since my mother died, it's Ivor who kept the rule —even over my father. You see, my father was a bit spoiling us, easy going; it was Ivor who kept the firm hand. 'Daddy Ni'—you pronounce it like your knee—was Christmas every day to all of us.

"When Richard was a baby, Tom and Ciss were away married, so that from our house in Dan-y-bont only my father, Ivor, and Will were down the pit. That left six of us under fourteen. David, Verdun, and I were at school, so my mother had to cope with Richard and two toddlers, Cassie and Edie. Well, it's a village where everybody helps one another, and looking back I can never remember going without—not even during the Big Strike of 1926. If the older ones were not getting enough to eat, they never let on. The house was always happy. In the kitchen we had two tables—one square and one round, both with scrubbed tops.

All the children under fourteen had to go to the round table. Of course, once they were fourteen and started work they went with my mother and father to the square table. At fourteen, you see, you were grown-up.

"My mother was very chapel and a great one for cleanliness and the best of food. Good plain food she liked. But my father was a complete agnostic. He loved his drink. Loved it. He was a loving man. A little man he was, very small, and we idolized him because there was nothing nasty, ever. I can see my mother laughing at his stories now, and Richard in his arms looking nearly as big as Daddy Ni was. He was the baby, but there was something very special about him. Bright as a button and a real little Welshman.

"But, oh, those stories! We loved his stories and believed nearly everything. Rich would listen to him by the hour, and when Daddy Ni had taken a drop his stories were farfetched, to say the least. But I think it was true, what he used to say about my grandfather's death. He told us that grandfather won twenty-six shillings on a horse called Black Sambo and then went to the Miner's Arms to celebrate. Well, the old man was paralyzed in both legs from an accident in the mine and was confined to a wheelchair. Anyway, he got completely paralytic in the pub, and on the way home he let the wheelchair run down the hill and was pretending to be the jockey and shouting, 'Coom on, Black Sambo' when he crashed into a wall and was killed. I believe it, because my father was just as mad. In those days there were terrible fights. Men stripped to the waist on the mountain and hitting each other 'til they bled. It was commonplace. They were terrible for drink and argument."

The Miner's Arms, in a switchback of houses on the road to Neath, is a blast-oven of stove coal, and the nicotine-stained walls are decorated with neatly framed sepia photographs of faded football teams, all alike, row upon row with different dates, but always the same shuffle of fifteen names with initials to distinguish a Davies from a Davies, an Edwards from an Edwards, an Evans from an Evans, a Jenkins from a Jenkins. The regulars are typically Welsh, wearing flat caps buttoned to the brim and white silk mufflers hiding the stud of their flannel shirts without ties. The backs of their hands are mottled with the blue tattoo of coal scars, and their faces puce-veined and gray. They all look like Spencer Tracy without his front teeth. The only way for a stranger to clear the Welsh from the throats of the pub is to drink a pint in one. And then another and another, and talk with loud knowledge of rugby football and such local saints of Cardiff Arms Park as Tommy Mainwaring, and to ask with sly innocence whether it be true that Gerwyn Williams was in the same youth team as Richard Burton.

"Born just down the road was Richard Burton," one ancient miner volunteered. "His father, Dic-bach-y-saer, was always in here. Used to sit over by there near the fire. Wicked little bugger. Full of fun. Isn't that right, Bryn?"

"Aye," said Bryn Davies, who used to drink with Richard's Daddy Ni. "But I don't know why he was called Dic-bach-y-saer. The translation is 'Richard the son of a carpenter.' Of course, we'd give each other nicknames, and come to think of it, I remember Ivor telling me one time that the grandfather was also Dic-bach-y-saer and he was a miner who did the roofing at the coal-face. He'd put in the timber props, you know, when they were cutting the seam. So there's some connection right enough. Now Dic-bach-y-saer's great pal was John Jones. Well, John Jones in Wales is like Pat Murphy in Ireland. So he was called Shoni Cochyn, which means 'Redhead.' Terror those two were."

The pub became loud and friendly, ripe and sulfuric. In the explosion of twelve-pints-a-man detonated by great jars of pickled onions, a gentleman with the Runyonesque name of Hopkin Morgan the Bread exclaimed, "Christ Almighty! They're farting the Hallelujah chorus. You could bottle that, boy, and send it to Richard Burton, and he'd sniff at it and say, 'Miner's Arms, late vintage.' "

"Now let's have a bit of hush," said Bryn. "You were asking about Richard's father. Well, duw! Dic was a real sweet man. No harm in him at all, but a right terror for his booze. Only this size, tiny, couldn't be five-two out of his boots. But drink! Bloody hollow legs. Now in the old days he'd really go on the batter with Shoni. After a match on Saturday they'd be in the Bird in Hand, which is the HQ of the Neath rugger club, and they'd drink their way back to Pontrhydyfen via Swansea by early Sunday, if they weren't thirsty. Beer, shorts, everything. He'd drink like a six-footer and had no fear in him. Wouldn't come up to a real big man's middle shirt button, but he'd pull them down and wag his finger and say, 'Remember, boyo, the bigger you are the harder you fall.' Oh, a lovely man was Dic.

"But if you look around here now you can't imagine what it was like when Richard was born. No pithead baths, you get me, and this place packed with miners soaked to the skin. You see, you'd have to work with the pick on your side in six inches of freezing water, and with only a two-foot clearance above you. All the Jenkins were bloody good face-workers. Dic, Tom, Ivor, Will, and then later, David and Verdun. In fact, Richard who never went down the pit was going to buy a mine for them years ago. That's a fact. Anyway, in those days there were pubs all over the valley. Up here was the Heart of Oak, then the Boar's Head, two others that were a bit of a step, and this place. It was a white-washed pub then—just one toilet, three walls around, you know; couldn't hold two exactly. We'd take it in turns or just piss out the back. The drinking was tremendous and cheap. No ladies. No need was there? Because they wouldn't be seen dead in here. You get me? Significant. There was only two ways of life. You were either going to the chapel or to the pub, and most of the miners went to the pub, and the women understood because miners' work is hell. But the Calvinistic Methodists were very strong here, and exceptionally strict. If a girl were in the pudding club—having a child and not married—she was out. Sent away from the village altogether. Denounced by name in the chapel. That was the accepted thing. No miner would argue. On a Sunday as a boy you couldn't even use a scissors to cut your nails. And the deacons of the church! Duw, boy, you were mortally afraid of them. See them coming! Hide, run away. The men of the ministry are practically actors, and we thought Rich would be one, but he knew better. They had a tremendous influence on the congregation. Tremendous. The Welsh gift of language is a sad gift of God. He inclined us all towards poetry and then buried us in coal.

"Dic-bach-y-saer, like most miners, was an agnostic. All the women, without exception, were chapel, and all the children had to go. Particularly Sunday school. The fathers would kick their little arses out of the house. Older ones as well. Stands to reason if you think. Only time a mother and father could be alone. Look at these houses. Three bedrooms at the most. Always nine children at least.

"When Richard was only a baby there was the General Strike. There were sixty-six collieries in these parts, and twenty-one of them had already been closed because of the Depression and the export of cheap Polish coal. At that time this was the most revolutionary place on earth. You can imagine, with fourteen thousand miners doing bugger all and helpless for their families and not getting enough food and being threatened by the bloody army. We marched to London—two hundred miles on the boot. Remember it like yesterday. I was in Charing Cross Road looking for them. 'They've been this way, boys,' I cried. 'Look at the gob.' The miners' trademark was a trail of gob yellow and black with specks of red. Terrible year. We had soup kitchens here in the village. See a sheep on the mountain? Ten minutes later it's in the fucking pot, head and all. No messing—the children were getting what they could. Some of the lads had a lamb bleating its bloody head off and with the law chasing us. We dived into Mrs. Owen's, and the old grandmother who was sitting by the fire wrapped it in a shawl. Seconds later we were out the back with the coppers chasing us and not bothering about the old lady nursing tomorrow's roast.

"It was only the strong who were surviving then. Read the newspapers of that time, even those of bloody Swansea and Cardiff. All Tory and not a mention of the conditions, really. No communications. Not like now. Take Aberfan and that terrible disaster. In America they saw them burying those miners' kids as it was happening. But in those days there were miners humping their children in little white coffins on their backs. But no photography, no telephones, no television. Not even wireless, which was a crystal set—the cat's whiskers that nobody had. No bugger cared. The coal owners wanted longer hours for less money because the Germans and Poles were flooding the world with cheap coal. The miners' slogan was 'Not a penny off the pay, not a minute on the day.' But in the end we were driven back by starvation. We had to take lower wages and longer hours, which meant there was always unemployment. And this was all during the time that Richard was growing up. But I tell you, man, such is the resilience of the Welsh miner that Richard never knew what it was to go without. He never tasted bread-and-sop."

Outside the Miner's Arms, a single-decker bus waits to take on passengers going two miles south to Cwmavon, the first village of the valley, or on another three miles to the industrial and commercial bustle of the sprawling steel-town of Port Talbot. The first stop is in the hollow of Pontrhydyfen, hard by Dan-y-bont. It was there, in 1928, that a bright-eyed little boy was lifted aboard, and the family waved until the bus disappeared round the giant S-bend sweeping down through the Afan valley. Richard Jenkins, just two years old, was on his way to Taibach, adjoining Port Talbot, to live with sister Cissie and her miner-husband, Elfed James.

"It was a terrible time," recalls Hilda. "It was heartbreaking when my mother had Graham and died. We were all so happy for Richard to have a little brother and then, my God, Mam was dead. I was the eldest girl at home and only ten. It was like a bad dream, the funeral and everything. Graham in a cot and Mam in a coffin. It was a long time before we got over it. Tom took Graham to live with him at Cwmavon and my sister Ciss took Rich to Taibach. Ciss and Tom were marvelous. They took on Richard and Graham as their own children. But you see, Graham was a newly-born baby and grew up to know no other life than with my brother Tom and his wife. In fact, a lot of children in Cwmavon, just down the valley there, thought that Tom was Graham's father. But different it was, see, with Richard. He was already speaking nothing but Welsh, and although Taibach is not too far away, it's too far to walk. And they are English-speaking down there around Port Talbot. He had no English and spoke all Welsh to my sister, while her husband Elfed, although he is a Welshman, always spoke English. So you can imagine how strange it was for Richie. It was like going to a foreign country."

Taibach

Richard Burton, lounging in the luxury of his private yacht in the Bay of Naples, was asked where he would like to be if the world had only thirty minutes to run. Without hesitation he answered, "Up on The Side, with the old miners and tinplate workers, squatting one-kneed around a fire, and telling yarns and peeling the sooty skins off finger-burning baked potatoes. Those men of my childhood are the salt of the earth."

The Side—it has no other name—is just the side of a plum-pudding grass mountain that walls off the fag-end of Port Talbot in an untidy bundle of terraced sidestreets called Taibach. And here, sandwiched between mountain and sea, Richard's childhood memories began, with brother-in-law Elfed carrying him piggy-back over the footbridge of the tiny Dyffryn railway and on up The Side, and through the dwindling tiers of streets to the upper gallery of wooden bungalows called The Constant, so named, they say, because the white walls reminded sailors of Constanti-nople as they rounded Mumbles Head and entered Swansea Bay from the west.

A strange place of strange faces and strange words to a two-year-old who understood nothing in English and only the odd monosyllabic sound when his sister Cissie spoke in Welsh to in-troduce new aunts and uncles and cousins. From the front win-dow he looked out across the rooftops of Taibach to the awesome backdrop of the blast furnaces and rolling mills of the monstrous Margam Steelworks, an inferno belching black clouds by day and lighting the sky at night with grotesque silhouettes of great pecking-birds that were dockyard cranes and the fingers of Gargantua that were chimney stacks. It was too much, and that first week Richard ran away. Auntie Margaret Ann Dummer, who lived next door and is Elfed's sister, remembers them searching The Side and around the old army barracks and in the wasteland of boys' dens at the ends of Inkerman and Balaclava Row, and how her old Uncle Dan found little Richie down on the main Commercial Road, and humped him home on his back.

Later, on weekends, Cissie or one of the brothers would take Richie back on visits to Pontrhydyfen. "Because, you see, he loved the atmosphere," says Hilda. "He liked being with us. We adored him, of course. And Ivor, well, he was devoted to Rich, and still is. He knew baby Graham was all right with the eldest brother Tom, but Richie was that little bit older and more old-fashioned, and he grieved for the village. We loved having him. He would sleep with us girls on weekends and holidays. The boys were all down the mine with my father, so it was natural that Richie would be with us girls most of the time. When he got older he would sleep downstairs on the sofa."

Richard never lost touch with his father and all the brothers and sisters who crowded Dan-y-bont. They were strictly a family unit, and he felt completely at home there. Somehow it was never quite the same in Taibach. He loved Cissie as a mother, and when her first daughter, Marion, was born, he looked upon her as a sister. But he knew that Uncle Elfed was not his real father, and Elfed knew that Richard could never really be his son. It was different in the case of baby Graham; he had been taken into a family where his own brother was the breadwinner. But Elfed was having a hard enough struggle to make ends meet for his own growing family without this added burden. Indeed, there were members of the James family who criticized the Jenkins family for having thrust such a responsibility on a young, meagerly paid miner. Amid this undercurrent of resentment, Richard, with his free and easy disposition, was the one person able to enjoy the best of two poor worlds. While Elfed had the unrewarding task of providing for the boy's basic needs, Dic-bach-y-saer, released from parental obligations, could assume a grandfatherly image and spoil his visiting son with occasional gifts.

It was therefore little wonder that Richard favored the more carefree atmosphere of Pontrhydyfen, where the boss was Ivor, who had postponed his own marriage until Hilda had become old enough to leave school and look after the other young ones. Here he was surrounded by adoring brothers and sisters, and he reveled in the wild, open-air life, proving himself to the village boys by heel-and-toeing along the narrow parapet of the bridge, one hundred and twenty feet above the swirling Afan, and then punching his way into the gangs. Gangs were everything from the moment a boy was old enough to toddle into new territory and feel the first bloody-nosed shock from bunched knuckles, and Daddy Ni would look proudly at Rich after a fight and say, "You've got a face like a boot—everybody wants to put his foot in it."

Every boy had his particular buddy, which the Welsh call *butty,* and Richie's butty in Taibach was Auntie Margaret Ann's son, Dillwyn Dummer. Call Richie, and Dilly was there. Richie's toys became Dilly's toys, just as Dilly's grandparents, Mam and Dad James, became Richie's Gran and Gramp. Long before the chant of the alphabet started to singe them with education, Richie and Dilly roamed The Side together. They played marbles in the gutters that were kept naked of dog-ends by Old Nash the Road-sweeper, who wore a bowler hat; they charioteered down The Side in Dilly's sister's doll's pram until one day Richie smashed into a wall and landed in the hospital—surprisingly, with appendicitis; and when Richie got the measles, Dilly sneaked into his bed in the vain hope of sharing his spots and missing school. "Oh, right little terrors they were," says Auntie Margaret Ann, remembering, too, how they pinched the ladder of Old Nod the Lamplighter and left him stranded in gas mantles at the top of his pole. And the little girls running and crying in undone pigtails to "tell my mammie" after playing "doctors and things" with Richie and Dilly on the wasteground behind Inkerman Row, up where the old miners wheezed in their tombstone lungs as they waited for Tom Hock-the-Clip to bring out his kitchen chair and shear them in the middle of the street. And Richie was with Dilly on the day the men heaved their handcarts up to The Constant to help Cissie and Elfed move to the larger four-bedroom house in the long terrace called Caradoc Street.

"Why are they shifting, Uncle Dan?" asked Dilly.

"For a better view of the gasworks, silly."

But the reason wasn't clear to the boys, not even when Mrs. Tabor TB, who wore a man's cap back to front, arrived in the house and rolled up the sleeves of her unboiled lobster arms and made the back-kitchen steam with hissing kettles. Old Uncle Dan, sly of winks, took Richie for bull's eyes in Mrs. Thorne's sweetshop, and then high up The Side where the miners crooned hymns and played pitch-and-toss by the flames of a bonfire as the sun slipped down the wall of the world at Mumbles Head. And Richie was afraid because everybody knew that all Mrs. Tabor's children died of TB and she had tuberculosis in her wallpaper. He was cold and it was later than supper, and Uncle Dan was drinking too much medicine from the flat bottle in his inside pocket, and he remembered that his mother had suddenly left him.

"Is my sister dying, Uncle Dan?" he asked.

"We're all dying," he replied. "She'll last the night."

And when Richie got home, there was a baby crying, and he couldn't understand when Elfed blew out a candle and said, "Go to sleep now, Uncle Richard." Uncle Richie was only five and so was Uncle Dilly, but neither cared much about their new niece the next morning. They were out early, and hanging over the tiny Dyffryn railway that ran below the back-garden of 73 Caradoc Street. And as the little engine steamed under the footbridge, they squeezed their eyes tight and took deep breaths and tried to blow the smoke out through their noses, and when the smoke cleared they looked down eagerly to see whether their half-pennies on the line had been turned into pennies by the loaded coal trucks that clattered on down to the Rio Tinto Copper Works.

A short run across the footbridge was school. Eastern Infants' Elementary was dark, gloomy, and leaky. Just behind the school was the rodeo of cowboys—the Picturedrome, generally known as the *Cach,* and despite the carbolic, not altogether unworthy of a nickname which translates as "The Shithouse." The story was always told that it was given the name because a woman was so absorbed in a film that she ignored the act-of-nature pleas of her child and said, *"Cach myna!"* (Shit here). Schoolteacher Evan Morgan, who was at school with Richie, says, "I don't know whether that story is apocryphal, but I know for a fact that the owner of the place [Mr. Roberts] had a slide made which he used to flash on the screen regularly that said anyone heard using this name instead of the proper name, Picturedrome, would be prosecuted."

For Richie and Dilly and the gangs from The Side, a whole week of turf-fights, swapping cigarette cards, reading *The Hotspur* and *The Wizard,* spinning yo-yos, and smashing conkers could not measure up to the sheer riotous joy of the Saturday "tu-'penny rush" at the *Cach* [pronounced "cack"] with Bertie the Torch frisking the customers like he was the sheriff. "Our kid's boxer and he'll do you, Bertie," and Bertie not taking a blind bit of notice and handing over the arsenals of The Side gangs to Old Man Roberts who piled the catapults, spud-guns, water pistols and peashooters behind the row of flattened cocoa-tins he called the footlights.

Charlie Hockin, who was in Len Nettle's gang because he was his cousin, says, "If you came from The Side, there was a chance you would be banned from the *Cach,* but if you knew Len you were in because Len was too tough and too big to keep out. And if you were clever, so clever you could escape from Sing Sing, you could get into the *Cach* for nothing. Some five-star general in the gang managed it—maybe Richie—but I'd find it easier to rob a bank."

Though the talkies had arrived, the *Cach* was still showing silent serials, where the wagon wheels went backward in slow motion, but the lack of dialogue was a mere detail amid the din of "look out behind you" warnings to Tom Mix, Ken Maynard, and Buck Jones. Periodically the hysteria was brought to a painful hush as Old Man Roberts marched up and down the aisle banging heads with his great knobkerrie and thumping the cocoa-tin foot-lights as his final warning. But at the interval it always started up again with the appearance of Leonard the Squirt from Caradoc Street, whose job was to go around with his special fire extinguisher and drench the pong of customers with strong scented deodorant. The kids would scream and jeer and stand on the seats, pretending to soap themselves under the armpits and posing with hands on hips like Jean Harlow. Then the lights were dimmed, and when the film rolled again, the projected beam was filled with flashing lights as the boys flicked balls of silver sweet-paper into the air and slung apple stumps at each other and invited another performance by Roberts the Stick.

It was always the same at the "tu'penny rush," and all Richie and Dilly needed to complete their Saturday heaven was a third penny from an auntie or sister, enough for a bag of boiled sweets and a couple of licorice strips to suck in the flea-pit of the *Cach*. With their bonus penny they went to Thorne's sweetshop, or else to the funny little backroom shop kept by an old lady who lived in Inkerman West and was called Mrs. These-Those-and-Them. Just inside the passage of her tiny two-up two-down house she had a chest of drawers. "What do you want, love?" she asked, pointing to three drawers. "These, those, or them?" And the answer was always, "These, please," for she kept her soggy dolly mixtures in the top drawer, the soggier ones in the second, and the rank putrid ones in the third.

If Richie didn't have the price of a seat at the *Cach*, there was always as much joy to be had by catching the bus back to Pont-rhydyfen for a penny. "In the backyard of Dan-y-bont," says Hilda, "the boys had made a gym in the sort of washhouse where the men bathed when they came up from the mine. Boxing was the great thing, and Ivor was a great athlete, a champion really. He played rugby for Neath and Aberavon, and he swam from Mumbles to Port Talbot in races. The whole village used to bet on him. It's a hell of a swim, I'll tell you [about ten miles]. But Ivor was the pinup. I still remember how my mother would watch him going out all dressed up, and she would say, 'Oh, look at him. Isn't he handsome?' And, of course, he was a much stronger character than my father, and he became the big white chief. The only one who could get away with anything was Rich. We had a big apple tree at the bottom of the yard and we'd get Rich to climb and pick some for us because we knew Ivor wouldn't say anything. You wouldn't think they were brothers— more like father and son. I remember the boys took Rich every- where. Across the mountains—they were great for walking—and Rich would chase wild ponies and hang onto their tails. It was a thing boys did. And they taught him to swim in Pwll-y-Ropyn pool, and they would let him fight his own battles, even if he was taking a terrible beating."

It was not often that Richie came off worse in a fight. In the street or on the hillside, kids settled an argument with the rival gangs gathering around to form a ring and shout encouragement to the bare-knuckled scrappers. One old boy of Eastern Elemen- tary remembers the day Richie came up against one of the Powell boys, who were identical twins. "About eighteen or nineteen of us formed a ring in the street, and Richie went completely wild. I can see him now. He was stocky, and his great leonine head went down as he charged forward, swinging both arms and following his feet, as it were. Well, there was this tiny gap in the ring and Gwynfa—or it could have been Afan, they looked so much alike —backpedaled like mad, and when he came to the gap, he turned and ran. But Richie kept swinging punches at thin air, and the Powell boy must have been gone eighty yards before he noticed that he was fighting nobody. Completely wild was Richie when he lost his temper."

During those bleak depression years of the thirties, Richie still reveled in family life back at Dan-y-bont. Times were hard but never tedious. Sometimes there was plenty of work; sometimes the cupboard was bare. There were days when Daddy Ni filled the house with laughter as he launched into outrageously colorful stories; equally often there were disturbing nights when he tot- tered back down from the Miner's Arms, stupendously stoned out of his mind, or else he didn't come home at all. He was always liable to take off on some gigantic jag around the valleys with his mates, staggering and singing from one pub to another and irrigating the land for miles around. And the family used to worry for him because, despite what the old man said, he wasn't perfectly capable of taking care of himself. Villagers still talk about the time he was in a straitjacket of bandages after being badly burned in the mine. With his arms useless, he insisted on going up to the Miner's, where his mates poured the beer into his mouth. And then at closing time, stumbling down the hill, he came face to face with an old and mortal enemy. They lashed each other with their tongues, and then his enemy struck with his fists. Richard recalls, "My father was defenseless and he took a terrible beating. He had his teeth kicked out, and then he was bundled over a wall. They didn't find him until the morning. But later the two men became great friends, and they used to laugh about it."

One of Dic Jenkins' most memorable lost weekends ran on into three whole weeks of appalling, mounting despair and anxiety for the family, but it ended in laughter when finally the impossible, errant Daddy Ni presented himself at the kitchen door before the whole assembled family. His eyes were bloodshot and glassy. In one hand was a rope, and at its end a half-living skeleton of a greyhound called Paris, the most mangy, toothless, gasping animal imaginable. "Boys," he cried, "our troubles are over."

Their troubles were not over, not until 1936, when Richard was ten, and the miners' wages at last began to rise. Even earlier, however, during the worst of the depression when the miners ran soup kitchens in the street, the young ones were never cruelly deprived. The adults took short rations and sometimes lived on a diet of *siencyn* (bread and cheese toasted like a Welsh rarebit with perhaps a strip of fried bacon and drenched in a bowl of sweet tea) and Laverbread (made from seaweed gathered around Oyster Bay and fried in bacon fat with a little flour to stop it from sticking to the pan). But, contrary to popular legend, they never raised the children on *siencyn*, although, as it happens, Richard loved it and would share a bowl with Lewis the Chips, a miner who lived two doors away in Caradoc Street, and who made a little extra by serving in the fish-and-chip shop, just as Richie made a little spending money by delivering newspapers for Miss Dangerfield, who was six feet tall and wore big boots and made a lot of extra by teaching at the school.

By the rough standards of The Side, Richard was quite the privileged boy. He had roller skates with ball bearings and a bicycle, and he sometimes wore shoes. Stanley Baker, the filmstar, then a boy having a tougher, more austere life across the hills in the Rhondda Valley, explains: "To have shoes instead of boots was the subtle difference between butter and margarine. It didn't give you any more muscle, but it gave you a shade of class. Let's face it, Richard was bloody lucky with two fathers and five brothers down the pit. But if you had one father who'd lost his leg in the mine, like I did, and brothers still at school, then you were a Means Test family. I dressed in the uniform of the poor—head shaved like a convict with a clump of fringe in front, gray jersey made of steel wool, sturdy short trousers with bloody great patches, and boots, those bloody great clodhoppers, always a size too large."

But the bicycle was Richie's most prized possession; it made him, he says, "a prince of the valley." Other boys ran behind, shouting, "Gis a ride then Jenks!" Young Jenks always did, because he enjoyed the power and generosity that possessions allowed, and anyway it was the way of The Side to share, and anyone who didn't was likely as not to be given a rattle made of his own teeth. Rich was one of the boys. He had not the remotest notion of acting then, and how he had squirmed when they dolled him up as John Bull for a St. David's Day Infants' School pageant. His dream of glory was wearing the red jersey of Wales and scoring the winning try at Cardiff Arms Park while fifty thousand voices lifted the roofs of the stands with "Richard Fach" and "Cwm Rhondda." Ivor the Forward was his idol, his prototype of all a Welshman should be, and having learned to tackle low from a thousand eye-jabs from Ivor's elbow whenever he went in high, Richie became another savage in the pack of the Eastern School junior team. "He wasn't a great rugby player in those days," says his schoolmate Charlie Hockin, "but wild as a bloody hawk he was. I remember him breaking a wrist in a match. Heard it fifty yards away. And no sooner had he come back than he broke it again. No, not a great player, but very enthusiastic."

Except for Sunday-school outings from Nodfa Chapel to the hurdy-gurdy fun-fairs and donkey rides of Porthcawl, playing rugby was the only excuse for organized trips outside the Welsh towns and villages. Yet a Taibach boy with a bike had the whole wide sea-bobbing world of Dylan Thomas within the compass of his pedals. Down Talbot Road, across the bridge, round to Aberavon Beach, along the front, and on, on to Swansea where the oldest passenger train in the world used to run around the coast to Oystermouth and Mumbles Head, with small boys clinging to the open-sided carriages to save a penny, and singing:

> *Mumbles is a funny place—*
> *A church without a steeple.*
> *Houses built of old ships wrecked*
> *And a most peculiar people.*

Most peculiar—including Dr. Thomas Bowdler, buried without eulogy in the churchyard and remembered for all time by the verb *bowdlerize,* after he had done just that to Shakespeare with an expurgated edition of Othello that had Iago talking of "trumpet's plague" instead of "strumpet's plague," and in such a way excised all passages "calculated to deprave the youthful mind." But here, where sea and country collide in cockleshells and fishwives, wild ponies and milkmaids, there was nothing to deprave the mind of a ten-year-old boy. Nor was there harm when Richie went back to the village and joined in the bawdy verses of rugger songs that his brothers sang as they tramped north in their navy-blue, Sunday-best serge, high over the brim of Pontrhydyfen to the ruins of Margam Abbey, where once lived the miners' patron saint of exaggeration, *Twm Celwydd Teg* (Tom of the White Lies). The story goes that a young man on his way bird's-nesting once mockingly inquired: "Well, Tom, what lies have you got for me today?" Said Tom, "You will die three deaths before nightfall." The young man laughed at the mad notion of the monk, but as he reached into a kite's nest that overhung a river he was bitten by a viper brought up by the bird to feed her young, and he tumbled out of the tree, broke his neck, and was drowned in the river.

Richie and his gang went up that way, but not for birds' eggs. They were snaring rabbits, knocking down chestnuts, and scrumping apples on the private Margam Estate with an eye cocked for Old Styles the Gamekeeper who had a double-barreled shotgun and a fair turn of speed. "He would shoot, given half the chance," says one of the boys, "so we were all magnificent cross-country runners and did the four-minute mile long before Bannister."

All this was Richie's childhood world, but it was the people more than the places that left an indelible mark. Characters like Mrs. "Blod the Beard" Williams with two enormous moles on each side of her chin, and a generous sprout of hair on both. ("If you see Rich, tell him Blod was asking after him. He'll know me if you mention the beard. I've bathed him, you know. I've seen all what Richard has got, which wasn't much then, mark you.") There was old George Church who lived in the barracks up on The Side and only went to the doctor once in his life and came out disgusted. ("Bloody don't know what they're about," he told the boys. "They took down my trousers and looked up my arse to see if my ears were on straight." It was piles that he had.) There was Dave Williams with the cauliflower ears who could have been a world boxing champion if the drink had not got him, and Freddie Williams who became a world champion twice (as a speedway rider), and schoolmate Gerwyn Williams who boxed Richie's ears in the gym and later played rugby for Wales; and there was Annie Mort, the tomboy of Taibach, who wore a tweed skirt and short jacket and collar and tie, who could drop or place a goal with either of her lace-up shoes from forty yards, and who dreamed of playing representative rugby but had to settle for international hockey instead.

And, most extraordinary of all, there was Meredith Jones.

Meredith Jones

Meredith Jones was taking his scholarship class at Eastern Elementary School one afternoon when he was interrupted by a visitor. She was a woman of about thirty—blonde, strikingly beautiful, and (unusual for Taibach) dressed in an elegant fur coat. But the image was marred by the tightness of her mouth and the purposeful narrowing of the eyes. The schoolteacher recognized her at once. Only that morning he had given her son a severe beating.

"Quiet now, boys," he said. "I shall be just outside." Then he stepped into the corridor to suffer a torrent of personal abuse that pinned back every straining schoolboy ear in wonder and delight. Old Mered was cornered by an alley cat protecting her young, and he was being called names that hadn't even been used to lash foreign referees at Taibach Football Club.

Mr. Jones waited calmly and silently. And when she finally paused for breath, he spoke: "Have you quite finished, Madam? I do hope so, because I want you to know that whenever I have passed you on the street, or you have passed me, I have always had to turn to admire you. You see, physically, you must be the smartest and most attractive woman in Taibach. But when you open your mouth and speak like that! Well, Madam, I shall never turn in the street again."

The woman blushed like a young virgin, and then she apologized. Mr. Jones held up his hands, beamed a disengaging smile, and courteously escorted her out of the building.

Soon all the school had heard the story of the splendid confrontation of Mr. Jones and Mrs. Fur Coat. "You've got to hand it to

Old Mered," they said. "He may be a hard nut in the classroom, but he can charm the birds out of the trees when he takes a mind to. And that's a fact."

This was Meredith Jones, essentially a man of overwhelming self-confidence; also a teacher of spellbinding oratory and considerable vision. In 1936, when a new airplane in the sky was occasion enough to allow boys out of school to see it pass overhead, Mr. Jones reveled in painting word pictures of the future horrors of war in the air. "The sky will be black with planes," he told his boys. "There will be mass bombing and destruction of whole cities on a scale that defies the imagination, and a holocaust the like of which the world has never seen before. Imagine it, gentlemen, if you can, and consider the revolutionary implications—the incredible power and responsibility thrust on man when he can wage war with weapons of such deadly capability as would be fit for the final conflict of Armageddon. . . ." Nobody in the Taibach streets could match the electrifying gift of gab of Meredith Jones at full voltage, and he knew it. Local people remember the day he returned to his home village of Cwmavon after his appointment as Further Education Officer for the county of Glamorgan. The village was only four miles up the valley from Taibach, but when he addressed a large meeting in the village hall, he began: "I feel like a prophet come back to my people."

Meredith Jones was a little Caesar of education, loathed as much as loved; a teacher who employed controversial methods, but who never spared himself in his service to youth in Taibach, and who was wholly dedicated to saving his pupils from the hell of the mines or the limbo of the haberdasher's mausoleum of Welsh flannel knickers. Ginger in color and bristling by nature, he cuffed and crammed his boys into higher seats of learning, but he also served as an inspirational force to the few of sufficient wit, intelligence, and ambition to appreciate the merits and advantages of a man who could flourish words and arguments like an Excalibur. Richie Jenkins was one of the few.

Richard was ten years old when he entered the scholarship class of Meredith Jones, and in time he fell completely under his spell. Until then he had not been an exceptional boy; he had never been top in his class. But as his primary teacher Mr. Tom Howell says, "He was a bright boy and a very avid reader of anything." Cissie, too, remembers his bookworm leanings. "Sometimes my husband, the girls, and myself went to bed before him, leaving him reading before the fire. 'Don't be long now, Richie,' I would say. But when my husband got up at five o'clock next morning to go on the early shift to the mine, there would be Richie still reading or else asleep in a book. It used to worry me, but it was no use. If he went to bed, he'd only read with a torch under the blankets."

"That was my father's doing," says Hilda. "He was a great reader, and you know, for a man without education he was extraordinary. Never without a book. If he had had a proper schooling he could have been anything, though only in a literary way, if you follow me, because he wasn't very good with money."

Daddy Ni, in fact, was downright hopeless with money; he also had an extraordinarily perverse mind and could be alarmingly unpredictable. But he respected education above all things, and he encouraged Richie to listen and learn, and he helped develop his love of poetry when he bought an old book from a traveling salesman. In it, the boy found a George Herbert poem he would never forget:

> *"Sweet day, so cool, so calm, so bright,*
> *The bridal of the earth and sky. . . ."*

Richard, at the age of ten, was already remembering most everything he read, including enormous Bible quotations, word for word; he had an inborn feeling for poetry and language and was in love with words long before he could understand them. But it was Meredith Jones who began to give those words deep meaning and power, who stretched the muscles of his mind far beyond the "tu'penny rush" of the *Cach*, and who lit the fuse to his ambition. And if, like most other slave-driven boys of the scholarship class, Richard did not fully appreciate Mr. Jones at first, he at least recognized the immeasurable advantages of being one of his chosen few. It meant that with reasonable effort he could expect to be the first of his family to enter grammar school and gain qualifications for something more than coal miner or shop assistant. He was going up in the world; most others who stayed behind at Eastern Elementary would be going down the mine. When he was wearing bicycle clips to keep oil off his cricket whites, they would have string around the knees of their corduroys to keep out the rats.

There were two "grammar" schools in Port Talbot—the County and the Secondary. Richard, in 1937, entered the latter. The Great Depression was over now, and it was a time of much change for the Jenkinses of Pontrhydyfen. Daddy Ni had left Dan-y-bont, the house he had always rented and never owned, to move into Penhydd Street with Hilda, her husband, and their baby son. Miners Ivor and Verdun were married, and so was David, who had become a policeman. Willie had joined the Regular Army, and Tom was still providing a home at Cwmavon for young Graham. They were years of weddings, christenings, and no funerals, and the worst to happen was Verdun having his right foot crushed down the mine. It left him partly lame; he bought a grand piano out of the compensation money, even though he couldn't play a note. Daddy Ni roared about the four-legged pride of Verdun's parlor—"Ooh Verdun!" he used to say. "How grand he is with that coffin of music."

On weekends, however, Richard and Graham often practiced their music there. Both boys were now taking private singing lessons from a Cwmavon tin-miner, and Graham was the star pupil, known locally as the wonder-boy soprano. Richard's voice was impressive—"he sang as if he had a bell in every tooth," said Cissie—and yet not quite so outstanding. But when the brothers clashed in the Port Talbot Eisteddfod, it was Richie who took the prize. Graham, who had dreamed of beating his brother at something, was in tears at the end. The challenge had unnerved him and he had sung far below his best to finish second. Richard, in contrast, outdid himself. It was typical of him; he always had to play to win. But when Cissie pointed out how heartbroken little Graham was, Richard quite nonchalantly let him keep the first-prize ribbon.

Brinley Jenkins, son of their singing teacher, and now a BBC actor and lecturer in drama, says, "My mother used to tell me the story of how Richie beat Graham at the local eisteddfod. He won by sheer determination, and it's not surprising. I remember playing Richard at tennis. I'd be up 5–1 in a set, and then he'd grit his teeth and manage to win somehow. He always looked on me as a rival at the eisteddfod. He'd come up to me and say, 'You beat me in the speech-and-character competition, but I beat you in the reading, boyo.' Richie just wasn't interested in second place."

Richard's bulldog determination showed again when he struggled before an eisteddfod with the intricacies of Sullivan's *Orpheus with His Lute*. He did not hesitate to solicit the help of his new English master at the secondary school, and the teacher, a tall and refined gentleman named Philip Burton, generously agreed to stay behind with the boy after school. But this time he could never win; his once shrill soprano voice was irreparably cracked, and Mr. Burton at the piano finally dissolved into helpless laughter. Richie, as furious with himself as with the master, stormed off the stage and stalked out of the assembly hall. As he went, he growled, "I'll show you. Some day, I'll show you."

Philip Burton was amused, nothing more. He faintly admired the pride of a miner's boy because he was one himself—the son of an Englishman killed in a pit-fall at Mountain Ash. But otherwise Richie was just another rough-spoken kid from The Side to him, and he thought no more of it. He had other things on his mind. In his spare time he was busy working on radio scripts for the BBC and soon, in April 1939, he was sailing to New York on a six months' traveling scholarship awarded by the Guild of Graduates of the University of South Wales. (Twenty years later, Mr. Burton would be in New York again—for the Broadway opening of the musical *Camelot*. And Richard would turn to him in the dressing room and say, as though it were only yesterday, "Well, I showed you, didn't I?")

Richard was nearly fourteen at the outbreak of World War II. The next few years brought nights of fire-watching duty, and from the heights of The Side he had a grandstand view of the Wagnerian *son et lumière*—the searchlight beams crisscrossing the sky, the ack-ack guns barking, and the Heinkels and Dorniers showering incendiaries on Port Talbot or else droning on westwards to burn the heart out of Swansea. On three successive nights in February, 1941, the bombers came, and though mostly the war was a stirring adventure for Richie and his friends, the horror of the blitz sometimes became shockingly real. One night, returning from Swansea, a lone German bomber climbed over the twelve thousand feet of Foel Fynyddau mountain and released its last high explosive. It was the only bomb to fall on Pontrhydyfen during the war, and it obliterated a house on the hill above the Miner's Arms. A boy Richard knew was orphaned by that raid, and he subsequently moved to live with his grandparents in Taibach. His name was Ivor Emmanuel, and he sang like an angel.

Richie's own singing days were over now—not that he cared. In the first flush of post-pubescence, he was going regularly with girls and scrounging cheap Woodbines which (to the horror of Auntie Margaret) he shared with Dillwyn Dummer. And beyond rugby and cricket, which he took far more seriously than girls, there was something entirely new to attract him—the Taibach Youth Center, a hive of recreational activity that had opened in the evenings at the old Eastern Elementary School. The skylight roof percolated rain and played havoc with the blackout, and the classrooms were dimly lit by antiquated, half-broken gas mantles, but on club nights the whole center shone with the personality of Meredith Jones. As Richard later expressed it: "He was all electricity, sparkling and flashing; his pyrotechnical arguments would occasionally short-circuit, but they were never out of power." It was a time of rationing and that infamous phrase, *"Don't you know there's a war on?,"* but Meredith Jones waged his own war on behalf of the youth club. His members were the best and he saw they got the best—the best part-time instructors, a canteen, and immaculate new gear for the sports teams. The club was one of three experimental centers set up and subsidized by the Glamorgan Education Authority in 1941, and with County Councillor Llewellyn Heycock, an old boy of Eastern School, as its President, it eventually had a staff of five, including paid part-time instructors in arts and crafts, music, and drama. But Meredith

Jones, as the first Club Warden, was always the great overriding personality, and his impact on Richie Jenkins was extraordinary.

Fifteen years later, as Richard Burton the Hollywood filmstar and prince of the Old Vic, he would be invited by the *Sunday Times* to contribute to a series in which distinguished men and women recalled people or occasions that changed the course of their lives. And though he owed more obvious debts of gratitude to other men, he chose to dedicate the whole of his published essay to *The Magic of Meredith Jones.* This was his heartfelt tribute to the man:

> Meredith Jones was a schoolteacher, a recognizable spiritual descendant of Geraldus Cambrensis and Shakespeare's Fluellen—passionate, fluent, something of a scholar, mock-belligerent, roughly gentle, of remarkable vitality and afraid of nobody. He was the concentrated essence of a kind of bilingual South Walian, unknown perhaps over the border, who speaks the alien English tongue with a loving care and octosyllabically too! No short word for them if a longer one will do—men of brilliantly active vocabularies who love an audience.
>
> In the more suspicious and austere North of the Principality we South Walians are described with an amused tolerance as "Shwnni Hoys," a rough translation of which would perhaps be "Johnny Shouts"— makers of great flaming gestures for the love of it, who turn all things from rugby football to a walk over the Brombil to T. S. Eliot, into powerful drama in the telling of it.
>
> I remember Meredith Jones talking, for instance, of "The Love Song of J. Alfred Prufrock" and holding us all, a group of young boys, spellbound as he unfolded with conscious looks of wonder the marvelous courage of the man Eliot to write the poem "Prufrock" at the time that he did. *"No, if I should die boys think only this of me or Sassoon and Owen and Thomas*

*with their beautiful bitterness but I have measured out
my life with coffee spoons. What a gesture, gentlemen.*"
Meredith would, in the high flow of his talk, describe
anybody of whatever age or sex as "Gentlemen," as if
at a council meeting. *"What quiet bravery, and who's to
say, who will argue with me, who will deny that Pruf-
rock's slow death was not the more terrible."*

His stage was an elementary council school, leaky,
and many years condemned, with buckets and bucket-
boys at the ready for the ever-threatening rain. He
worked hard. All day long he taught eleven-plus boys
the rudiments of Arithmetic and English to prepare
them for entrance into the local Grammar Schools,
and at night he presided in the same school over a
Youth Club. And always he talked and couldn't bear
to stop.

At night when the club was shut he would invariably say "Walk home with me, boys," and delightedly
we would; for we all knew that some lecture to be delivered would be only half-completed by the time of
our arrival at his house, which would mean a further
half-hour of talk while he offered to walk us back
home. A further walk even might be necessary while
he talked and talked. His subjects were legion.

*"Consider the tax on the brain gentlemen of the great
mathematician pondering in his chill chambers at Cambridge the incontrovertible fact that there is no square root
of a minus quantity. Let us examine the mystery of numbers, let us involve ourselves with him, let me explain."*
And he would. And astonishingly we potential corner-
boys and billiard markers would catch a glimpse of the
glory of man from Meredith's play with the assump-
tion that two and two makes four.

He had a trick, too, of reducing the most august and
Olympian figures to the familiar, the known, and the
nudgeable: *"Honest and ugly old Van, boys, smoldering*

like slag, painting in the high sun until it burned his brain. Put your hat on, Van, they told him, put your hat on."

His manner was such, perhaps, as few adults could tolerate, and his seemingly deliberate dismissal of facts, dates, and figures as trivial was perhaps maddening to the more educated. He defended the local habit of exaggeration, which approached sometimes very near mendacity, as if it were a virtue. He would argue that it was the unconscious and poetic shaping of a story that sometimes distorted its more prosaic accuracy, and how relieved were the secret liars and stretchers of fact.

Indeed his description of Truth as a shadowy wing three-quarter running forever down a ghostly touch-line was an acting tour de force. *"Nobody will ever catch him,"* he would say, *"and he never will go into touch. Great artists, philosophers and poets eternally corner-flagging will never get their arms around the legs of Truth."* He would actually do the run in small, playing all the parts himself—the majestic philosopher, the mad artist, the wild crying poet, and Truth royal, immutable, faintly effeminate and untouchable. It was a remarkable performance.

His impact on me was decisive but not immediate. It was cumulative, not a blinding moment of revelation. I felt with him that my mind broadened with every step I took. I couldn't believe this week that I was so ignorant last week, or this year that I wandered for twelve months in the darkness that was last year. He taught me to love the English language without actually talking about the English language. He taught me to be a reader without actually being much of a reader himself. I became, indeed, an under-the-bed-clothes-with-a-torch-reader, bequeathing to myself, no doubt, a legacy of bad eyesight in my middle age, while Meredith, because he was too busy, became a

past master at the art of "glancing-through." He had
"glanced-through" everything, and could elaborate on
it and was extremely difficult to fault.

Since I left Meredith Jones's circle I have enjoyed
the talk of many pretty talkers; notably the gifts of the
gab of failing actors, at large in the nearest pub, and
unpublished writers, bitter among the gas-rings and
the dirty dishes, and Oxford undergraduates who
rarely took firsts. They were thru'penny thinkers all,
dealers in warped platitudes and twisted clichés, but
none had the huge personality of this man, or possessed the dark-eyed insolence to take on an opponent
in the opponent's special subject and destroy him with
a fire of improbable and, to the specialist, infuriating
irrelevancies. To his death, and lamentably he is dead
now, I never saw him matched.

My debt to this man, and my devotion to his memory, are, I hope, apparent in this article. Without him I
would have missed a large slice of life—I would not
have gone to a great university and I would probably
not have become an actor. I would not have had the
courage to answer an advertisement and I would never
have gone to London except possibly in a leeked red
beret and with an enclosure ticket for Twickenham. I
would, I suspect, in some unpleasant job, have become
morose, suspicious, bitter, and impossible to live with. I
might even have become a politician.

Not everyone remembers Meredith Jones with such exaltation.
Gerry "Luther" Lewis, a classmate of Richie, is now a Taibach
schoolteacher and a professional football referee. He says, "Jones
had certain qualities—fair do's. But I didn't like him. He was
quick with the lip and a bloody sight quicker with the fist. Wonder was that nobody filled him in. You see, he ran the scholarship
class. You got into his class when you were ten and sat for this
monstrous national examination when you were eleven. If you

failed, you stayed on at Eastern School until you were fourteen and then went into the steelworks or down the mine. No chance. But if you passed you went to Port Talbot Grammar School until you were sixteen, with university to follow if you were exceptional. Now the difference between being a grammar school boy and an elementary school boy in these parts is the difference between an officer and a buck private. Well, there would be thirty-odd children in a scholarship class, and in theory the odds of them getting into the grammar were about six to one against. But Jonesie had the highest pass record to the grammar of any elementary school in the area. And why? Because he handpicked the clever little buggers and ignored the dumb ones.

"I got there without his help and that's when I really got to know Richard. But even then Meredith Jones ran the Taibach Youth Club at night and had his chosen boys following him about the streets. Bar Richard, they were right regular arse-hole creepers. Do anything he asked. I remember we were playing Neath. Unbeaten at the time. All we had to do was throw the ball about and we were there. But no. Mered was running up and down the touchline, shouting, 'Keep it tight, boys, keep it tight.' And Richard, the skipper and a bloody good loose forward, knew he was wrong but made us keep it tight. We lost 6–3. No, I didn't like Jones. It wasn't jealousy or anything. I just felt it was disgraceful the way he treated boys who were not in the magic circle. I can see him now, striding along with his mac flapping and waving his arms and his tribe following him like he was Jesus. I thought he was slightly off the latch."

Charles Hockin, also a Taibach schoolmaster, was top of the class at Eastern in Richie's day. But he declined his first chance of going up into the scholarship class because of his distaste for Meredith Jones. "He was a slave-driving teacher. He used the cane regularly, and you sat there afraid to bat an eyelid in case it rattled. You did nothing else except English and arithmetic with him, and the period of joy was once a week when he took Welsh in another class and we had Tom Howell, who read us *Night Must Fall.* You either liked Mered or you hated him. He had the gift of the gab all right, and if you wanted a fellow who was verbose and could step in front of five hundred people and hold them—then, yeah, this was the fellow. But he wasn't a great guy to me. To me he was a bully of a man.

"He took rugby at the school, and if you couldn't play rugby you were no good at all. He drove everybody. He bristled. He had a ginger moustache and this purple temper. We had the rudiments of rugby in Mered's class. You went out in the yard and the touchline was a wall. I can remember the ball being kicked out and there was a savage horde descending on me, and because I was near the wall I stepped to one side, because I would have been crushed. You know—discretion is the better part of valor. Well, Mered just blew the whistle and he walked up and said, 'You should have taken the ball, boy.' And I said, 'But the wall, sir.' And then he stood me in the middle of the yard with eight boys in front of me and he kicked the ball up in the air and said 'Right.' And as I took the ball I fell back three times, not once, and I was flattened into the ground. Nowadays, as teachers, we would never do anything like that by a wall, because we would be afraid of claims and all sorts of things against us. But in those days it was different. You didn't go home and complain to your father about him because you were afraid of the fellow.

"But in many ways he was a real character. I went on to the County school and I remember once we were drawn against Eastern in the quarter-final of the Cup competition. Well, we beat them, and Mered was literally fuming. He was patrolling the line, shouting and bawling, and if any boy got in his way he got a clip on the earhole. The following Saturday he canceled his school's game and brought the entire team to watch us play. He marched them up and down the touchline, pointing and yelling, 'See, that's how forwards should pack.' It didn't end there, you see, that they were beaten. They were going to learn from it."

One ex-pupil still recalls with horror how Meredith made a boy with a turn in his eye and a limp stand on a chair in front of the class and told him: "Turn up your north eye, Danny Boy, and say after me—Twinkle, Twinkle, Little Star. . . ." Yet another ex-pupil, Trevor George, now a primary school headmaster in Devon, does not view the incident in the same sadistic light. "I found Mered nothing but wonderful as a man and a teacher. He was the sort of person who wanted to make men of boys and boys of sissies. He was understanding, tolerant, but very hard. I well remember the incident when he made Danny recite 'Twinkle, Twinkle, Little Star' with actions. Apart from his other deformities, Danny had a very bad speech impediment. During his 'performance' many of us were laughing our heads off. On completion Danny was sent back to his seat with a pat on the head and 'Well done, boy' from Mered, who then turned on the merrymakers. 'Come out, the boys who laughed.' We were each given six of the best. I often thought that Mered was particularly cruel with Danny to insist he undergo such an ordeal. I realize now that he was teaching the rest of the class not to laugh at anyone less fortunate than ourselves. That lesson has remained vividly in my mind and was typical of his teaching. There was always a reason for his actions."

Putting Meredith's rare personality down on paper, it has been said, is like trying to pick up quicksilver with a fork. And this is true. It is impossible for the neutral observer to judge the man, and any jury would be confounded by the conflicting evidence of witnesses. There are memories of jolly Meredith, gaily dancing a gypsy tango at a club party; of kind-hearted Meredith, holding the hand of a child who had nervous fright when speaking a poem for the first time at a club concert; of hard-hearted Meredith, wielding the cane with a vengeance; of happy Meredith, wreathed in smiles, as he swung the baton while his choir sang his favorites, "Rise Up, O Men of God" and *"Iesu Dyrchaefedgig"*; of eccentric Meredith, so transported by the music that he got his choir disqualified at an eisteddfod by taking them through their performance a second time; of fearless Meredith, who, when there was a great hubbub at the back of the hall during a youth club meeting at Sandfields, got up and told the parents: "You ought to be ashamed of yourselves—adults behaving like that in front of teenagers"; of proud and dedicated Meredith, who would proclaim to officials visiting the club: "My members are not cultured and refined—yet—but they're *here* and they're *alive.*"

Whatever the personal failings of Meredith Jones, whatever

the injustices of his private form of educational separatism, he was, above all, a mover of mountains whose drive and leadership made Taibach Youth Center the most widely known and respected youth club in Glamorgan, a prototype for a hundred more to follow. In his peculiar, part-Machiavellian way, he realized what he set out to achieve. His dynamism built up a recreational laboratory that widened the horizons of many members, and the wizardry of his words lit fireworks off the penny-comic candles of their minds. And no one was to be more dramatically influenced by him than Richie Jenkins.

Though Richard was soon drawn into the dramatics section of Taibach Youth Center, his first stage role happened to be in a school play production—Shaw's political comedy *The Apple Cart.* In the minor role of veteran ambassador Mr. Vanhattan, he briefly attracted attention by the way he fiddled with his waistcoat—as sly a piece of upstaging as ever there was—and he effectively assumed an American accent. But he failed to make any lasting impression; indeed, members of the cast have little or no memory of his stage debut.

Susie Preece, a later girl friend, played the part of the queen. She says: "Richie didn't do much in the play as I remember. It was the boy who played the king that we all thought was great. Morgan Griffiths was his name. He had the star part and he was very good. But Richie was just another one of the boys then. Quiet. Not spectacular. You see, he was one of the younger ones in our form—about nine months younger than me. And it makes a difference at that age. I remember he used to fool about a bit during Welsh—our teacher was a real old spinster—and that he was full of fun. But otherwise he was quite ordinary really." As for producer Philip Burton, he was pleased enough with Richard's first acting effort, but not ecstatically so. He had other drama pupils of obvious flair—well-spoken boys like Hubert Clements of Aberavon, and little Rubert Davies who lived just around the corner from Richard in Brook Street. The following spring they would play the roles of bully and hero in Mr. Burton's radio production of *How Green Was My Valley.*

By now Mr. Burton had become quite the local celebrity. He

had arrived at Port Talbot Secondary two months before Richard was born—an unqualified teacher fresh out of university with a double-honors degree in pure mathematics and history, and a passion for English literature and drama. At first his creative work was confined to the YMCA amateur dramatic society which he co-founded, but in 1937, following the success of his spectacular pageant to mark the 800th anniversary of Margam Abbey, he began to write radio scripts for the BBC in Wales. He also became a spare-time actor and producer, and now, following his sabbatical in America, he had been given the rank of flight-lieutenant, commanding officer of Port Talbot's 499 Squadron of the Air Training Corps. Besides this, Mr. Burton had shown a flair for developing fine juvenile actors, including one boy of recognized star quality—Thomas Owen-Jones of Bryn who, after winning the Leverhulme Scholarship at the Royal Academy of Dramatic Art, had gone on to the Old Vic, acting with Olivier, Redgrave, Vivien Leigh, and Edith Evans among others, and then making his film debut in *The Four Feathers*. Owen-Jones was now a dashingly handsome six-footer, a Battle of Britain pilot. He had been dedicated to acting since his schooldays, a boy beautiful in both speech and manner. But Richie had none of that; still bearing traces of the jagged vernacular of The Side, he was a world away from Owen-Jones and the polished and donnish Mr. Burton, whose pupils sometimes read in immaculate English for "Auntie BBC."

At the youth club, however, he was soon displaying a certain flair as an all-around entertainer. He and his closest friend Trevor George used to sing "Drummer Boy" at club dances; they improvised with an impersonation of Hitler and Mussolini when the main lights failed at a club concert; and as a comedy act for a parents' evening, they devised a crazy boxing match, larking about for two rounds and then fighting for real in the third when Meredith Jones whispered, "Have a go." Rich and Trev were both prominent in the school under-fifteen rugby team, and they were inseparable friends during the early years of the war. Today Richard still tells the story of how Trevor was injured during a rugby training session and lay rolling in agony on the ground.

"It's my knee," he groaned, and the math master knelt down beside him and proceeded to massage his right knee furiously. Finally he asked, "Is that better?" "No," George replied. "It's the other knee." And Trevor remembers the day Richard impressed everyone by talking back to their headmaster. "On entering the school grounds Richie noticed the headmaster entering without his gas mask. After assembly, the headmaster asked all those who came to school without gas masks to remain behind. He gathered all of us near the stage, glowered at us, and pointed to Richie first and said, 'Jenkins, where's your gas mask?' Richie stared back and said, 'Where's yours?' Taken aback, Mr. "Pop" Reynolds dismissed us all."

In November, 1941, as he approached his sixteenth birthday, Richard's immediate future seemed obvious. Next summer he would sit the School Certificate examination of the Central Welsh Board. He was bright; there was every reason to suppose that he would pass with distinction and qualify for further education, bidding for the Higher School Certificate, perhaps even winning a university scholarship. The family talked vaguely about him going on to the ministry college and training to become a Baptist minister. After all, his Bible knowledge was prodigious; he loved singing the towering Welsh hymns, and in his rough way he had an arresting style when he took his turn at Bible reading in the quarterly chapel meetings. Perhaps he could make a fiery pulpit orator. Perhaps not. But whatever, as most everyone agreed, Richie Jenkins would never have to go down the mine like his brothers and father.

And then, suddenly, his whole world fell apart. It was Christmas. Elfed the family breadwinner was unwell and temporarily out of work. Money was desperately short. The family talked, argued, debated, but however they looked at the problem, the conclusion was the same. It was impractical to keep Richie on at the secondary school. The boy was already two years beyond the minimum age for leaving school. He would have to earn his keep. It was a decision which touched off old sores among some members of the Jenkins family, who felt that Elfed had never been enthusiastic about taking in Richie as a baby. Graham explains:

"When Tom's first wife died, I stayed with them at Caradoc Street for a while, and I came away with an uneasy feeling. There was no doubt in my mind that not only Elfed but most of the Jameses had originally been against Richard coming into the family. The feeling was, Why should we have to have this boy? We've got enough problems of our own. With hindsight, this reaction is now understandable when you consider what hard times they faced and the fact that they were living on peanuts."

At the time, however, it seemed a cruel and ruinous blow to Richard's future prospects. Brooding and silent, he now accepted the inevitable and cleared his desk of all aspiration. "I had a wild ambition to go out into the world and starve," he said later. "I didn't know what I wanted to do. I liked talking, so I thought of becoming a preacher. But it was pointed out to me that I had no religious feeling and I gave up the idea." In fact, he never had a choice. The ministry was out of the question now; he had to take paid work immediately, and wherever he might find it. So, full of apathy, he went to serve behind the counter of the men's outfitting department of the Taibach Cooperative Wholesale Society. He hated it, and his mind was an unspoken confusion of bitterness and regret. Just seven months short of matriculation, with the chance to secure career credentials, and here he was—the first of his family to reach grammar school—"a bloody haberdasher" at the age of sixteen. And all for thirty bob a week.

Jenkins the Co-op

There was no great surprise when Richard Jenkins failed to return to Port Talbot Secondary School after the Christmas holidays in January, 1942. Boys from working-class homes were continually dropping out of grammar school because of hardship at home, and especially in wartime when there was a marked lack of parental control and a blunting of purpose and ambition. Fathers and elder brothers were in the armed forces, mothers were in factories, and boys were drifting aimlessly until they received their call-up papers at the age of eighteen. In Port Talbot there was such growing concern about juvenile delinquency and the accident risk for unguarded children that a campaign was now unsuccessfully waged for the schools to remain open during holidays.

It was a time of changed values and crazy contradictions. Shop assistants had become heroes in uniform while the miners, in reserved occupation, rubbed shoulders with conscientious objectors who had been sent down the pits. The public was exhorted to restrict their bath water to five inches depth, but as Daddy Ni was never slow to protest, they were pouring more and more water into the beer—so much that while beer consumption soared, the national intake of alcohol fell. There were warnings about the alarming shortage of prams, nipples, and fireguards, and yet the birth rate continued to rise. And while the great patriotic appeal was for belt-tightening self-sacrifice, the black market flourished by demand. It was a time of peak austerity. White bread had become a luxury. There were stricter controls of food, sweets, soap, and petrol. And the Board of Trade had introduced standardized utility clothing.

Jenkins the Co-op, as he was called, was directly involved in the controlled sale of clothing. But in the vernacular of the later forties, he "couldn't care less." "Really and truly, he hated that job," says his sister Hilda. "He only went there because Cissie's husband Elfed was out of work and they were a bit hard-up. You know how they were in those days—somebody had to go out to work. Well, Richard detested it more than anything else in the world. He used to come and tell me, 'I hate that bloody job.' And the things he did were worrying. There was clothes rationing, and when an old miner came in wanting a suit, Richard would give it without taking coupons. That was typical of him. He'd take the shirt off his back to give it to you. But of course Cissie, a lovely girl, was terrified. She worried herself sick about Richard.

And the trouble with grammar school is that normally once you've left, that's it. You can never get back."

Several times Richard was threatened with dismissal from the Co-op, but it was his general attitude to life that worried the family most. They could understand his temporary disappointment and despair at being denied full education, but it went deeper than that. His moody frustration darkened the house in Caradoc Street, and he now took perverse satisfaction in catching up with the street-corner boys who had been hanging around the billiard rooms and the dance-halls since the age of fourteen. He was sixteen, big and tough for his age, and overnight he buried the schoolboy image and assumed the slick assurance of an independent youth who could do as he pleased. He smoked and he drank, and in the "cattle market" of YMCA dances, where the girls sat around the walls and boys cluttered at one end and made distant appraisals, he was the one who could be relied on to cross the floor of girls dancing with girls and walk away with the one his pals judged unobtainable. And later, when the gang sat around the stove in Berni's, the Talbot Road ice-cream parlor which smelled foreign with crushed coffee beans and where old Joe Morozzi's pretty daughter served yellow ice cream in tiny boats flooded with raspberry sauce, they would press him for intimate details of the last-waltz girl he had escorted home. But Richard was discreet, and old Joe, who liked him a lot, even though he wasn't too pleased about him going out with his Catholic daughter, said, "Richie's a very nice boy. But too quick he wants to be the man."

Besides the family, one other person was deeply concerned about Richard's future—Meredith Jones. On the day he called in the Co-op he couldn't believe his eyes: that one of *his* Eastern scholarship boys was condemned to dead-end dealing in miners' long johns. "Why, Why, Why?" he thundered in front of two startled girl assistants. And the girls listened in wonder as the customer with the ginger moustache and liquid tongue poured out Welsh wails of invective that purpled the department store and made Richie Jenkins shrug his shoulders like the schoolboy he really was. What could he do? "Do!" Meredith exclaimed. He thumped the counter. "We've got to get you back to school, boy.

But if you want me to help you, you've got to help yourself. There is no place in my scheme of things for parasites awash with self-pity. And, you know, in the final analysis you make your own luck in this world. You can achieve most anything if you want it badly enough and pursue it with industry and imagination and unbending single-mindedness of purpose. But you have to have fire in your belly. You have to believe intensely in life, in the future, and most of all in yourself."

Meredith Jones did not possess the authority to have Richard readmitted to school, and though he was Secretary of the Port Talbot Youth Committee and had some influence with the local education authorities, it was not easy, even with his facile tongue, to convince everyone of the crying need to return to school a boy two years short of his National Service. Richard had to give him ammunition for argument by demonstrating that he merited treatment as "a special case." Richard did because, as he expresses it, "Meredith Jones, with his breathtaking effrontery and his eloquent and dazzling generalizations, hurled and swept me into the ambition to be something other than a thirty-bob-a-week outfitter's apprentice."

Through his friendship with Susie Preece and her family, he knew all about cousin Tom Owen-Jones who had joined the Old Vic and gone into films, and he had met other boys Mr. Philip Burton had helped to develop as actors through school plays and radio work. Moreover, in January, 1942, he had collected the princely sum of three guineas for appearing with eight other Port Talbot Squadron cadets in *Venture, Adventure,* a radio documentary written by Flight-Lieutenant Burton as an account of the Air Training Corps and the effect on lives of boys in South Wales. Now he saw acting as an attractive escape from the insignificance of the Co-op, even though when he had previously approached Burton, the teacher had only laughed at his notion of going into drama. ("He made it seem the most impossible thing in the world. And that only made me more determined to persevere.")

Richard persevered by throwing all his spare-time energies into the activities of the Taibach Youth Center, and he got into acting by helping to form the new drama section, with himself and a girl called Violet Hook as the elected junior leaders of the group.

Until now, the Center had been seen simply as a splendid means of keeping young people off the streets and out of the juvenile courts. But Meredith Jones was never to be satisfied with running a play-center; he intended that his club should win kudos throughout the county. With this aim he invited a Mr. Leo Lloyd to take charge of the drama group as a part-time instructor, and a few weeks later he asked him to enter the club for the first Youth Eisteddfod to be held at Pontypridd in June, 1942. Lloyd responded by calling together five boys and two girls to prepare a production of *The Bishop's Candlesticks.* The education of Richard the actor began.

In tribute to Mr. Lloyd, he says: "He gave me a leading part in the youth club play and persuaded me that acting was infinitely fascinating. He taught me the fundamentals of the job; to stand and move and talk on the stage with confidence. He taught me unsparingly and I learned quickly. He taught me discipline and he taught me, by inference, and from his devotion to the craft, that 'reality' can be greater *on* the stage than *off.* He taught me the power of the spoken word and the rudiments of its use. He channeled my discontent and made me want to be an actor."

Leo Lloyd worked in the steelworks, but lived only for the theater. One ex-pupil describes him as "a hard taskmaster with a heart of pure gold," and schoolmaster Evan Morgan, once one of Philip Burton's star pupils, rates him as "one of the most dedicated producers I've met in twenty-five years of professional broadcasting." He was held in such high repute that he staged Shakespearean plays for the Glamorgan Education Authority, in which schoolmasters from all over Wales were invited to take part.

"He was the original thespian," says Charles Hockin. "Tall and all nose and Adam's apple. I can see him now—walking the pavements of Taibach in his large velours trilby, completely oblivious to passersby, with his head buried in a book and throwing his arms about as he spoke his lines. If you didn't think, eat, speak, and live drama, you were of no use to Leo. I remember I was helping behind the stage in a one-act play, and a quick dim-out had to be done at a precise moment, and Tommy Lane, who was in charge of the lights, missed, probably by 1.576 of a second. There was a centurion waiting to go on and Leo grabbed his spear and thumped poor Tommy with it. 'You bloody fool,' he cried. 'I can't trust anybody. Everybody lets me down.' This was his favorite expression. Next night he did the job himself, and he forgot the lights completely. That was Leo; always the great ham on stage. If the door didn't open, he would walk straight through it. A bit forgetful, but a great producer! Really professional. I don't think Richie ever got on the roll of honor for anything until he met Leo."

Richard experienced a new excitement from the moment he met this gaunt and bespectacled man of stern expression, who blazed a passion of words and focused the boy's ambition. Lloyd told his class: "Good acting is good drama; good drama is beauty; beauty is truth; and the truth of the matter is that we are going to win the first Youth Eisteddfod at Pontypridd this year." He cast Richard as the convict in *The Bishop's Candlesticks,* a leading part that demanded the imagination of a silent screen actor since the play, adapted from Victor Hugo's *Les Miserables,* was to be presented as mime. And then, quoting from *Hamlet,* Leo exhorted: "Nor do not saw the air too much with your hand, thus; but use all gently; for in the very torrent, tempest, and, as I may say, the whirlwind of passion, you must acquire and beget a temperance that may give it smoothness."

Night after night, Richie remained late at the youth club, rehearsing with Lloyd, or else developing his mind by joining the discussion group that huddled around a classroom coal-fire. And heeding the advice of Meredith Jones, he did much more. During lunch hours he crossed over from the Co-op to the Taibach public library and buried himself in Shakespeare and sandwiches, and librarian Dai Eaton, who also met him on fire-watching duty, remembers how the boy was even pumping him during an air raid for information about the Welsh changing consonants and the intricacies of Welsh poetic meters.

Though he enjoyed the independence of a wage earner, Richard could see clearly the opportunities and advantages he was missing out of school. So much was happening that summer at

Port Talbot Secondary. Philip Burton was busier than ever with radio work in which he often involved his pupils. He was producing a series of documentary programs, and in April, 1942, he achieved a new accolade of success: Ealing Studios bought the film rights of his outstanding radio play about wartime action involving the oil tanker *San Demetrio.* The following month Burton was in the news again when a BBC recording van came to the school to record three scenes of the radio play of *How Green Was My Valley.* Burton was the associate producer. He also took the role of the brutally sarcastic schoolmaster, and two of his boys played the wrestling scene in the schoolyard while the rest of the school cheered them on. Richard, locked in the pins-and-needles cramp of the drapery counter, could not even go along to watch. Yet he wasn't worried now. Soon he would have his own chance in the Youth Eisteddfod at Pontypridd.

As the date of the Eisteddfod drew near, one fact continually worried Leo Lloyd—that the company of *The Bishop's Candlesticks* hadn't been given a tryout on a real stage. As usual, Meredith Jones found a way. "Build a stage for the night," he said. "We've got tables and blackboards, and we can use the school desks." So classrooms were cleared and desks carried into the main hall, and they laid bricks on the sloping desks so that the blackboard stage would lie flat. The trial performance was almost ruined when the combined weight of the cast—Richard, Phyllis Williams, Sally Thomas, Bruce Vincent, Trevor George, Tom Lane, and Brian Tashara—loosened the bricks and sent the players see-sawing crazily on rocking blackboards. But Lane gave up his walk-on part to save the day by rounding up other club members to crawl under the "stage" and support the blackboards with their backs. Hockin was one volunteer—"You can literally say that Richard Burton started his acting career on the broad of my back."

After the tryout, Meredith Jones was brimful of confidence. "Well done," he said, enthused. "When we go to Ponty we'll hit 'em for six." And so they did. The adjudicator called it "a masterly production" and it took first prize. Moreover, against the talent of major Welsh towns and cities, including Swansea and Cardiff, Richard himself won second prize in English reading, third prize in English recitation, and second in solo singing. It was a remarkable all-around achievement, and one that could not fail to impress Philip Burton, who had heard all about the saga of the Jenkins family from Meredith Jones, his fellow officer in 499 Squadron of the A.T.C.

That summer Richard devoted all his time to the youth club, serving on the editorial committee that launched the club magazine *The Bridge* and appearing in a series of one-act plays presented at the Wesley Hall as part of Taibach's stay-at-home holiday campaign. And by now Meredith Jones had rubbed it into everyone concerned—relatives, local dignitaries, and teachers— that here was a boy of exceptional scholastic potential. Most important of all, Richard's case won the sympathy of County Councillor Llewellyn Heycock, President of the Youth Center, and a Governor of Port Talbot Secondary. It was Heycock who finally used his wide powers to have Richard readmitted to school in September, 1942.

There remained the problem of whether the family could afford to keep Richard at school, but they agreed to try, and Burton promised Meredith Jones that he would keep a watchful eye on Richard at school and encourage him in plays. Since then the legend has grown that Mr. Burton discovered the wild genius of Richard Jenkins. But it was never as simple as that. "He didn't discover me," Richard has said. "I discovered him." And so, in a sense, he did.

Philip Burton

The return of Richard Jenkins to Port Talbot Secondary set the teachers gossiping in their teacups during the first morning break of the 1942 autumn term. It was absolutely unprecedented for a sixteen-year-old boy to come back in this way after ten months' absence, and they all knew it was not really the doing of his family, or of Pop Reynolds, the head. Jenkins was back because Meredith had pulled strings. Apparently Alderman Heycock and the other school Governors judged this boy to be a special case, but there were a few teachers that term who concluded that he was strictly a difficult case.

Richard had not been ten minutes back at school before he was caught standing at a shattered classroom window with the evidence of the broken glass still in his hands. He had smashed it with a gym shoe that some butter-fingered boy had failed to catch. But when the master, George Hapgood, entered the room, Richard didn't bat an eyelid. Unabashed, he smiled sweetly. "Good morning, sir," and simultaneously he let the glass drop into the yard outside. "Less dangerous, sir," he said briskly. "I'll get it swept up at once."

Phyllis Catherine Dolan, the only other pupil in Richard's class to take up acting as a career, remembers that day vividly. "All the girls were terribly excited, and there was endless whispering— 'Have you heard . . . have you heard Richie Jenkins is coming back?' Funnily enough, I couldn't place him at all, which was odd, because I am related to the James family and had vague recollections of having met him as a child in Cissie's house. But I was as intrigued as the rest, because it was quite unique for a boy to leave school for a year, go to work, and then come back as a pupil. And his entrance that day was fantastic. He opened the door and hurled a gym shoe right across the class and smashed a pane of glass. So Richard was back; you can imagine the effect on us girls. He was such an attractive young man. Extraordinarily so. And despite his mass of pimples and acne, and those boils on his neck (he even had nicknames for them), no other boy had a chance from that day on. He'd cock those green eyes and it was obvious that no girl would ever hold him. That first day during the play-break he asked me to go to the pictures and I turned him down because I was going with a boy called Roy Jenkins. In fact, I went to the pictures with Roy and regretted it very much. So the next time Richie asked I said yes straight away, and we shared a double seat in the *Cach*. I don't remember a thing about the film,

I was trembling so much. And he didn't even touch me, although
we were sitting in a double seat designed for courting. But then
Richie was never a toucher. Not one of your gropers. He had
more class than that. In a strange way I became his 'bird,' but it
was all very innocent."

Like Mr. Hapgood, other teachers soon discovered that Richard had greatly changed in his year out of school. He was patently different from most other boys; more self-assured and
worldly-wise. He would come back reeking of beer after the
lunch break, and always at half-time in rugby matches he would
have the rest of the team gather around him while he coolly
smoked a cigarette. After rugby matches he would travel the five
or six miles to Briton Ferry to attend the Saturday night hop at
The Pavilion, and once, after drinking too many beers and lingering too long in saying goodnight to a girl, he missed the last
train and walked home in the early hours. Cissie and Elfed worried about him, naturally, but more than they needed. As his
classmate "Luther" Lewis puts it: "Richie was a man among the
boys—a hell of a character. He was put in a class where we were
all a year younger, but he was university material all right. No
doubt about that. Brilliant. A normal person who had academic
ability and the right potential would have to swot hard, but he
could do it without seeming to do anything but drink and that.

"I initially became friendly with him because we played rugby
together. I remember we were playing Llanelly Grammar School
and I got really done up in the scrum by my opposite number in
the front row. A big bugger was putting the boot in nonstop. I
was taking a fair bit of hammer, and then this character banged
me in the belly when I was going up for the ball. I was nearly
sick. Richie picked me up and said, 'Right, Luther. Change
places.' Well! We went down and Richie yelled, 'Okay, boys,
let's have some shove.' And when we broke there was this poor
bugger stretched out unconscious. After that Richie looked after
me.

"I remember another time he was telling us about the night he
took a girl up the mountain. We were all standing around in the
playground, waiting for him to come to the juicy part. Well, he

used to suffer something chronic from boils, and he had this big one on his arse, and the girl suddenly grabbed him right on it. And Richie let out such a yell that she ran hell for leather down the mountain and left him there. That was Richie all over. Always telling stories against himself. Never a show off, if you get me, and yet somehow he'd never let anyone get the better of him."

There was one boy who tried to his cost. It happened after he had seen Richard put well and truly in his place by sweet Miss Griffiths, who took them for Welsh. While she was writing on the blackboard and had her back to the class, Richard had been slipping from desk to desk, until he was next to a particular girl. And without turning around, the schoolmistress snapped, "Richard Jenkins! Go back to your desk, you soppy ha'porth." He acknowledged the chastisement with a wry grin and later bore the jibes of his classmates as they waited for Miss Best to take them for geography. But there was this one boy who interpreted Richard's ability to take a joke as a sign of weakness. He was a big lad and something of a bully, and he was notoriously glib with his excuses for leaving school early. He was leaving early now, and as he passed Richard's desk he mussed his hair and slyly whispered, "soppy little ha'porth." Richard immediately stood up. "May I leave the room, Miss?" he asked. And Miss Best said, "Yes, all right." The class watched him leave and listened. Then they heard running footsteps and a loud crash from down the corridor. Seconds later Richard came back. His hair was neatly combed, and he was sucking a knuckle.

Most boys came to regard him as their natural leader, but despite his cavalier style he was grimly aware that his unique second chance at school could end at any time; that he needed to look beyond ordinary schooling if he was to ensure that he never again had to work behind a counter. Acting was the one career that attracted him and Philip Burton was the one man with the means to help him, whether he remained in school or not. Now, deliberately and calculatingly, he set out to impress him, and his first opportunity came in November with the school production of *Gallows Glorious,* a play about American abolitionist John Brown that Burton was putting on in the YMCA hall. Since the play had been partly cast the previous term, there was only a small role for Richie—that of John Brown's brother, Owen.

Dennis Burgess, who was Richard's best friend in school, says: "Rich told me that he was going to be an actor and that he was going to get Phil Burton to help him. That is why he did such a tremendous scene in *Gallows Glorious*. There is a terribly emotional thing at the end when Owen imagines he has seen the army of John Brown marching through the clouds. I am teaching drama now, and when you can get boys of fifteen or sixteen to let themselves go, with tears, chokes in the voice and the rest, it is a remarkable thing. And Rich did it without being coached. He brought it out himself.

"And he was clever with it. He didn't do this in rehearsal—only on the night of the performance. I shall always remember Burton's face. He was in the wings and he couldn't believe it. He turned round to me and said, 'Good God, is that Richard? I'll kill him!' And he did. Afterwards he tore into him saying, 'What do you think you were doing out there? Did you think that was good? You do realize you've probably ruined the play!' And he went on talking about dramatic balance and how he had sweated blood over rehearsals to get the balance absolutely right. And he ended by saying, 'Don't do it again.' But Rich did. Every night. I asked him if he was going to stop and he answered, 'No. Once I'm on stage there's nothing anyone can do.' I think it really tickled his sense of humor to see Philip Burton helpless in the wings."

While Mr. Burton didn't approve of Richard's forceful playing of such a minor role, he was far too experienced to miss the boy's enormous potential as an actor. Brinley Jenkins, who was outstanding in the main role of John Brown, says, "Richard didn't have much to do, but he always had this walk, this magnetism—the power to draw people's eyes to him. We did a lot of things later, but after that play Richard always took the lead. We were rivals. Phil Burton used to organize these competitions for speech-and-character, acting out a Shakespearean character, and when Richie came back to school I used to win. I was probably the only boy who could beat him at anything, because he was a brilliant student and the captain of rugby and cricket. But then, after a month or so, he could even beat me at that. Yet he'd let me win the reading prize, because he always had this generosity which was very rare in that type of competitive boy."

Richard revealed his promise as an actor at an especially propitious time in the life of Philip Burton. This versatile teacher was possessed by what he has since called his "Pygmalion complex," a compelling urge to establish a close personal identification with a pupil and to fulfill his own acting ambitions through that person. Many of his prodigies had bridged the gap between amateur and professional acting, and yet he was still without that one bright star who might achieve lasting brilliance. Flying Officer Tom Owen-Jones was his one pupil who had seemed destined for greatness; now, tragically, he was gone. The previous year this young man of infinite promise had died of sarcoma, a rare cancerous condition, after damaging his hip in a parachute fall. He was twenty-eight. Another pupil Burton had had high hopes for was Vivian Allen, a Cwmavon tinplate worker's son. He was born into appalling poverty, but with Burton's guidance he developed into an accomplished actor, outstanding in the school production of *St. Joan*. Now Allen was in the Army, and although Burton still found him radio work, he knew he was not the one to fulfill his dreams of glory. The young man was simply not dedicated enough to acting. He wanted to become a teacher, and ultimately he did.

Could Richard Jenkins be the one? There was no denying the boy's natural flair for acting. But Burton had serious doubts about working closely with him. He was unlike other pupils he had had; more strong-willed, independent, and difficult to control. He remembered how the boy had reacted during *Gallows Glorious* after accidentally smashing the large bottle of wet-white. The bottle with the gold stopper was precious to Burton because this stage make-up was almost unobtainable during the war, but when he cried out in horror at finding it broken the boy only roared with laughter at his theatrical histrionics. Richard had apologized since. But was this the kind of youth who would fully cooperate and re-

spond to months, possibly years, of hard disciplined drama training in after-school hours?

What finally influenced Burton was the sheer determination
and apparent dedication of the boy. He had done everything possible to dissuade him from the notion of acting—all to no avail.
The boy had persisted, and when he had finally sent him away to
learn Hotspur's "My liege, I did deny no prisoners" as a test
speech, the boy with the rough Welsh accent had practiced for
weeks on the tongue-twisting words, delivering the speech to the
teacher each day until he was perfect and precise in every pro-
nunciation, pause, and emphasis. Burton liked that. It showed
spirit, and he gave Richard all the help he could.

Then, at the end of that autumn term, a fateful situation made
it possible for Burton to work more closely with Richard than he
had done with any other student. It came about because of a new
family crisis over Richard's education. Meredith Jones had been
wonderfully persuasive in arguing the case for sending the boy
back to Port Talbot Secondary, but his rhetoric didn't alter the
harsh economic fact that Elfed could not afford to keep his wife's
brother, who was nearly seventeen and who would be nearly
eighteen before he left school. Moreover, there had long been an
uneasy relationship between Richard and his brother-in-law.
Richard looked on Elfed's daughters, Marion and Rhianon, as his
sisters, and he adored Cissie and never wished to do anything to
upset her. "But he and Elfed just didn't get on," says brother
Graham. "I remember when I stayed there that Elfed used to fall
asleep on the sofa in the living room and Richard would look at
him with contempt. The atmosphere was very strained, and in
the end I reckon Richard just walked out."

Phil Burton's landlady, Mrs. Elizabeth Smith, and her two
daughters, Elizabeth and Audrey, remember Mr. Burton coming
into their house at No. 6 Connaught Street, which was a few terraced streets lower down from The Side, and saying that he had a
pupil outside who had nowhere to spend the night because there
had been trouble at home. Thereafter, events moved at a pace
that surprised even Richard. Mr. Burton was virtually one of the

Smith family because he had been with them for seventeen years
—ever since he had arrived in Taibach and they were living in
Broad Street. And within a few months Richard was one of the
family too, with Mr. Burton as his ward. Recognizing the enormous advantages for Richie, his family had eventually agreed to
his legal adoption. As it happened, full adoption proved impossible
because Mr. Burton, born on November 30, 1904, failed by
twenty days to fulfill the legal requirement of being twenty-one
years older than the boy he wished to adopt. But a legal document
was drawn up and executed to make Richard his ward, and at the
same time Richard's surname was legally changed, though to
avoid confusion he was to be known as Jenkins until he left
school. The problem of his education was finally resolved.

Today Audrey Smith reflects, "It is amazing to think how
Philip Burton came home on a winter's night and asked mother if
she would have a boy called Richard Jenkins to stay here, as he
had nowhere to go; and that had she refused to have him there
might never have been a Richard Burton. Little did we know
then what fate had in store for him. Richard came to stay the
night and this was his home for the next two and a half years. He
had this little room upstairs and in the evenings he worked with
Mr. Burton in the room downstairs at the front. He was a nice
boy, and the one thing I always admired was that he would never
ask Mr. Burton for anything. He was often very broke, but he
was never a sponger. I remember, too, how he would go down to
the bottom toilet to smoke and drink. Mr. Burton would come in
and say, 'Where's Richie?' And I used to say I didn't know, and
then we'd look out of the window and see smoke coming from
the outside toilet."

"Ma" Smith lost her husband in 1918, a victim of the world's
worst influenza epidemic after he had served at sea throughout
the war. At the age of ninety-six, still wonderfully alert and
bright, her eyes lit up with pride at the mention of Richard Jenkins. "All I can say about Richard is that I glory in his success.
He has worked so very hard. You know, Mr. Burton would be up
with him at all hours, talking and studying. They would learn a
play between them in a night. And sometimes they would wake

me up and I would think they were quarreling in the front room. Then I'd tap from the bed and I could hear them tiptoeing up-stairs.

"When Richard came here from Caradoc Street, he had noth-ing at all. Mr. Burton bought him his clothes. He coached him, trained him, did everything. Richard's got to thank him for everything in the world he's got. He was a pretty rough boy then, and we had to polish him up a little. I taught him everything in manners—how to hold a knife and fork, how to eat his soup. But really he was the type of boy you couldn't alter. He had his own character and he was quite set in his ways even at that age. I remember once he stayed out all night after he and Mr. Burton had had a little bit of a fuss. He slammed out and said, 'You'll see me when I get back.' Mr. Burton waited up half the night. I hap-pened to be down early in the morning, and there was Richie at the door, looking bedraggled and very sorry for himself. 'Where in the world have you been?' I said. And he answered: 'Sitting on my grandmother's grave all night. Meditating.'

"Now that other boy who used to come here, Owen-Jones, he was very different; exceptionally handsome-looking, and defi-nitely a gentler, more cultured type. Yet he also came from a mining family, and so did another boy Mr. Burton helped. That was Viv Allen, who has got on very well. He lives in a lovely house in London, and he is headmaster of a school. But oh, if you saw the miner's house he came from—a lean-to place with a toilet at the bottom of the garden. And when you think of those lads, where they were born and how they were brought up, it is extra-ordinary. Now Richie is entertaining in the Dorchester.

"He was a rougher type altogether when he first came here. Very outspoken. What came into his mind he would say, and he didn't care who he offended or what happened. Ask his opinion and you would get it. He had a wonderful memory. Yet he could be so forgetful about his clothes. Somebody gave him a new mackintosh, and he immediately lost it when he went down to the YMCA for a rehearsal. And, oh yes, I remember, he had such smelly feet. His socks! I used to say to Mr. Burton, 'Take those things out in the backyard.' And even then you couldn't go near them for a couple of days. Oh, but Richard had so many good points. You had to like him. He was always in a rush, leaving it until the last minute to go to school. And I remember he used to like shredded wheat for breakfast, and Mr. Burton was so spoiling that he used to sprinkle the sugar on for him."

Living in that comfortable house in Connaught Street, Richard Jenkins virtually became the most privileged boy in Taibach. He shared a private study with the benevolent man who was his English master and his commanding officer in the A.T.C. He had private tuition from a playwright, actor, and drama coach of rare patience and understanding. He had Ma Smith to fuss over him as lovingly as any real mother. At the same time he was undoubtedly the hardest working boy in Taibach. When he came home from school, his concentrated studying had only just begun. Far into the night Mr. Burton was soaking his mind with the stage of the world outside, discussing the characters of the great plays, the meanings of words, the rhythm of lines, and where the emphasis lay, and all the time correcting the boy's elocution and striving to rid him of his industrial Welsh accent. He fed him with a reading list of important books. And on weekends, in the startled loneliness of flocks of sheep on the high mountains, master and pupil, more father and son, sent birds soaring with the soft magic of clear-ringing Shakespearean verse. *Out, out with shout and the panting antics of ranting preachers. Let the voice speak clear and gentle and twitch the ears of that rabbit wrapped in one hundred yards of stillness.* Meticulous speech was Philip Burton's obsession; maximum effect with minimum effort his first principle. There was little he could teach Richard about stage movement—the boy's ability to move and to hold an audience with his physical presence was a gift to be recognized, not taught. Instead he concentrated all on the understanding and delivery of language; the control and discipline needed to achieve princely power in speech without any obvious strain. No opportunity was missed of broadening Richard's drama education. To strengthen his coordination and mathematical precision in speaking, he made him play again and again the part of a bank manager who, in a scene of a play, has to hold five separate telephone conversations, switching in rapid succession from one phone to another. And even when the boy took a girl to the cinema, Burton's influence was upon him, for his task-master would direct him to study certain films, such as *The Moon and Sixpence,* after which Richard went home to give him a brilliantly acted account of George Sanders as Maugham's Gaughin-type anti-hero.

Obviously, a boy enjoying such a close personal relationship with a master could have been bitterly resented by his school colleagues. Yet Richard never was. For one thing, he never courted privilege. And secondly, while Burton worked wonders in improving his mind and speech, Richard's basic character never changed; in school he was as strong-willed and unmanageable as he had been in his Caradoc Street days. "Luther" Lewis says, "I remember him coming to school one day when he was completely cut. He had been in the Grand Hotel all lunchtime and he reeked of beer. Burton was taking the class and he said to him, 'Richard! Get home at once.' Another time Richie belted a master who was knocking me about for something I hadn't done. He was reported to old Reynolds the headmaster, and any other boy would have been expelled. But somehow Richie got away with it. I think Phil Burton wanted to control him, but I don't think he ever did."

Burgess agrees: "Richard was working very hard with Phil Burton, and there were a number of occasions when it was perfectly obvious that they hadn't come to school on the best of terms. There had been a row or something. At these times, when he might be remorseful, Burton could be very amusing in class, and he would have everyone laughing at his jokes. Everyone, that is, except Richard, who would deliberately stay granite-faced. It was rather sad in a way, and these were the only occasions when I felt like telling him to come off it.

"But mostly Richard's reaction to things was remarkable for his age. He had this extraordinary adult attitude, this maturity and almost worldly sophistication that made him different from other boys. I was terrified of Phil Burton, and as for the headmaster Mr. Reynolds, he would have awed Frankenstein. But not Richie. There was a rule at the time that the main doors were to be used only by staff, sixth formers, and prefects. Richie always used the main doors and eventually he was caught. Reynolds called him up before the entire assembly at school, and he walked down the aisle and up on to the stage as though he were about to receive the Oscar.

" 'You know you are not allowed to enter by the main entrance?,' said the headmaster.

" 'Yes, sir.'

" 'You realize that only sixth formers and prefects are allowed to use that entrance?'

" 'Yes, sir.'

" 'Are you a sixth former?'

" 'No, sir.'

" 'Are you a prefect?'

" 'No, sir.'

" 'You're a big boy, Jenkins, aren't you?'

" 'If you say so, sir.'

"The school waited in suspense for his punishment. Then, after a deliberate pause, the headmaster said, 'Well, in this case, Jenkins, I think I had better make you a prefect here and now.'

"And he did. For Reynolds this was completely out of character. Even in the ordinary way, boys were never made prefects in front of the entire school. But Richie was. You see, these things just happened to him all the time. Nothing was ever ordinary. As a schoolboy he was ten times larger than life, and whatever happened to him was invariably dramatic. He didn't really look for it; these things just came to him. For example, after playing rugby against Abertillery away, we were coming back in a non-corridor train when Richard desperately wanted a pee. Someone suggested that the only place was out the window, and so he did. Just at that point we roared through a station with people lining the platform. And that was the first public appearance of Richard Burton in Wales.

"But Richard's most outrageous behavior at school was in the physical training classes. The regular P.T. master had been called up for the Army, and his replacement was unpopular with the boys and not very good at his job. Richie used to give him hell.

He was a big boy, and he always turned out for P.T. in the smallest possible pair of shorts he could borrow from a boy in Form II. When we changed he would take off his shirt but leave on his collar and tie, plus socks and suspenders, and he would do all the exercises in this monstrous outfit, swinging on ropes, climbing wallbars, vaulting the horse. This master didn't know what to do, and Richie plagued him for God knows how long. The climax came when the master was bending over the large chest in which we kept all the sports gear. For some reason he got inside and as he was stooping Richie closed the lid and sat on top of the box. The master was beating and hammering from inside and making all kinds of terrible threats. But Richie just sat there. The rest of us were a bit scared and then I looked out of the window and saw the headmaster approaching. 'Watch out,' I said, 'Here comes the boss.' Now everyone was terrified of the head, including this master. So Richie knocked on the lid of the box and simply said, 'Mr. Reynolds is on his way over.' Silence. Then Richard whispered into the box, 'You do realize, of course, that when the boss comes in I shall have to stand out of politeness?' Still dead silence; it was like something out of an Abbott and Costello film. And when the headmaster entered, Richard made a great noise of getting off the box, but the lid didn't open.

"The headmaster, obviously suspicious at the silence, went up to Richard. 'Have you seen the P.T. master?'

" 'Yes, sir.'

"The box loomed large and still.

" 'When?'

" 'In the lesson, sir.'

"The boss looked quizzically at Rich. 'Why are you dressed like that, boy?'

" 'Changing, sir.'

" 'Those your shorts?'

" 'No, sir. Borrowed them.'

" 'From a midget?'

" 'No, sir.'

" 'Well,' said the headmaster, 'when you see your teacher, tell him I want him.'

"The boss looked at the box, looked at all our tight-lipped expressions, and then walked out. I think he secretly guessed what was going on. Anyway, Rich lifted the lid of the box and said, 'You can come out now.' It was a joke and we laughed about it tremendously. But when it was all over, Richard said to me, 'What do you think of that then?'

"I said, 'Think of what—you or him?'

" 'Him.'

" 'I don't know,' I said. 'I don't really see what else he could have done. I would probably have done exactly the same.'

" 'Ah,' said Rich. 'But you wouldn't have got yourself into that spot in the first place. That's the difference. For a person to allow himself to get into such a position with boys like us! The lack of dignity!'

"It all seems a childish prank now, but the point is that no other boy thought of it in the way he did. To us it was just a hell of a good joke. But he saw the implications. He had this incredible maturity and awareness. He used to say, 'What is it? Is it something we've got? Or is it something they lack?' I have met Richard many times since our school days, and looking back there is so much of his character that shows in little things that happened then. His reactions were never the sort you would expect from an ordinary schoolboy.

"That P.T. master never forgave Rich. But it didn't worry him. He could get away with things, and because we were with him, so could we. He wasn't really malicious. He gave respect to the masters and he expected respect in return. If it wasn't given, as it wasn't given by that P.T. master, Richie would react in his own way."

Richard's wild ways became a constant source of anxiety for Burton and especially, says Burgess, whenever they had a play in rehearsal. "I remember when Rich was about to do *Youth at the Helm* for the Air Training Corps. Burton had flatly forbidden him to play rugby or do anything that would endanger his well-being. He was cosseting him to a ludicrous degree. Well, Rich could never resist a rugby ball, and on the day before the first performance we were sitting in the schoolyard when somebody kicked a ball over the hedge. Richard had to get up and take a running kick at it. But he missed it entirely and instead kicked the bench that was fixed on concrete. Oh, the histrionics! He collapsed, roaring and writhing. And it was like a corny film, for at that moment Phil Burton came round the corner. Rich was still doing his act, clutching himself and groaning that he had probably broken his foot. Then I told him Burton was approaching and I have never seen such a reaction. He put on a fixed brave smile and said, 'Pick me up.' And with Rich still wearing this ghastly fixed smile, Burton passed on by. Afterwards Rich said, 'I can't go home. My foot! I can't walk! I'll have to come back with you for tea.' We had tea together, but that evening we had to go on to see Phil Burton appearing in his own play—some terrible thing called *Cedars So Strong*. In the YMCA hall we sat at the end of the row so that Rich could stretch his leg out in the gangway. When the play ended they played 'The King.' Richard tried to stand for the national anthem, and then crashed flat on his face in the middle of the gangway. He got up, and then fell down again like a tree. I said, 'It can't be as bad as that.' And Richard said, 'It is. It's gone! Finished! I'm crippled for life. I can't go home like this. You'll have to walk me round the block until everything returns.' And it was absolutely pouring with rain, but still we trudged around the block at least a dozen times until he felt he could stand on it without support. Finally he said that I would have to help him home, prop him up against the front door, ring the bell, and then run away. And I did. Of course, it was probably all an act, but then that was typical of Richie, making a great performance out of it."

Shortly afterwards, Richard was starring in *Youth at the Helm* at the local YMCA, and Trevor George remembers how the production was mysteriously undermined by some practical joker. "Richie was the very energetic young secretary who forced himself onto the board of managers of a company without anyone realizing what was happening. During one performance chaos broke out on and off the stage, resulting in 'P.H.' poking his head through a door on the left and shouting at all on stage. It happened in a scene when the board was having its annual general meeting. The treasurer was presenting his report while his annual statement was being passed around. This statement consisted of a torn piece of paper the size of a postage stamp on which was printed the word *BALLS*. As each member of the board saw the statement he was convulsed, and it took many minutes before we were able to continue normally. No one ever found out who printed the offending word."

While George was Richard's constant companion on the sports field, at club dances, and in the coffee bars, Burgess was his closest friend on a more serious plane. They compared their end-of-term reports (both boys always achieved high gradings), tested one another for examinations, and studied drama together. Richard especially liked to try out his speech delivery on Dennis, and once, seeking privacy, they spent an hour rehearsing in the boys' lavatory. Richard was preparing his Macbeth piece for the verse-speaking at the local eisteddfod and he launched into the lines:

> *Is this a dagger I see before me,*
> *The handle towards my hand? Come let me clutch*
> *thee. . . .*

"It was incredibly funny at the time," says Burgess. "I leave it to your imagination. But the paraphrasing that went on in that speech, with the boys coming to and fro to use the toilet, was brilliant—coarse and filthy, but very, very clever. We had a lot of fun working together, but, mind you, underneath was always a great deal of seriousness."

During his year back at school, Richard went out with Catherine Dolan more than any other girl, and some people viewed them as a young couple with an idyllic relationship. Richard's younger brother Graham was one. "I was a year younger than Cathy, and at that time a year made all the difference. I used to dream of having something going like Richie. To me it was the biggest romance since Nelson Eddy and Jeanette MacDonald. I thought Cathy was the most beautiful girl in the world, with that red hair and that shape and style. I was terribly jealous."

Miss Dolan, as Catherine West, wife of an American novelist, laughs about it now. "Graham may well remember it as a great love affair, but it was no such thing. There was never anything serious like there is today. Things that you can see in films now would not even be mentioned between a boy and a girl in the Port Talbot of those days. I know that Richie and I would dodge the school dental inspections on a Friday and always end up on the wooden pier where we read poetry to each other. I know that I make it sound like something out of *Peg's Own Paper*, because I was a very emotional young woman and he was a very sexy young man. But this was just the way of the time, our particular society. Why, we didn't even kiss! Richard would say, 'My hands are awfully cold'—and for gawd's sake I'd offer him my gloves. It wasn't being frigid or anything. It was just that we both recognized that things could have become too hot. Richard was never a lecher. He was attracted by thoughts, feelings, ideas. And anyway, he was more attracted by rugby football than he was by me. I was sixteen and innocent and gormless about sex, and he liked me just for what I was."

Despite all the time he gave to sport, acting, and girls, Richard did not waste his second chance at school. In that one year he was never away sick, and he studied to such good effect that in September, 1943, he achieved matriculation standard in the Central Welsh Board School Certificate examinations, with "very goods" in English literature and math, "credits" in English language, history, Welsh, and (surprisingly) chemistry, and a "pass" in geography. At the same time, Philip Burton had demonstrated his confidence in Richard's finely tutored diction by casting him as Professor Higgins in the school production of Shaw's *Pygmalion*. Cathy played a supporting role. In October the play ran for a week of full houses at the YMCA, and the critic of the *Port Talbot Guardian* hailed it as a triumph for Richard: "As the Professor, he displayed dramatic talent that made him a dominating personality and brought out all that was best in the acting of his opposite number Dilys Jones as the London flower girl."

The Jenkins family was there to cheer and to celebrate afterwards with Philip Burton and *Richard Burton,* for it was time for Richie to begin using his adopted name. He had left school again, but not to return to the Co-op. His guardian had already introduced him to radio work in Cardiff, and now Richard had the chance to go straight from school on to the professional stage. On August 21, 1943, when they were with 499 Air Squadron at a summer camp at St. Athan's, Flight-Lieutenant Philip Burton had come across the following advertisement in the *Cardiff Western Mail*:

EMLYN WILLIAMS WANTS WELSH ACTORS

Mr. Emlyn Williams is looking for several Welsh actors and actresses for small parts in his new play which will open in the autumn. Types wanted vary from young people to character actors and actresses. A Welsh boy actor is also required. Boy applicants must be 14 years by December 1, but are expected to look younger. Those who think they can fill these roles should write within seven days to Mr. Williams at 15 Pelham Crescent, London, S.W.7, giving age, qualifications, and enclosing a recent photograph.

Flight-Sergeant Richard Burton successfully applied.

II
Richard Burton

The Druid's Rest

The day Philip Burton recognized Emlyn Williams's advertisement as a breakthrough for Richard, some fifteen miles east, as the miner crawls, another dedicated teacher, Glyn Morse, saw it as an opportunity for his own wild prodigy. His pupil, also a miner's son, was a pugnacious boy of fourteen who had none of Richard's penchant for poetry and scholarship. But he had presence, a strong personality and remarkable self-confidence for his years, and Morse was determined that he should not be condemned to the coal pits of the Rhondda Valley.

Today that boy's "pit" is a palatial eleventh-floor executive suite with a wide-screen view of the Thames stretching from the Houses of Parliament to the Tower of London. And as Stanley Baker, the British producer, television tycoon, and filmstar, he looks back in humble wonder at the way the Glyn Morses and Philip Burtons helped underprivileged boys in South Wales. "The dedication and self-sacrifice that goes into that sort of life is truly amazing. I suppose they were moved by the sheer hopelessness of life in those valleys. There was bugger all in my town of Ferndale but to go into the pits—unless you wanted to be a draper's assistant or work in the Co-op. The natural move at the age of fourteen was to buy an axe, a strong pair of boots, and an old suit, and sign on. And that was it! Your whole future, your whole way of life. If you didn't do that you were regarded as a sissy, and in a way that was a bloody sight worse.

"To go down the pit was a sign of manhood. You revolted against anything that suggested effeminacy. My father was an agnostic. A one-legged coal miner and a great character. I worshipped him. But it was my brother, ten years older than me, who really raised me. He bought the first pair of boxing gloves, the first pair of football boots; he took care of you, screened the girls you were going with, and clipped you around the ear if you were cheeky. In the same way it was Morse who really made me in my career. He had a family of his own, and yet he gave me private elocution lessons, took me to London for my first film part, got me into my first play.

"After I left Wales, he sent me one book every week, and I had to read it and every Sunday write at least eight pages about it. Then he got me into Birmingham Rep, and though I was working very hard there, he used to send me two books each week to read and discuss. This went on until I was about twenty-five years of age and after I became successful. In a strange way he guided my career. I don't know what it was. Some strange kind of instinct about what one should do, what moves one should make next. He's retired now and half-blind. But to this day I still take his advice. An extraordinary man."

Baker describes himself as being a dropout in his Rhondda Valley days. "Until I was twelve I was totally hopeless at school. Got into awful trouble. Then I met Morse, the arts-and-crafts master, and for the first time in my life I wanted to go to school. I didn't do ordinary lessons like arithmetic, English, and science. I just went to his class every morning and stayed there all day long."

What Morse saw in Baker was the resolution of a natural born fighter; a boy of character—proud, self-willed, and overspirited. He found an outlet for his cocky exuberance by putting him in end-of-term plays, and within a year the rebel schoolboy was a promising boy actor in an earthy nonclassical mold. Baker, contemptuous of limp-spined play-actors and proud of his rough masculinity, even regarded the name Stanley as being somewhat unmanly. But the opportunity of any kind of life outside the Rhondda made him soldier on with a fistful of knuckles as the quick answer to anyone foolhardy enough to call him a pansy actor.

It took Baker another twelve years to establish himself as Britain's top tough guy in such films as *The Cruel Sea* and *Hell Drivers*. Yet briefly at the age of thirteen he slipped ahead of Richard when film producer Sergei Bolbandov saw him in a school play

and told Glyn Morse to bring him to London for a small part in
Undercover. In this respect, young Stan was the professional and
the older Richie the amateur when they answered Emlyn Williams's advertisement. But it was Richard who made the big impression, especially on casting director Daphne Rye, and he was
chosen to play the boy Glan in *The Druid's Rest.* Stanley, three
years younger, was hired as his understudy, with every hope of
stepping into the role after Burton's call-up to the services. Both
boys looked too old for the other juvenile part of Tommos, and
this went to a youngster called Brynmor Thomas.

Ted Upton, stage director for the production, remembers boys
coming in droves to auditions at the Prince of Wales Theater,
Cardiff. "It was an extraordinary sight, all these mothers turning
up with their children, and mad to get their boys in the theater.
But Richard wasn't among them. He had already clinched the
part. Directly Mr. Williams saw him, it was a cast-iron certainty
he would get it. He was a natural. You couldn't miss it. Nobody
could. He was more mature than any of the others, very sophisticated, and knowledgeable. But the most amazing thing that
struck one straight away was his wonderful repose. When he
hadn't anything to say on stage, he was still very much in the
play; absolutely still and yet you were aware of his presence,
which was most unusual with young people. Stanley had nothing
special about him then, though my God, he's got it now."

Richard had only one scene of any significance in the play, and
his role seemed microscopic after playing Professor Higgins in
Pygmalion. But all that mattered to him then was being accepted
and having a professional career. As Baker says: "At that stage I
feel sure Richard couldn't sit back and say there was a burning
ambition to become an actor. I certainly couldn't. One's main
ambition from the earliest sort of remembrances was to get out of
the valleys. It didn't matter which way—through football, boxing, anything so long as you left the valleys and improved yourself. There was no passionate desire to be an actor, great or bad.
It was simply an opportunity provided at the right time and coincidental with everything else that was happening. An opportunity
to go to London at an early age and earn money. I always used to

think as a kid that Cardiff was England—and yet it was only twenty miles away. That's how far withdrawn we were. We just had to grab the chance to widen our horizon.

"I didn't even know who Emlyn Williams was. I knew he was the boss, that he had written and directed the play. But there was a sense of unreality about the whole bloody thing—to be suddenly taken out of a Welsh valley and thrust into big cities, totally alone. When I think about it now, I would never have let my son go off under those circumstances at the age of fourteen. Maybe that attitude is too protective, but it never occurred to my parents. All that concerned them was that I was earning the princely sum of five pounds [$22.50] a week."

Unlike Baker, Richard at seventeen knew all about Emlyn Williams. Here was the mercurial little man of many talents who was regarded in Wales as the outstanding symbol of success; the prototype for the great ideal—the underprivileged Welsh boy, armed with native drive and wit and his own peculiar brand of genius, who reaches a pinnacle of fame and fortune across the border. True, Williams hailed from the pastoral north of Flintshire, not from the strike-torn industrial south. Yet his origins were no less humble, his achievements none the less great. Richard had idolized him ever since he had been among the eight-year-olds at Eastern Elementary listening to old Tom Howell's beautiful reading of *Night Must Fall*.

Richard's debt to this white-maned wizard of the arts is now immeasurable and irredeemable. If Philip Burton guided him towards the stage door, Williams was the one who flung it wide open. He could not have done more to accelerate Richard's progress and growth if the young man had been his own son. His contribution went far beyond taking an unknown, untried boy from the Afan Valley and giving him his first opportunity on the professional stage. He was to become a father, teacher, and inspirational force. Both socially and professionally he was to be the guiding star. Just as he introduced him to the theater, so he would later launch him on his film career—writing his first movie role, directing him, starring alongside him. He would be instrumental in Burton's meeting of his future wife; he would become a god-father to their first child.

Emlyn Williams is the classic example of a Welsh talent fostered and fed by a dedicated teacher. He was ten years old when Miss Sarah Grace Cooke recognized his bright-eyed curiosity amid the rows of her pupils. She satisfied and shaped it to such an extent that she served, years later, as the inspiration for the character of Miss Moffatt in his play *The Corn Is Green*. Her invested time also paid dividends for countless other Welsh talents. Before Williams, the Welsh had made little impression on the English stage. Those who were potentially great actors invariably emerged as fire-breathing orators in the chapel pulpits. There was, of course, Ray Milland, born up the road from Richard in Neath, and the incomparable Dame Edith Evans, but neither was essentially Welsh. By writing plays with authentic Welsh backgrounds and characters, Williams paved the way for many more of his countrymen to make their mark as actors and gain experience to move on to a wider range of parts. He did the same for Burton, giving him a Welsh vehicle for both his stage and screen debut.

Appropriately, in the light of his subsequent reputation as a saloon bar storyteller, Richard's first professional appearance as an actor was in a play set in, and named after, a village pub; and in it the author poked affectionate fun at the Welsh tendency to give preference to the truth of their imagination rather than their eyes. Williams's comedy of eccentricities centered on the village of Tan-y-maes, where the landlord of *The Druid's Rest* and the local constable suspect they are harboring Smith, the notorious "Brides in the Bath" murderer. But they are prepared to postpone his arrest until he had helped the local choir to win a 200 guineas ($900) prize at the National Eisteddfod. In the end, Smith turns out to be a local peer who wants nothing more in life than a book of verse and a pint of beer. Richard's small role was that of the stolid older brother of the overimaginative boy who feeds the villagers' suspicions about the stranger in their midst. There were only seven others in the entire cast—Michael Shepley as the mysterious wayfarer; Roddy Hughes as the innkeeper; Gladys Henson as his wife; Neil Porter, a Welsh tramp bard; Lyn Evans, Nuna Davies, and Brynmor Thomas.

Miss Henson, who played Richard's stage mother, remembers well the first time she met him at rehearsals. "He was the most beautiful looking boy. He was lovely. And he seemed so calm and collected. I thought perhaps he would be nervous, but not a bit of it. You would never have thought it was his first professional part. He was really a natural from the word go, from the first rehearsal almost. He was always lolling about, always so calm. He took everything in his stride. He may have been more excited than he pretended to be. I don't know. But certainly the theater was quite secondary to his interest in rugby; he never stopped talking about the game.

"I remember one day he was lying on the sofa at rehearsals, dozing off. And I said to him, 'Oh Richard, you're never going to be an actor if you go on like this. You must keep your place. Don't go to sleep in the middle of rehearsals.' And he said, 'Oh you know me, Glad. I go my own way.' Yet he was never a precocious boy; just an ordinary boy with a great talent."

On November 22, 1943, twelve days after his eighteenth birthday, Burton made his first appearance as a professional actor at the Royal Court Theater, Liverpool, where one week before Michael Redgrave had appeared in *A Month in the Country*. Though pretentiously publicized as the world premiere of *The Druid's Rest*, it was a modest beginning, and his debut went unmentioned by the critics. Yet it was not completely unrecognized. Joshua Logan, the distinguished American director and dramatist, happened to be in the audience, and he predicted a great future for Richard. Emlyn Williams, too, was impressed. "He was obviously going to be a great actor because he had the looks, the ease, the deportment, and the natural flair. But you couldn't foresee his future precisely because he only had this one small comedy scene, which he played with tremendous assurance, as if he had been in the theater for years. It is a paradox in a way that he never became a great comedian rather than a serious actor, because it was the comedy scene that persuaded me that the potential was there and that he had tremendous reserves of natural timing."

Those days in bomb-scarred Liverpool, with the flotsam of sailors and the jetsam of girls eddying together in the notoriety of Lime Street just around the corner, gave Richard and his understudy an excitement they had never felt before. For the first time they were free in a big city with money to spend. An odd pair, Burton and Baker. Richard, infinitely more mature, was soon away with a pretty program-seller, and he mixed easily with the cast in the Magic Clock bar. Stanley, though equal in size, was very much the junior and was treated as such, but not by Richard, for they were bonded together by their identical backgrounds— the Welsh mining village, the tough hard-drinking father, the idolized big brother.

The tour moved on to Nottingham and Brighton. And then, in mid-December at the Swansea Empire, Richard took his first professional bow on a Welsh stage. This time he was noticed by the *South Wales Evening Post* critic: "Richard Burton as Glan, who incidentally is made to act as interpreter for the Welsh in an unobtrusive manner, is an accomplished performer." Next morning he caught a bus into Port Talbot and took identical gifts to sister Ciss and Ma Smith—two small prints of the Mona Lisa in simple wooden frames. "It's not much," he said as he gave one to Ma, "but never mind. When I'm rich I'll buy you a house."

"Good heavens," said Phil Burton. "Why buy Ma a picture? Why not a bag or a pair of stockings?"

Richard hugged Ma. "I bought it so that she can always remember me." And he was right. When she was in her nineties, it would still be her most prized possession.

The climax of the pre-London tour came in Cardiff, where they stayed for a three-week Christmas season, and Daddy Ni came down for a matinee and a night out on the town. "It was really wild," recalls Stanley Baker. "I remember especially a night at the Prince of Wales when Richard was making up to go on stage and we suddenly started fighting in the dressing room. I was thrown back against the window, about four floors up and overlooking Queen Street. It was a windy night and the whole window frame went smash and fell right down in front of a bus queue. We were terrified, and I remember the stage manager saying he'd have to report us. Then Emlyn Williams read the riot act: 'If this happens again one of you will have to leave. You're uncontrollable kids. Always fighting. Terrible.' They put the window back. And do you know the very next day we did the same thing exactly! But you know how it was. Cardiff and all that, and nobody to say no."

"Cardiff and all that" was every Welsh boy's wicked dream: The capital of the Principality with not a deacon in sight, and the blacked-out tram rocking down Bute Street, where the girls are so sweet, to Tiger Bay and the pub of the Six Tits which kept the world's jolly-rogering sailors amused in booze while they waited to collect their blisters in the upstairs snigger rooms of pot-scented Chinese cafés. Taibach and Ferndale were over the hills and far away as the young Burton and Baker roamed the city with eyes like blowlamps.

The play was becoming a glorious game that Richard couldn't take altogether seriously, until they arrived in London. Then the nervous tension mounted, and he was made profoundly aware of the sense of occasion and the importance of an opening night in the West End (London's equivalent of Broadway) to players who acted for a living. The first night at St. Martin's Theater was January 26, 1944, and next morning he eagerly combed the newspapers for reviews. They were hard to find. The newspapers were restricted in size, and much of the space was given to the struggle for Leningrad and the battle of Cassino. There was a handful of short, reasonably favorable notices, with two mentions of Burton. The *Times* critic wrote: "Mr. Richard Burton (or should it be 'Master Richard'?) is consistently droll as the small boy whose starved imagination spins the web of misunderstandings." And later the *New Statesman* concluded its review with the line: "In a wretched part Richard Burton showed exceptional ability." Burton loathed being called Master Richard, and more galling was the fact that the praise in the *Times* was entirely misplaced since the critic had obviously identified Richard with the part played by

Brynmor Thomas. But he glowed with pleasure on reading the *New Statesman*. "It's the only notice I can remember, and that last line changed my life. I thought, 'Well, all right then, I'll stick to this business.' "

When Burton was working in London, the worst days of the blitz had passed and the lingering terror of the doodlebug missile and the other German secret weapon, the V2 rocket, was still to come. The West End theater was slowly returning to life; the cinema was positively booming. At last the great flood of war films was abating, and after so many moviegoers had enjoyed the exquisite catharsis of weeping for Bette Davis and Paul Henreid in *Now Voyager*, the accent was now on sentiment and romance, and especially youth. Mickey Rooney was still going strong as Andy Hardy; Margaret O'Brien was everybody's kid sister and the current star of *Lost Angel*; and at the Empire, Leicester Square, in January, 1944, an eleven-year-old girl called Elizabeth Taylor was stealing a film from a dog in *Lassie Come Home*.

On the stage, Michael Wilding was enjoying a brilliant success in Rattigan's *While the Sun Shines*, and next door to Richard's theater, at the Ambassadors, Hermione Gingold was starring with Henry Kendall and Bonar Colleano in *Sweeter and Lower*, the second in a series of popular revues. It is the show Stanley Baker best remembers. "Towards the end of spring the chorus girls used to sunbathe on the roof and our theater looked down on them. So Richard and I—it shows how childish we were—used to aim peashooters at them, trying to hit their tits. They didn't know where the artillery was coming from. We lived in digs in Gower Street, and the things we got up to are indescribable when you look back. We were like wild animals let loose to enjoy the birds and the booze, everything that the money and glamor of being in the theater could bring; two Welsh kids, totally disorientated, absolutely free of any sort of control at all. In these days if a kid comes into the theater, there are all sorts of laws and regulations; they have chaperones and all that bollocks. We had none of that. We ran totally wild.

"You don't lead a sheltered life in Wales anyway, and a boy of fourteen, in terms of ordinary living, is as advanced as a seven-

teen- or eighteen-year-old in other parts. So we nearly drank ourselves to death at the age of fourteen and eighteen. We really did.
Quite seriously it was a bloody gay adventure. Though I was
fourteen, I looked much older, and both of us used to get into
trouble when we went into pubs. When we walked into a bar
and ordered a pint, some idiot would say, 'Hey, why aren't you
in the Army?' We couldn't answer that we were too young for
the Army, because then we would be too young to be in a pub. It
got to such a state that either we had to fight about it or else we
had to shoot a line. I got to saying I had a weak heart and was not
medically fit. Hell, we got through some boozing in those days.
Only last year Emlyn Williams told me another story about this
period. We were rehearsing at the Scala Theater, and there was a
day when Richard was missing. So Williams called for the understudy. But I wasn't there either. 'Where the hell are they?'
Emlyn asked. And somebody answered, 'I shouldn't be surprised
if they're behind a flat having a wank!' "

Mr. Upton does not recall the incident. "It seems very unlikely, because the boys would have been slightly in awe of
Emlyn Williams then, and they would have scarcely dared to
miss a rehearsal. Young boys are always difficult in the theater because their heads swell out, but I don't remember them as being
worse than many others. Of course, Richard was very good-looking, something quite extraordinary, and the girls went for him in
a big way. I know there was a certain amount of trouble."

During one scene in the play, Glan and his stage mother had to
go upstairs, ostensibly to get ready for church. "Every performance we went up to a kind of landing," says Miss Henson. "We
always had about a quarter of an hour wait together, and while
we were up there Richard used to tell me all about his love life.
'Oo, I met the most lovely nurse last night, Glad,' he would say.
And I should think he did have a love life because he was gorgeous to look at."

After the curtain Richard liked nothing better than joining the
cast at the Two Brewers pub just around the corner and meeting
the chorus girls from the Ambassadors. It was there in the spring
of 1944 that they gave him his farewell party before he joined the

RAF. "Philip Burton was there," says Ted Upton, "but it wasn't a big party. After all, in a way, we were a flop. We were never really away with that play, never. At that time managements were damned glad to keep anything on, and having something coming in as opposed to having a dark theater was fine. It was a charming little play, but it was not a great money-maker.

For young Burton, however, those months in *The Druid's Rest* were nearly idyllic. In 1944, the West End's square mile of theater and pubs was about the most exciting place on earth for a teen-age adventurer never short of friends or a pound in his pocket. The war was being won. Days and nights were never dull. Life was not all watered-down beer and pea-peppered chorus girls; with nightly performances and matinees, he had been made to earn his keep. All the same, whenever he thought of his brothers, back in the cramped crouch of the mines in Cwmavon and Pontrhydyfen, he could not help reflecting that he was absurdly overpaid. "Play acting! That's not work," they said. Yet it had brought him in a tenner ($45) a week—exactly double the new minimum wage for underground miners doing hard labor. And that minimum ($22.50) a week was only for the men. For Richard, at eighteen, the pay for going down the mines would have been three pounds ten shillings ($14) a week, with increments of five shillings ($1) a year. Instead he was earning almost triple that sum without the strain and the sweat and the hacking cough from coal dust.

Now peacock proud and an officer-cadet to boot—the Royal Air Force had posted him to Oxford to take the wartime University Short Course—he was going home to Wales to show them. But the old miners were not impressed. "*Iesu Mawr!* (Great Jesus)," said old Will Dai, a much-loved Cwmavon character who wore the peak of his button-down cap flat on his face and had an impediment in his speech. "J-j-just look at young D-d-douglas F-f-fairbanks in his f-f-fancy suede shoes. G-g-get yer hair cut, Richie." They didn't understand, and they would never understand, just as Daddy Ni would remain ignorant of acting until the day he died. But Richard didn't mind. He instinctively slipped back into the rough vernacular and matched pint for pint.

He loved to be back in Afan country, and whenever he returned, his heart would race as he rounded the lip of the mountain on the road to Pontrhydyfen. Yet he knew now that his future lay far beyond the valley of his childhood. Acting offered the one real hope of fame and fortune. And if there was little demand for Welsh-accented actors, well, he could mouth the King's English as purely as the best of them. At Oxford they might call him Taff, but given a stage he aimed to show the privileged public-school types just who was master of the spoken word.

Oxford

In the fall of 1944, Nevill Coghill, Merton Professor of English Literature at Oxford and Sub-Rector of Exeter College, was updating the college undergraduate card-index file, noting examinations passed and trying to make some perceptive comment on each student. The difficulty was to assess those students received from the Armed Forces for only six months on the special war-time University Short Course, but when Coghill came to the name of an eighteen-year-old Air Force cadet from Wales he wrote unhesitatingly: "This boy is a genius and will be a great actor. He is outstandingly handsome and robust, very masculine and with deep inward fire, and extremely reserved."

This, after six months' acquaintance, was the learned don's opinion of Richard Walter Jenkins Burton of Taibach. Time has not tempered his judgment. More than a quarter of a century later, he comments: "I have had many students of very great gifts and many of very little. But I have had only two men of genius to teach—W. H. Auden and Richard Burton. When they happen, one cannot mistake them."

Robert Hardy, the Shakespearean and popular British television actor, was at Oxford with Richard, and he too chooses the word genius to describe him. "He was a genius in the effortless way he attracted everybody—the most attractive creature I have ever come across, in the true sense of that adjective. It was the size of his personality that made me think of him as a great man. Everything was larger than life, but not in an actorish way. He did not give the impression of an actor throwing it on. He was a fine athlete, brilliant talker, superb drinker, everything. A sort of Renaissance man. We read things like Castiglione's *The Courtier* —sixteenth century instructions on how to be a perfect man— and it seemed to some of us at Oxford that this was just the sort of man he was. A natural-born prince."

Prince? Genius? Ostensibly they are extraordinary words to describe the son of a miner and a former barmaid, who was to leave Oxford as he had arrived—without any academic distinction of note. An officer-cadet undergraduate of Exeter College, he was reading English literature and Italian, but there was never time to achieve an advanced standard in these subjects. Nor could he make his mark on the sports field, since he was there out of the rugby season, and cricket was organized only on a casual basis during the war. Yet still he had an impact on Oxford, leaving an indelible impression on his tutor and fellow undergraduates.

Richard went to Oxford under the system whereby recruits to the Armed Forces who had gained a high enough school certificate standard could take a six-month university course, living in college as undergraduates in the usual way, but also undergoing basic service training on two days a week when they attended drill parades and lectures on such subjects as aircraft recognition, navigation, weapon training, and engines. On a Friday night, whenever possible, he returned to Taibach on a seventy-two-hour pass, and Ma Smith and her daughters would blanco his belt and gaiters, brasso his cap, badge, and buttons, and send him back infinitely smarter than when he arrived.

"Well, Richard, what have you learned at Oxford?," Ma Smith asked him on his first weekend leave.

"Who can drink the most beer," he said.

And it was true. At first, any reputation he had at Oxford rested entirely on his prodigious drinking capacity. "Beer" Burton they called him, and he laid claim to the Exeter sconce record—part of a dining-hall punishment for bad etiquette in which the offender must drink nearly two pints of beer in thirty seconds or pay for it. According to Richard, he learned to drink without swallowing and could sink a sconce in ten seconds. Drinking records were the only honors open to him at Oxford. But he was resolved at least to widen his acting experience in the short time he was there.

In the summer of 1944, Oxford's famous but bankrupt University Dramatic Society was midway through its decade of suspension, and a substitute company, "The Friends of the OUDS," was staging a series of productions to raise funds to pay off the society's debts. The moving spirit behind The Friends was Professor Coghill, who was destined to become the father figure of the Oxford theater. Richard tackled him with the same single-mindedness of purpose that he had displayed in approaching Philip Burton.

"What do you want?," said Coghill when the young Welshman knocked at his door.

"I have come to say some poetry to you," Richard replied.

"Well, there's a dais over there. Stand on it, and say it."

Richard recited the soliloquy, "To be or not to be . . . ," and Coghill was impressed. "Well, you need no help from me. That was perfect. But what do you want?"

"I would like a part in *Measure for Measure*," said Richard.

"I'm afraid it's fully cast," said Coghill. "But wait a minute. There is likely to be a vacancy in the part of Angelo. If you care to understudy for it, you can have it, if the vacancy occurs."

Richard moved towards the door. "Thank you then. I will."

"Hey, what's your name, by the bye?" the Professor called out.

"Richard Burton."

Coghill explains: "I do not often recall conversations verbatim, but this one impressed itself on me. I can still hear the melodious Welsh voice and the way of speaking, which was at once changed to received standard English when he started on 'To be or not to be.' The change was utterly convincing and instantaneous. Out came the most perfect rendering I had ever heard, except that given at that time by John Gielgud in his Haymarket *Hamlet.* But it was not just an imitation of Gielgud."

Typically, Richard has a dramatic tale of how he moved up from understudy to play Angelo. According to his version, told on BBC television, he was a fairly ruthless young man, and he prayed that one night the leading actor might not appear. "Eventually the man playing Angelo was so impressed by my earnestness that he said I should play half the performances and he would play the other half. Then he became ill—nothing to do with me, with the Welsh and wizardry; he became ill and I played the whole thing, all the time." As Professor Coghill remembers it, Burton moved into the lead because the actor, an RAF officer, was posted away from Oxford. He was the late Hallam Fordham, who had modeled himself on Gielgud, and who had won distinction for his BBC readings of *The Prelude* of Wordsworth, which Coghill judges as being the best he has heard with the exception of readings by Gielgud, Burton, and Robert Donat. "He had already played Oberon and Horatio for me. When I cast him for Angelo, he warned me that he expected shortly to be posted elsewhere, and I was on tenterhooks for fear that he would be taken from me—until Richard appeared, so that my king was guarded by an ace. In due course Hallam was posted away, and Richard stepped effortlessly into the part."

Richard was determined to shake Oxford with his performance of Angelo, and he literally did so. He recalls that he became so passionately involved in one speech that he hammered a fist against the wall of Christ Church. "A piece of centuries-worn masonry broke off, dust flew into my eyes, and, half-blinded, I stumbled off while the audience roared with laughter." Coghill remembers the incident in less dramatic terms. "Richard unfolded a performance of great feeling and passion as Angelo, often surprising me with some gesture, such as the famous wall-bang that brought down a little bit of moldering stone. . . . It didn't really dislodge the masonry in any dangerous sense, and I think the anecdote has got mixed up with another, which was also true. The performance was in Christ Church's inmost quad, east of the Hall steps, the cloister quad; it had Gothic revival crenelations, and one of these fell down during the night in the week of performance. If it had fallen down a couple of hours before, it would have killed three or four people at the back of the audience. But this was not Richard's doing. Richard's hammering of the wall with his fist was on the other side of the 'theater,' the stage side, and though a bit of wall flaked off, it was no danger to anyone."

Coghill was so impressed with Burton's Angelo in rehearsal that he invited Mr. Hugh Beaumont, the suave managing director of H. M. Tennent Ltd., to come down and see him act. Tennent's was the major producing company responsible for presenting *The Druid's Rest*, and Beaumont, once assistant manager of the Cardiff Playhouse and nicknamed "Binkie" (in Welsh, "darkie") since his childhood days in Wales, was fast on the way to becoming the most powerful theater manager in London. After seeing Richard's performance, he told him to call at his London office as soon as he had finished his service in the RAF.

Once again, Philip Burton had assisted Richard's progress, for he wrote to him regularly, advising him by letter about the playing of Angelo, and he visited Oxford for the final dress rehearsal and spent half the night with his prodigy, going over the part with him and working out subtle variations. After the opening, Mr. Burton went to his room at Exeter College and waited for his ward to visit him in triumph. Richard never came. With other members of the cast he went to a party given by a wealthy woman. Her home was stocked with a whole range of different brands of whiskey and "Beer Burton" could not resist sampling the lot. Finally he passed out, and when he came round it was long after calling hours. Climbing back into college, he slipped into Philip Burton's room after dawn. Mr. Burton was horrified when he saw the state of his ward. Richard looked deathly pale and both his clothes and flesh were torn. In climbing back over the railings he had become impaled on a spike. "As I remember it," says Robert Hardy, "the spike went slap up his arse. He was badly injured and had to be lifted off the thing. But he refused to see a doctor because he knew he'd be gated."

Richard had other wild escapades at Oxford, but he was never in the same league as his famous namesake Richard Francis Burton, the poet, explorer, soldier, diplomat, and author, who was sent down prematurely from Trinity College, Oxford, and who, on his departure in a tandem, drove his horses over the flower beds, tooted his horn, and blew kisses to shopgirls in the high street. Beyond heavy drinking, Burton the Second was a reasonably serious student, and the one significant event in his half-year at Oxford was his performance in *Measure for Measure*.

How strong was Richard in his first major Shakespearean production? A student critic wrote: "Mr. Burton is pretty, with a good voice and nothing else." But Coghill insists that he made an excellent Angelo. "Student critics are notable for their cattiness and bitchiness, and have an art to combine what is foul in both dog and cat. Moreover, they have little experience or judgment, and are more interested in drawing attention to their own personalities than to their subject. There was nothing 'pretty' either in face or manner about Richard; he was simply the most manly-handsome boy I can remember, and, from the start, acted with distinction and strength.

"Richard's 'stillness' was overwhelming while he (as Angelo) was being unmasked, in the last Act, by the Duke. He stood absolutely erect, facing the audience with all the anguish in the world in his eyes, and with his arms at his side, his fingers clenched, yet ever so slightly unclenching and clenching again—an almost invisible, yet overwhelming movement; his features motionless, like stone. I think I may have told him this gesture, but he did it so much more grandly (if that is the right word for something almost imperceptible) than I had expected, that it was one of those things that made me know his greatness as an actor. You couldn't not look at him. You couldn't not feel with him."

The value of those five months in *The Druid's Rest* were self-evident now; Richard had hardened his dramatic muscles, had successfully experimented with his delivery and stage movements. Still, he was constantly exercising his voice, seeking more subtle power and control. The man he purposefully sought to emulate was Sir John Gielgud, who in the autumn of 1944 was playing *Hamlet* at the Haymarket theater. This was the outstanding Shakespearean production of the year, and during a short visit to London, Richard went five times to see the performance, noting the master's every gesture, assiduously studying his verse-speaking technique.

The Druid's Rest had closed. Its leading man, Michael Shepley, was still in town, starring with Roger Livesey in *The Banbury Nose*, a comedy by a promising new playwright called Peter Ustinov. Stanley Baker was moving on to Birmingham Repertory to work with such bright new talents as Paul Scofield and Peter Brook. It was a time of great opportunity in show business. The cream of the profession's young talent had been skimmed off by the war, and yet more and more theaters were reopening; and though nearly eighty percent of the movies were American in origin, the renaissance of British films was clearly under way with the booming box-office power of such stars as James Mason, Stewart Granger, Margaret Lockwood, John Mills, Deborah Kerr, Michael Wilding, Anna Neagle, Phyllis Calvert, and Patricia Roc.

Richard, however, was now condemned to anonymity in the Royal Air Force. Yet he was never a reluctant warrior. Almost nineteen, he was brimful of native aggressiveness, and in his Walter Mitty dreams he rather fancied himself as the dashing young fighter pilot, scrumming down and scrambling for his squadron with Errol Flynnish élan. What he could not stomach, as a man of action, was interminable service as an understudy, forever marking time in the wings and never moving on to center stage. And that was precisely what the future held for him. He was a belligerent bantam fated to stand and serve in a war without seeing one shot fired in anger.

The RAF

When Richard left Oxford for full-time RAF service in the fall of 1944, he was one of twelve prize-winning cadets in the passing-out parade of the University Air Squadron. On that parade was another top cadet of humble origin—a Jewish boy called Mick Misell, who had been born over a fish-and-chip shop in East London and was now studying to become a scientist. Misell didn't like Burton the first time they met. "I can't think why we were among the prize cadets, perhaps because he was an actor and I was something of an athlete. Anyway, we sat at the same table in the mess and the first words he spoke was in having a dig at the number of Jews who controlled the West End theater. I said, 'Hey, come off it, we're fighting a war against that sort of thing.' And then we had a terrible stand-up argument and I accused him of being highly anti-Semitic."

Nevertheless, the Jew and the Welshman became friends, and during the next three years they were stationed together for long periods. Afterward Mick Misell was to become an actor, too. (Years later he would change his name by deed poll to Warren Mitchell and establish himself as one of Britain's best-known television personalities through his portrayal of Alf Garnett, the foul-mouthed bigot of the series *Till Death Us Do Part*.*)

In the normal way, Burton and Misell would have left Oxford for Grading School to train on Tiger Moths, becoming pilots if they soloed, and navigators if they did not. But the RAF now had

---

* In America, the CBS version of this series has been called *All in the Family*, and the central character named Archie.

an embarrassment of pilots, so this selection procedure was abandoned. Instead, the Oxford cadets were given a general classification of PNB (pilot-navigator-bomb-aimer) and sent to Torquay for a series of aptitude tests, physical and mental. At the end of it, Burton and Misell disappointingly found themselves stuck with the label of navigator. Their war was virtually ended before it began. After six months of being shuttled from one RAF training station to another, they arrived in Canada for advanced training just in time to celebrate VE Day, and when they were due to pass out it was VJ Day. The only fighting Richard ever saw was in barrack-room and public-house brawls, and his worst injury was inflicted by a commando who settled an argument over a tough steak by breaking Burton's nose with his fist.

Misell remembers Burton as one of the wildest young rebels in Canada. "He came back one night with his face smashed to pieces after a fearful punchup. And I can remember him doing up a sergeant. It was terrible; I mean the boots went in as well. This sergeant was not a disciplinarian. He was a Welshman trying to disguise his Welshness by putting on an American accent, and this infuriated Richard and another Welsh bloke. So they did him up.

"There were drink restrictions in Canada at that time and we couldn't buy liquor easily. But Richard found a way round that. He used to stay in this Home Hospitality Center run by a woman they called Aunt Sally. She was very strict, church-going and proud, and on one occasion Richard was out the whole night and he came home blue-chinned and bleary-eyed. Aunt Sally said, 'Richard, have your breakfast. Then I want to talk to you in the study.' Aunt Sally gave him a right lecture on the perils of the flesh and damnation. At the end of it all, Richard looked back and said, 'Aunt Sally, an old doctor friend of mine once told me that if you want immortality, you must find it in the gutter.' Then he swept out.

"But you know, it was always fun to be with Richard. People tend to gravitate towards where the action is, and there was usually action when he was around. Whenever you went out with Dick, you knew it was going to be a ball. Why, in Torquay, he formed a Welsh male choir—even though he was the only

Welshman there. I can still remember the harmonies now, and at that time I was very keen on becoming naturalized Welsh. I felt that if you were Welsh and Jewish you couldn't miss."

In the RAF Richard drew his friends mostly from the hard-drinking, rugby-playing types—the closest was a Welsh mountain of a man called Dai "Dinger" Evans—and the only part of his noncombat service activities that he did not regard as completely profitless were his many hours on the rugby field. In fact, his only proud memories of those Air Force years are of the few occasions when he played in matches with Bleddyn Williams, the legendary international center-threequarter of Cardiff and Wales. Today he still treasures a reference to his rugby potential that was made by Williams in his biography *Rugger, My Life*, and, as he says, when his copy of the book is taken from the shelves, it automatically springs open by custom at page thirty-seven, where in the first paragraph Williams writes, "I played with a wing-forward who soon caught the eye for his general proficiency and tireless zeal. His name: Richard Burton. But it was in Cinema-Scope that he caught the eye after the war. A pity, because I think Richard would have made as good a wing-forward as any we have produced in Wales." It is the only notice Burton has troubled to keep.

The other notable experience of Burton's RAF days was his first visit to the United States. In June, 1945, he and "Dinger" Evans had a month's leave, and together they set out to hitchhike from Winnipeg to New York with only two dollars between them. They reached Buffalo, and from there they were driven by a Mrs. Spencer Jones who was going to New York to do some shopping. ("I thought this the most American thing that ever happened," says Richard. "That a woman should drive four hundred miles to shop.") His aim in New York was to look up an old friend of Philip Burton—a Mr. Alfred Baruth, teacher of English literature at the Horace Mann School for Boys. Mr. Burton had become a great friend of the Baruths on his 1939 visit when he joined them on a fourteen-thousand-mile automobile tour of America and Mexico. The Baruths were not in New York now, but Richard finally traced them to Vermont. Before that, however, he and his friend spent nearly three weeks living on handouts in New York. The first night they slept on the steps of the city's main post office, and then Richard telephoned Columbia University during vacation and persuaded the authorities to put them up in a fraternity home. The rest was easy. Their RAF uniforms were a passport to hospitality. In bars they sang in Welsh in exchange for free drinks and food. They were also given free tickets to a Toscanini concert and to the musical *Oklahoma*, and in Greenwich Village an old lady was so moved by their singing that she gave them fourteen dollars, so that they went back to camp richer than when they had left. "We all hitch-hiked somewhere at the end of the war," says Misell. "I went to New York myself. And Tim, Robert Hardy as he is known now, hitched thousands of miles just to see Paul Robeson in *Othello*. Of course, he was really dedicated to acting. Why, he used to fence two hours a day to develop his thigh muscles so that he would look good in tights."

In the fall of 1945, Richard and his group were flown back to Britain and posted to the RAF station at Bircham Newton in Norfolk. They brought back with them kit-bag loads of gin, and in November Richard celebrated his twentieth birthday there by getting impossibly stoned along with four wild Irishmen. Running amok through the barrack block, they took it upon themselves to demonstrate conclusively and scientifically that it is altogether possible to put one's fist through a closed glass window without getting the smallest scratch on the skin. "It was all quite innocent," says Burton. "But we did smash one hundred and seventy-nine windows and we got seven days' jankers."

At this time, Mick Misell told him he could secure him a posting in London because he had a friend who had an uncle who could pull strings in the Air Ministry. Richard declined. "He said he would sooner stay on there. He said he wanted to play some rugby, translate a novel from Welsh into English, and go on studying Shakespeare. You know, he used to read the complete works from cover to cover every six months.

"Anyway, my friend and I went to London for about six months, and eventually we were posted back to Bircham Newton. Richard met us at the guard room and said, 'Come on, boys, I've got you all fixed up in my billet.' And when we got there he opened this bloody great locker filled with dozens of eggs, meat, milk, everything. He'd got it bloody well organized there. It was a complete skive. And he loved it. He just wanted to be out there in the country—reading, fucking, and playing rugby."

Robert Hardy also met up with Richard in Norfolk during the interminable two years after the war when they were virtually marking time until demobilization. "I remember going into the pub on the night I arrived and looking for Richard. I found him surrounded with the usual clutch of followers, all listening to him. There was an atmosphere of excitement and danger in the air, and half of them had air marshal stripes chalked or painted onto their sleeves, and wings painted onto their chests. It was unbelievable, incredible, a fantastic period when they were on a detached station and they had got rid of the sergeants or whoever was in charge, and they were absolutely left alone.

"At one time they had been involved in a terrible pub battle when people were injured, and they were hauled up for disciplinary action. But suddenly it all stopped and they wondered how the hell they had got away with it. Richard then discovered that a directive had arrived from the Air Ministry to the effect that all these disappointed young stallions who were roving the countryside were to be given as much rope as possible. Let them play rugby or whatever, but don't fuss them—because they had been trained up like racehorses and then suddenly dropped. Thereafter, they lived an unbelievable life of absolute autonomy at the main station at Bircham Newton and the substation at Docking. They lived on the countryside; poached the pheasants and cooked them, ate like kings, and drank in the pubs. Yet we had no rating still. Really, we were neither fish nor flesh nor fowl."

By now, Misell, the student of physical chemistry, had a certain vague aspiration to become an actor like Burton and Hardy, and curiously, during those wild-living days in Norfolk, he had his first successful acting role—playing Richard Burton.

He explains: "As usual Richard had got himself involved with too many women, and he asked me to take this part on. There was a girl he had only met once, very briefly, in the dark; and he rang her up to say that he was coming to meet her. 'By the way,' he said, 'you've got no racial prejudice, have you? Because I'm Jewish.' She said she hadn't and so, posing as Burton, I went to meet this lovely girl. She was a hairdresser; very sexy, and she had money. And when we first met, she remarked, 'You're very tiny to be skipper of the station rugger side.' And I said, 'Well, you don't have to be big, girl. It's how hard you hit 'em that counts.'

"You know, I actually learned my first lines of Shakespeare to play that role. She knew he had been an actor and so I learned:

> *'Tis now the very witching time of night*
> *When churchyards yawn, and hell itself breathes out*
> *Contagion to this world: now could I drink hot blood,*
> *And do such bitter business as the day*
> *Would quake to look on. . . .*

"I quoted it to her down by the river bank in King's Lynn, and as we walked around King's Lynn people said, 'Hello, Mick,' and when she asked what they had said, I told her, 'they said Dick. Dick.' I kept this up for about three weeks, and all the time she really thought I was Richard Burton the actor."

As a navigator, Richard was virtually superfluous during two years of peacetime service. But there was rugby in the winter and cricket in the summer and girls the whole year round, and the RAF was generous with leave, during which he sometimes took on radio work. By now Philip Burton had quit teaching to take up an appointment as BBC Features Producer in Wales. He helped Richard get radio parts, together with other ex-pupils like Vivian Allen and Evan Morgan, and on one leave, in the summer of 1946, he took him to Stratford on Avon for a week to see various productions, including Marlowe's *Dr. Faustus*, with Hugh Griffith playing Mephistopheles. Richard was fascinated by the play and dreamed of one day playing Faustus. Afterwards, Burton senior and junior went to work on the great spellbinding speeches, and in the back garden of the guest house where they were staying, Richard poured out with extraordinary feeling and power his favorite lines, among them:

> *Why, this is Hell, nor am I out of it;*
> *Thinks't thou that I, who saw the face of God*
> *And tasted the eternal joys of heaven,*
> *Am not tormented with ten thousand Hells*
> *In being deprived of everlasting bliss?*
> *Oh Faustus, leave those frivolous demands,*
> *Which strike a terror to my fainting soul.*

Here was the kind of magnificent rhetoric that had first attracted him to the notion of acting; the power of language which, spoken with commanding tongue, could even hush the black-and-tan bustle of a Naafi bar. Both sound and meaning of words held deep fascination for him, but he was naturally drawn more towards the dancing words of the senses than the disciplined words of reason. He loved the melodious phrases of *cerdd dafod* ("tongue song"), such as he had discovered in the poetry of a bright new star of Wales called Dylan Thomas, with whom Philip Burton had worked in preparing a radio program.

In November, 1946, Richard celebrated his twenty-first birthday with another gigantic drinking spree, but this time he controlled his natural urge to punch in window panes. The long wait for demobilization was now becoming an unbearable drag; he was restless and bored, and eager to get on with advancing his career. Moreover, he was soon to have one very special girl friend he could only see on weekends by making marathon journeys by third-class rail, and no sooner were they together than it seemed to be time to make the loathsome journey back to the station again. The girl was an actress called Eleanor Summerfield, and he met her in London when he had special leave to play in a BBC television production of *The Corn Is Green*.

Eleanor was fun to be with; a slim honey-blonde, warm, vivacious, witty, and intelligent. Before the war she had won a scholarship to the Royal Academy of Dramatic Art, where for two years she trained for Shakespeare and the classics. Now, following wartime service as a secretary at the War Office and then at the secret American headquarters, where plans were laid for the D-Day invasion of Normandy, she was busy establishing herself as a highly versatile stage actress and comedienne.

Richard called her "Boots" and wrote to her regularly during his Air Force service, and after a time they became unofficially engaged. "I thought he was absolutely marvelous," says Miss Summerfield. "I had never met anyone with quite his sort of appreciation of words, and I thought there was no reason why he shouldn't become the greatest actor in the world. He had all the kind of Welsh passion for the theater, which was fantastically invigorating. He used to come and see me every weekend he could get off from the RAF, but quite honestly I was awfully busy working in those days, so that our social life didn't really amount to much. We had so little time, you know, that we just mooned about and stayed at home or went to the pictures."

In April, 1947, they managed to have five days together, but again Eleanor was busy in the theater in the evenings. She was touring with the play *Dr. Jekyll and Mr. Hyde,* and Richard joined her in Scotland, sharing digs with Donald Houston, a Welsh actor who had completed his RAF service. Donald was then agonizingly in love with actress Brenda Hogan who, he recalls, "didn't want to know." But ironically he eventually wooed and won Miss Hogan, while Eleanor and Richard went their separate ways. "I honestly can't remember why we decided not to go on with it," says Miss Summerfield. "Our temperaments really didn't fit or something—anyway we decided that this was not going to work."

The following November—the month Richard ended his Air Force service—actor-director Leonard Sachs, now well known in Britain as the genial, loquacious host of television's music-hall *The Good Old Days,* telephoned Eleanor to invite her to appear in the revue *Players Please* that he was producing at the Players' Theater. She declined, but he persisted, and finally she went along simply to pacify him. It was their first meeting. A month later they married. Although Miss Summerfield went on to establish herself as a star of stage, screen, and television, she was destined to meet Richard only once more—about a year later when he was appearing on a radio show with her husband. "It all seems an awfully long time ago now," she says. "After all, I've been happily married for twenty-three years, you know."

Meanwhile, as Richard came to the end of three years' National Service, he could be forgiven a degree of cynicism in his reflections on what a farcical time-wasting business it had been. There was comic irony, too. For he took perverse delight in recalling that his one achievement of distinction in all that time had been in the service of the enemy—helping to defend an Italian prisoner of war accused of raping a Land Girl. Air Force officials controlling a prisoner-of-war camp had called him into a court-martial when they urgently needed an interpreter, and Richard, who had studied medieval Italian at Oxford, saw it as his great theatrical moment. When he arrived in court, however, he discovered to his horror that the defendant spoke in an obscure dialect that he couldn't understand at all, and he recognized the plaintiff as none other than "Docking Lil," a local roll-in-the-hay girl whose character he understood all too well. But Richard on stage wasn't going to fluff his lines or bow out for anyone. He looked at Land Girl Lil, as husky as a Texas Ranger in her boy-scout hat and riding breeches, and then at the sad-faced Italian in patched prison uniform, and he could only conclude that *she* had raped him. So, as the Italian answered questions, Richard based his hazarded translations on this single premise—and the man was acquitted.

Richard didn't go on with his Italian after that. Following demobilization, those servicemen who had taken the University Short Course could return to the university if they wished and complete their studies. Robert Hardy went back and took his degree; Misell and Burton did not. Richard had always planned to resume university life, but his principal motive was to win a "Blue" for rugby. Now he was advised that the competition from the colonials—the South Africans, New Zealanders, and Australians—was so great that it was doubtful whether he could get into the Oxford team. He planned to wait two years until the postwar pile-up of students had declined. But Richard would never get back to Exeter College. Within two years he would be completely committed to a new way of life—a married man and an actor constantly in demand for films, theater, and radio.

The London Years

S hortly after being demobilized in November, 1947, Burton and Misell happened to meet in London's Shaftesbury Avenue. "Well," said Richard. "What are you planning to do in civvy street?"

"I'm going to the Royal Academy of Dramatic Art," said Misell.

"Good God!" Burton exclaimed. "Don't tell me you're going to become a bloody actor."

"That's right. And what are you doing?"

"Bloody marvelous," said Richard. "I've got a contract with Tennent's. Five hundred quid a year! Guaranteed! Ten pounds [$40] a week whether I work or not."

Misell, now Warren Mitchell, recalls their conversation with a wry grin. "It was really funny, because a few months later I went backstage to see Burton, who was appearing in his first West End showpiece, and I congratulated him on doing so well. 'Like hell, I am!' he said. 'Do you know what these bastards are paying me? Just ten quid a week!' "

It would be a long time before Misell saw ten quid a week, and it was the same for Stanley Baker. Both would serve in the West End as waiters before making their names as actors. But Burton was never to know unemployment, since immediately after leaving the Air Force he was put under contract by "Binkie" Beaumont. Moreover, he had the benefit of three loyal mentors: in radio, Philip Burton, whose work often took him to London and who would later become Chief Instructor in the BBC Staff Training School; in films, Emlyn Williams, now working closely with Sir Alexander Korda, czar of London Films Productions; in the theater, Daphne Rye, Tennent's casting director, who had first auditioned him for *The Druid's Rest.* Miss Rye, a loving and dynamic woman with exceptional knowledge of the theater, gave him the most practical help at this time. When he was looking for a London flat, she offered him rooms at the top of her house in Pelham Crescent, only five doors from the Kensington home of Emlyn and Molly Williams. And when he returned to the London stage three months after his demobilization, it was in Daphne's production of *Castle Anna* at the Lyric Theater, Hammersmith. Richard had an insignificant role, but he was also understudying the leading man, who had been summoned to appear before a Conscientious Objectors' tribunal and was in danger of being removed from the play. On the day of the tribunal hearing, Burton played the lead through a full rehearsal. Immediately everyone could see that he was infinitely better in the part.

Actress Pauline Letts was on stage with him that day. She recalls: "He walked on in the dull light of a Wednesday morning after the opening night, and everyone was feeling a little jaded and unhappy. Then something electric happened. He was quite brilliant in the part. Since then, over the years, I have worked with many actors and actresses who went on to become very big stars, but he is the only one whom one knew absolutely from the beginning that he was destined for greatness. I can only tell you the feeling I had about him—the impact of this tremendous brain and talent. That day we sat around talking and became very deep about personalities and the psychological aspects of life, and I remember very well him saying that he had a sort of other-half sitting on his shoulder and watching everything he did all the time, and that never under any circumstances was he non-objective. This objective self was watching everything he did. Most good actors do this, but he had developed it very early. It was there then. And I remember everybody's dilemma, because they would have liked him in the leading part, but at the same time they were very fond of the leading man and didn't want him to go to jug."

The leading man didn't go to the jug and Richard didn't get his part. But shortly afterward, while touring in *Dark Summer*, he received an urgent call from Emlyn Williams to come to London for a screen test. His chance to enter films arose because Williams, who had been asked to write and direct a picture for Korda, happened upon a plot while bumping around the Welsh countryside in a bus. The writer heard the driver call out: "Over there is the reservoir. They couldn't make it, you know, without flooding the valley. Everybody was evacuated and the village had to go under." It inspired *The Last Days of Dolwyn*, his story of a doomed Welsh village and an old lady's fight for its survival against a villainous land agent. Williams had written leading roles for himself and Dame Edith Evans. Now his problem was to cast the hero of his story, the old lady's foster son, Gareth, who accidentally kills the agent in a struggle to prevent him burning down the village.

Richard arrived at Williams's house in the middle of the night, tested before the cameras in the morning, and was back on his provincial stage in the evening in time to open a one-line cable: YOU HAVE WON THE SCHOLARSHIP. It was a quote from Emlyn's *The Corn Is Green*, and it signaled the beginning of Burton's film career. He did not even trouble to reply.

When he arrived for his first day's work on a film set, Williams cracked, "Oh, it's you. We were just about to replace you because we thought you hadn't accepted the part."

Richard apologized, and said lamely, "I just didn't know what to say," but the truth was that he was hopelessly unbusinesslike when it came to small details. Not intentionally so—just hurtfully so. Forgetful, careless, and outrageously casual. Three years of RAF routine had failed abysmally to bring any marked sense of discipline and order into his life. He impressed men in different ways. Most saw him as the great extrovert and a splendidly highbrow peasant who lived only for rugby, beer, women, poetry, and song. Others saw him as a generous touch, but failed to recognize the very private person beneath—contemptuous of ill-mannered words and fastidiously disdainful of boorish people who tried to emulate him. To the opposite sex he was totally appealing—ruggedly handsome, masterful by nature, and yet seemingly helpless in little everyday things; the kind of man women longed to organize but never could.

Recalling the first time he was with a woman, Richard characteristically tells a story—like the episode of the girl on the mountain who clutched his boil—angled against himself but nevertheless revealing. It happened during his RAF service when he and a girl were in a half-bombed house in Liverpool. They lit a fire to keep the room warm. "Eventually I fell asleep in front of the fire, and my feet were right up against the flames and in time my boots became terribly hot. Well, I had this terrifying dream that my lost soul was being consumed by hellfire, and because I had had this strict chapel upbringing and had learned all about the wages of sin, you can imagine what an alarming experience it was." Not that it deterred Richard. "Having discovered sex," as he later expressed it, he began "looting and plundering it with great delight." And the opportunities were limitless.

One lunchtime at the London Film Studios, Isleworth, when the cast of *Dolwyn* was lazing outside in the summer sunshine, Williams asked, "What did you do last night, Richard?"

"Oh," said Burton, "nothing special. I took some floosie to a nightclub."

Williams frowned. "Really, you know it's time you settled down. Why don't you take out one of these nice girls who are in the picture. That one, for instance." And he pointed out a slim, young girl sitting on the grass nearby. "Now she's a really sweet girl. Her name is Williams, too. Sybil Williams."

Richard laughed. "Yes, all right. Why not? I'll introduce myself." He did, there and then.

Sybil Williams was an eighteen-year-old drama student, also in her first film, but only just. After the auditions, Mr. Williams had eliminated her from his short list because of her inability to speak fluent Welsh and a tight budget that restricted him to six girl extras. But he had relented when her Professor of Music telephoned, begging him to reconsider because the girl was so hard-working and desperately keen. "I thought—oh to hell with it. Korda can afford it, for heaven's sake. Another £8 ($32) a week won't hurt." Now Sybil was meeting the young actor who most everyone agreed had a great career ahead of him. She found him utterly charming, and Richard was attracted to Sybil from the start. It was not just her good looks. He had all the glamor girls he wanted. But this one was different. She had genuine personality. She could converse on an intelligent level. Moreover, she was Welsh. After shooting a love scene with Andrea Lea, he talked to her again, and she explained that she wouldn't be there tomorrow because she was taking her gold medal test at the drama academy. Richard was interested and concerned—and insistent that he should have her telephone number so that he could ring the next day and hear how she had fared.

Sybil won her gold medal. And back at her London apartment she waited eagerly for his call. She waited until after midnight. He never rang. Next morning she resolved to cut him dead; he was, she concluded, just another philandering, self-centered actor and all the gossip she had heard about him was true. But the moment they met again on the set, she was knocked off balance. "What the hell's wrong with your telephone?" he said. "I tried again and again to get you but couldn't get through." Sybil was too wise to the devious ways of the Welsh to swallow that story, but the Burton charm melted her icy resistance, and the following evening he took her to the theater. Thereafter they were inseparable—on and off the set.

Briefly at this time, Burton and Stanley Baker were sharing a Thames houseboat at Chiswick with a couple of girl students, but now Richard ignored them and eulogized the wonderful Welsh girl he had met at the studios. "I didn't take much interest at the time," says Baker. "After all, I reckoned there must be about a hundred thousand girls in Wales called Sybil Williams. But about two days later I met this Sybil. And it was incredible. I had gone to school with her in Ferndale. She was the daughter of the local under-manager of the pit, and I used to go around with her as a kid. Richard was right. She was a marvelous girl, the most attractive girl in the village, the most mature, the most interesting, the most friendly. Richard was absolutely dotty about her."

In Sybil, Burton saw a young woman who combined beauty, intelligence, wit, and charm, and who in a strange way reminded him of his sister Cissie in her youth. There was nothing artificial or precious about her, unlike so many starlets he knew, and having kept house for her father and two older brothers, she could relax easily in the company of men who drank beer by the gallon and talked endlessly of a religion called rugby. Sybil had been born in the small mining village of Tylerstown, twenty miles east of Richard's birthplace, and though her background was not so humble (he joked that she represented the bosses of the Rhondda while he represented the men who crawled between heaven and earth) they had much in common. She, too, had lost her mother as a child and had been brought up by an older sister; and like Richard, she had made her mark in amateur dramatics, playing the lead in Clemence Dane's *A Bill of Divorcement* at the age of thirteen. Two years later her father had died, and for a time she worked as an assistant in a village dress shop. But, like Richard again, she had longed to escape the anonymity of life behind a counter. She dreamed of becoming an actress, and at seventeen she gained a place at a London academy of music and drama.

Sybil had no real acting opportunity in *The Last Days of Dolwyn*, but she was thrilled just to be involved—working at London's Walton Hall studios and then on location in Rhydymain, an enchanting setting that Williams had chosen after inspecting some sixty Welsh villages to find his *Dolwyn*. Here Burton played his last big scene—a struggle to the death with Emlyn Williams, who becomes soaked in paraffin, rolls in the embers of a fire, goes up in flames, and dies of shock. Then, to an accompaniment of heartrending harp music, Dame Edith had to save her foster son from a murder charge by climbing to the great dam above the village, and with trembling fingers let loose the mighty flood to engulf her beloved *Dolwyn*. Burton's first film had reached its ironic, overmelodramatic end.

Richard had seen Sybil almost every day of that long romantic summer, and he had come to take their relationship for granted. But now, as they came to Dolwyn's last days and it was time to go their separate ways, he became acutely aware of how vital and important a part of his life she had become. To his own surprise, too, he realized that he had no desire to go back to the bachelor roundabout of girls once seen and never remembered. He wanted roots again. He wanted to be organized, fussed over and loved; to be able to share his ambitions with someone. He needed Sybil. And for Richard the next stop was instinctive, inescapable, spontaneous. "Boot," he said, "we're going to get married."

He often called her Boot, a bastardization of "beautiful," and when he showed her off to the family at Cwmavon and Pontrhydyfen, they were all agreed—brothers, sisters, and Daddy Ni— that she really was a "beaut." Apart from her inability to converse in *Cymric,* she impressed them as being absolutely perfect for Richie. Sweet yet not without spirit; intelligent yet not intellectual; proud but not passive, and proficient in all the essential domestic arts. Above all, she worshipped Richard and understood his moods.

It was difficult for them to make wedding plans. He was heavily committed to radio work and a modest role in the film *Now Barrabas Was a Robber*; she was an assistant stage manager and understudy in *Harvey,* then playing in a West End theater. So, without much forethought, they fixed the wedding day for February 5 and hoped for the best. It would be a quiet, informal ceremony at Kensington Registry Office—just a few intimate friends and relations, and held early in the morning in case of professional engagements. By then, however, Sybil had stepped into a minor part in *Harvey,* and as the wedding day was a Saturday, she was required on stage for a matinee that afternoon. More horrifyingly, from the bridegroom's fanatical point of view, the date clashed with the Scotland versus Wales rugby international at Murrayfield.

Richard, never a great one for formalities, was predictably casual about the whole ceremony; relaxed to a degree that verged on indecency. By nature he was inclined to leave tedious organizing details to others, and now, once again, Daphne Rye came to the rescue. She gave them a wedding reception at her London home, and at low rental she offered them a small furnished apartment at the top of her house. It was an ideal situation for the newlyweds. They were ten minutes from the theater lights of Shaftesbury Avenue. And they would almost be neighbors of Emlyn and Molly Williams.

After the wedding, the champagne flowed at 24 Pelham Crescent from eleven in the morning, but early in the afternoon the bride and Sid Field had to leave for *Harvey,* and Emlyn had urgent dubbing to do on *Dolwyn.* At twenty-past-three Richard and the remaining guests settled down by the radio to hear the BBC commentary of the rugby international. Hours later the bride returned. But the bridegroom just sat there, brooding in gloomy silence, a dead bottle at his side. For the moment he had completely forgotten what day it was. The Murrayfield result had stunned him into "we-wuz-robbed" incredulity. It was impossible. The Welsh pack had dominated up front; fed by that great-rumped genius of a scrum-half called Haydn Tanner, and spearheaded by Richie's old mate Bleddyn Williams, the backs had launched wave after wave of assaults. Yet, on that foggy afternoon, entirely against the run of play, the Scots had conquered by six points to five. "Bloody hell!" Richard snarled at the end, and the rest was moody silence. It was too painful even to discuss.

Sybil just laughed at his theatrical despair. She understood Welshmen and their extreme attitudes to all things they held holy. And Richard quickly came round, shrugging off his gloom and fussing over his bride before she returned to the theater. It was not an ideal start to a honeymoon at home, but then Sybil happily accepted it because she was accustomed to the crazy, disorganized actors' life, and because in her own way she was even more dedicated to the theater than Richard was; not so much for her own sake as for his. Though she would have loved to be a star, she was a practical woman without pretensions to being a new Sarah Bernhardt. She recognized that she had only a fraction of Richard's gift for acting and, believing in his passionate desire to become the greatest actor on earth and living for its fulfillment, she would always put his interests before her own. Sybil was, in Richard's own word, "impeccable."

For Burton, life soon became a steady progression of growing opportunities and rising fame. Within four years he would be a Hollywood star. But, intensely ambitious as he was, he never dreamed of such progress at the start of their married life, since it coincided with the first notable disappointment of his career. Early in 1949 he was eagerly anticipating his first appearance in an important West End production: Terence Rattigan's *Adventure Story*, a play about Alexander the Great. His role of Hephaestion was a minor one, but at least he was assured of being seen by all the leading critics, and he would be working alongside an actor he admired immensely—Paul Scofield, three years his senior, and far more experienced after two seasons of Shakespeare at Stratford. Burton shared his good fortune with Stanley Baker by helping him get a walk-on part carrying a spear and by lending him £10 ($40) to buy a new suit for the out-of-town tour. Then, entirely out of the blue, came a shattering blow. After three days of rehearsals he was fired and replaced by Robert Flemyng. "I felt suicidal," says Richard. "Everybody had told me 'This is your big chance.' It made me fighting mad, and I vowed it would never happen again."

Producer Peter Glenville (years later he would direct Burton in *Becket* and *The Comedians*) explained that Richard looked too young to play Scofield's senior. But Noel Willman, who was playing Darius, takes an extreme view of the affair. "Richard was sacked simply because he was far too interesting; not because he was bad or inadequate at all. In his part he was meant to be a shadowy figure and Richard was never going to be a shadow no matter how hard he might try, and he was jolly well not going to try. I don't mean he was being naughty about it. He was simply a star personality who was riveting, and to play a shadowy kind of figure behind Alexander just wasn't on."

As it happened, Glenville did Burton a good turn, because immediately afterward he was offered a part in *The Lady's Not for Burning*, a new Christopher Fry play that Daphne Rye had recommended to Sir John Gielgud. But Richard was not entirely consoled. As much as he welcomed the chance to work with Gielgud, he could not envisage this play enjoying the commercial success of *Adventure Story*. Rattigan and Scofield were then very much in vogue, while the Fry play, though beautifully written, was essentially a ballet of words, a comedy in blank verse unlikely to gain popular appreciation.

Burton's ruefulness was still showing when he went to meet Frank Hauser, a BBC drama producer, to discuss the possibility of playing the title role in a Saturday night radio version of *Henry V*. Robert Hardy, a contemporary of Hauser's at Oxford, had arranged the meeting, and they talked over dinner at a restaurant. It was a stormy discussion. Richard, impatient for success, had drowned his humility in booze and was now fiercely aggressive. At one point, he told Hauser that no one was going to tell him how to play *Henry V*, and he threatened to throw the producer through the window. Hauser retaliated, "I don't want to hear anything from broken-down Welsh actors like you." Yet, as other diners failed to appreciate, it was basically a cheerful row. Hauser was a Cardiff man, and he understood the Welsh actor's drink-generated dramatics and his feigned hostility toward a semi-Anglicized Welshman with a pronounced Oxford accent. Finally they agreed that he should audition for the part.

Richard was well in liquor again when he arrived at the Broadcasting House for the trial reading. "He was still gloomy at being sacked from what was obviously going to be a great huge success," says Hauser, "and I think he had deliberately not studied the text. He did a good reading, though nothing like as good as he could have done. But something of the personality came across, and Archie Harding who was my boss said, 'Okay, why not? If you're keen on using him, use him. It might be interesting.' So we did the production and he was very good in it. Very honest, and very hard working. I thought he was more successful in the quiet bits, but then on radio it's almost impossible to be successful in the loud bits of Shakespeare."

Burton was the youngest actor ever to play Henry V on radio. His performance was well-received. But if he was reasonably pleased with himself, his pride was quickly deflated by a ghost from the past.

"Well," Richard asked. "What did you think of my Henry V?"

"You want me to be forthright?"

"Of course."

Meredith Jones prodded him in the chest. "My boy," he roared. "You were a weak, pale, piping, pusillanimous imitation of Olivier."

That same month brought another major milestone in Burton's career—the release of his film debut. *The Last Days of Dolwyn* was first shown at the Empire, Leicester Square, where, one month later, Michael Wilding was to be seen romping with Anna Neagle in *Maytime in Mayfair,* and where, three months later, an overdeveloped sixteen-year-old girl called Elizabeth Taylor would be seen in her first adult romantic role as Robert Taylor's wife in *Conspirator.* Richard, listed below Emlyn Williams, Dame Edith Evans, Allan Aynesworth, and Barbara Couper, was not given star billing, but at least his impact was immediate. He was hailed as "an exciting new discovery" . . . "a most excellent newcomer."

Ewart Hodgson (*News of the World*) was the most enthusiastic critic. "This twenty-two-year-old possesses the fire of great acting allied to good looks, a manly bearing—he's played rugger for the London Welsh and Aberavon—and an innate tenderness that renders his love scenes so movingly real. Emlyn Williams, Edith Evans, Richard Burton—this column salutes you. Whether you like it or not, you are destined for the pinnacles of screen fame." And Welshman John Ormond Thomas wrote in the old *Picture Post*: "A mixed film, in fact, but a better film about Wales than I've seen before. If I were a film producer I'd rush, contract in hand, after Richard Burton."

It was not a vintage year for British films following the outstanding 1948 crop that included Olivier's Oscar-winning *Hamlet, Oliver Twist, The Red Shoes, Fallen Idol,* and *The Winslow Boy.* But at least *Dolwyn* was counted among the few artistic successes. Before it was even begun, Korda, puffing a cigar and surveying the scene from his office window at 146 Piccadilly, had said to Williams: "I leave it all to you, my dear Emmaleen. You know what you want. It will make a nice film. Of course, it won't make a fortune. But it's worth doing." And now he was proved absolutely right. It was not a box-office smash, and it did not make Burton a star. However, at the Venice International Film Festival it earned the only prize for Britain—the award for the best musical score (composed by John Greenwood). The prize for the best actress went to Olivia de Havilland for her stark portrayal of a mental patient in *The Snake Pit*. Within three years Burton would be her leading man.

One month after the release of *Dolwyn,* Burton was seen on the screen again. His role was smaller, his impact greater. In *Now Barrabas Was a Robber* he played Paddy, a taciturn Irish saboteur serving a ten-year prison sentence. Bitterness and despair in confinement had transformed the man into a bully, and the part gave Richard an opportunity to create a characterization of real depth and subtlety. He seized it brilliantly. It was exceptionally difficult for an unknown film actor to command attention in this particular picture, since it was a well-scripted study of a dozen different characters during the days before an execution. Richard Greene, Sir Cedric Hardwicke, and Stephen Murray were the stars, and vying for honors was an extraordinary host of other talents—Kathleen Harrison, William Hartnell, Ronald Howard, Glyn Lawson, Beatrice Campbell, Betty Anne Davies, Leslie Dwyer, Alec Clunes, Harry Fowler, Dora Bryan, Dandy Nichols. In a microscopic part was a newcomer called Kenneth More. Yet, amid so much competition, Burton made this film his own special triumph.

Many members of the cast were singled out for special mention by the critics; Burton no more than others. But he gained the notice of greatest significance. C. A. Lejeune, then the most celebrated and respected of all British film critics, wrote in *The Observer*: "Mr. Burton, in particular, is an actor whose progress I shall watch with great curiosity. To my mind, he has all the qualities of a leading man that the British film industry badly needs at this juncture: youth, good looks, a photogenic face, obviously alert intelligence, and a trick of getting the maximum effect with the minimum of fuss."

Philip Burton glowed with as much pleasure as Richard at recognition of the "trick" he had impressed on his ward from the beginning of his drama training. Yet, strangely, the British film industry would never fully utilize the new discovery as Miss Lejeune suggested. Meanwhile, Richard was more immediately concerned with establishing a reputation on the stage. Not that it manifested itself in his behavior. His demeanor was always deceptive. He talked more passionately about rugby than the theater, and during rehearsals of *The Lady's Not for Burning,* as when he had been preparing for *The Druid's Rest,* he seemed relaxed and reserved to the point of disinterest. Gielgud, both producer and leading man, became angry with him because he always began to yawn prodigiously when one o'clock lunchtime arrived.

"Come on," said the producer. "We're going to do that scene again."

"No," said Burton defiantly. "I must have my lunch."

And Gielgud, the gentlest and most sweet-natured of men, was finally compelled to enforce his will and to scold his young puppy-actor for being so greedy. Richard's attitude stemmed from a private conviction that he had his role well under control and that there was no great urgency for further rehearsal. In this sense, he was not the easiest of actors to direct. Yet his judgment of how to handle his role was basically sound and quite remarkable for a twenty-three-year-old who was comparatively new to the stage. Sir John still regards this play as one of the finest things Burton has done.

"Beaumont rang me up one day and said, 'We've got this wonderful boy Richard Burton for the part of the apprentice in *The Lady's Not for Burning.*' And I said, 'Oh really'—rather unimpressed. And then he came to the first rehearsal and, of course, I was absolutely bowled over by his immediate understanding. He was perfect looking for the part. He spoke it beautifully. And in the second act we had this great poetic scene, rather long, between Pamela Brown and myself, when he was the boy scrubbing the floor. I always remember this. It was very difficult to do

—with the boy stopping at intervals to come into the scene with a line or two. And when he had these lines to speak, he knew exactly without my telling him. I didn't direct him at all in that play. He played the love scenes with the little girl and this scrubbing-the-floor scene, in which he kind of came into the scene and then retired from it, in the most wonderful way. Absolutely, you knew instinctively, even if you had your back to him, that he was feeding the scene exactly right."

Following a provincial tryout, *The Lady's Not for Burning* opened in London in May, 1949, and Richard bought forty seats for friends and relatives from Wales. Afterward, they all retired to the nearest pub, and Richard set up the pints and then asked, "Well, what did you think of that, boys?"

"Great," said Tom the Fullback. "You were very good. But tell me, lad, what the devil was it all about?"

The question seemed to confirm Richard's suspicion that Fry's poetical fantasy might be too obscure for popular tastes. He was proved entirely wrong. Ironically, the play was a far bigger success than *Adventure Story*. It ran for more than a year, and such were its high artistic qualities that it attracted a procession of celebrities of stage and screen to the Globe Theater.

The Burtons made many new friends during the long run, among them Alec Guinness, the Scofields, and Stewart Granger and Jean Simmons, who that summer had a great film success with *Adam and Evelyne* and who starred together on the London stage in Glenville's version of Tolstoy's *The Power of Darkness*. And they had many other friends in town. There were Sybil's colleagues from *Harvey* and Richard's from the Fry play, including Richard Leech, Peter Bull, and a sweet eighteen-year-old girl called Claire Bloom. Donald Houston was back in town and for the moment he was a more prominent film star than Richard, following his involvement with Miss Simmons in a spectacular unintended comedy called *The Blue Lagoon*. Philip Burton, who had regularly visited Richard from Cardiff, was moving to London permanently, and Vivian Allen of Cwmavon, now married, was living there too.

Dennis Burgess and Brinley Jenkins were among old school

friends who came to see the show at the Globe. Ma Smith and daughters Betty and Audrey made the journey, and another visitor from Port Talbot was Ivor Emmanuel, the boy who had been bombed out of Pontrhydyfen. After two years down the pit, Ivor was now serving an apprenticeship in the steelworks, but his dream was of becoming a professional singer. He stayed the night with the Burtons and was back on the afternoon shift at the steelworks when a telegram arrived from Richard: AUDITIONS FOR OKLAHOMA STOP BE AT DRURY LANE TOMORROW NOON. "I traveled up by bus all night," said Ivor. "And, do you know, Richard was waiting for me at the theater. We had a couple of pints in the Opera Tavern, and then I faced the auditions. I was thinking I was the only one, but there were about sixty other fellows there. The show had been running for a year or more, you see, and they were sending the American boys home. Anyway, I started to sing something, and when I was halfway through Gerry White the producer said, 'Okay. You're in.' I couldn't believe it until I signed the bloody contract. Eight pounds ($32) a week it was then, but it was a beginning. And Richard did more than that. He and Sybil let me live with them at Pelham Crescent for several weeks until I had found my own place."

While in *The Lady's Not for Burning,* Richard continued to take on a prodigious number of radio parts and poetry recitals, and by the end of the year he was working under greater pressure than ever before—appearing at the Globe every night, starting at Pinewood Studios on his third film, *Waterfront,* and rehearsing another Christopher Fry play during the day. His second Fry play was *The Boy With the Cart,* based on the old legend of the shepherd boy Cuthman, who hears a call in Cornwall and then trundles his elderly mother across England in a homemade wheelbarrow to reach the Sussex village of Steyning, where he builds a church with his bare hands. It was only a one-act play, but a formidable test for its two central characters—Richard as the boy and seventy-two-year-old Mary Jerrold as the mother; virtually alone, they had to make the story credible and deeply moving. It was so testing that understudy Paul Daneman remembers it as his worst moment in the theater. "Richard got influenza at the time of the first run-through, and I was terrified at the prospect of taking over so soon. But happily he recovered in time for the opening because he was absolutely perfectly cast for that play.

"We were young actors striving to achieve some kind of presence at that stage, but Richard had got it already. Extraordinary presence and quite fantastic repose. It was very unusual to see a young man walk on stage with all the maturity and quiet assurance of a middle-aged man. He seemed to know, either by experience or by instinct, exactly what *not* to do. He came into a very middle-class theater as a kind of regal peasant who would tell wonderful stories about Old Dai holding up the pit-prop with his bare hands, and how his father stole food so that his sons could grow into the strongest in the valley.

"But it was strange how he tackled that part. At the first rehearsal he read beautifully and we were all impressed. But as we rehearsed for another six weeks, which was much too long, he never did another thing with it. We kept asking, 'When is he going to do something?' We were all trying new things, yet he never did. And when we came to the first night, Richard's performance seemed to be exactly as it had been at the first rehearsal. But it was an enormous success. People came backstage with tears in their eyes to say how moving his performance had been."

Gielgud, who produced the play, thinks that Burton could not have been better. "It was one of the most beautiful performances that I have ever seen, and he and Mary Jerrold together were absolutely divine. It was a very simple miracle play that Fry had written for an amateur festival somewhere, and Richard's simplicity and shining sincerity were deeply moving. He knew himself how good he was in it, and he talks of it now with such affection, as if it were his great moment and the part that made him into a star. But I don't remember it causing all that impact in London. It was a charming play, but it ran only for a few weeks at The Lyric, Hammersmith."

Richard was praised by the critics, and Mary Jerrold insisted that he take a solo bow each night when they were called back again and again. But one-act plays, especially one-act miracle plays, are not good box office, and *The Boy With the Cart*, though a little gem of theater, was strictly small Fry compared with the richness and sophistication of his new *Venus Observed*, which had just opened with Olivier at the St. James's. Certainly it did not make Burton a star. It ran for one month and he followed it in April by playing Tegeus the soldier in an out-of-town production of Fry's *A Phoenix Too Frequent*. He had yet to play a leading role on the West End stage.

Burton was due to make his Broadway debut in November when *The Lady's Not for Burning* would be transplanted to New York. Meanwhile, he returned to his film career. In *Waterfront* he had a prominent romantic role, but the script based on John Brophy's novel was an inferior one. The setting was the Liverpool docks between the wars, and Robert Newton was predictably cast as Peter McCabe, the beer-sotted, good-for-nothing ship's fireman who deserts his wife (Kathleen Harrison) and leaves her unsupported with two daughters and a son. Richard was Ben Satterthwaite, a ship's engineer who falls in love with a McCabe daughter (Avis Scott) but cannot marry her because he is unemployed during the depression of the thirties. It made a very ordinary film, but he successfully captured the misery and stubborn pride of the unemployed, and once again he was well-treated by the critics, who variously described him as "magnificent" . . . "very talented" . . . "a very promising newcomer." After three movies, he had still to get a bad notice, and at last the messages about his potential were beginning to get across. That year, Korda signed Burton on a long-term contract at £100 ($400) a week. Remarkably, this onetime Hungarian peasant, who became the first knight of the British film industry and the maker of a hundred stars, was never to star Richard in a film of his own. Always he subcontracted him to others.

Richard and Sybil now bought a house in Hampstead, North London, which was only a five-minute walk from Philip Burton's apartment. But they were careful with their money and lived only in a self-contained upstairs apartment, subletting the rest of the house. Richard still refused to take success for granted; after all, he had yet to star in a really successful production, either in films or in the theater. He was about to start on his fourth British movie, and at last he was playing opposite a top box-office star, Phyllis Calvert. But he was pessimistic. For the third time he was cast as the young lover, and this time he was to be killed off early in the plot. The film, based on the novel *Happy Now I Go* by Theresa Charles, was a wartime weepy, *The Woman With No Name,* and he had the part of Nick Charmerd, a Norwegian RAF officer who falls in love with amnesia-case Yvonne Winter when they meet in the hospital after being injured in the same air raid. He invites her out to tea, marries her a few days later, and gets killed in action twenty-four hours afterward, leaving his widow to search for a forgotten past that produces another husband (Edward Underwood). The female lead was a natural for Miss Calvert. Shrewdly, she recognized the sentimental story as such a sure winner for a woman's picture that she invested some £10,000 ($40,000) of her own money into its making.

Richard was to win rave notices for his brief appearance in that film, but before its release he made one more British picture, and it was a gigantic flop. He should never have become involved in it because he had been urged to take a long rest before leaving for New York in October. Instead, having worked on two films, three plays, and various radio productions within the past seven months, he postponed his holiday until late August so that he could appear in a comedy based on Howard Clewes's novel, *Green Grow the Rushes.* The project was publicized as "the most exciting venture in the history of British film production."

At a time of mass unemployment in the film industry, the Association of Cinematography and Allied Technicians had set up ACT Films Ltd., a cooperative company, to make their own pictures. With financial support from the government's five million pounds (twenty million dollars) National Film Finance Corporation, the workers, as it were, would be employing themselves, and *Green Grow the Rushes* would be the first film of their own. The plan was nobly conceived and nobly supported. Technicians limited themselves to the minimum union rate; artists agreed to work for modest fees and on a deferred payment basis, receiving the balance of their money if and when the film made a profit. According to plan, it provided work for nearly four hundred technicians. It was made at about half the cost of comparative British feature films, and it was shot in twelve weeks, nearly a month less than average. But enthusiasm and teamwork were not enough. There remained the major problem of distribution, and with a stockpile of thirty-eight British films awaiting release, it had to be an attractive commercial product in its own right if it was to get on to the circuits. *Green Grow the Rushes* was anything but that.

Reissued years later as *Brandy Ashore,* it was a pale imitation of *Tight Little Island,* a comedy about a marshland community whose traditional interest in smuggling is disturbed when three Ministry of Agriculture officials arrive to investigate local farming conditions. A freak storm improbably lifts the smugglers' trawler over the seawall and deposits it full of brandy in a farmyard, and the familiar battle against bureaucracy ensues. Roger Livesey, direct from an Old Vic tour, was the principal star, Capt. Biddle, a hard-drinking old salt. Honor Blackman, in her first screen comedy, played a local reporter. Burton was the adventurous operations chief of a gang of smugglers. After the pressures of the London stage, it was a lighthearted frolic for Richard, filming in the invigorating summer breezes of England's southeast coast in and around Rye and New Romney. But the film was a disaster; it was rejected for circuit release and was reviewed by only the trade press, who dismissed it as "an artless British comedy."

Fortunately for Richard, this film had such an obscure fate that its failure did nothing to detract from his fast-rising reputation as an actor. In January, 1951, *The Woman With No Name* was released, and though the reviews were not wholly enthusiastic, he was consistently praised. He was likened to "a British edition of Montgomery Clift," and once again Ewart Hodgson was the most passionate in praise: "I predict here and now; hand on heart, that with proper handling, Richard Burton is destined to become one of the new faces the screen is calling for. With his perfectly simulated Scandinavian accent and demeanor, his is the most impressive performance. . . . There is something so 'rich and strange' about this young man's acting that he is able to make any situation convincing."

Now the movie magazines and annuals joined in tipping Burton, along with Elizabeth Sellars, Petula Clark, Laurence Harvey, Herbert Lom, and Sally Ann Howes, as major British stars of the immediate future. But it was too late. Richard was in New York and the Hollywood film scouts were already efficiently sniffing around after *The Lady's Not for Burning* had opened to rave notices at The Royale on Broadway. Five British films had failed to launch Burton as a major movie star. The Americans would need only one. Not that they discovered him entirely on their own initiative. Stewart Granger played a valuable supporting role. After visiting Burton backstage and praising his performance, he came back again and again, bringing with him such Hollywood stalwarts as Nunnally Johnson of 20th Century-Fox, and Sam Zimbalist of Metro-Goldwyn-Mayer. "Why don't you sign him up?" he asked. And Hollywood offers immediately followed.

There was also a proposal that he should play Romeo to Olivia de Havilland's Juliet on Broadway, but Richard surprisingly shied away from what would have been the most prestigious role of his career. The truth was that he regarded Romeo as an unbearably prissy character; and while he had played mild romantic parts on the screen, he couldn't face playing "that mawkish lover" on a stage. Years later, talking to Kenneth Tynan on BBC television, he explained: "I can't play with girls. I'm not a romantic actor in that sense. I think I'm recognized as a sort of sexual actor in some senses of the word. But Romeo, for instance. I've never played it, but it's beyond my capacity, because the acting urge to kiss somebody on the stage is beyond me. I can't do it. I can't bear to be touched, physically touched, on the stage or the screen. It has to be very carefully arranged. I really cannot bear to be touched and I very rarely allow myself to touch other people—physically touch them, I mean. When I have to kiss a woman on the stage or on the screen, horrors start up."

Burton was now sorely tempted by Hollywood offers, but he was cautious and uncertain about making long-term plans, and anyway he could only refer them to Korda, who still had him under contract. For the moment he was too preoccupied with a more immediate challenge to give much thought to his future in films. His next commitment was a six-month season with the Memorial Theater Company, Stratford on Avon. He would be facing the awesome test of playing Prince Hal and Henry V and acting alongside such masters of Shakespeare as Michael Redgrave and Anthony Quayle. Richard approached this work more seriously and more nervously than anything he had done before. Until now, acting on stage had come easily to him, and working in films had not impressed him as being a serious art. Stratford was different. This, he judged, would reveal the true caliber of his acting. It was his moment of truth.

Stratford

Every star entertainer—actor, dancer, musician, athlete—can nail that precise moment in time when he stepped from the shadows into the full glare of the public spotlight. For Burton that moment came on April 3, 1951, at the Memorial Theater, Stratford on Avon, when he was praised to the skies for his Prince Hal in *King Henry IV,* Part I. "A young Welsh boy jumped on the back of this play as if it were a fiery charger, and rode it to triumph," wrote John Barber of the London *Daily Express.* "His Prince Hal is noble without arrogance, graceful without effeminacy, handsome without dullness." Other notices were no less enthusiastic, and the keenest perception of all was displayed by Kenneth Tynan of *The Observer,* whose judgment of that Stratford debut still stands, twenty years on, as the finest appraisal of the style and gifts of Burton the actor:

> A shrewd Welsh boy shines out with greatness—the
> first this year. . . . His playing of Prince Hal turned

interested speculation to awe almost as soon as he started to speak; in the first intermission the local critics stood agape in the lobbies. Burton is a still, brimming pool, running disturbingly deep; at twenty-five he commands repose and can make silence garrulous. His Prince Hal is never a roaring boy; he sits, hunched or sprawled, with dark unwinking eyes; he hopes to be amused by his bully companions, but the eyes constantly muse beyond them into the time when he must steady himself for the crown. "He brings his cathedral on with him," said one dazed member of the company. For all his bold chivalry this watchful Celt seems surely to have strayed from a wayside pulpit. Fluent and sparing of gesture, compact and spruce of build, Burton smiles where other Hals have guffawed; relaxes where they have strained; and Falstaff (played with affectionate obesity by Anthony Quayle) must work hard to divert him. In battle, Burton's voice cuts urgent and keen—always likeable, always inaccessible. If he can sustain and vary this performance through to the end of Henry V, we can safely send him along to swell the thin company of living actors who have shown us the mystery and the power of which heroes are capable.

A quarter of a century after his entrance into the dark, depression-world of Dan-y-bont, Burton had burst into prominence as a Shakespearean supernova, illuminating the Stratford scene with a brilliance not even surpassed by the young Olivier. And Sybil was on stage to share his first moment of true glory. As Lady Mortimer—coached by Richard to make "Welsh as sweet as ditties highly penn'd, sung by a fair queen in a summer's bower" —she spoke in her native tongue and played one small scene sufficiently well to prompt speculation on the development of a notable husband-and-wife stage partnership. But it was never to be. Unlike her Welsh friend Rachel Roberts, also gliding prettily on the nursery slopes, Sybil would not aspire to progressively

greater heights. At the end of the Stratford season, she was to retire from the stage to dedicate herself to her husband's interests.
Richard joked that he encouraged this because she was upstaging
him, but it was strictly a logical step. To continue her career
would have involved long and frequent separations, and it simply
did not mean that much to her. In keeping with her Welsh upbringing, she chose to put her man's career before her own.

Sybil had no deep yearning for the spotlight on stage, but she
loved the behind-the-scenes involvement as Richard's manager,
secretary, and general aide. She loved, too, the camaraderie of
theater life, which was spiced with an unusually strong Welsh
flavor during the seven-month season at Stratford. The un-
crowned king of the Welsh clan was Hugh Griffith, who with
enormous presence was playing Shakespeare's "great magician,
damned Glendower"—the legendary Owain Glyndwr. He held
court at a rambling old country house at Oxhill that he and his
wife Adelgunde shared with two other Welsh couples—the Burtons, and Osian Ellis, the famous harpist, and his wife. Adelgunde
was a magnificent cook, and though it was rather wasted on Richard's chips-with-everything taste, she kept a wonderful table and
entertained a procession of actors and actresses, including Michael Redgrave, Charles Laughton, Nora Swinburne, Rachel Roberts, and Rachel Kempson. "We had cultural parties," recalls
Ellis, "when everyone threw bouts of poetry at each other—what
we call in Wales 'a merry night.' Laughton recited passages
from the Bible from memory; Richard did poetry by Robert
Frost."

Robert Hardy, a junior member of the Stratford company and
by private arrangement Richard's makeup man, stayed at the
"Welsh country club" for some weeks, and he insists that it was
haunted by a ghost he met in one of the corridors that so terrified
him he dropped a fully loaded tray of food. "That was a mad-
house," he says. "There would be extraordinary people like
Laughton staying at weekends, and I found them all so much
larger than life that I used to have difficulty in keeping pace with
them. There was one marvelous occasion when Osian was hidden
under the staircase, and suddenly, in the middle of the night,

when everyone was pissed and talking about the place being haunted, these weird strains of a harp filled the house. It was a beautiful Elizabethan harp and people were absolutely staggered. They really thought they were in on something amazing."

One weekend, Humphrey Bogart came down to the Old House with his fourth wife, the tall and sultry Lauren Bacall, for whom he had fallen while filming Hemingway's *To Have and Have Not.* Burton was fascinated by the lip-twitching, sad-eyed veteran of over sixty movies, and he turned on the charm and won himself a valuable ally for the day when he would become ensnared in the Hollywood rat race. Another visitor was Alan Badel, who was playing Poins in *Henry IV,* Part I, and who mischievously used to tease Richard about his tendency to imitate Gielgud's stage gestures. "You're doing it again," Badel kidded one day in rehearsal as Prince Hal flourished an arm while exclaiming, "The land is burning; Percy stands on high. And either we or they must lower lie." Another time, Richard was waving an arm in the center of the stage when Badel promptly stuck a sausage roll in his hand. "It was strictly a joke," Badel says today. "He didn't really copy Gielgud that much. In fact, he was brilliant. He had enormous presence, and he fitted in like a glove to Henry IV and Henry V."

Richard took the ragging in good spirit, but secretly he wondered and worried whether there might not be an element of truth in Badel's mock criticism. And certainly, in rehearsals, there were members of the company who were unimpressed by his Prince Hal. It was not the usual thigh-slapping, laughter-roaring Prince of Wales they had come to expect; he seemed to be doing so very little. But that was Richard's way, and this time it was astutely devised—a prince he sought to project as "solitary and removed and cold." Once again he was playing to his own strengths, and when it came to the performance, his interpretation was seen to be exciting and highly effective. In a company that included Redgrave as Hotspur, and Quayle as Falstaff, his was the personality that dominated the stage.

His adaptability was less apparent when next, in June, he briefly escaped the cares of future kingship to play the young

Ferdinand in *The Tempest*. Though his impact was great, it was misdirected—perhaps inevitably so, because his natural forcefulness scarcely fitted so nebulous a character. He simply had a personality too strong and too individual to be suppressed—a limitation to his craft that, some say, has scarcely diminished over the years. Never, it seemed, could he be the complete chameleon on stage or screen; and the scar is still tender from Tynan's neat rapier thrust: "It's the first time I have seen Ferdinand played by the bull."

As Ferdinand, the new boy at least overshadowed more celebrated players—to such an extent that one critic predicted they soon would be calling the town "Burton on Avon." On the other hand, while Richard was hailed as heir apparent, he was not yet crowned, and after the two parts of *Henry IV* he faced a far sterner test on graduating to kingship. His youth and freshness and vigor, so fine for Hal, were not such powerful allies now, and the crown never sat easily on his Henry V. As a Van Gogh of storytellers, instinctively painting in bold and positive and exciting colors, he recalls how he felt suicidal over the panning he received for his Henry V: "It really depressed me. The critics gave me a terrible roasting. They said I couldn't walk, couldn't talk, couldn't do anything well. But Olivier told me, 'Don't worry about it. The main thing is that they took such a long time saying it.' " The truth is less dramatic. His king was judged neither brilliant nor bad, and the critics were never savage.

P. L. Mannock (London *Daily Herald*) wrote: "His manliness, looks, youth, and attack carry off a personal triumph. But something is lacking—the full music of spoken poetry, the power to sustain ringing heroics, and the creative use of a fine speaking voice. In other words—nothing that experience will not cure. I felt exactly the same about Olivier's Henry V at the Old Vic before the war. Feeling is there, and full expression will flower." Alan Dent (London *News Chronicle*): "He has the moral if not the physical stature for the part, the voice rather than the authority . . . the performance is a deeply interesting one, handsome, varied, and with some highly original pauses and looks and gestures. But no amount of intelligence can prevent this king having the appearance of a bantam surrounded by full-sized cockerels."

Many young actors would have rejoiced at emerging from their first Shakespearean campaign with so many spoils and such superficial wounds. Not Burton. By his own impossible, uncompromising standards, the tempered praise of the critics, and especially reservations about the music of his spoken poetry, represented nothing less than abject personal failure. He had no interest whatsoever in being a brilliant second best. And while his sensitivity to criticism emphasized his immaturity as an actor, it at least spurred his determination to return to Shakespeare and one day set the heavens ablaze.

Nevertheless, this season was a spectacular success for the Memorial Theater. By late October, when three stage kings took their final bows—Redgrave as Richard II, Harry Andrews as Henry IV, Burton as Henry V—more than 332,000 people had attended the performances, pulling in a record £132,000 ($390,000) at the box office. Richard's own financial gain was a modest £35 ($105) a week. But as had happened before, and would happen again, the theater on the Avon had taken a good, efficient actor and projected him as a star. In 1948 it had been Scofield, aged twenty-six and playing Hamlet in his second Stratford season. Next year, 1952, it would be the flamboyant Lithuanian-born Laurushka Mischa Skikne, aged twenty-four, and going by the name of Laurence Harvey, who won acclaim as Orlando. Five years on, Richard Johnson would arrive as Mark Antony and would attract the film talent scouts. But it did not take the Stratford showpiece to convince the Americans of Burton's potential. They had recognized it in *The Lady's Not for Burning,* and already he was booked for a return to Broadway.

Twenty-four hours after the final curtain fell on Stratford, Richard was sailing with Sybil to New York to play the lead opposite Dorothy McGuire in Jean Anouilh's fantasy, *Eurydice*—a modern variation of the legendary romance of Orpheus (an impoverished strolling musician) and Eurydice (an unhappy actress). In London, where Dirk Bogarde took the lead, this *pièce noire* was entitled *Point of Departure*. On Broadway it was *Legend of Lovers*. Burton had his first leading role on the American stage

as Orpheus, and though the production was a severe disappointment to all concerned, he made a big enough personal impression
to have the columnists hailing him as "another Laurence Olivier."
The *Herald Tribune* called him "an actor of tremendous promise"; *The New York Times* judged his performance to be "intelli-
gible and persuasive"; the New York *Daily Mirror* described him
as "one of England's most gifted actors" who played Orpheus
with "sensitivity and powerful impact." Yet the Theater Guild
production was a flop, and was seen by the critics as "cheerless,
cynical, and muddled."

It opened at the Plymouth Theater during Christmas week,
and it closed two weeks later. Noel Willman, who played Monsieur Henri, recalls: "It was the classic example of an American
management mucking up and mishandling an English production.
By the time we opened, we were all so discouraged and so fed up
because most of what was best in the play was gone. It was the
old story of an American management saying that American audiences wouldn't understand it and that they knew best what was
wanted, but this was just rubbish. Moreover, Dorothy McGuire
was simply not right for the role. She is a darling, and in many
ways a very good actress. But in this instance she was badly miscast. Richard was so intense about the way they treated the play
that he became discouraged from giving his best, and even if he
had, it wouldn't have made any difference. They had mucked the
play about to such an extent that its original intention was lost."

Hugh Griffith, for whom it was an unfortunate first experience
of the New York stage, was the most demonstrative in his disgust.
He had played the part of the father with great distinction in the
London production, and as far as he was concerned, this was not
the same play. In his beetle-browed fury, he proclaimed his intention of catching the next boat home, and he headed straight for
Pier 90 where the Queen Mary had been. But when he arrived,
there wasn't a ship in sight, and he reluctantly stalked back to his
hotel. "Hello!" said Burton. "I thought you were going home."

"Dammit," growled Griffith. "I'm not Jesus. I can't walk the
bloody Atlantic."

Richard shared his disenchantment. He called the production

"A Streetcar Named McGuire" and made it abundantly clear that he looked forward to jumping off at the first available stop. At twenty-six, he was impatient to further his career, still hungry for his first major triumph on the London stage. And with this aim, he now plunged directly into the title role of *Montserrat*, an adaptation of a harrowing French play that projected a battle of wills between two Spanish officers during the Venezuelan uprising of 1812. Once again, his stage was The Lyric, in the London borough of Hammersmith. This time it was hoped to transfer the play eventually to a West End theater.

Soon after rehearsals began, Richard concluded that this grimly depressing play was doomed to fail, and he advised all his friends and relatives to stay away. But on the opening night he was agreeably surprised to be playing to a full house, and more amazingly, the audience applauded wildly at the end. Afterward, Beaumont and a few old faithfuls came back to his cubbyhole of a dressing room and sang his praises. Then they all left, and the star suddenly felt depressed and alone. He sauntered off to the pub across the road and was relieved to see a familiar face there. It was his "charming but vicious" old friend, Alan Badel.

"What's yours?" said Burton.

"A Guinness," said Badel.

For a few minutes they stood abstract and silent at the bar. Then a thought dawned on Richard. "Were you out front tonight, by any chance?"

"Yeah," said Badel.

Another long silence. Richard became impatient. "Well, what did you think of it?"

Badel gave a noncommittal shrug. "All right."

Another pause, and Richard could not restrain the question any longer. "What did you think of *me* then?"

Badel looked at him coldly. "You need a haircut."

In *Montserrat*, Richard played a rebel-sympathizing officer being pressured by the fanatical Colonel Izquirerdo (Noel Willman) into revealing the hiding place of rebel leader Simon Bolivar. As a young idealist racked by his own conscience, he had enormous scope to demonstrate how profoundly he could move an audience, and he and Willman superbly captured the grisly conflict between the two protagonists. Yet the production was only successful in that it achieved its first objective: to convince the audience of the appalling horror and tension of the situation. Three years earlier Emlyn Williams had appeared on Broadway in Lillian Hellman's adaptation of the play; it proved too over-whelmingly grim for American tastes and had a comparatively short run. Now, in London, the reaction was precisely the same. Critics praised the acting, but theatergoers were unwilling to pay for the pleasure of being emotionally shattered. The play closed after a month.

Willman, who reluctantly directed the play in which he co-starred, remembers it as a magnificent failure. "It was very odd. Nobody came to it, and yet the first night was an extraordinary experience because we had an absolutely wonderful ovation. It was a great flop, and yet the people who did come came again and again. The trouble was that it was basically about six people going to be shot one after another, and after the first ten minutes there was no doubt that this was going to happen. I think this was the weakness of the play. It was very strong and passionate, and it had some marvelous things in it. But there was only one way it could go.

"As in *The Boy With a Cart*, Richard had a surprisingly inactive part, a very unrewarding part. I had the showy part. And yet he was infinitely superior to me, because apart from being a much better actor, he can achieve this absolute stillness, this inner strength, like no other actor can. It was not that he played a serene or placid character; simply that he could be so dynamic while yet doing nothing.

"It was fun to work with him, but he was very whimsical in the sense that you were never quite sure how he was going to behave. He would work like an absolute dog one day, and the next day he would be absolutely impossible. Very often he would discuss things and excitingly respond to certain bits of direction. At other times he would not have it at all. He would carouse, play the fool, and carry on and absolutely disrupt the rehearsal. But not badly. I did not mind it. He had these whims rather more than most actors, but then he had rather more of everything than most actors.

"He was curious. He took direction, but from a kind of affection for the person giving it rather than because he wanted it. He is a great flatterer. He would say, 'You're so marvelous. So beautiful. You know absolutely everything.' All that kind of rubbish. One doesn't take it seriously because it's a great giggle really. But clearly he had his own way of doing things. I think this is true of almost every remarkable actor. You can accept a great deal from people in certain ways, but their own way of doing things must not be impinged upon because it's harmful to them. If they feel that is happening, and they often feel it instinctively, and for the most part rightly, sometimes wrongly, then they'll fight like anything. Paul Scofield I find just the same. He is a marvelously cooperative actor and wonderfully disciplined—far more so than Richard. But if he felt at a certain time that a certain process only he knew about was being interfered with, even with the best intentions, then he simply wouldn't have it. And this is true only of real star actors. It's not true of most actors. It was particularly true of Richard.

"He was terribly disappointed that *Montserrat* didn't get to the West End. He became very involved in the play and he thought it was a marvelous part for him, which in a sense it was. It was a very close-knit company and he felt that it should have been a success, and he was terribly hurt when it wasn't. I remember him being very passionate about that. He would say in a determined voice: 'Just wait . . . just wait. One day they'll be fighting for the chance to see us.' "

And he was right. Meanwhile, as with his sacking from *Adventure Story*, his disappointment was immediately turned to advantage with an irresistible offer from 20th Century-Fox—the promise of leading roles in three films at the rate of $50,000 a picture. Richard jotted down the figures on a piece of paper that he kept as a constant reminder of his absurdly good fortune. A sum total of $150,000 was, at the current rate of exchange, over £54,000—more, he calculated, than a mining Jenkins had earned in a lifetime. He was fascinated by the idea of so much money for what he judged to be so little work, and Korda agreed that the opportunity was too great to be missed.

Korda subcontracted Burton to Fox on a basis that enabled him to make a profit out of his hitherto under-exploited investment, and on the eve of departure he threw a big party in his honor. Richard, like a once dedicated bachelor on his wedding's eve, stayed up until dawn, singing, dancing, telling stories, and finally drinking himself into a stupor. The following afternoon his wife and a few friends put him on the plane, and the arrangement was that Sybil should join him in a few weeks, when he had found them a house and settled into the new routine. With a king-sized hangover, Burton was Hollywood-bound.

Hollywood

Richard Burton the movie star came onto the market in 1953, tinsel-wrapped and bearing the unmistakable "made in Hollywood" label. He may have been groomed in British studios, but the credit for launching him belonged exclusively to the Americans, who had the cash and courage and know-how to take an embryonic star and package him as an international screen idol from the onset. At home, Richard's progress toward film fame had been a slow haul in economy-class vehicles, a five-picture apprenticeship that had not taken him remotely near to becoming a box-office figure of James Mason or Stewart Granger dimensions. Yet, after one year in Hollywood, his pockmarked features were familiar to audiences throughout the world.

During that year he was seen in nineteenth-century frills as a young gentleman investigating the mysterious death of his foster father; in twentieth-century khaki as an heroic commando officer

winning the war at Tobruk; and in a first-century toga as the arrogant Roman tribune who superintends the crucifixion. And in
each film—*My Cousin Rachel, The Desert Rats,* and *The Robe*—he
received the full star-spangled treatment. In the first, the Hollywood hunch-players gave him Olivia de Havilland, twice an
Academy Award winner, as his leading lady; in the third, they
entrusted him with the key role in an epic that was launching the
CinemaScope wide-screen process to which all the vast production resources of the 20th Century-Fox empire were committed. None of these films was a masterpiece, but the sheer magni-
tude of the presentation ensured that he would not be ignored.

In the candyfloss fifties, when trivia was so much in vogue in
the press, Burton was projected in Britain as the young innocent
abroad and some writers still called him "boy." In reality, he hit
Hollywood with all the innocence of a Molotov cocktail. It was
an early summer morning when he arrived in Los Angeles; he
was unshaven, crumpled, and irritable after more than twenty
hours' flying. By evening, however, he was switched on for his
first performance. Refreshed, well-scrubbed and dinner-jacketed,
he made his entrance at the luxurious home of producer-writer
Nunnally Johnson before faces he knew only on celluloid. After
an uneasy hour of weighing up the synthetic sex appeal of these
exotic, perfumed cuttlefish, the booze bounced him into his all-
conquering party style, and he launched into tales of Wales with
a power and rhythm of language that held his listeners spellbound. And then, with the party in full swing, he broke into
Welsh song and recited Shakespeare, plus a few irreverent verses
more suited to a rugby club stag night. Some guests wrongly concluded that he couldn't hold his liquor; others rightly judged that
he was working overtime to make an impression. But it was not
an exceptional act. It was just Burton being Burton, and the great
majority found him enchanting. Most important of all, he was refreshingly different in a film colony where life could be unbearably tedious.

To Richard, the Hollywood Boulevard of his dreams in the
Cach was a vulgar neon strip of tatty shops with the sidewalks in-
scribed with famous screen names that were never seen outside a

Cadillac. He, however, was on the inside looking out at the bus-
loads of rubbernecks that daily trundled past the pseudo-mansions
of screen idols, and it was all so unreal. The stars were in their
gilded cages, amusing themselves with the deadly dull gossip of
themselves. Who's in what? Who's having who? Have you heard
the latest?—and the latest was a young Welshman who could talk
on a seemingly inexhaustible range of topics without danger of
becoming a bore. The word quickly got around, and within
twenty-four hours of his arrival the "innocent abroad" was pro-
fitably established as a rare personality.

Sybil joined him two weeks later, and until the novelty wore
off, life for them seemed like something out of *Alice in Wonderland*. At one party, Richard's eyes kept straying toward a remote
beauty seated in a corner of the room. He murmured a few words
of appreciation, and then Sybil whispered, "But you know who
that is, don't you? It's Garbo."

"Good heavens!" said Burton. And immediately he made his
way across the room to introduce himself. They exchanged a few
courtesies; then, as he took his leave, he bowed deeply and gently
squeezed her knee. Afterward he recalled how he and his sister
used to pay sixpence to see Garbo the goddess in The Regent of
Taibach. "When I write home and tell Cissie that I've squeezed
her knee, she'll know that I've really reached the heights."

Stanley Baker met the Burtons soon after their first year in
Hollywood. He says, "Both of them were star-struck when they
first went there. They were meeting people like Joan Crawford
and Bette Davis, stars they had only seen from their seats in
Welsh flea-pits. Yet Richard quickly made a fantastic impression
out there. Hollywood is a pretty dull bloody place and the Americans were amazed to meet a man who could talk really well besides being a marvelous actor. He absolutely enchanted them with
his wit and his stories. Long, long before he met Elizabeth Taylor, he was set on the road to great success in this business."

While the Burtons were fascinated by the super-living of Beverly Hills, they found it difficult to adjust to life on the lavish
scale. Richard, though generous to his friends, remained instinctively cheeseparing over personal spending. He saw that they

were very much the poor relations in millionaires' row, and haunted by an easy-come-easy-go vision of $150,000 being frittered away, he guarded his dollars with almost eccentric caution. He took pride in wangling free lunches out of the 20th Century-Fox commissary, and later, rather than buy a car of his own, he borrowed either the Masons' Cadillac or the Grangers' Jaguar. Once Stewart Granger gently chided him for turning up for lunch in an ill-fitting, twenty-two-dollar suit. Burton smiled, and simply explained, "I'm no glamor boy, you know."

Richard's style of living was contrary to all the known rules of the Hollywood way to success. Yet he thrived, because while some social snobs regarded him as a peasant devoid of taste in clothes, food, and wine, many more people accepted him as an eccentric and intellectual wit of rare talent. His thrift became a subject for Jack Benny jokes, though he displayed it with flair—like inviting everyone to a nightclub, but sending the invitations too late for anyone to attend. In fact, it was impossible for the Burtons to entertain on a grand scale in the little house they had rented on Hollywood's unfashionable side, and it would have been reckless extravagance for them to have held a party elsewhere. So they kept more and more to themselves, and restricted entertaining to a small group of intimate friends.

One of their most regular guests was the ubiquitous Badel, then in Hollywood for the first time to play John the Baptist to Rita Hayworth's *Salome*. He detested the place, left after three months, and never went back. "I couldn't stand it. I really couldn't," he says. "And Richard wasn't very happy there at that time either. But he and Sybil really saved my life in Hollywood. I was always round at their apartment. We used to play liar dice an enormous amount, just for cents, and Richard always won. My salient memory of that time is that they were terribly kind to me out there, and that Sybil was absolutely marvelous. I always had tremendous admiration for her as a woman.

"Every Sunday we used to foregather at the Grangers. They had a very big house and grounds, and an enormous swimming pool. It was the usual Hollywood sort of thing that went on all day; one did very little—just swam, talked, or went off to the playroom and played records. It was all very English—Deborah Kerr, Stewart Granger, Jean Simmons, Richard and Sybil, Michael Wilding, Elizabeth Taylor, and so on. I don't think Richard got to know Elizabeth very well then. He didn't seem to have very much to do with her. She used to sit with her feet dangling into the water, very pregnant, and alone. She was a loner, absolutely."

The purpose of those quiet English Sundays at the Grangers' retreat was largely therapeutic—the one day in the week when the stars could forget about their images and relax among genuine friends without fear of publicity and petty intrigues. For Richard, especially, it brought welcome relief, since he was working under enormous pressure and strain. His first star role for Fox had him in more than ninety percent of the scenes, and though he scorned the artificiality of Hollywood life, he was involved in the rat race as much as anyone. He knew that on the strength of this one performance he would stand or fall as a highly paid actor, and he tackled it with the same intense determination he had shown as an undergraduate in his first Oxford play. Early in the filming of *My Cousin Rachel,* even such an experienced director as Henry Koster was surprised by the Welshman's aggressive approach. In one scene Richard had to climb the ivy-covered wall of a mock mansion and halfway up pause to speak to Rachel on the balcony above. When he reached that point, the actor lost concentration and fluffed his line. Immediately he dropped to the ground, beat a fist against the wall of soft stone-colored plaster, and shouted: "What's the matter with me? Why can't I do it right?" Then he calmed himself, apologized for his failure, and offered to try it again. The film crew applauded such self-critical histrionics; normally, it was the way of the stars to shrug off a missed cue with a perfunctory four-letter word and casually pass on to the next take.

Richard G. Hubler, writing for the *Saturday Evening Post,* reported from the film set: "The passion and energy which he crams into his role makes Burton a throwback to the grand old ideals of acting—in the tradition of John Barrymore, Sir Henry Irving, and Edmund Kean. Not that Burton's style is theirs—he is more intimate, less flamboyant—but his concept of the profession is the same. He is not afraid to emotionalize off stage as well as on. . . . It is hard for him to open a door, pour a drink, or blow his nose without making a small dramatic scene out of it. The world is literally a first act for Burton and no matter what his lines—which, thanks to his Celtic wit, are usually good—he likes to dominate it."

Burton was tackling Hollywood with as much delicate finesse as he brought to his wing-forward play. Not for him the quiet reserved image he had displayed in the theater. This was a bold, brassy world, and his approach was the same. "By heaven," he loudly proclaimed, "I'm going to be the greatest actor, or what's the point of acting?" He was in no position to play the remote, aloof star, and so he shrewdly took the opposite stance, ignoring the spacious studio quarters provided for him as the leading man, and hanging around on the set to swap yarns with technicians and show genuine interest in their work. The crewmen thought his attitude was marvelous. But not everyone in the cast was endeared by his flashy displays of enthusiasm and exuberance—his leading lady, for example. Publicity stories quoted Miss de Havilland as saying, "I shudder to think of the fame awaiting this young man. There isn't another leading man like him. In my opinion, Richard Burton is the greatest leading man in a decade. I'd love to do a stage play with him." But Richard had declined to play Romeo to her Juliet on Broadway the previous year, and studio gossip had it that she now found his occasional bursts of *braggadocio* a little too vulgar for her tastes. "That was a strange business," says Burton now with deliberate vagueness. "I remember how her husband (Marcus Aurelius Goodrich)* announced that he didn't want anyone referring to his wife as Livy, and I thought this was very odd."

Miss de Havilland was at that time very much the superstar. Though only thirty-six and still a strikingly handsome woman, she was virtually a veteran of the cinema, a star since the midthirties, twice an Oscar winner, five times an Academy Award

* The marriage, Miss de Havilland's first, was dissolved in 1953.

nominee, and ever-remembered as sweet Melanie of *Gone With the Wind*. She had played opposite the leading screen heroes—Gable, Robert Taylor, Leslie Howard, and Errol Flynn—and she had done her share of Shakespeare on stage, and with such all-round experience she was not so readily impressed as others by Burton's background, showmanship, and larger-than-life personality. She recognized his talent, but she was not going to join in the fussing over a co-star infinitely less experienced than herself.

There was an uneasy relationship between the refined First Lady of Hollywood and the rough-cut diamond from Wales, yet they worked well together. Indeed, the team assigned to *My Cousin Rachel* was totally professional; it had a distinguished director, and the producer-screenwriter was Nunnally Johnson, an extraordinarily prolific writer who was regularly being told by Humphrey Bogart to get out of Hollywood and stop prostituting his rare gifts. All these talents, however, could not make a classic film out of a did-she-do-it mystery plot in which all interest would ultimately be stifled under an avalanche of red herrings. In the script, based on the novel by Daphne du Maurier, Richard was the romantic hero Philip Ashley, a young Englishman who falls in love with his guardian's widow, even though he suspects she may have murdered her husband. The setting was reminiscent of Miss du Maurier's *Rebecca,* but the film, for all its fine direction and acting, would never achieve the gripping suspense of that superior work.

Nevertheless, the story broke soon afterward that Richard had been signed up for ten years and a million dollars by Fox, payable at the rate of $100,000 a year. The report was premature. He was not going to rush into committing himself for a whole decade ahead, not even for a million dollars. As Fox was to discover, he could be a tough and canny negotiator. But the offer was a significant commentary on the impression he had made in Hollywood. After all, *My Cousin Rachel* had yet to be seen by the critics, and his box-office pulling-power remained to be measured.

Burton's next starring role was in *The Desert Rats,* a story set to the background of the siege of Tobruk by the German Afrika

Corps. It was important that he make a success of it because Fox was then considering his bold request to star in their biggest film project, *The Robe*. It was also a film fraught with obvious dangers. The Air Force cadet who had never risen from the ranks was now playing a super-efficient, much-decorated Army officer who rises from captain to temporary lieutenant colonel within a few months, leads fifty-four handpicked men far behind enemy lines to blow up an ammunition dump, escapes from the Germans, walks wounded across the desert and back to his own lines, and then takes charge of a crack battalion that must hold a key position against impossible odds. It was a role ideal for his brand of authoritative masculinity. And it was a superman yarn that could easily have dissolved into farce.

Earlier, Hollywood would not have dreamed of using British and Australian actors to play British and Australian desert rats. Errol Flynn would have saved Tobruk single-handed, or else Bogart would have brought an American tank into the campaign, as he had done in *Sahara*. But this was a time when more and more American stars were filming abroad, while more and more Britons—Mason, Granger, Niven, Rennie, and the rest—were living in Beverly Hills. So *The Desert Rats* was properly cast with Commonwealth actors, including Robert Newton as the cowardly, alcoholic private who was once Burton's housemaster, and Chips Rafferty as the Australian sergeant. And though an Englishman, James Mason, appeared as a skin-headed Rommel, he spoke mostly in German to add to the film's authentic touch. The picture was not a sensational success at the box-office, but it could scarcely have been more skillfully made. It was well acted, given greater realism through Michael Rennie's narration and the subtle use of old newsreels, and, above all, intelligently directed by Robert Wise, who had been nominated for an Oscar after his first assignment as a full editor on the classic *Citizen Kane*. Years later Wise would collect an Oscar for the best of all musicals, *West Side Story*, and then would direct the second biggest money-making movie of all time, *The Sound of Music*.

Richard enjoyed making *The Desert Rats*. He liked working with Mason, and regarded him as a British actor who had handled his career supremely well; he liked carousing with Newton, a hangover soulmate from his *Waterfront* days. One weekend, while on location, Burton and Newton assumed American accents and crossed the border into Mexico without visas. "We became absolutely paralyzed with tequila," says Richard. "But on the way back we were so stoned that we completely forgot about our accents, and we landed in the pokey for the night."

Richard was more relaxed in Hollywood now. He gaily invented outrageous stories to meet the gossip columnists' insatiable appetites for anecdotes, and when a female photographer kept asking him for one more different pose on the beach, he impulsively threw himself into the sea fully-clothed. He was the most extrovert member of the British Beverly Hills clan, and though some had advised him to remain remote and aloof, he favored the approach of Victor Mature, who told him: "Love everybody. Talk to anybody. Pose with anybody. Don't listen to the English; after all, they stifled Welsh culture, didn't they?"

The man he listened to most was Humphrey Bogart, who had recently departed from his eternal tough-guy image to score his great Oscar-winning triumph as the gin-swilling owner of a tramp steamer in *The African Queen*. In 1952, Bogie of the leathery face and sorrowful eyes was king of the film colony where the great god was success, but he wore his crown jauntily. In his fifties, he remained the hellraiser and instinctive showman who could not resist playing up to people who expected him to be as tough and fearless off the screen as on. Burton found in him a kindred spirit.

To know Bogart is to know much about Burton. Their backgrounds were poles apart; a generation divided them. Bogie, born into New York high society, disrespectfully spat out his silver spoon to pursue life in his own rough-and-ready fashion; Burton, born into comparative poverty, blew the coal dust out of his nostrils to do the same. And somewhere between their diametrically opposed origins they collided as almost twin personalities—devil-may-care individualists, drinking hard, playing hard, working hard, each with the rawness of life etched on his sandpaper face. Bogart lacked the Welshman's poetic flair; he had neither his handsome features, nor, despite four marriages, Richard's peculiar power over women. Yet they were similar in many respects. Bogart could be arrogant and bawdy and cynical, but behind the tough facade was a sincere and generous man who loved kids, was immensely proud of his family, and profoundly conscientious about his work. The way friends affectionately remember the Bogart of the forties and fifties is strikingly similar to the way friends describe Burton in the sixties and seventies. Like Burton, Bogie belonged to the immobile school of acting, displayed that same gift of stillness that enabled him with eyes alone to project a sense of menace or despair. Similarly, he had the ability to swig buckets of scotch without keeling over or impairing his work the next day. Like Burton, he was basically a man's man; and, like Burton, he came to the films via the theater.

When they met up in Hollywood, Bogart said to Richard: "It's unusual to get a trained actor out here. Most of these young glamor boys in the movies today used to work as gas station attendants. They aren't actors. Go into any major studio and shout 'Fill her up' and all the leading men in the place will instinctively come running." It was a favorite theme of his. Burton heard him contemptuously spouting about the artificialities of the film colony, describing the actresses as the dumbest broads in town and most of the young actors as pretty-faced nonentities. A strong, individual personality, he said, was the vital ingredient for lasting fame. He praised the indelible personalities like Tracy, Cooper, and Gable; scorned the "Races, Rocks, and Lances, or whatever they're called"; rued the dwindling number of old-time Hollywood hellraisers and rebelrousers; detested the phony personalities created through the devices of publicity men. "Acting's a professional business, and that's how I treat it. I don't go for this art-form stuff. I'm ready when they want me, and I'll take a drop of scotch when they don't."

Burton fitted in rather well with Bogart's conception of what an up-and-coming film star should be: individual, utterly natural, fearless of authority, and too powerful a personality to be malleable in the hands of the studio bosses. A man whose opinions were entirely his own; a man solely motivated from within. "I don't trust anyone who doesn't drink," said Bogart. "I think the world is three drinks behind and it's time it caught up." And that, too, was a view that Burton heartily endorsed.

He loved Bogie's style, and since both liked nothing more than sharing a late-night bottle with a fellow freethinker, they had marathon drinking sessions together. "He was a great character," says Burton. "If you challenged him to put his fist through a plate-glass window he would do it. And he'd still keep on drinking with the other hand." Once Richard had the gall to challenge him over a point of acting, and the superstar stormed out of the room and came back with his Oscar, which he thumped down on a table. "You were saying?" he growled.

Burton can enliven endless drinking hours with his memories of Bogie, though not all the outrageous stories reveal the man in an endearing light. He liked to shock people; at times he could be crude to a fault. Like the occasion he walked up to a stranger at the bar of New York's 21 Club and said loudly, "Are you a homosexual? We've got a bet going at our table." Afterward he realized he had been unreasonably malicious; it was just that he couldn't resist the temptation to shatter someone with the unexpected remark. Richard recalls such a time when he was with Bogart at a smart Bel-Air party in honor of an overseas diplomat. "It was a full dress affair, the kind of stuffy occasion which never appealed to Bogie. But he was asked to be on his best behavior and quite properly he sat all through dinner, listening and scarcely saying a word. Then, at the end of the dinner, he very correctly complimented the foreign visitor on his excellent command of English. 'Thank you,' said the diplomat. 'You see, I had the benefit of an English governess.' Bogie looked at him interestedly. 'Oh yeah. Did you fuck her?' "

Burton has a similar dislike of formal occasions, and while his language is rarely so basic, he has, with advancing years, grown more like Bogie in that he will not suffer fools and bores gladly, and in that he is capable of being outrageously curt when company becomes tiresome. He has also acquired Bogart's knack of brinkmanship, possessing sufficient bloody-mindedness to provoke someone deliberately, and usually having sufficient wit and charm to forestall an ugly incident with the swift remark or subtle gesture that reduces drama to the realms of farce.

There is a story about Bogart having a fearful row with his neighbor and onetime regular drinking companion, Sid Luft, then Judy Garland's husband. Grossly insulted, Luft had threatened to punch Bogie on the nose. But as he advanced, Bogart's face suddenly creased into a puckish grin. And the actor famed for his unflinching gangster roles said, "Sid, you ain't gonna lay a hand on me." Momentarily puzzled, Luft held back his fist and asked, "Oh yeah. Why's that?" And Bogart switched to a tender, touching voice—"Because, Sid, you're my friend." Recalling the affair, Richard said, "It was a magnificent moment. Arms around each other, Bogart and Luft strolled over to the bar, raised glasses, and the incident was closed. Bogart's brinkmanship had defeated Luft as it did many others."

Toward the end of 1952, Burton himself was getting no mean reputation as a Hollywood hellraiser. His big year was drawing to a dramatic close, the party season was in full swing, and no one in the film colony had more cause for celebrations. That December, *My Cousin Rachel* was released, and though many critics panned the film, they were almost totally enamored with its forceful male star, who always commanded attention with his resonant voice and who did much to save the picture by making his involvement in the absurd affair somehow credible. On both sides of the Atlantic the reaction was the same. Hedda Hopper welcomed "one of the most exciting actors I've seen in the past ten years"; Jympson Harman (London *Evening News*) hailed him as "the most exciting thing in movies since the advent of Gregory Peck eight years ago." Britain's leading film critic, C. A. Lejeune of *The Observer*, wrote of him as "so closely resembling a fiery young Laurence Olivier that he is bound to set Hollywood ablaze." And *Star* magazine concluded: "Mr. Burton from Glamorgan justifies all the hullabaloo which has been made about him in this his first Hollywood part. He has looks and a sturdy individuality and acts with enough fire to make you overlook a suspicion that the young man he is playing is the silliest film hero of the season."

Burton's role in *My Cousin Rachel*'s unmemorable ninety-nine minutes of pedestrian mystery brought him three press and magazine awards, and an Oscar nomination. "He is one of the few talents that can vibrate and glow," said director Koster. And when Don Hartman, head of Paramount studios, arrived in London that December, he described the Welshman as "the most promising actor since Laurence Olivier" and bracketed him with Alec Guinness and Audrey Hepburn as the three outstanding young people in films.

Any remaining doubt about Burton's stature in Hollywood was vanquished when he landed the coveted role of Marcellus in *The Robe,* the film epic of the late Lloyd C. Douglas's novel about the Roman tribune who takes part in the crucifixion of Christ only later to be converted to martyrdom. This was not just another big movie. It was the forerunner of a whole new style of film presentation—the first picture in CinemaScope, the latest process, following close on the heels of Cinerama and 3-D, to be developed in Hollywood's struggle for survival in the face of ever-increasing competition from television. Producer Frank Ross had bought the film rights of *The Robe* for $100,000 when the manuscript was half-written. Now 20th Century-Fox had more than four and a half million dollars staked in the filming and promotion of this make-or-break epic; and untold millions more were committed to the further use of the revolutionary wide-screen process.

In these circumstances, it was extraordinary that Fox should entrust the key role in their prototype film to a comparatively inexperienced actor with only two Hollywood movies in the can and neither of them outstanding successes. Moreover, they made the decision before either of those two films was released. Since Burton was the main pillar on whose strength the film could stand or fall (he had 313 speeches out of some 700 and appeared in 96 percent of the scenes), Fox's faith in their potential star was indeed prodigious. Ultimately, the credit for the gamble belonged to Darryl Zanuck, the five-foot, five-inch cigar-puffing czar of the studios who had launched a host of legendary stars since first making a name for himself with the Rin-Tin-Tin dog dramas. Zanuck was quite a practical joker; one evening he put a trained ape in his chair, dimmed the lights, and called executives to a conference. But there was no mischief in his approval of Burton as star of *The Robe*. Zanuck's whole future depended on the film's success.

Richard responded with appropriately solemn remarks about the "awesome responsibility" and the "enormous challenge" of a role which he said might almost be compared with the infinite variety of Hamlet. But he didn't really believe it. There was more high-flown publicity talk about how he was going into strict training, with weight lifting and fencing to get into peak condition for the part. In fact, immediately before tackling this "deeply meaningful religious role," he was throwing himself wholeheartedly into the whirlwind round of parties. At the Bogarts' Christmas party (Bogie was fifty-two on Christmas Day), he rhythmically recited speeches from a variety of Shakespeare plays while old-time musical star Jack Buchanan went into a tap-dancing routine and another guest banged out jazz on the piano. On to daybreak they caroused, with Richard consuming enormous quantities of drink and displaying astonishing range and stamina as an entertainer. Then came a bean-feast with a more dramatic climax—the lavish, exclusive New Year's Eve party given by Mr. and Mrs. Charles Lederer. Here the magic midnight hour struck in memorable style for Richard. He was dancing with Jean Simmons, the dark bewitching beauty with whom he would be starring in *The Robe,* and according to time-honored custom, they kissed as the New Year tolled in. Unhappily, he had overlooked Sybil, who as tolerant as she was, at least expected him to rejoin her for that sentimental moment. She now walked purposefully to the center of the floor, slapped his face, and left. The Burtons, who had been house guests of Stewart Granger and Jean Simmons, subsequently moved out and rented a small house from Pamela Mason.

Was Burton the incorrigible playboy and ladykiller that some Hollywood columnists would then have him to be? If one accepted all the cocktail party prattling about his first years in Hollywood, he would rate as the greatest womanizer since Casanova. But so many stories about him rate as second-hand tittle-tattle.

Gossip was far and away the most popular pastime in the old Hollywood—a sport without rules or closed season. To be ignorant there of the latest scandals and intrigues was to be a social outcast, and more than once it was demonstrated that you could invent a vague story about one star having an affair with another and later in the day have the same story, much embroidered, retold to you as positive fact. Burton later remarked: "There's no libel law to speak of, and the things gossip writers can write are fantastic. I was honored by one article accusing me of breaking up nine happy homes. I hadn't even met one third of the couples concerned. Do you know what Sybil did with that article? She papered the smallest room with it."

Perhaps she did it as a telling reminder, for Richard's appeal to women in the film colony was undeniably great. He was a good listener as well as a wonderful talker. He took a healthy masculine pride in his facility to charm and fascinate the ladies, and he did little to discourage the legend of Burton the Great Lover. But never was he a furtive, two-faced philanderer. He charmed, teased, and delighted the ladies, but he did so openly and spontaneously. Though Sybil was sometimes deeply hurt, she was sufficiently adult and sophisticated to shrug aside the impulsive, ego-feeding exercise of a young man producer Ross once described as "a born male coquette." At the same time, she was too proud, too spirited a personality, to remain impassive when her position seemed threatened. *Saturday Evening Post* reported that she then had a fixed formula for dealing with his little escapades. "The first week she tells him: 'She's a nice girl; don't do anything to hurt her.' The second week: 'Richard, don't do anything to hurt us.' " The truth was that she adored her husband, and Richard regarded her as the perfect wife, which she was.

During the filming of *The Robe,* Emlyn Williams stayed with the Burtons and saw a great deal of Sybil. But he scarcely ever met Richard, because one was working at the theater at night and the other was up at six every morning to go to the studio. "But there were two nights when Richard came to the Los Angeles theater where we were playing Dickens, and this was marvelous of him, because he had to work early next morning. Moreover, he roped in many others: Lauren Bacall, Humphrey Bogart, Stewart Granger, Robert Newton, Clifton Webb—they all came and they were very nice. But I knew they didn't come of their own accord. That was real Welsh loyalty for you. But otherwise all I saw of Richard was an enormous pile of clothes left in the bathroom every day for Sybil to wash. Everything was covered in bole* because he had been wearing togas and things, and everything was naturally caked in this brown stuff."

Curiously, while Burton was now much talked about in Hollywood circles, the publicity he received was minimal for a star actor. Only *My Cousin Rachel* was so far released, and his status with the filmgoing public was no more than that of an interesting newcomer. His fan mail totaled less than a hundred letters a week—low by Hollywood standards. He was not hounded by autograph-hunters. He was rarely sought out for serious interviews. And not a word about his hellraising antics was reported in Britain. Inevitably his publicity increased as Fox assigned the unusually large number of four public relations officers and two publicity photographers exclusively to *The Robe*, but it was the film itself that got the lion's share of coverage. We learned that a vast army of workers had toiled for 2,404 man-hours to recreate Golgotha for the crucifixion scene; that the seamless robe was one of four, insured for $100,000, and handwoven by Mrs. Dorothea Hulse, a trucker's wife and a minister's daughter—yes, the same Mrs. Hulse who had actually woven Susan Hayward's costume for *David and Bathsheba*! We were told how many tons of sienna-dyed dirt were suctioned-up by wind machines to make dust storms, how 193 technicians created thunder, lightning and blizzards, how 10,000 props were brought from museums, and how 402 research books were consulted to ensure absolute authenticity (though they hadn't bargained with Mrs. Maggie Rennie, wife of Saint Peter, having a baby during the shooting). Amid this plethora of statistics neither Burton nor Miss Simmons could hope to gain much attention. Here was an epic bigger than

* An unctuous clay for face and body makeup.

its stars, a film destined to be seen as a triumph for technicians more than its actors.

Richard, at work on *The Robe,* was much the same as he had been on *Rachel*—intense, determined, self-demanding. He was still prone to fly into rages when he fell short of his own high standards, and once, after several failures in tackling a stunt, he deliberately charged headfirst into a plaster wall. "I'm the kind of ham who wants to rush into every scene and chew the scenery," he said. Another time he told reporters, "Half the fun of playing other parts is getting away from your own disgusting self." To the casual observer, he seemed refreshingly frank and humble. But to those who knew him well, humility was never one of his most striking characteristics. He could promote himself as well as anyone if need be, and once he proclaimed: "After what I am and what I've come from, where can I go but to the top?"

In private, Richard described the part of Marcellus as a "prissy role." Nevertheless, his performance won the approval of the critics, who praised his dynamic vigor and forceful acting, and the film was a runaway box-office success—a lifesaver for Fox and the indestructible Zanuck, then facing his first big proxy fight in the boardroom. The company was so delighted that they made a sequel, promoting Victor Mature from common slave to superman and tossing him to the lions and man-eating Susan Hayward in *Demetrius and the Gladiators.* Yet *The Robe* was no classic. Its huge attraction lay essentially in its original filming technique; all else was subsidiary. Vast, extravagant sets dwarfed the players. Jean Simmons, coming direct from *Androcles and the Lion,* had little to do but give wide-eyed looks, and ancient Rome creaked under the weight of Yankee accents. As for Richard, while the film's success justified Fox's faith in him and made his name far more widely known, it did nothing to enhance his reputation as an actor.

There now came conflicting reports of a new long-term deal between Burton and Fox, but Richard was still unwilling to devote himself exclusively to films. He thrived on challenge, and his budding genius needed to grow beyond the confines of the Hollywood hothouse of gossip and intrigue if it was to achieve full flower. Moreover, he had a deep-grained suspicion of soft and easy living, having been indoctrinated from childhood with the need to work hard and play hard. At the same time, with his ever-growing respect for riches, he could ill-afford to isolate himself from Hollywood. Seeking the best of both worlds, he now contracted to make more films for Fox, while retaining the freedom to work for long periods on the stage. *The Prince of Players* would be his next film. Meanwhile feeling the need for experience and discipline in the Old Vic school, he grabbed the chance to tackle the most searching test of an actor's art—*Hamlet*.

The Prince of Players

Few actors, once they have reached the heights of Beverly Hills, return to their humble origins. Richard Burton did, and still does. "My valley is vulgar but honest," he says, and it is that raw honesty which helps to preserve his sanity in a crazy, artificial world. It balances his values, and it brings him down to earth as surely as it did when he returned in July, 1953. One weekend he was sunning himself in the Grangers' luxury pad; the next he was in the gray, rainswept grimness of Cwmavon, knocking back pints with his brothers in the old Copper House. He arrived as a Scheherazade—back home with a thousand and one tales of nights at the Mocambo, Ciro's, Grauman's and Romanoff's, of sly chin-wags with Louella Parsons, of Brando whooping it up along Sunset Boulevard on a motorbike, of Bogart and Broderick Crawford hoaxing house guests with mock fistfights, and . . . but who cared? Not the miners around him, who were more concerned with selecting a World History Rugby XV than with listening to stories of Hollywood and Hedda Hopper. "Hedda Hopper?

Who's that then Richie? Sounds like a bloody soccer-playing kangaroo. Now, as we were saying, Ivor bach, we'll have Napoleon at fullback and Hitler as hooker—a bit dirty like but effective—and old Lloyd George at scrum-half. . . ." And as they rumbled on, debating with absurd passion and intensity the respective rugger merits of Mussolini and Alexander the Great, Richard listened spellbound. It was as if he had stepped back in time—into a Glamorganshire *Brigadoon,* where values remained ever constant and where men pursued pleasures with a simplicity and sincerity that defied analysis in a world of growing materialism and sophistication. Suddenly Hollywood seemed alien and remote and totally irrelevent.

The miners knew about Burton the filmstar and they were proud of him, but it wasn't their way to treat him as anything special. They liked his fancy car though; and Sam the Drop, whose idol was Pierrepoint, and whose one great ambition in life was to become the public hangman, climbed into the back of the new Jaguar Mark VIII and just sat there for hours, feeling the leather, examining the dashboard, and then sinking back and tugging at the handstrap and dreaming of ropes and trap doors. It was quite an event to see him *outside* a pub during opening hours, for Sam the Drop was also known as Sam the Schooner, and his passion for the local "iron ore" was so great that he had even shocked the agnostic miners by trying to sell his parents' gravestone to raise beer money. "Would you like me to drive you somewhere, Sam?" the filmstar asked. "Ooh no, Richie. I'll just sit here and enjoy myself."

Approaching on the other side of the road Richard spotted the unmistakable shuffling figure of old Will Dai, and knowing he was always good for a laugh he crossed over. " 'ello," said Will, peering out from below the drooping peak of his button-down cap. "W-w-well, if it isn't b-b-bloody D-d-douglas F-f-fairbanks 'imself." His stammer was worse than ever, and he looked unusually glum.

"Hello," said Richard. "How are things going then?"

"It's t-t-terrible," said Will. "I've l-lost s-s-seventy f-five th-thousand p-p-pounds."

"However could that happen?"

"W-well, I had s-s-seven d-d-draws on the f-f-football p-p-pools. And j-just one t-team let me down."

"Really? Which team was that?"

"Fuh-fuh-fuh . . ."

"Fulham?" suggested Richard.

"N-n-no. Fuh-fuh-fuh . . ."

"Falkirk?"

Will grinned wickedly. "N-n-no. Fuh-fuh-fuhking Swansea."

Richard accompanied him into the Copper House and bought a fresh round of beer, and there he became "just Jenks" again as the public bar chat burbled on to the unforgettable exploits of the Cwmavon Boys School "Wonder Team" that never conceded a point in three full seasons of the thirties and scored over a thousand against. "Unbeatable they were in League and Cup, and there was a prize of a gold watch and a holiday in Porthcawl for every member of any team that scored against them. Bloody geniuses some of those little buggers were. Remember Viv Allen then, Richie? He was one of Phil Burton's little actors. But duw! What a scrum-half! Fast as greased lightning! Remember when they played Meredith Jones's Eastern team and Viv came up against young Joe Drew, who was slow off the mark, and Viv flattened him every time they got the strike? And he was giving him such a hammering that old Mrs. Drew ran on to the pitch and belted him across the ear'ole with her brolly." Richard remembered; and his thoughts wandered ruefully into wondering how on earth he could ever scrum down again in the number eight shirt if he was geared to filming schedules with precious millions to be lost at the crack of a collarbone.

Back in Port Talbot, the welcome was different. Small children with autograph books came running to knock at 73 Caradoc Street, where he and Sybil stayed with Cissie and Elfed James; and when he went into pubs, teenage girls followed him and giggled and ordered small ports. "I suppose they're fascinated by my pockmarked face," Richard told his brothers as he bought the beer and then entertained them with stories of Bogie and Brando and all the dumb broads in town. But as far as Daddy Ni knew or cared, Richie's homecoming was just another excuse for a rip-roaring piss-up. "I think my father believed Hollywood was a small place on the other side of the Welsh mountains," says Richard. "He just greeted me with, 'Well, Rich, how are you getting on?' As if I'd been down to Swansea for the weekend."

Daddy Ni was now seventy-seven, and only once had he seen his son in a film. The brothers explained that there were seventeen pubs on the way to the cinema and that the old man had called in every one. And when he saw Rich pour himself a drink on the screen, he said 'That's it,' and was away for a pint. "He just wasn't a film-going man," says Hilda. "When my eldest brother Tom took him to see *My Cousin Rachel* he thought it was disgusting—so much lovemaking going on. He couldn't grasp it, that they were acting. And Tom was laughing because he kept saying, 'What the hell is all this kissing? What does Sybil say?' And Tom said, 'but it's only acting, father.' 'Acting be damned,' he said. 'It looks real enough to me.' He never could understand the film business."

"In fact," says Graham Jenkins, "Daddy Ni did go once more to see Richard in a film. Contrary to opinion, he got past the seventeen pubs to the old Plaza cinema in Swansea, now demolished to make way for the new Odeon Center. He went to see *The Robe,* and rather than get complimentary tickets organized for him, he stood in the queue for a couple of hours. The management invited him to come inside, but he said, 'No, no. I'll stay in the queue and wait my turn. It won't be long now.' Later some Pontrhydyfen people insisted on getting him in ahead of the queue, for he was now in his late seventies. But that was typical of Dic-bach-y-saer. He was well loved by everyone."

Though Richard pretends to eschew sentiment, great waves of nostalgia swept over him as he went around Taibach and Port Talbot, and Cwmavon and Pontrhydyfen. This was his valley, and he knew it would never be his home again. It had changed a lot, but superficially not at all. There were the same YMCA dances and Sunday-school outings to Porthcawl, the same gaggle of teen-agers in Morozzi's "caff," the same old sun slipping down beyond Mumbles Head. And everywhere familiar faces—Leo Lloyd, still dynamically dedicated to amateur dramatics; Alderman Heycock (later Lord Heycock of Taibach), ascending new dizzy heights of local government; old boys back at school as masters. Philip Burton was away in London; he had resigned from his BBC post and was currently playing a small role in Wilde's *A Woman of No Importance*. But all around there were brothers and sisters, and a whole new generation of little Jenkinses. He visited Ma Smith and Betty and Audrey, who were still in Connaught Street, and he drove up the hill to see Dennis Burgess. His great school chum was reading in the garden, surrounded by bread crusts his wife had put out for the birds. "Jesus Christ!" said the star direct from the religious solemnity of *The Robe*. "I hope to God she feeds you better than that!" And he hugged Dennis's mother who had always adored him. "Been halfway around the world, luv, and nobody makes steak-and-kidney pud better than you."

When friends asked him about Hollywood, Richard told them: "Hollywood is a toy town. An enchanted city where every moment you think you're going to wake up to reality. It's a great place for a short visit, but a disturbing place for long stays. You would forget there were any poor people in the world. You would forget how to walk. Even to go a hundred and twenty yards from one studio to another, people take their cars." And he was refreshingly honest about his attitude to films: "At one Hollywood party I heard director Billy Wilder refer to actors as 'a pack of bums.' Bogie got mad at him over that. Anyway, I asked Wilder to explain his remark, and he said, 'Look, I can photograph Gregory Peck's face from four different angles, put them into a film anywhere I like, and make them mean anything I choose.' And, you know, I had to admit he was right. I'm strictly in Hollywood for the fame films bring, and especially the money. But I don't take films that seriously. The theater is magic, but somehow I can't believe in films. It all seems a bit of a lark."

With overtime, that "lark" had earned him about $230,000 from three Hollywood pictures, not including a living allowance of $400 a week from the studio, and it therefore seemed an admirable gesture of dedication to the legitimate theater that he and Claire Bloom should be joining the Old Vic company in the summer of 1953 for a ten-month season on the maximum wage of $116 a week. But Burton couldn't help laughing about the talk of self-sacrifice and altruism. He was learning all about the artificialities of life in the super-tax bracket, and he painfully calculated that British income tax would consume all but $17,000 of his Hollywood earnings. He explained, "You can't keep the big money anyway, and an actor must feed his ego somehow. So the lower salary on the stage is compensated for by the applause every night. That's just as good as money in the bank." The man within, however, was far from certain of winning applause; he was as nervous as an Olympic runner returning to top athletics after a year of soft living. He desperately wanted to succeed. And he knew full well that after his filmstar buildup the critics would not swing velvet gloves if he failed.

Typically, he sought no graduated path back to stage stardom. He was starting at the top, boldly playing his first *Hamlet* at the seventh Edinburgh Festival. There was some talk of Philip Burton playing Claudius, but this was dropped because producer Michael Benthall, who had also directed the Wilde play, rightly feared that Richard might be inhibited by sharing a stage with his tutor-guardian. Instead, "P.H." sat out in the front row on the opening night, quietly fuming because his seat at the side gave him a rear view of Richard at critical moments.

The "thrust stage" of the Church of Scotland's Assembly was wholly ill-suited to the Old Vic's production. It was composed of steeply built-up stairs and rostra, and it demanded athleticism almost as much as acting ability on the part of players, who had to charge round the corridors and up and down the jagged elevations. Moreover, the first act was marred by an irritating, high-pitched whistling sound that filled the hall. (Two people in the audience, it was discovered, were seated at opposite sides of the stage with their hearing aids tuned into the same frequency.)

Burton got the applause he wanted that night, but the notices were disappointing. His athletic, sharply alert Hamlet gave insufficient attention to the psychological aspect for some tastes, and only one feature of the performance evoked unanimous praise—the extraordinary realism of the final dueling scene. But then his adversary, as Laertes, was Robert Hardy, his regular fencing partner in Oxford days. After that lukewarm opening, Richard anxiously sought to polish his performance before they moved on to the Old Vic and his first star appearance on the London stage. By the eve of the opening he was too nervous to sleep. He left his Hampstead home to meander the streets at night, and by four in the morning he had covered nearly ten miles and was standing on Waterloo Bridge, a few hundred yards from the theater. A policeman stopped him. Richard explained he was a terrified actor and then joined him in pounding his beat.

Burton's fears were largely unfounded. His "rugger-playing Hamlet," as one critic called it, was seen to better advantage on the orthodox apron stage, and while his Prince of Denmark was still judged too uncomplicated, too full of dash and verve, it also won many qualified words of praise. "Burton adds a new dimension as an important Shakespearean actor," wrote David Lewin (London *Daily Express*). And Harold Conway (*Evening Standard*) described it as "the most effective—and authoritative—Hamlet that any actor under thirty has achieved on the London stage since Gielgud's first performance twenty-four years ago." Others thought he had tackled the demanding role a decade too soon, but then that question of age is an ancient, much-masticated bone of contention. The late director Tyrone Guthrie always maintained that an actor of great merit should play Hamlet early in his career, even though he may lack the maturity to do it justice, so that he will be stretched to the full and strengthen his dramatic muscles. In this sense, Burton's "financial slumming" down the gray and dingy Waterloo Road was altogether worthwhile. And he was fortunate to have arrived when the Old Vic was beginning a great revival in popularity and prestige under the new direction of Benthall. This young producer of plays and operas had extraordinary flair as a theater administrator, and now he was launching the famous Five-Year Plan—a half-decade in which they proposed to present the whole of Shakespeare's first folio of thirty-six plays, nearly half of them to be directed by Benthall himself.

Under Benthall, who had co-produced an Old Vic *Hamlet* with Guthrie during the war, Richard became increasingly confident and convincing. And the moment he most fondly cherishes came nearly midway through the run. He had some sixty performances behind him and was eager to break the Old Vic record of a hundred and one consecutive appearances in the role. At this point, when bookings were beginning to decline, the house manager visited the star's dressing room and said, "Richard, you had better be extra good tonight. The old man's outside."

"What old man?" asked Burton.

"He comes once a year," the manager went on. "He usually stays for one act and then leaves."

"For God's sake, what old man?"

"Churchill, of course."

The Prime Minister was sitting in the front row of the stalls, and from the moment Richard spoke his first line, "A little more than kin, and less than kind," he could hear a soft mumbling coming from just beyond the footlights. "Churchill, I soon realized, was following me line for line, word for word, all through the play. I'd try to shake him off. I went fast. I went slow. But he was always right there beside me like a faithful old dog. And every now and then you could detect a growling sound where he was irritated to find a line or two had been cut. I was tremendously impressed."

During the second interval, Sir Winston wandered backstage. And Richard still delights in majestically miming the first words spoken to him by the grand master of the English language. "My Lord Hamlet," he rumbled. "May I use your lavatory?"

That night Burton took eighteen curtain calls, and Churchill reportedly remarked that "it was as exciting and virile a performance of *Hamlet* as I can remember." But the power of his performance, so appealing to Sir Winston, was interpreted by others as a weakness, because it made Hamlet too forceful a personality ever to have been tormented by indecision. This view was endorsed toward the end of his record-breaking run when Burton was visited by another idol of his youth—Sir John Gielgud. They were to take supper together after the show, and Richard recalls how this foremost authority on *Hamlet* waited for him to change in his cramped, drab-brown dressing room. "I was trying to hurry but was continually being held up by well-wishers, hangers-on and freeloaders. John got bored and suddenly said, 'Well, dear boy, shall I go ahead or shall I wait until you're better—um, er, I mean ready?' The truth was out." Gielgud confirms his little indiscretion.

While Burton's acting was impressive enough, his huge box-office success obviously owed something to his aura as a filmstar. "The Tommy Steele of the Old Vic" was how he frankly described himself. The young fans loved him. They thrilled to the authority and resonance of his voice, the magnetic quality of his presence, and they were happy that his virility and strength were not to be subdued. But if he won the popular vote, he missed the purists' approval. Bluntly, his *Hamlet* gave no striking evidence that his artistic skill had markedly advanced since his conquest of Stratford two years before. So far we had seen only minor variations on a theme; the same burning eyes and deep intensity and sonorous tones came across in *Hamlet* as they had done in *Rachel* and *The Robe,* and the man Hollywood called "the newest gift to womanhood" had done nothing to disturb his film image as the handsome romantic hero.

As concerned as anyone about being typecast, Richard bravely attempted to broaden his image and widen his experience. In February, 1954, while still playing *Hamlet,* he took on the extra strain of preparing to play *Coriolanus,* and here he did achieve a truly memorable performance. The role of the eloquent Roman noble, with its succession of heroic speeches, suited his technique admirably. Olivier generously told him that no one else could ever play the part now, and that first night of *Coriolanus* confirmed his position as the new idol of the cultured bobby-soxers. In the gallery they were screaming for him, just as they used to call for "Larry" years before. John Neville, who has done more Shakespeare with Richard than anyone, judges *Coriolanus* to be one of his really great achievements. "He was quite brilliant in that part. Unfortunately, none of us ever had enough time to study in rehearsal; otherwise, I think that with a little more work on it, Richard could have been absolutely earth-shattering."

One man carries a permanent reminder of the vigor with which Richard attacked that role—Paul Daneman, who played Tullus Aufidius. In the final scene a Third Conspirator tells Aufidius, "Let him feel your sword." But in an earlier scene Richard reversed Shakespeare's action. On the opening night he tore into his adversary with such fury that his fellow actor had to be taken to the hospital with a severely slashed hand.

"Richard was terribly proud of his skill with the sword," says Daneman. "He used to tell us how some stuntman had fought him in *The Robe* and had gone berserk, attacking him like a lunatic, and yet he had managed to hold him off. Well, I rather fancied myself with a sword as well. We rehearsed our fight scenes very fully, and Richard was terribly keen. 'We'll make the sparks fly,' he said. We had short Roman swords, no gloves, and the lighting was very low for dramatic effect, which made it rather difficult. Anyway, in our enthusiasm, we fought rather too furiously, and I suddenly felt a pain and then the hand went numb, and it wasn't until I was at the bottom of the steps underneath the stage that I saw the hand was streaming with blood. The nurse at the theater bound it up and we finished the performance. Later I went to Charing Cross Hospital and found that the blow had cut right through the tendon of the index finger of the right hand. For the next six weeks I had to go on stage wearing this great plaster, and I was still wearing it when we were playing *Twelfth Night*. I still can't completely bend that finger. But Richard was terribly sweet about it. It was not really his fault. And it did at least achieve one thing: after that, it became a firm rule at the Old Vic that gloves should always be worn for sword fights."

Though he shrugs off the fact, Richard himself often came off the stage with blood running from his sword hand. He accepted it as part of the game. As the man of action, he was completely fearless. It was only the acting that sometimes filled him with dread, and to relieve the tension he invented absurd omens, such as taking it to be a favorable sign if all the traffic lights were green when he drove down Kingsway to the theater. "Early on in that season he was terribly nervous," says one member of the company. "He tried to character act a bit, to do touches of Olivier and Gielgud, and then it was a disaster. At that time one felt there were several more accomplished actors in the company, people like John Neville and Robert Hardy. But Richard had this remarkable presence. And the less he put on this pure kind of Gielgud accent the better he became. One of his best parts was as the Bastard in King John. He was on the bottle then, and in a way it was a good thing, because it helped his repose."

Burton moved on to other roles less obviously suited to his talents. In April, he appeared as the savage and deformed slave of *The Tempest*, spending two hours each day donning his grotesque costume and makeup. One critic judged that "Burton's Caliban, looking like a black-faced comedian in a sewer, eschews pathos for farce," and the inclination to farce was not checked during one performance when his false nose curiously appeared white to the audience. It was froth of beer he was supping from a jug.

The following month, at his own suggestion, the cinema's glamor boy padded his stomach, puffed out his cheeks, and crowned himself with a semibald pate to emerge in the improbable role of Sir Toby Belch. It was a gay little romp but not really his style. Nevertheless, he had run the five-role gauntlet at the Old Vic with courage and panache and not inconsiderable distinction. His performances had varied from night to night from the mediocre to the inspired, and his Hamlet was at least unique in that he was the only Prince of Denmark to take a weekend off to return to Wales to scrum down with a village team of miners. It was his first rugby match for four or five years and his last, and one he has lovingly recorded for posterity in 3,500 words of supremely poetic prose.

Ambitious, ruthlessly self-demanding, Burton drove himself at an impossible pace over the last laps of that Old Vic season. Besides the five Shakespearean roles, he undertook broadcasts, charity benefits, Sunday-night plays and lectures, and, above all, he busied himself with tributes to the late Dylan Thomas. He did the first BBC radio broadcast of *Under Milk Wood*, playing the First

Narrator in a cast that included Hugh Griffith as blind Captain Cat, Sybil as Miss Myfanwy Price of the loving hot-water-bottled body, with Phil Burton and Rachel Roberts taking several parts. He also joined in public readings on behalf of the trust fund for the education of Dylan's children, and during one evening of homage at the Globe Theater, reading with Dame Edith Evans, Hugh Griffith, and Emlyn Williams, he wept unashamedly on stage as he read *Fern Hill*.

Richard deeply mourned the passing of that wild, strangely inspired Welshman whose earthy genius filled him with awe, and he was shattered when the poet died prematurely in his fortieth year. He remembered how, as a seventeen-year-old boy in Taibach, he had leapt the low fencing skirting Ma Smith's house and had run in waving a copy of the old *Sunday Referee*. "Listen to this," he cried, and poured out to Phil Burton: "The force that through the green fuse drives the flower." And when his guardian asked what it meant, he said, "I don't know, but isn't it beautiful?" He remembered, too, how Dylan had stayed with him and Sybil at Hampstead during his last year and had sometimes treated him like a dog—"he absolutely dismissed me unless he wanted something." And there was the sad, lingering memory of that October day when Dylan telephoned him for a touch for the last time. He was speaking from Phil Burton's London flat, and he wanted to borrow two hundred pounds.

"What do you want it for?" asked Richard.

"For the education of my children," said the self-styled 'podgy pub-crawler' from Wales.

"Come off it," said Richard. "Don't give me that."

"All right then. For two hundred quid I'll give you the rights in my new play."

"Oh yes. Where is it?"

"Well I haven't actually written it yet," said Dylan. "It's the story of a love affair between two streets."

Burton gazed sadly into his tall vodka-and-tonic as he recalled their last dialogue. "It was strange because he then unfolded a story of extraordinary fascination that held me completely spellbound for a while. But something inside me told me that it didn't ring true; some dark suspicion that for all the brilliance and fluency of his story, he was making the whole thing up as he went along. Anyway, I didn't have the money. I suppose I could have sold something, but I didn't, and he didn't get the two hundred pounds and immediately afterward he went to America, and the next month he was dead. I've felt slightly guilty about it ever since.

"He was the only real bohemian I had met. If he wore odd clothes, it was because he had no others. And as a joke he would hire a dress suit, bury it in the garden, then dig it up and return it. He saw my *Hamlet* at the Old Vic three times, but he only saw the third act each time. He hated intervals, and he told me that he would walk in with the crowds after the second interval and get a free seat. He never got caught."

In mourning the loss of a friend who had so enriched his life with great tumbling words and telescoped images, Richard readily joined in efforts to raise funds for Dylan's dependents, and ultimately he drove himself too hard. For nine months there had been no letup. As *Hamlet,* he had been giving two performances within nine hours on matinee days, and his program steadily increased until it proved too much. He collapsed at home after one performance and was told by his doctor to restrict his engagements to the Old Vic.

His marathon finally ended with a short provincial tour and performances of *Hamlet* at Elsinore and in Zurich. In July, he returned to London—sun-tanned, refreshed, and fit for a last round of parties before going back to Hollywood. By now his first three films for Fox had been widely screened in Britain; he was established as both movie star and champion of the Old Vic. He and Sybil mixed with the cream of London society. They veritably glowed with realized ambition. And then came a new accolade of recognition—an invitation to a Buckingham Palace garden party. He was one of seven thousand, but as usual Richard stood out in the crowd. Among all the tails and toppers on the Palace lawns, he appeared in a blue pin-striped suit and yellow gloves, and dragging a mane of long unruly brown hair cultivated in pre-Beatle days because he was loathe to wear wigs on stage.

After an all-night party given by Old Vic producers Benthall and Robert Helpmann, Burton now flew off to Hollywood to make *The Prince of Players,* based on Eleanor Ruggles' biography of America's foremost Shakespearean actor, Edwin Booth. Twentieth Century-Fox saw this as a great chance to exploit his Old Vic background. He would be completely in his element, strutting on a stage and ranging from the gentility of Romeo to the soul-searching of Hamlet, from the virtues of Henry V to the villainy of Richard III. Equally, in the offstage scenes, he would be a natural as the actor who is tormented by fear of becoming a mad alcoholic like his father and who is finally disgraced as the brother of Lincoln's assassin. *Life* saw it as "the most effective piece of Hollywood casting in years" and described him as "the most promising young classical actor alive today," and that was the general view in Hollywood. Director Philip Dunne and many others on the set were hypnotized by his poetic eloquence and felt that an Oscar-winning performance was in the making. Even when rehearsing, Richard dazzled and delighted those around him. He danced ankle-deep in the Pacific surf off Santa Monica as he practiced Ariel's song from *The Tempest*; he recited blank verse to the improbable tune of "Frankie and Johnny," explaining: "It sharpens the wit and strengthens the throat. You sound like nothing at all. Then you go into the studios and deafen the sound men."

He was full of conjuring tricks. But then they went into the projection room to see the rushes, and it was discovered that he wasn't a magician at all. The forcefulness and magnetism of his presence on the set simply did not come across on the screen. Snatches of Shakespeare, thrown into a film like song-and-dance numbers in a musical, were totally without effect when taken out of context and without proper dramatic balance and buildup. Some critics raved over Burton's performance, but overall the film was a colossal bore, ill-conceived, poorly executed, and not even historically accurate in visual details of the President's assassination. Despite a strong cast, including Raymond Massey, Maggie McNamara, and John Derek, and a screenplay by Moss Hart, it was the first notable box-office flop in CinemaScope.

When *The Prince of Players* was complete but not yet released, Darryl F. Zanuck, the wiry little fifty-one-year-old boss of 20th Century-Fox, made a shrewdly perceptive judgment of Burton— "I put him among the three finest actors in the world. But this doesn't automatically make him a star, although *The Robe,* his first big starring picture, was among the biggest box-office money-makers of all time. Burton has *acted* all his parts so far, but what about his personality? No opportunity to show it yet. I think that he, like Olivier years ago, will have a stuttering start and creep up on people slowly." Zanuck defined a star as "a person who can make people pay money at the box office, even if the film is not much good." By this definition, as *The Prince of Players* showed, Burton was not a star yet. He himself recognized this, and for the moment he still felt that his real home was in the Waterloo Road. "I'm simply not the Oscar-winning type," he said. "As Bogart always said to me: 'Kid, you leave the Oscar-winning to your Uncle Bogie.' "

While in Hollywood, Richard was briefly reunited with Phil Burton who, during his annual summer holiday in the United States, had been persuaded to take charge of the script department of a new film company. His first assignment was to try to interest Richard and several other stars in projected films, but all his efforts were to come to naught because after six months the company was dissolved following differences between the two controlling partners. Although Mr. Burton had no such intention at this time, he was destined through a chain of events to remain permanently in America, lecturing on Shakespeare, directing plays, and eventually becoming President and Director of the American Musical and Dramatic Academy in New York. In this way, he would only see Richard on rare occasions in the next few years.

In February, 1955, Richard and Sybil celebrated their sixth wedding anniversary with wine and song in a village near Madrid. They were on a motoring tour of Portugal and Spain—the first real holiday abroad they had shared together. These were blissful romantic weeks, driving across wild and unspoiled countryside and stopping wherever their thirst and fancy took them;

and, away from the temptation to booze with his buddies and flirt with the butterflies, Richard could be an extraordinarily dutiful and considerate husband, while Sybil possessed just the right mixture of gaiety, worldliness, and common sense to match his unpredictable, boyish exuberance. Moreover, there was a pot of gold at the end of the trail. In Madrid, Richard was to star in his second big-screen epic, *Alexander the Great.* His fee: $100,000.

For the first time in ten movies, he was experiencing the "working holiday" of a star on location with all expenses paid, and after the cloistered pressures of theater routine, he thrived on a healthy open-air life on the plains near Madrid and in the lofty Guadarrama Sierras. The publicists projected him as a bronzed he-man, riding bareback as he had done as a boy on pit ponies in Wales, stripping off his leather armor for lunchtime swims in the cold-rock-streams from the mountains, and springing onto his Bucephalus, which had come direct from Olivier's Richard III. It wasn't quite that attractive. Burton was no great horseman, and he found the battle scenes distinctly uncomfortable, leaving him with severe bruising to the back of his legs and feet. Still, it was better than working.

There were plenty of leisure days, since the scripting was still in process. Claire Bloom, for example, staying in a twenty-dollar-a-night luxury suite at Madrid's lavish Castellana-Hilton, enjoyed weeks on the payroll before she was needed; then Richard's familiar leading lady from the Old Vic arrived on set wearing a near-topless hostage's gown and gently purring about how she had always wanted an X certificate. The period was 338 B.C., but all modern comforts were close at hand—a fleet of cars to take players between battlefields and luxury hotels, refrigerators, and high-class cuisine on the set. This was to be another epic to end all epics, a film possessing all the ingredients for a mighty blockbuster—a great heroic story ideally suited to the wide-screen color treatment; a $4,000,000 budget; a cast of thousands that included such genuine professionals as Fredric March, Danielle Darrieux, Bloom, Peter Cushing, Harry Andrews, Michael Hordern, Peter Wyngarde—and Stanley Baker.

Baker and Burton chuckled over the memory of their last involvement with Alexander, in the Rattigan play when Stanley carried a spear and Richard got the sack. Now, seven years on, Richard believed that Alexander might provide his chariot to super-stardom. He had no illusions about the past: "I've done absolutely nothing worthwhile as a film actor," he said, but he was genuinely excited about this one. He was perfect for Alexander, a man of stocky physique, powerful personality, and lionlike courage. And the author, producer, and director was Robert Rossen, the New Yorker who had won an Oscar with *All the King's Men.*

Rarely had so much scholarship gone into the making of an epic. Prince Peter of Greece was technical adviser. Rossen spent two years on the research. He hired nearly four thousand foot and cavalry soldiers from the Spanish Army for battle scenes; called on five hundred extras a day; hired three hundred and fifty horses, thousands of suits of armor, shields, blunted swords, and rubber-tipped spears. The result was a breathtaking spectacle, faultless in visual detail. Yet it would not win over the critics. Like so many epics, it lacked pace. An hour and twenty minutes passed before Burton came to the throne; then in one hour and twenty-five minutes he set out to conquer all the known world.

It was to be almost a year, however, before *Alexander* hit the wide screens, and in the meantime 20th Century-Fox took their star prodigy out of the Spanish sun and plunged him directly into *The Rains of Ranchipur,* a modernized version of Louis Bromfield's novel, *The Rains Came.* This was originally filmed with Tyrone Power in the lead, and the only possible justification for refilming the story was that the great tempests and flood would be so much more breathtaking in CinemaScope. But a remake scarcely demanded an actor of Burton's vocal power in the role of the taciturn, philosophical Dr. Safti who seeks the spiritual awakening of a selfish and spoiled Western woman. Turbaned and tanned, he was required to do little more than rumble Sellers-like impressions of an Indian gentleman, flash the whites of his eyes in exchanging meaningful glances with the satin seductress Lana Turner, and allow the special effects men to drench him in gallons of water. Richard quipped, "It never rains but it ranchipurs," and he later described the film as rubbish that was "beyond human belief." But it didn't worry him. He was no longer the intense young man straining to dominate every scene. He had learned to accept the lack of emotional satisfaction in trying to create a role at the rate of a few minutes each day. Filming was strictly a job that offered enormous rewards quite disproportionate to the effort involved and that afforded him the periodic luxury of working in the theater.

Richard splashed through the mediocrities of *The Rains of Ranchipur* as professionally as he could and took his pleasures on the side. He surfed and bathed off Malibu; he caroused through scores of parties; he got a great kick out of bringing over brother Ivor and his wife and showing them the wonders of the west coast. But once filming was complete, he didn't stop to socialize or see the final product. Within two hours of his release by producer Frank Ross he was jetting off to New York, where he and Sybil took Ivor and Gwen on a day-and-night junket around the city before sailing for England. It was eighteen months and three movies since Richard had left the Old Vic. Now, in the late fall of 1955, he was ready to go back and earn a mere pittance for the most nerve-racking test of his entire career.

The Bobby-Soxers' Idol

Burton was in a curious and distinctly uncomfortable position when he returned to the Old Vic. He was a major Hollywood star, yet it served him no advantage at all; quite the reverse. In this "back to school" period he had to develop his craft in a blaze of publicity. More distressingly, he met with some hostility within the company. There were actors who strongly resented the way this much-publicized Alexander could casually return after eighteen months absence and step straight into the leading role of *Henry V.* They saw him as a carpetbagger picking plums that long-serving players deserved more, and they were sickened by stories of how he was sacrificing nearly $10,000 a week to be working with them.

The pressure upon him was enormous. There was the strain of striving to justify advance publicity which was too impressive for him to be forgiven failure. And life was not made any easier by the senseless contest which developed between his fans and those of John Neville, who had become the Old Vic bobby-sox idol during his absence. That season one half of the house cheered every entrance and exit by Neville; the other half vociferously supported the visiting star. It brought a kind of Beatlemania to the Waterloo Road, the like of which has never been seen there since.

"It was incredible," says Neville. "Those crowds were really enormous, stretching right across the Waterloo Road, stopping the traffic, and blocking the way from the station. I think the first manifestation of this sort of thing was when Johnnie Ray came over here. They screamed and wore all sorts of things, such as scarves and jumpers with our names on. I was playing Chorus and Richard had the leading role, and because we weren't playing scenes together I suppose we could be separated, as it were, in the mind of the audience."

In a sense it was natural that these two Old Vic stars should gain rival factions. Though both had humble backgrounds— Neville as a lorry driver's son—they contrasted sharply in physical appearance and personality. Richard was the fiery Celt, dark, stocky, thickset; John the studious, soft-spoken Englishman, tall, lean, and fair. Both were thirty years old, and both in different ways were handsome and charming and talented. Their careers had followed quite separate paths. After a triumph as *Richard II,* Neville had been inundated with film offers, but he had turned them down because he had made a gentleman's agreement with Benthall, that come what may, he would stay with the Old Vic through the whole five-year plan.

Here then was a situation neatly designed for razor-edged rivalry spurred on by the gallery. Indeed, after the opening night of *Henry V,* one or two critics judged that Neville had absurdly overdone his task of emceeing the show, and so insinuated that he was straining to steal Burton's thunder. It was a good box-office angle; it also happened to be totally untrue. Neville, the most amiable of men, was an especially close friend of Richard, and after each performance they would trek across the Thames to sink pints and swap stories in the Savoy Tavern. "To say I was trying to compete with Richard while playing Chorus is absolute balls," he says. "I certainly don't look upon acting as a competition, and Richard and I were always great friends. Yet there was still this invented rivalry between us, and it seemed to us that many of the notices were preoccupied with this aspect rather than the play. In *Henry V* we were rather hurt by the notices. There was one critic in particular who said, 'Well, of course, I always remember Laurence Olivier in this role in the late 1930s at the Vic, and, of course, he was magnificent. He had poetry. He had the virility; he was a soldier and he was a king." It was a sort of eulogy, and so Richard and I thought it would be quite interesting to look up the notices of this particular performance by Olivier. We did, and you know they were not very good at all. In fact, this same critic, who was still writing for the same paper, gave him almost the worst notice of all, and said he'd be better off selling cars in Berkeley Street. Anyway, the fact is that Richard was really damn good in the role from the word go."

Burton was especially determined to triumph as *Henry V* because he had never forgotten how critics had pinpointed his shortcomings at Stratford. And he did triumph, even if the notices were not wholly enthusiastic. Tynan wrote in *The Observer*: "By stressing the 'gently gamester' aspect of the part and delivering the rest as a trumpet voluntary, many actors have been able to blind us to the barbarity of *Henry V.* Richard Burton takes a steeper path. He gives us a cunning warrior, stocky and astute, unafraid of harshness or of curling the royal lip. The gallery gets no smiles from him, and the soldiery none but the scantiest commiseration. Though it sometimes prefers rant to exuberance, this is an honest performance, true and watchful and ruthless."

The *Times* critic also noted a marked improvement. "Mr. Burton's progress as an actor is such that already he is able to make good all the lacks of a few short years ago. The Harfleur speech remains mere ferocious rant, but this is the only conspicuous flaw in a performance which excitingly combines all the qualities of Shakespeare's ideal king. The whole performance—a most satisfying romantic one—is firmly under the control of the imagination. The only parts of it that occasionally slip out of control are the sudden vocal transitions. Mr. Burton has a Celtic impetuosity which tempts him not to look before he takes a vocal leap, and the effect is now and then to startle us in the wrong way."

Richard skillfully avoided the pitfall of making the king insufferably virtuous, and in time he honed a Henry V of such polished fineness that it won the coveted Evening Standard Drama Award for the best performance by an actor in 1955. At thirty, he had finally arrived—recognized as a Shakespearean actor of the first order. Yet he did not stop there, resting safely on his laurels. In February, with a degree of masochism, he allowed himself to be persuaded by Benthall to undertake the awesome feat of alternating with Neville in the parts of Othello and Iago on successive nights. With his intuitive box-office sense, Benthall recognized the idea as a commercial winner, but it was less appealing to the actors. Olivier, at twenty-eight, was alternating the roles of Romeo and Mercutio with Gielgud, but here was an infinitely greater challenge, involving far more lines and a far more testing range of character interpretation. It was the toughest and most mentally exhausting work that either actor has ever tackled.

At first, Neville hesitated to accept the challenge. "In a sense it meant that we were rehearsing two plays, two enormous classical roles, in six weeks. Normally you would get four weeks to rehearse one play. We did both in six weeks; moreover, we didn't have a week between the openings. We opened one night and swapped parts the next. Neither of us really had enough time to study, but it was easier for me in a way. I was originally asked to play Iago, and so we rehearsed it that way for three weeks before changing round for another three weeks. Now, Iago is one of the longest parts in all Shakespeare, and it has the added difficulty of being predominantly in prose, which is far harder to learn than

Shakespeare's verse. So I got the more difficult part out of the way first. It was just Richard's bad luck. He was marvelous in both roles, but when it came to rehearsing the other way round, he was put under the greater strain. I always thought he was a little behind in his learning, not through any fault of his own, but simply perforce of circumstances. Certain things in Iago are fiendishly difficult to learn. For instance, there's the famous street scene where he kills Rodrigo—a great mix-up in semidarkness, and it's a bloody awful scene to learn. Iago is the *deus ex machina* there; he simply has to keep going. And Richard had to do this in the last part of our rehearsals."

Dramatic dueling was a popular sport in the English theater of a century and a half ago. The Othello–Iago exchange was presented as long ago as 1816, by Macready and Young at Covent Garden. In the old days, it was often an exercise of bitter rivalry between flamboyant egotists, each jealously guarding his reputation and seeking to eclipse the other. For Burton and Neville, however, it was strictly a friendly exchange. Both had a demonstrative gallery of doting fans with whom they could do no wrong, and inevitably their performances were studiously compared. But neither actor made a conscious effort to outshine the other, simply because they were far too preoccupied with the struggle to discipline themselves, and master their parts, to be concerned with theatrical sparring.

The double challenge did not come easily to them, and, for all the rapturous applause, the interchange of parts could not be described as a total success; nor was it failure. They were making an assault on an Everest of the theater without sufficient experience on lesser peaks, and they simply lacked the dramatic muscles, with subtle variations of style and pace, to carry them to the summit. For courage and effort, however, they merited the highest marks. They were the youngest Othellos to appear in London in this century, and in the entire history of the stage it is doubtful whether any actors so young have tackled such a marathon with a comparable degree of professionalism. Though Burton, by a narrow margin, was judged by critics to have slightly the better of the exchange, it is invidious to dwell on comparisons. Both men, in their individual styles, had their moments of glory and greatness. Tynan observed:

> Temperament alone is not enough for Othello, nor is physical beauty. The essence is that unfeignable quality which some call weight and others majesty, and which comes with age. Frederick Valk had it, a great stunned animal strapped to the rack; but neither Mr. Burton, roaring through his whiskers, nor Mr. Neville, a tormented sheik, could give the Moor his proper magnitude. . . . Tuesday's performance, with Mr. Burton blacked up and Mr. Neville a capering spiv, was a drab squabble between the Chocolate Soldier and the Vagabond King. . . . On Wednesday we were in a different world. Mr. Burton was playing Iago, and the production rose to him. Paradoxically, the only way to play Iago is to respect Othello. Let Iago mock the Moor with cheap laughs, and the play collapses: it becomes the farce of an idiot gull instead of the tragedy of a master-spirit. Mr. Burton never underestimates Othello; nor, in consequence, do we. His Iago is dour and earthy enough to convince any jury in the world. He does not simulate sincerity, he embraces it; not by the least wink or snicker does his outward action demonstrate the native act and figure of his heart. The imposture is total and terrifying. Like his author, Mr. Burton cares little for the question of Iago's motive; mere jealousy of Cassio's rank is not enough, else why should Iago go on hounding Othello after he had supplanted Cassio? Discarding this, Mr. Burton gives us a single, dirty smoldering drive towards power without responsibility. With a touch more of daemonism in the soliloquies, this will be an incomparable performance.

In conclusion, Tynan gave an appreciation of Burton's acting talents that subsequent performances have fully endorsed.

> We may now define this actor's powers. The open expression of emotion is clearly alien to him: he is a pure

anti-romantic, ingrowing rather than outgoing. Should a part call for emotional contact with another player, a contemptuous curl of the lip betrays him. Here is no Troilus, no Florizel, no Romeó. Seeking, as Othello, to wear his heart upon his sleeve, he resorts to forced bellowing and perfunctory sobs. Mr. Burton "keeps his heart attending on himself," which is why his Iago is so fine and why, five years ago, we all admired his playing of that other classic hypocrite, Prince Hal. Within this actor there is always something reserved, a secret upon which trespassers will be prosecuted, a rooted solitude which his Welsh blood tinges with mystery. Inside these limits he is a master. Beyond them he has much to learn.

As on the stage, so again and again on the screen, Burton's performances would reinforce the view that, while he can exude immense physical power and express inner torment supremely well, he is strictly limited by his true self in affecting displays of tenderness and deep affection. The stark slag-heap roots, the sheer virility and instinctive anti-sentimentality of the man shone through too strongly to be completely obscured by the actor's mask.

Several critics now stressed that Burton was no second Olivier yet; that he would need to dedicate himself more to the stage if he was going to scale such Olympian heights. Yet, in a sense, he was ahead of Olivier, whose legend was becoming bigger than the man. In his formative years, Olivier had acquired greater experience through school Shakespeare productions and repertory, but at thirty he had made several films without remotely approaching the stardom achieved by Burton. He was two years older than Richard when he had his first season with the Old Vic, then playing Hamlet, Henry V, Macbeth, and Sir Toby Belch. At thirty-one, he was Iago. The following year he went to Hollywood to make *Wuthering Heights* for Sam Goldwyn, followed by such successes as *Rebecca, Pride and Prejudice,* and *Lady Hamilton,* and he was thirty-seven before he really settled down to prolonged work in the theater. So there was time for Burton yet.

Moreover, while critics rued that he was not seen more on the stage, the truth was that he had devoted only one-third of his working time to films in the past five years. His absence from the theater only seemed longer because so much of his stage work had been out of London, at Stratford and in New York, while his films were given West End prominence.

Nevertheless, there was validity in the argument that Burton was nearing the crossroads of his career. Korda said that the vital decision of Olivier's career was made when he gave up the chance of making $5,000 a week in Hollywood to work at the Old Vic for $70, and then moved toward a loftier fame. Though Burton was younger, he was also approaching the critical point between two powerful magnetic fields. He could continue to flirt with both stage and screen, but he could not hope to realize his full potential in one without giving it clear-cut priority at the expense of the other. This was Burton's dilemma. He would not face it in quite such simple terms; he would not at any one moment of time make an outright choice. Circumstances and interests, however, would now gradually draw him more and more towards the cinema. Two key factors influenced this movement. First, while he loved the theater, he had never been wholly dedicated to the stage. Second, he had the highest respect for money—rather, the comfort and security it bestowed—and he could never completely dismiss financial interests for art's sake.

His financial position was peculiar and not entirely understood by his critics. He had the gross income of a Hollywood star—as much as $150,000 for a film taking no more than three months—and yet he did not live like one. In California, he and Sybil rented a simple two-bedroom house without a swimming pool, and they hired a utilitarian car. He said they had calculated that with extreme economy it was possible to survive in Hollywood on as little as $90 a week. "They like you to spend a lot of money in Hollywood because that way you get dependent on them, and then they can do what they like with you. But I don't want to be dependent on anyone." And this was partly true. No one could manipulate the canny Celt, not even Darryl Zanuck. He had furious rows with the boss of 20th Century-Fox and won his respect because of it. But the Burtons also lived modestly in London. They were still occupying only two rooms of their large tastefully furnished Hampstead home, and were renting the rest to cover the mortgage payments. In the lounge, Richard kept a giant painting of Pontrhydyfen—a constant reminder of harder times.

Burton, however, was not the scrooge that some people supposed. His real friends knew him as a man of extraordinary generosity. When he returned to the Old Vic he brought back a crate of presents for friends and relatives, including twenty nieces and nephews in Wales. He gave large cash sums to relations in need, and made many more gifts that were never reported. His generosity was instinctive and spontaneous. Tired of hearing Neville's noisy comings and goings in an old jalopy, he asked him how much he needed for a new car, and then, immediately and unsolicited, he loaned him the money. When Frank Hauser was forming Meadow Players Ltd. to reopen the Oxford Playhouse, and desperately needed funds, he went along to the Old Vic to ask Burton if he could help him by appearing in a production. To his amazement, Richard gave him $5,600 instead. "It was by far the biggest donation and it was what enabled us to launch the company."

Yet, as Hauser says, Burton was not really super-rich at this time. So long as he had residence in Britain, or visited the country for more than six months in any fiscal year, he would be fully liable to income tax there. Disregarding all the tax deductible "expenses," it meant that as a married man without children he was liable to pay over £42,000 ($117,600) tax on an income of £50,000 ($140,000) a year, or some £88,300 ($247,000) on £100,000 ($280,000). So there was no great incentive for him to make more than one film a year. Of course, he could live very comfortably on that and spend the other nine months of the year living in Hampstead and working for modest rewards on the stage. But this made little sense to a hedonist, who for the most part worked to live, rather than lived to work. Above all, he was deeply aware at this time that there was no guarantee that his prosperity in films would last, and with his inborn fear of insecurity, he felt a desperate need to secure his enormous earnings. In this sense, he would never really have a choice between stage and screen.

Ironically, while Burton was being hailed as the crown prince of the English Theater, his development as a film actor fell far short of expectation. He was at the Old Vic when *The Rains of Ranchipur* arrived, and for the first time he was persuaded to attend a premiere of one of his films. He always felt uncomfortable seeing himself on the screen; so he met the guests of honor and slipped out by a side-door as soon as the lights were dimmed. It would not have served his morale to stay. His talents were largely wasted, and the picture was coldly received on both sides of the Atlantic. One month later, the eagerly awaited *Alexander the Great* arrived in the wake of massive publicity. This one was panned as "a crashing flop . . . a colossal bore . . . an epic with elephantiasis."

In his blond wig, Burton looked the complete Greek, and he captured the intelligence, virility, and nobility of the man. But with his carefully modulated voice, deliberate and resonant, he was accused of making Alexander so impossibly dull that the screen was dominated for two and a half hours by a robot. More reasonably, the film's failure could be attributed to a script so obsessed with historical detail and accuracy that the audience was taken into superbly recreated battle scenes and immaculate period settings, but rarely into the inner thoughts of the characters. Burton had plunged into another pool too shallow for his talents, but if he struck his head on the bottom, his reputation was not seriously impaired, and by the sheer extravagance of this movie his public image was greatly magnified. Most everyone had heard of Richard Burton now.

Meanwhile, the Old Vic season had been extended until mid-July (a record of forty-five playing weeks), and there was more talk of the greatness Richard could achieve if only he concentrated on the stage. As Tynan later remarked: "We all thought he was the natural successor to Olivier. We thought he could be another Edmund Kean, that he was going to be the greatest classical actor living." But the star of the Old Vic was physically fading. Again, he was striving too hard to prove himself in the company of stage regulars, who were not under the same pressures, and he was near breaking point. He was already playing three leading roles in the repertory when he prepared to take on a fourth part—Thersites in *Troilus and Cressida*. Now he had to give this up on medical advice, and Clifford Williams took over. Burton soldiered on until mid-May; then, a few hours after taking his final bow as Henry V, he left London with Sybil to catch a slow boat to Jamaica.

Richard had now had a five-year surfeit of classical and costume drama, and at the end of a restful two-week voyage he welcomed the chance to toss aside his turbans and togas and get down to a contemporary story in which he could smoke a cigarette. But his next picture, though given a modern setting, was no better than the rest. *Seawife,* adapted from J. M. Scott's novel, *Sea Wyf and Biscuit,* was the story of three men and a novice nun adrift in a rubber dinghy after being torpedoed by a Japanese submarine. Burton was playing the shipwrecked RAF officer nicknamed Biscuit; others involved were Basil Sydney as a fascist-minded businessman, calypso-singer Cy Grant as a Negro purser, and, in the most imaginative casting of all, the torrid Joan Collins as the young novice nun. Miss Collins, whose obvious assets had not been fully utilized by Britain's dear old Rank Organization, was now a top-salaried Fox star. Three years later she would be the original choice to play history's most alluring siren in Walter Wanger's *Cleopatra,* but for the moment Italian film director Roberto Rossellini had reportedly looked beyond her 37–22–35 statistics and perceived "the face of innocence" suitable for his nun at sea.

Seawife was in trouble from the start. Rossellini quit the picture after two days on location, and when they got back to Elstree Studios, Richard spent his happiest hours on the adjoining lot where Bob Mitchum, Rita Hayworth, and Bernard Lee were filming *Fire Down Below,* with great quantities of liquor at the ready for regular visitors like Burton and Trevor Howard. Richard's one vivid memory of *Seawife* is the time they wandered into the New Inn near Lord's Cricket Ground to meet a few Welsh cronies and found Rita Hayworth in a wild party mood. It was an L-shaped bar, and the landlady called Richard over and asked in a whisper whether the rugged man in the corner really was filmstar Robert Mitchum. Richard confirmed that it was indeed, but before he had time to make introductions a parson came in, leading a little dog which immediately started to make menacing growls at the resident Rin-Tin-Tin. The dogs were finally separated, and the parson said, "Dear me, that was a close shave." Bob Mitchum looked down his drooped eyelids at the frustrated little dog sulking between the parson's legs. "Pity," he drawled, "your dog nearly got fucked."

For Richard, everything came to life after the day's shooting, and following his Old Vic achievements he found *Seawife* a pretty trivial exercise. He was so full of Celtic gloom that he told Richard Hampton, who was about to star in the Youth Theater's production of *Henry V,* "If you eventually come into the profession, steer clear of films. The attractions are very great, but the live theater is the most truly rewarding to the actor." Yet he refused to follow his own advice. Financially, he was as hooked on the movie-making merry-go-round as were Mitchum and Hayworth. And he knew he could only hold on to his wealth by living abroad.

"I Need Never Work Again"

The Swiss family Burtons had hardly settled into their new villa at Celigny on the west side of Lake Geneva when a bearded portly figure rolled up at the front door. "Who shall I say is calling?" a servant asked.

"Blenkinsop," said the visitor in a brisk Whitehall manner. "Blenkinsop of the Inland Revenue."

Richard, standing in the background, overheard him and was momentarily unnerved. But seconds later he was sharing in the joke. Behind the beard was the crumpled, impish face of Peter Ustinov, a neighbor who had become used to making jest of British income tax without fear of reprisal. Now Richard could laugh, too, because he estimated that his escape to this tax haven was saving him some $250,000 a year. Yet, despite this compelling inducement, some of his friends argued that his move was a grave error, that his financial gain would add up to an artistic loss by divorcing him from the English stage. After all, his film work was scarcely winning him new glory. In April, 1957, *Seawife* was released; another indifferent work. And now he was doing no better by returning to the North African campaign for *Bitter Victory*, with Curt Jurgens and Ruth Roman. Director Nicholas Ray injected some realism into this improbable story of two commando officers in love with the same woman. Burton had a few strong dramatic moments. But the film as a whole did not advance his reputation one iota; indeed, Columbia did not even bother to give it a West End release.

Why did Burton become involved in such a procession of mediocre films? The old alibi of a lack of good scripts did not stand up. Before doing *Seawife,* he had failed to grab the chance of playing the legless Battle of Britain ace, Group Captain Douglas Bader, in *Reach for the Sky.* The role, so suited to his talents, went instead to Kenneth More and did wonders for his career. Before *Bitter Victory,* he was in line to play Lawrence of Arabia. The part went to Peter O'Toole—another box-office smash. Next came talk of Burton playing Warwick in Otto Preminger's *St. Joan,* but amid much personal acrimony, negotiations broke down and Gielgud stepped into the role. At the time it was reported that Burton backed down because he was under contract to make *The White Rabbit.* But he didn't do that one either. In the case of *St. Joan,* he rightly believed he was too young and too earthy to play the arrogant, blue-blooded Warwick; and sometimes he missed meaty parts through a clash of commitments. But there were times, too, when he passed up great opportunities either through misjudgment of scripts or through failure to study them in advance.

Four years after his Hollywood debut Burton had reached the stage where he no longer needed to worry about making money. Yet 1957 was a highly unmemorable year in his career. It was the first year in which he made no real advance as an actor. It was also a year of sadness. In January, he mourned the loss of a great friend, Humphrey Bogart. He had died of cancer in Hollywood at fifty-seven. Richard's admiration for Bogart, as a man and an actor, was profound. He recalled how he had watched him working with Rod Steiger on his last film, *The Harder They Fall*—"Steiger was acting with everything he'd got. Bogie was doing absolutely nothing. When I got home that night I said to Sybil: 'You know, Bogie must be getting old. That new chap Steiger's acting him off the screen.' Then the film came out and Steiger was absolutely nowhere. Bogie was the only one you looked at. I always remember that when someone who's watched me doing a scene comes over and says, 'You were great.' I get worried. For the person you look at on the screen is the one who usually appears to be doing nothing." It was an important lesson for Burton whose gift for stillness, so evident on the stage, had not yet been put to such telling effect on the screen.

Four months after Bogie's death, Richard was saddened by a greater personal loss. Daddy Ni was dead. Shortly before he died in Neath General Hospital, the old man asked feebly, "Where's Richie?" And one of his sons explained, "Richard is far away and can't get here. But he sends his love." And so Dic the son of a carpenter passed on, with a smile on his lips. He had seen eighty-one years—fifty of them as a working collier. His one last order was that if his funeral coincided with one of Aberavon's home matches, then the funeral was to be postponed. Scores of friends and relations attended the funeral at Pontrhydyfen—sons, grandsons, sons-in-law, cousins, and nephews; and by tradition, the womenfolk remained at the house of mourning in Penhydd Street. Richard and Ivor were away in Switzerland, but they were there in spirit. "My father was a very unsentimental person," explained the sixth son. "He would be shocked if he knew I had traveled more than seven hundred miles to go to his funeral." Together, the two absent sons solemnly toasted his memory and thought back on happier times.

Richard's last memory of Daddy Ni was of the old man in his penultimate year going up to the Miner's Arms on a wild drinking spree, just as grandfather William Jenkins had done half a century before to celebrate his twenty shillings' win on Black Sambo. He was eighty years old, and he was celebrating a much bigger winner coming home. "Rich had just come home," says Hilda. "And you know what he was—always filling father's pockets with money. I used to be very annoyed because my father was always straight over the Miner's and saying, 'Drink up, boys, Rich is home.' And, of course, he'd come back paralytic. Well, I felt responsible because Daddy Ni had been living with me in this house ever since 1938, and I knew his little weaknesses. And I would tell Rich, 'Don't give it to him. Give the money to me to dish out.' But he said, 'No, I can't do that to Daddy.' Anyway, Richard comes home this day, and apparently he had given my father a wad of notes. Off like a flash to the pub. Rich went over with him and then went on back to Taibach.

"Now whenever my father was going for his medicine—his polite way of saying he was going on the booze—I'd tell him to walk the long way round by the road, rather than the bridge, because he was such a short man that he could easily fall through the railings and down the embankment. Well, he was very drunk this night, and that is exactly what happened. We couldn't find him for hours. Then a relation of mine found him very late at night. He was lying at the bottom of the hill. It was pouring with rain and there was blood all over him. I had such a shock when I saw him. My son helped to bring him in and put him in the bath, and then the doctor came and sent him to hospital. Well, the doctor reckoned it was the end. So I rang Rich and he went to see Daddy at four in the morning. Then Rich turned up here about four-thirty and said, 'Daddy's okay. I've taken him a bottle of whiskey.' In a week my father was out like a two-year-old and straight back up the Miner's."

Life ends, life begins. After eight years of marriage, Sybil was now expecting her first baby, and in August she left their Geneva villa to enter the State maternity clinic. For several months, the Swiss director, Professor Hubert de Watteville, had prepared her for "painless birth," and on September 11, Richard became the father of a 6 lb. 4 oz. daughter—Katharine Burton. She arrived ten days prematurely, which was fortunate in a way, because the next day Burton was due to fly to New York to appear on Broadway in Jean Anouilh's romantic comedy *Time Remembered (Leocadia)*. Sybil and the baby were to join him there eight weeks later.

Time Remembered opened at the Morosco Theater in mid-November and represented Burton's one notable achievement of the year. Here he was playing opposite a Cleopatra of the twenties—Helen Hayes, the First Lady of the American Theater; and a bright new star of the fifties—Susan Strasberg, who had been acclaimed for her leading role in *The Diary of Anne Frank,* and who was the teen-age daughter of Lee Strasberg, founder and artistic director of the New York Actors' Studio and principal exponent of the method school of acting. The play, one of a series of *pièces roses*, tells of a duchess who hires a young milliner to shock her son, Prince Albert, out of his melancholia over a dead enchantress. It is not one of Anouilh's celebrated works; yet, with such a cast, it could scarcely fail. It won rave notices and only lost money because the production costs, especially the salaries for the stars, were impossibly high.

Burton had a wild life on Broadway. He thrived on New York's swinging late night life, and there was no lack of stimulating company. So many familiar faces were in town—Ustinov in *Romanoff and Juliet,* Noel Coward in *Nude With Violin,* Laurence Harvey and Julie Harris in *The Country Wife,* Olivier repeating his London triumph in John Osborne's *The Entertainer,* Julie Andrews and Rex Harrison in the smash-hit *My Fair Lady.* And the Welsh clan was prominent again, with Hugh Griffith enjoying a huge success in *Look Homeward Angel,* Donald Houston doing *Under Milk Wood,* and Philip Burton living there permanently, writing and directing plays. Osian Ellis was also in town, playing with the Philharmonic Orchestra at Carnegie Hall, and one night Richard asked him to bring his harp over to the Park Hotel for a party. "I wasn't keen to move the harp, and so I hired another one for which Richard paid through his brother Ivor. We had a really jolly evening, and I became aware of how terribly Welsh Richard really was. I found him quite a different person. He spoke to me in Welsh, but he had never done so at Stratford. Before, he was getting away from his Welsh background, but now he had obviously developed as a personality, and as he matured he turned back more to his roots. He was also far less reserved, but then these two aspects are typically Welsh—periods as a deep introvert, then as a great extrovert."

The last big party in New York came in May, when Olivier entertained two hundred celebrities on a midnight cruise up the Hudson, and Richard arrived wearing a red jersey with "HMS Olivier" written across his chest. It was a colorful Cockney-style outing, with barrels of stout and a buffet of jellied eels and fish-and-chips served in English newspapers, and as Richard pounded the deck in a wild version of "Knees-up-Mother-Brown," he bumped into the actor who had become famous as England's angry young playwright. The man was John Osborne, who, like Richard, had a Welsh father and a barmaid mother, and whose play *Look Back in Anger* said everything that Richard felt about the intolerant class structure of English society. Osborne had created a new antihero in the rough shape of Jimmy Porter, an intellectual from the slums who spat on English china. It had been a tremendous success in the theater, but despite the brilliance of Kenneth Haigh in the stage production, it needed a bigger marquee name for the screen version.

Burton was an obvious choice for the part, but would he grab the chance? So often he had lost all sense of direction in the Hollywood jungle. There were plans for him to appear with Carroll "Baby Doll" Baker in *The Miracle* and in yet another epic *Solomon and Sheba,* with the box-office clockwork of Gina Lollobrigida and Tyrone Power. Also Milton Sperling, the Hollywood producer who had brought him to New York for *Time Remembered,* had signed him to star in the film *The Bramble Bush.* But for once Burton's judgment was sound; he recognized the Jimmy Porter role as offering him the best of both worlds of cinema and theater, a film in which the basic ingredients of the stage play would not be lost by transfer to the screen.

In August, 1958, after a two-month holiday in Switzerland with Sybil and baby Kate, Richard returned to Britain to start work on the film. It was his first visit as an overseas resident and his newfound wealth was obvious. They had a nanny for the baby, and when he drove back to Pontrhydyfen it was at the wheel of a $15,000 Rolls Royce. He talked proudly about his beautiful villa, of the luxurious Cadillac convertible he had left behind, of the million dollars he had earned from eight Hollywood movies, and the $300,000 he had under his number in a Swiss bank. "I need never work again," he told his friends. As he frequented his favorite pubs, there was a suspicion that he missed the British way of life, but Richard insisted that Switzerland was near to heaven. He had plenty of British neighbors, like Deborah Kerr and Alistair MacLean; he could swim and ski, and if he wanted to watch rugby, there was a fine team nearby at Grenoble. Paris was only forty-five minutes away, Rome just a couple of hours. As for Sybil, he said, she much preferred it because she didn't get hay fever.

Britain, however, can react like a wasp-stung beekeeper toward those who desert her for tax reasons. Noel Coward felt the sting, or rather the barbs of the British press, when he moved abroad. Now it was Richard's turn. He argued his case soundly enough: "If I made three pictures in a year I would earn about £100,000 ($280,000), and in England I'd pay £93,000 ($260,000) of that in tax. But now I'm a Geneva resident all I pay is £700 ($1,960). Do you wonder that I don't want to live in London again? Ours is an uncertain profession. We make a lot of money for a few years, then nothing." He spoke frankly about Britain's "vicious, punitive tax situation," and expressed the wish that someone like Olivier would leave and "really shake the Chancellor of the Exchequer." Unfortunately, people took him too seriously when he remarked: "I'm not against the high taxes for Britain. I believe everyone should pay them—except actors." After that remark, the criticism mounted sharply, even though a social directory of other famous British names had skied quietly into Switzerland via other countries.

At this stage, he rather badly needed some worthwhile achievement to restore his popularity, and his part in *Look Back in Anger* fitted the bill very well. The role of Jimmy Porter, the intellectual barrow-boy who sneers at the middle-class background of his wife, was tailor-made for him. Moreover, he had a first-rate director in Tony Richardson, who would later win an Oscar for *Tom Jones,* and he was working with three fine actresses—Dame Edith Evans, now seventy and Grand Dame of the English Theater; Mary Ure, then Osborne's wife; and, most familiar of all, Claire Bloom, with whom he had worked through hundreds of Old Vic nights, on tours from the provinces to the battlements of Elsinore, and on through the campaign of Alexander.

In mid-September, they were busy filming in the poor East End of London, lunching each day at a cheap restaurant, but they were attracting precious little publicity. The show-business columns were now dominated by the continuing story of the Taylor-Fisher-Reynolds triangle. Six months earlier, Elizabeth Taylor had been widowed by the tragic death of Mike Todd in an air crash. Now all sympathy had passed; she was being pilloried in the world's press over her romance with crooner Eddie Fisher and was blamed for the breakup of his "storybook marriage" to Debbie Reynolds. The Fishers' marriage had been running into troubled waters before Liz came on the scene, but no matter. Miss Taylor, soon to marry a fourth time, was now firmly typecast as the *femme fatale* of the century.

Hollywood at this point was outdoing itself as a hotbed of intrigue, and gossip flourished like rhubarb forced on manure. When Richard returned after *Look Back in Anger,* he saw the change, and he changed gear himself. For the first time, he began to behave and live like a full-fledged star. He demanded and got twin Cadillacs, one for himself, one for the family, and insisted on having the best dressing room in the studio. Inevitably, too, he became the subject of malicious gossip. Publicity-seeking starlets clung to him tighter than their minks when photographers were around, and when Sybil was back in Switzerland, preparing for the arrival of her second baby (Jessica), gossip-writers were linking him with the absurdly improbable young ladies he had in tow. In the case of one teen-age actress, he was asked about a rumor that he planned to take her with him when he returned to Europe. "It's true all right," said Richard. "I'm crazy about her. So is my wife."

In Hollywood, he was now committed to two films far below the merit of *Look Back in Anger*. The first was a totally forgettable picture called *The Bramble Bush*, based on the best-selling novel about euthanasia. He starred as the doctor on trial for taking the life of his best friend, whose wife he had made pregnant, and others involved were Barbara Rush, Tom Drake, and a sadly miscast Jack Carson. This was, without much debate, the worst film Burton ever made, and the only consolation was that it was made on a small budget and therefore was not a financial disaster. The same could not be said about the second film, *Ice Palace*, a Warner Brothers version of Edna Ferber's outsize novel about feuding families in Alaska. It was absurdly overlong, and much to Richard's financial profit, ran far into overtime. This time not only was the picture bad, but Burton was bad. As Zeb "Czar" Kennedy, the ruthless canning-factory tycoon, he employed his woeful, guilty glances and his fixed, soul-searching looks to a degree more suited to a silent movie. In the early scenes his voice wavered from faint Welsh to phony American, and at times he appeared to be giving a caricature of James Cagney. It was an incredible performance and a barely credible story. His co-stars were Robert Ryan, Martha Hyer, Carolyn Jones, and Jim Backus (a great drinking pal). None of them emerged from this monstrous misconception of a movie with their reputations more sadly tarnished than Burton.

While Richard was slipping on these icy slopes, *Look Back in Anger* was released, and at least in Britain it gave his reputation an invaluable, much-needed boost. Some critics judged it to be the best British film for many years and easily Richard's greatest screen performance. For the first time he could identify himself closely with the character he was playing—someone from roughly the same working-class background, yet possessing a powerful command of language; and for the first time in fifteen films he came across with something like the impact and smoldering fire that he achieved in real life. Yet the American critics took a very different view. Amid a few rave notices, there were blistering attacks on his Jimmy Porter; they argued that he was too strong a face and personality to play such a whiner, too old and too mature and too well-bred in accent. *Time* magazine said he had turned the character into a "seething, snarling Elizabethan villain."

By mid-1960, with the release of *Ice Palace,* Burton's stature in the American film industry had sunk lower than it had been for years. Too many of his films had fallen below expectation; for too long, directors had talked of his exciting potential but had failed to capture it on the screen. That summer, as he luxuriated in Switzerland with Sybil and the children, he desperately needed a blockbusting success if he was to continue attracting $150,000 fees. And, providentially, it now came from the most surprising quarter.

King on Broadway

S hortly before he became involved with *The Bramble Bush* and *Ice Palace,* Burton was asked what was the most important lesson he had learned from his pictures. "Just this," he replied. "If you're going to make rubbish, be the best rubbish in it. I keep telling Larry Olivier that. It's no good playing a minor role in an epic like *Spartacus,* which he's just done. Larry had a dressing room half the size of Tony Curtis's on that film, and he got about half Curtis's money. Well, that's ridiculous. You've got to swank in Hollywood. When I go there, I demand two Cadillacs and the best dressing room. Of course I'm not worth it, but it impresses them."

In adopting this approach to movie-making, he was simply playing the Hollywood survival game according to the age-old rules—never sell yourself short; never allow yourself to be upstaged by other stars; never concede privileges once gained; never be obviously tractable. In short, behave like a star to be treated as a star. Vanity did not enter into it; for the canny Welshman it was essentially a matter of economic truths. He would prefer not to make rubbish, but pride in the films he made was no substitute for cash in the bank, and for him the number of zeros on a paycheck was a more reliable measure of success than the column inches of critical acclaim. All talk of the artistic merit of *Look Back in Anger* left him cold. Film-making remained in his eyes a craft and nothing more, and he was strictly in it for the loot. Given the opportunity to rest from movies without financial loss, he would gladly take it. "But where else can you get that kind of money?" he asked.

Burton now had his answer. And it came from a totally unexpected source. Director Moss Hart, lyricist and librettist Alan K. Lerner, and composer Frederick Loewe were seeking to repeat their smash-hit *My Fair Lady*, and when they came to casting a new musical tentatively called *Jenny Kissed Me*, they reached the astonishingly farsighted conclusion that Burton, with his experience of playing kings in Shakespeare, was just the man for the leading role of King Arthur.

"But you don't even know I can sing," said Richard.

"Yes we do," replied Lerner and Loewe. "We once heard you singing a duet with Olivier at a party. Anyway, we only want an average bathroom tenor."

Burton couldn't recall such a duet, but then he had sung at so many parties—cute calypsos with Sybil, charming Welsh ditties, and shocking rugby songs. Perhaps he had been impossibly stoned at the time. He checked with Olivier. "No, I can assure you that we have never sung together, drunk or sober. But the money's good, so I should say nothing and carry on."

Richard took his advice. It was the highest paid work he had ever been offered outside the movies. And not only the money attracted him. He was tickled pink at the idea of doing a musical, and the role of King Arthur was especially appealing. The play, based on T. H. White's novel, *The Once and Future King*, was retitled *Camelot*, and as rehearsal time approached Richard spent more and more time singing in his showers. Like Rex Harrison in *My Fair Lady*, he was an amateur singer stepping into a Broadway musical at a fee of $4,000 a week for his first year, with the promise of $8,000 a week if he stayed on for a second year. And as it happened, he proved worth every cent of his princely salary, for this was a production doomed to be beset with a series of crises so alarming that only a team of highly disciplined professionals could hope to meet them and avert complete disaster.

Here, reunited, was much the same team of fine talents that had been responsible four years earlier for the most successful of all Broadway musicals, *My Fair Lady*—the same authors and director, the same choreographer (Hanya Holm) and scenic designer (Oliver Smith), two of the same players (Julie Andrews and Robert Coote), and the same financial backer (the Columbia Broadcasting System). Miss Andrews was now infinitely more experienced, and there was not the same nightmarish struggle with her Queen Guinevere as there had been to make her a convincing Eliza Doolittle. But otherwise the cares of *Camelot* were far, far greater.

After rehearsals in New York, they opened at the new twelve-million-dollar O'Keefe Center for the Performing Arts in Toronto. Critics praised the performances of Burton, Miss Andrews, and the handsome Canadian baritone Robert Goulet, who played Sir Lancelot, but there were serious weaknesses in the script, and major cuts were imperative before the Broadway opening. Then came the disasters. The production was being reshaped in Toronto when Lerner was taken to the hospital with ulcer trouble that caused internal bleeding. The Broadway opening was postponed two weeks, until December 3. Next, director Moss Hart, the quiet perfectionist, suffered a near-fatal heart attack and was replaced by Lerner, now recovered. Meanwhile Loewe, who had had a heart attack two years before, was putting himself under a dangerous strain. And, incredibly, there were more misfortunes —not grave setbacks for the show, but no less serious for those involved. The husband of the wardrobe mistress died; the chief electrician was taken to the hospital with an internal complaint; another electrician was almost killed when electrical equipment fell on his head; a dancer suffered blood poisoning after spearing her foot on a needle.

In a foreword to the book and lyrics of the musical, Lerner later said it was miraculous "that *Camelot* stayed together in one piece and did not disintegrate like a decayed tooth." For this he largely thanked the star players. "Time after time in those seemingly endless weeks before New York I used to imagine the condition the play would be in if certain other stars of whom I had intimate knowledge had been playing the leads, rather than Julie Andrews and Richard Burton. I could imagine the reaction of a few of our darling ladies of the theater had they been given a new song two nights before the opening, as was Julie Andrews. A cold wind hit the spine when I thought of some well-known actors who occupy stellar positions being given a new second act two weeks before New York, as was Richard Burton. Agents and lawyers would have descended on me next day like the hordes of Genghis Khan. . . . I find I cannot write my last words to *Camelot* without first mentioning Miss Andrews, Mr. Burton, and the majority of the cast who were, thank heaven, professionals."

But the man who played a key role in holding the show together during the crisis never received a word of public credit at the time. This was Phil Burton. The man from Mountain Ash, who had helped Richard from the time he was in short pants and straining a cracked soprano voice for an eisteddfod, unhesitatingly put aside all other interests to come to the rescue when the production team was laid low. In those three weeks before they arrived on Broadway, he rehearsed the company for five hours a day, except on the two matinee days. He studied the performance every evening, made notes, and then conferred with Lerner late at night. Not least, forever bustling and fussing in the background, he successfully maintained the company's morale and sense of urgency. Many changes in reshaping the show were made at his suggestion, and the end result was a faster-moving musical, with new songs added and the running time reduced by an hour. Yet, from the start, he agreed not to be given any personal credit. "Why ever did you take on such a job?" he was asked. He simply replied: "Because Richie needed me."

Phil Burton thrived on his involvement with a major Broadway production, and he amazed everyone with his energy and enthusiasm. And Richard, drawing fresh confidence from having such an old ally at his side, was in his element too. The prince of players, who had performed Othello and Iago on alternate nights, who had fiercely studied Coriolanus in offstage moments while playing Hamlet, was hardly to be disturbed at having to grasp a new second act in two weeks. Indeed, during *Camelot*'s run at the Schubert Theater in Boston, Massachusetts, he was playing King Arthur every night, and every day was recording the voice of Sir Winston Churchill for the twenty-six-part television series *The Valiant Years.* For this the American Broadcasting Company was paying him as much as he had been paid for a full-length Hollywood feature film, and he made a great success of it. Though not trying to mimic the war leader, Burton skillfully projected the timber and rhythm of his voice. Studying an original copy of one of Churchill's speeches, he found that it was spaced out with breaks to mark the points where he wished to pause for extra emphasis and effect. "This way I discovered the way he spoke, and then it was a question of working in the underlying menace that he gave to his words, and, of course, his virility."

At the same time Richard was sailing through *Camelot* with all the hearty assurance of a vaudeville star, and when the musical finally hit New York there were some critics who judged that he stole the show. They were not wholly enthusiastic about *Camelot*, but they all praised its king. As the curtain came down, it was Burton, in his first musical, who won the bravos. Tynan, in his review, referred to the "ineffable banality" of Frederick Loewe's score and called the show an "adult pantomime." But he also wrote: "Richard Burton, of the furrowed face and accusing eyes, makes a peerless king. His singing is bold rather than beautiful, but his stage presence has that intangible quality of weight, as distinct from bulk, by which great actors always reveal themselves. This is a majestic performance."

Burton was good for *Camelot*, and *Camelot* was good for him. He enjoyed this novel challenge more than anything he had done before, and for once he had opportunities to reveal light comic touches. He seized them well. Everyone knew he could capture the nobility of Arthur. Few people, who had not seen him cavorting about at parties, could have guessed with what aplomb and whimsy he would glide through musical numbers, like the odd skipping dance of the opening scene in the duet "What Do Simple Folk Do?" It was part of his own design. Since he might never do a musical again, he wanted to experience it fully, so he asked for a little dance to be written in for him. He found the show a lighthearted romp, quite unlike any other in his career, so much so that he exclaimed in a moment of bold frankness: "We are ridiculously overpaid. Broadway will be in trouble if it keeps this up. I don't know why the managements do it."

This was not another *My Fair Lady*. It lacked such tuneful melodies. But it was skillfully played throughout, and above all, the spectacular settings by Oliver Smith made it a glittering spectacle—a musical always appealing to the eye, if not especially to the ear. It was so dazzlingly opulent that it became known on Broadway as "Costalot." Yet, financially, it was a smash; a half-million-dollar production, that after drastic rewriting and reconstruction, arrived on Broadway with an advance sale of three million dollars, the largest in history.

During the long run, a relaxed Burton revealed more of his less familiar side—as a leading man with a devilish sense of humor that made each performance something of an adventure in itself. In light musicals a star can indulge in breaches of discipline in a way that would be sacrilegious at the Old Vic, and Richard made the most of his new freedom. There was the time a large, shaggy dog in the musical paused to mess the center of the stage, just as

Julie Andrews was dancing around the animal singing, "It's May. It's May. The merry month of May." At that point an actor had to say, "I think there's a hint of summer in the air." In a moment of abandon, Burton split his sides laughing along with the audience. Another night he tripped during a dance number when Dame Margot Fonteyn was out front. Again, he only laughed, and afterward he told her, "I tripped on purpose to make you feel superior." More proudly, however, he recalls how Robert Preston and some others wagered that he couldn't drink a bottle of 100-proof vodka during the matinee and then a fifth of cognac during the evening show without Julie being any the wiser. He won the bet.

In *Camelot*, Richard was singing on stage for the first time since competing with brother Graham in youth eisteddfodau, and appropriately he now entertained his youngest brother in New York. Graham missed the opening night because he caught pneumonia as soon as he arrived, and when he left the hospital the doctor agreed that he could recuperate in Richard's apartment only on the strict understanding that he was never to get out of his pajamas to gallivant about. But at Richard's suggestion, Graham still saw *Camelot* without breaking his promise. He went to the theater with his dinner jacket over his pajamas. "Both Rich and Sybil were wonderful to me out there," he recalls. "I was accommodated for six weeks at the most palatial hospital I have ever seen— more a hotel than a hospital—in the Guggenheim Pavilion of the Mount Sinai Hospital. Cost a fortune I promise. Afterwards I saw *Camelot* four or five times and it really was a great joy to me."

As far as New York was concerned, *Camelot* did more for Burton's stature as an entertainer than all his seventeen movies put together. Elsa Maxwell called him "the best British actor in the world today," to which he replied that he didn't object to the superlative, but he would have her know he was not British but Welsh. In April, 1961, he won a Tony award for the best actor in a musical. In July he received the Hopkins Medal of the St. David's Society of New York. Later *Time* magazine recorded: "His talents were wastefully poured into *Camelot*, like a cataract into a thimble, but he was a more than magical king, giving a performance of vigor, charm, gaiety, melancholy, and controlled dash that made every audience fall in love with him."

Camelot brought many admirers to the Court of King Richard. As in those far-off, free and easy Air Force days in Norfolk, but on an infinitely grander scale, he became the central figure of a society of friends and sycophants that automatically and informally gathered around him. It was a Burton Admiration Society that glittered with celebrated names, and the drinks and the lively chitchat never ran dry. On matinee days a group of followers usually accompanied him to dinner at a nearby restaurant; outside, the procession would be halted by autograph hunters before passing regally on. For evening performances the focal point was the star dressing room at the Majestic Theater. During Richard's eight and a half months on Broadway, no night passed without his court being entertained there—before, during, and after the show. "Burton's Bar," they called it; a dressing room invariably packed with actors, agents, secretaries, and clinging, adoring females; a rendezvous for an assortment of characters, including such sharp wits as Phil Silvers, Mike Nichols, and Alec Guinness. "Why not?" said Burton, when someone remarked on the congestion in his dressing room. "After all, it's the cheapest bar in town." It was also the best free entertainment, with the king holding forth with his mimicking, recitations, songs, and seemingly never-ending stream of stories. You had to be around a long time to realize that Richard poured out stories in a great circling stream and not as a Niagara of anecdotes with its own eternal spring. As Julie Andrews confided to a friend: "He can entertain you nonstop for three weeks with his conversation, but in the fourth week he starts to repeat himself."

Screenwriter Mead Roberts, a roly-poly eccentrically dressed friend of Richard, used to sup at "Burton's Bar" when he was in town. "It was incredible," he recalls. "Any stage manager on a big musical has enough problems, but in *Camelot* I thought the stage manager had the worst job of all. Burton's Bar was not only a bar, but also a place where extra costumes were stored for other people and it was often a communal dressing room. How they got people on stage at the exact minute I shall never know, for everybody would be in there chattering and changing.

"And if Richard knew that any of his friends were in the house, he wanted to know where they were sitting, and then he would perform to them. When I came to New York from Hollywood all his house seats were gone, so he got me one of Lerner's tickets. But he didn't know where I was sitting because he only knew where his own house seats were. Anyway, there's a scene in *Camelot* when the main foreground action is the joust in which Lancelot first appears, and upstage is a canopy under which Arthur and Guinevere are sitting to judge the tournament. Richard and Julie Andrews just had to whisper to each other in that scene as though they were discussing the tournament. Well I can lip read, and suddenly I got such a shock for he was on stage saying, 'Where's Mead?' and Guinevere was saying, 'Who the hell's Mead?' "

Richard as King Arthur was the toast of Broadway, the most talked-about actor in New York. And like *My Fair Lady*, though to a slightly lesser degree, *Camelot* became the hub of social life, attracting everyone who was anyone in town. Among those drawn to the Majestic was producer Walter Wanger, who in June, 1961, was beset with problems in recasting and reshooting his jinxed *Cleopatra* epic. He badly needed an actor to replace Stephen Boyd as Mark Antony; a personality strong enough to stand undiminished alongside whichever star he found to play Caesar. Three years earlier, in the spawning days of the film that would not stop growing, he had envisaged as ideal casting: Elizabeth Taylor (Cleopatra), Olivier (Caesar), Burton (Antony). But 20th Century-Fox did not then share his grandiose ideas for a blockbuster; they wanted a modest-budget Cleo, using contract stars. Now everything had changed. He had secured Liz for a record million-dollar fee, and having seen the way Burton ruled *Camelot*, he was determined to sign him, too.

Backstage in Burton's Bar, Wanger waited for the crowd of courtiers and agents to disperse; then he and Richard, joined by a leggy blonde chorus girl named Pat, moved on to the 21. There he outlined plans for the new *Cleopatra* to be shot in Rome and Egypt. Burton liked what he heard. The script was barely started, but Joseph L. Mankiewicz, an old friend, was the writer-director, and he had promised him "a playable part." Moreover, for Caesar, they were trying to get Trevor Howard whom he had first met in an elevator and had joined on a mutually agreeable pub-crawl. (Later, when that deal fell through, Burton was equally happy to be working opposite another old friend, Rex Harrison.) It was, of course, tempting to stay on at the Majestic and double his salary by playing in *Camelot* for a second year. But the *Cleopatra* deal was even more tempting—a quarter of a million dollars guaranteed for three months' work, plus $1,000 a week as "living expenses," and the provision of a villa and staff in Rome for himself and the family. All this and the opportunity of playing opposite the dark enchantress who had fascinated him for years. Never before had he been offered such lavish rewards. They were irresistible.

Curiously, Richard had always had a secret yearning to play Antony in *Antony and Cleopatra*. He had confided as much to Pauline Letts thirteen years before, when he was an unknown actor straight out of the Air Force. "We were standing in the wings at the Lyric and he stated, quite categorically, that it was the one part he was really interested in playing, because he had this obsession for Cleopatra as a person. He was far too young then, but this was his ultimate ambition, and I remember thinking, 'Yes, and I would love to play Cleopatra to your Antony.' "

Now 20th Century-Fox wanted Burton badly enough for the role to agree to pay $50,000 for his premature release from his *Camelot* contract. And, much as he had enjoyed playing the King, he welcomed this early escape from Broadway. *Camelot* had been fun, but the honeymoon was over; the novelty had worn off. It was all becoming too easy, too automatic and repetitive. Even at double the money he could not contemplate playing Arthur throughout a second year; it would be like drinking flat champagne every day. So it was arranged. He would leave *Camelot* for *Cleopatra* in mid-September, 1961. At the outside, he expected to be involved with the film for twenty weeks. If he had known then that it was to occupy him for forty-eight weeks, he never would have signed.

Once he was committed, Julie and other friends kidded him about the challenge of playing love scenes with such a superstar as Miss Taylor. "Better watch yourself, Richard," they joked. "You may meet more than your match this time."

He laughed. "Nonsense. You know how well I can take care of myself." In more serious private moments, he told Julie that he really adored Sybil and the children and that he would never allow anything to break up his marriage. He was completely sincere.

For twelve years now Richard had successfully maintained his dual roles in life—in private, the happily married man and loving husband; in public, the gay, rumbustious extrovert, a hellraiser in the eyes of men, a romantic figure of deadly fascination to women. That he had been able to reconcile these two conflicting images was due largely to the exceptional qualities of his wife. Sharing his Welsh and theatrical background, and having been with him from the first day he stepped onto a film set, Sybil knew and understood Richard to a remarkable degree—better than many wives understand their husbands after a lifetime of marriage. It was not simply that she knew his likes and dislikes, his secret hopes and fears; she understood and appreciated his whole *raison d'être*, his inner compulsion to prove himself (to himself as well as others), his instinctive urge to dominate every scene in the life he was playing. More pertinent, Sybil had sufficient wit, intelligence, personality, and charm of her own to hold his undiminishing respect and affection.

The young Burton had been as a wild stallion, strong-willed, virile, independent, and a natural-born leader. He followed a course all his own, and if any woman had sought to hold him on a taut, short rein in those years of vigorous youth he would surely have broken loose to run fast and free. Sybil, then in many ways more mature than Richard, had the sense to recognize and accept her situation—not grudgingly, but gratefully. She worshipped him, yet was never absurdly possessive; she was familiar with his dark moods and impulsive ways, yet never sought to change him;

she lived for his interests, yet never slipped into the role of the passive "little woman." Sybil was quite a personality in her own right, and Richard knew it. Their closest friends regarded them as an absolutely perfect match. "They were wonderful together," says one old friend. "But perhaps because of her gray hair, one tended to see Sybil as a kind of mother figure to him." Richard, however, would later express an opposite view and describe his love for Sybil as more the love of a man for his daughter. "I felt protective towards her because she was very giggly and bright and sweet and innocent and selfless."

A few days before his big farewell night, the King of *Camelot* accommodated a photographer by making a rare public appearance with his family. He was persuaded to take Sybil and the children to a playground and pose for family shots. Burton had never been to Central Park with the kids before, and he found it an exhausting experience in the midsummer heat. Dutifully he guided Kate across the street on her tricycle, pushed Jessica to and fro on the swings. But for once he was patently ill at ease before the camera. Here was a Burton rarely seen—in the glamor-lacking role of the responsible middle-aged parent. The children adored their celebrated father. He genuinely loved his family. But when it came to a hectic family outing, he could become as flustered and impatient as the next man. The scene presented a striking contrast to his smooth performances at the Majestic. Richard seemed completely relaxed before an adult audience—on stage, in his dressing-room bar, or at late night parties. He reveled in being surrounded by other players and hangers-on, in having an appreciative audience to hold with his ready wit. But Sybil and the children were something quite apart. His respect for family life was deep-rooted, and he could never allow them to be dragged into his show business circus. They belonged to his other world.

On that farewell night at the Majestic, Sybil kept discreetly in the background, as was her custom on such occasions. It was his night, and one of rare emotion for the abdicating king of Broadway. He was pressed into taking a series of curtain calls alone, and the audience rose to him in tumultuous applause. Again and again they called him. And for once Richard the Ironheart, the rugged Celt who shied away from open displays of sentiment, was visibly moved, deeply saddened at the prospect of leaving a show that had won him so many friends and loyal fans. Then the theater emptied, and it was the turn of the *Camelot* company to fete him. The champagne never ran out and neither did Richard, even though he was due to fly the following afternoon to Switzerland before traveling on to Rome and *Cleopatra.*

That night the most impressive speech was made not by Burton but by Moss Hart, the celebrated dramatist, director, and author. This giant of the American theater, weak of heart, with only three months more to live, told the gathering: "Actors like Burton are born once in fifty years. Unlike most stars, he has an imposing personality offstage too. Most stars are not really people—their magnetism disappears away from the footlights. But this man Burton stays full-size."

Finally, Moss Hart the extraordinary starmaker added a few words of advice. He told Burton: "You're rich now. Don't waste your gift. The next five years may decide whether or not you'll become the leading actor of the English-speaking stage."

Richard was flattered. Privately, however, he was not thinking on quite the same ambitious lines; indeed, for the moment, he was not especially interested in acting. Rich and restless, increasingly conscious of his age, he was thinking more in terms of semiretirement, of making perhaps one film a year and giving more time to reading, writing, and generally savoring the second half of his life. He did not know precisely where he was going, but he did have a strange, unaccountable awareness that he was ripe for some dramatic change in his life.

Richard Burton's
parents—Edith and Richard
Walter Jenkins. (*Courtesy
Hilda Owen*)

Richard Burton in
Pontrhydyfen. Across the
river (extreme left front)
his childhood home of
Dan-y-bont; behind him the
viaduct where little Richie
proved himself to the local
gang by heel-and-toeing
along the narrow parapet.

1938–39. Port Talbot Secondary Grammar School Junior XV (under 14's) win the local Burton Cup competition. Richard Jenkins (second from right, second row); captain Trevor George (center); headmaster "Pop" Reynolds (left); Rugby coach and math master Jack Nicholas (right); Freddie Williams, future world champion speedway rider (center, back row).

Richard in an early studio portrait with Philip Burton, the teacher who gave him his name.

The girl friend in Richard's Air Force days: gay, vivacious Eleanor Summerfield—here with Richard Attenborough in a scene from the film *London Belongs to Me* (1948).

1948. *The Last Days of Dolwyn*—and the first film for Richard Burton, here with Andrea Lea.

1948. *Now Barrabas Was a Robber*. Burton (center) in his second film. On his left—Ronald Howard; on his right—a newcomer called Kenneth More.

1952. Burton's first star role—with Olivia de Havilland in *My Cousin Rachel*.

1954. Old Vic Days. Richard as Caliban—with Claire Bloom as Miranda. (*Keystone Press Agency*)

1956. As Othello, with John Neville as Iago. (*Keystone Press Agency*)

Burton's Old Vic debut—as Hamlet at the 1953 Edinburgh Festival. (*Keystone Press Agency*)

With Sybil, leaving
Waterloo Station en route
for Jamaica and the filming
of *Seawife*. (*Keystone Press
Agency*)

Burton's professional low
point—with Angie
Dickinson in *Bramble Bush*.

As a child star Elizabeth had to attend special classes at MGM studios . . .

. . . and she was still having compulsory sessions with her tutor between playing the wife of Robert Taylor in *Conspirator*. Here, aged seventeen, she was already being hailed as one of the world's ten most beautiful women.

Confrontation: Cleopatra meets her paramour Mark Antony . . . "and one only had to see them together to be aware that some strange chemistry was at work. . . ." (*Twentieth Century-Fox*)

His high point—as King on Broadway, with Julie Andrews in *Camelot*. *(United Press International Ltd.)*

With Sybil and daughter Kate, Richard arrives in Rome to film *Cleopatra*. *(Keystone Press Agency)*

High Jinks in Shepperton: Raymond Way saluted them . . . (*Keystone Press Agency*)

Archie the landlord toasted their health . . . (*Keystone Press Agency*)

Ruth served them. (*Keystone Press Agency*)

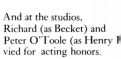

And at the studios, Richard (as Becket) and Peter O'Toole (as Henry II) vied for acting honors.

Burton and Gielgud chew over problems after a rehearsal for their record-breaking
Hamlet in New York. (*Friedman, Abeles*)

Three Burtons in rehearsal for the Poetry Reading by Richard and Elizabeth. It raised
$30,000 for Philip Burton's American Musical and Dramatic Academy.

The Burtons visit Oxford in the charity play in the charity production of *Dr. Faustus,* and here they stroll with Richard's former tutor, Professor Nevill Coghill. (*Syndication International*)

Between rehearsals for *Hamlet,* Burton returns to South Wales and sinks pint of beer with his father, Daddy Ni (center) in the Miner's Arms. (*Radio Times Hulton Picture Library*)

Richard in the classic shot from *The Spy Who Came in From the Cold.*

The Burtons score their greatest triumph together in Edward Albee's *Who's Afraid of Virginia Woolf?*

The Taming of the Shrew . . .

. . . is chosen for the 1967 Royal Film Performance where the Burtons meet Princess Margaret (Sir Michael Redgrave looking on). (*Keystone Press Agency*)

The picture they said could never be—Debbie Reynolds (now Mrs. Harry Karl) in friendly conversation with Richard and Elizabeth. The occasion: the annual Thalians Ball at the Beverly Hilton Hotel which raised over $100,000 to assist emotionally disturbed children. (*Keystone Press Agency*)

Richard and Elizabeth attend the wedding of their long-serving aide Bob Wilson who was best man at their wedding. (*Keystone Press Agency*)

Elizabeth pictured with her
two daughters—Liza (left)
and Maria (center).
(*Syndication International*)

On his forty-fifth birthday
Richard leaves Buckingham
Palace with his C.B.E.
With him the two women
closest to his
heart—Elizabeth and sister
Cissie James. (*London
Express News & Features
Ltd.*)

III
Richard and Elizabeth

Elizabeth

Burton, more Lancelot than Arthur toward women, has described with appropriate gallantry the stunning emotional impact of his first glimpse of Elizabeth Taylor. It happened, we are told, one Sunday morning in the grounds of a Bel Air millionaire's pad, where assorted celebrities soaked up the sunshine and swilled down their Bloody Marys and highballs around the inevitable pool. Richard had on a beautiful head of Welsh steam, and as the eager young gamecock strutted and crowed and gently flushed the ladies, many Hollywood eyes were upon him. But across the pool, not taking a blind bit of notice, was this gorgeous, aristocratic gypsy. He stopped talking and in the lull while hands idly agitated ice cubes, she looked up from her book, pushed her sunglasses to the end of her nose, and stared. Full of eyes and teeth and confidence, he grinned straight back at her. She smiled absently, very faintly; then pushed back her glasses and returned to her book. In those minutes of seconds, as Richard has since told the world, he decided this rare beauty was "the most astonishingly self-contained, pulchritudinous, remote, removed, inaccessible woman I had ever seen." In a much-quoted eulogy, he likened her to the Mona Lisa and to the Dark Lady of Shakespeare's sonnets; described her breasts as "apocalyptic," her body as "a miracle of construction." Now for the facts.

The year was 1952. The place was the luxurious mountaintop home of Stewart Granger and Jean Simmons. And Elizabeth Taylor, in Welsh Wales anyway, was then more to the liking of girls' magazines and a subject for the discussion of eye shadow application rather than a young miner's fanciful idea of a roll on the mountain. As Richard's school pal "Luther" Lewis says: "Ooh,

Bootiful! I'll give you that, fair do's. But I always saw her as a sort of Shirley Temple in those days." If Richard preferred to see her in terms of Aphrodite by Zeus out of Dione, it was perhaps because she was wombful of Eros at the time—pregnant, that is, by Michael Wilding. But no matter—the myth-maker will never concede that his first vision of Elizabeth in the flesh was anything less than earth-shattering.

After those casual first meetings on lazy Sundays at the Grangers', five years passed before Elizabeth and Richard met again. She was Mrs. Mike Todd then, mother of two, with a third one on the way. Nevertheless, Richard insists that he loved her from that first poolside meeting, "but she was unattainable." It is too late now to separate romancing from reporting; what matters is that his version captures the essence of the aura of unattainability that has surrounded this goddess of celluloid. In seeing her as "remote, removed, and inaccessible" he was only seeing her as untold millions would come to see her.

The Taylor allure on the screen far transcended the physical attributes of a pinup girl. The bust was sufficiently ample, the body gracefully proportioned, the facial features near perfect. Yet she was no Hollywood glamor queen; her beauty was of a more intangible, ethereal kind. The face, not the figure, arrested the eye—the well-shaped nose and generous mouth, the long, dark hair and, most striking of all, the fabulous violet eyes that had registered ten thousand emotions since those far-off days when she wept for her Lassie and rejoiced for her steeplechaser in *National Velvet*. Elizabeth, with the eyes alternately sparkling and saddening, was not strenuously faking high emotion in those animal weepies of the forties. The squeals of delight and the looks of anguish were virtually real as she became emotionally immersed in each dramatic situation and abandoned herself to a world of make-believe. And her acting has remained instinctive. She really feels what she is playing—really sweats. Similarly in real life, this woman of acute sensitivity has been genuine and extreme in her emotions. Countless operations, a journey to the brink of death, widowhood, divorces, funerals of loved ones, scandals, crucifixion in the press—she has run the whole gamut of tormenting experience and invariably her agony, whether mental or physical, has been excruciatingly real. Between the pain she has known equally moments of supreme joy. To the casual observer, it must seem that all her life has alternated between periods of black despair and sublime happiness, for it is these times of peak emotion which have commanded massive publicity. Only in brief, undramatic interludes has the curtain fallen on the star who has become a legend more through her performance in life than through her performances on the screen.

As a woman, Elizabeth Taylor has been adored, despised, ridiculed, and pitied. She has never been ignored. Where so many movie stars have gained publicity through gimmicks and stunts, she has done so through experiences, sometimes shocking, sometimes agonizing, but always authentic. Running through her life there has been a constant underlying element of danger—for herself, and for those drawn into her magnetic circle, and this is equally apparent on the screen. While the body is beautiful, somehow her sex appeal lies within the electricity that her presence generates—the sense of hidden perils, of unpredictable excitement, of sudden explosions.

Over the years, Elizabeth has been described in print as cruel, selfish, spoiled, and heartless. She has been painted as a witch, and more commonly, as the *femme fatale* of the century. But the overall picture that emerges is a gross distortion of the truth. In public, or on the film set, the born actress in her will respond instinctively to the artificial atmosphere around her; then she can be timid, tough, humble, or haughty as needs be. But meeting the real Elizabeth Taylor in private, the great mother figure fussing over her man, her children, relations, lifelong servants, and innumerable pets, is a delicious anticlimax. Cruel? Selfish? Heartless? Such adjectives dissolve into absurdity as one confronts a gentle, buxom woman of great warmth and at times surprising shyness. The legendary beauty is still there, the tremendous depth of feeling in the eyes, the overall impression of effulgence. Otherwise, she appears totally divorced from the tempestuous, man-eating, marriage-wrecking vulture of bygone headlines. Discuss her with anyone who knows her intimately, and immediately the same two adjectives arise again and again: sweet and generous. Stories illustrating her compassion and generosity are legion. She has poured a fortune into charities, and has fallen hopelessly for innumerable hard-luck stories. Small children absolutely adore her.

Could this be the Elizabeth who has flaunted a thousand conventions, outraged moralists, and reaped a wild wind of scandal? The two Miss Taylors are only irreconcilable when the woman and the actress are regarded as separate entities. In reality, the two are intertwined. The distorting mirror, fashioned by thirty years of sensational publicity, may present a different image depending upon the angle from which it is viewed, but basically only one Elizabeth remains—the woman who from infancy was encouraged to respond acutely to emotional situations; who has in her an enormous appetite for loving—loving animals, loving children, loving men. Ironically, while she has often been called heartless, her principal fault, if it can be so called, has been the possession of too much heart, too much feeling, too much love. It is her resilience, her ability to recover swiftly from seemingly impossible despair and start afresh on some gay, new adventure that has sometimes been confused with heartlessness. But this is entirely in character with the actress who since childhood has been called upon to register extreme emotion, compose herself, and start afresh on some new traumatic scene. The real Elizabeth is only to be accurately viewed within the context of her environment, her glamorous goldfish-bowl life; an artificial world with its own standards and values in which, as she herself has explained it, she came to regard love as synonymous with marriage and could never have one without the other.

Though seven times engaged, five times married, and once widowed, Elizabeth Rosemond Taylor has never lost that mysterious unattainable quality that so impressed Burton on their first meeting. Conversely, she is the eternal princess of the Hollywood fairyland, for whom all things have seemed attainable. She once called herself "the original spoon-fed child." Beauty, fame, fortune, love . . . everything came her way in abundance. From the beginning, February 27, 1932, she knew only wealth and easy living—nannied in London's upper-middle-class Highgate, toddling through a cozy pleasureland of pony romps on Hampstead Heath and chintzy strawberries-and-cream children's parties, pampering her innumerable little pets, dancing ballet steps before the Princesses Elizabeth and Margaret when she was a precocious three-year-old. Nothing was allowed to mar her idyllic existence. When war threatened, she was promptly removed to the safety and sunshine of Pasadena, California, and later to the luxurious heights of Beverly Hills.

Chance played precious little part in the making of Miss Taylor, filmstar. Nature lavishly endowed her with photogenic features; she inherited a spirited, artistic temperament. Her mother, former stage actress Sara Sothern, sent her to the best poise-and-ballet schools in London; in kindergarten in California she mixed with children of powerful film executives—Darryl Zanuck, Louis B. Mayer, William Goetz. She was nine when she made her first film for Universal, appearing briefly as a brat with Alfalfa of Our Gang in *Man or Mouse*. Two years later Mr. Francis Taylor, a successful art dealer, was on air-raid warden duty with producer Samuel Marx when he was told that MGM needed a girl with an English accent for a great dog-lovers' weepie called *Lassie Come Home*. It was to be Elizabeth's second film and amid a strong cast —Roddy McDowall, Donald Crisp, Dame May Whitty, Edmund Gwenn, Nigel Bruce, and Elsa Lanchester—she was an instant success. Then, after insignificant parts in *The White Cliffs of Dover* and *Jane Eyre*, her riding ability helped her to secure the coveted role of Velvet Brown, the boy-disguised girl who rides to Grand National victory in *National Velvet*. From that point, Elizabeth, aged twelve, was confirmed as a child star. Thereafter any similarities between her upbringing and that of an average child were purely coincidental. She now lived in a world of make-believe, outside of which she had a strictly sheltered and chaperoned social life. Where other girls went to school and had teachers, she went to the film set and had private tutors. Where other girls had boyfriends, she had carefully screened escorts. It was an approved escort, actor Marshall Thompson, who gave Elizabeth her first screen kiss in *Cynthia.* One year later, aged fifteen, she was playing an adult woman and was having a terrible schoolgirl crush on Peter Lawford, who gave her her second screen kiss in *Julia Misbehaves.* Unlike so many other child stars, including Mickey Rooney, her co-star in *National Velvet,* she grew all too suddenly out of juvenile roles. Her "problem" was delightfully apparent on the day she walked onto the *Cynthia* set with a thirty-seven-inch bosom flouncing beneath a low-cut blouse. Two years later, back in England to film *Conspirator,* she was playing a twenty-four-year-old woman, the wife of Robert Taylor, and after a love scene her tutor would be telling her, "Elizabeth, it's time for your lessons now." As she said later, "I had the body of a woman and the emotions of a child."

Life was absurdly artificial. She was presented with a Ford convertible years before she was old enough to drive. She missed ordinary school life, and yet when she was seventeen, and engaged to be married, she donned cap and gown to graduate from high school with the flashbulbs popping. Things did not just happen in her young life; mostly, they were made to happen. Hollywood, thriving on a postwar boom, was as garish and powerful as it had ever been—a giant factory of synthetic dreams and dramas, where it was still the Machiavellian style of studio publicists to foster, even invent, romance and scandal to stimulate the instinctive urge of fans to share in the larger-than-life adventures of their screen idols. Elizabeth Taylor needed invented romance like Casanova needed Cupid.

She was sixteen and a contract star at twelve hundred a week when she first experienced the indignities of romance played out like a film script under Hollywood direction. Her friendship with Glenn Davis, the all-American football idol, was the perfect publicity setup. He was handsome, young, and rugged, and bound from West Point to serve as a lieutenant in Korea; the fans loved the poignant situation of innocent young lovers separated by the Army. Elizabeth, already hailed as one of the world's ten most beautiful women, gave every appearance of being wildly, ecstatically, head over heels in love. On a gold chain round her neck she wore Glenn's miniature gold football. They posed together for photographers on Malibu Beach; then came the tear-jerking farewell as the hero left for overseas. In the months ahead, Elizabeth wrote almost daily to her first true love and longed for his safe return. The young lovers were genuine enough. But they were trapped in an artificial web of publicity and intrigue.

When Elizabeth returned to the States after filming *Conspirator*, the great Liz–Glenn romance was poised for the long-awaited climax. The hero was due home in March, 1949. His golden girl drove with her mother to Miami Airport and there, coat flying, she rushed across the tarmac and literally threw herself into the young lieutenant's arms. (Cut for close-up) "Glenn! Oh, Glenn!" She was near to tears. On the third finger of her left hand was a ruby and diamond ring. Now the soulless publicity machine swung into action, and their relationship that had never been allowed the chance to develop naturally soon died in the unrelenting glare of the public spotlight. They themselves could not explain rationally why it ended. Perhaps it was adolescent adulation, a frail fire that rapidly cooled, but the tears were real enough. Elizabeth was incapable of insincerity in love. She could only lose her heart completely and spontaneously. Once it was recovered, she could lose it as hopelessly all over again.

After Glenn, it was William Pawley, Jr., son of a millionaire and former ambassador to Brazil and Peru. In June, 1949, their engagement was announced; many times her speedboat-mad fiancé publicly declared his love. But this romance collapsed largely through the conflict with Liz's career. She had been prepared to give less time to filming, as Pawley wished, but then MGM loaned her to Paramount for George Stevens' production of *A Place in the Sun*. For the first time she enjoyed a meaty, satisfying adult role; she was seventeen and felt that at last she was becoming a real actress. Next Elizabeth was linked with her latest co-star, Montgomery Clift, a quiet, likable, and dedicated young actor of the method school. Monty was to become one of her closest friends, but there was never a romance. Instead, at seventeen, she fell for Conrad Nicholson Hilton, Jr., a Roman Catholic, son of the tycoon hotelier and heir to a $150 million hotel empire. He wooed her on the grand scale—$15,000 engagement ring, a trousseau worth $10,000, a Cadillac convertible, a white mink stole, a hundred Hilton shares. The wedding ring he slipped on her finger in the little Church of the Good Shepherd at Santa Monica on May 5, 1950, was worth another $10,000.

"I want all the people I have grown up with at the wedding," said the eighteen-year-old bride. So they were, plus a wondrous galaxy of stars—Greer Garson, Walter Pidgeon, Spencer Tracy, the Fred Astaires, the Van Johnsons, Loretta Young, the William Powells, the Gene Kellys, and more. It was the society wedding of the year, with all the kind of eleventh-hour frantic excitement that Elizabeth had already captured as Spencer Tracy's daughter in *Father of the Bride*: the hacking cough that kept her in bed almost until it was time to leave for the church; the last-minute car dash; and the trouble with her twenty-five yards of satin train. All went off with the appropriate joyful confusion, until the honeymoon. The rest was disaster.

The newlyweds dined with the Duke and Duchess of Windsor on board the *Queen Mary* when they sailed for their prolonged honeymoon tour of Europe. They went to Paris, to London and the Ascot races, to Rome where they saw the shooting of the then biggest epic *Quo Vadis*, and where Liz, for a stunt, took the part of a slave girl. And yet, incredibly, it was the saddest and most unromantic of honeymoons. Monte Carlo was the scene of their unhappiest times. The bridegroom found the Casino tables irresistible and went gambling night after night. Liz, never before away so long from her parents and friends, felt bored and neglected. Soon they were finding how greatly their interests clashed. There were quarrels, recriminations, disillusionment. Divorce followed swiftly in January, 1951, a month before Liz's nineteenth birthday. She charged him with mental cruelty, and she refused alimony.

The breakdown of that first marriage left a deep emotional scar on the teen-age actress. She had gone into it with genuine starry-eyed dreams of marital bliss, firmly believing at the outset that marriage was forever. Now, after eight bewildering months, she emerged from the experience brokenhearted and confused. Her latest film was entitled *Love Is Better Than Ever*. Then, as suddenly as she had fallen in love, she recovered her composure. Enjoying independence for the first time, she became a bachelor girl with her own apartment, and soon she was back in the social whirl—bright-eyed and gay and hanging on the arm of her latest escort, the handsome, young whiz-kid director, Stanley Donen. She was still searching for the perfect love. Now, for the first time, she became the target of the kind of petty and malicious gossip for which Hollywood was renowned. "I've been getting so many nasty letters, I don't read them any more," she explained. "They bawl me out for being a spoiled brat, for taking my divorce lightly, for hurting my parents by taking an apartment of my own. Well, I didn't take my divorce lightly; I cried my eyes out for three months." It was her fate that for years to come a mixture of love and tragedy would always be waiting around the corner.

At this point MGM executives decided that their bright young star would benefit from a few months abroad, away from emotional distractions and gossip columnists. They packed her off to London, to play Rebecca the Jewess in *Ivanhoe*, again with Robert Taylor. In the film she lost her man to Joan Fontaine, but off the set she got her man—Michael Charles Gauntlet Wilding, the dashing, debonair filmstar and son of a British Army captain. They had first met in London when she was sixteen and making *Conspirator*. Greatly attracted to him then, she found him irresistible now. Wilding, separated from his wife, Kay Young, was in love with Marlene Dietrich. But after their second meeting, he and Liz became inseparable. In February, 1952, mobbed by a thousand fans, the two screen idols were married at London's Caxton Hall, and how the busybodies prattled over that one. It hadn't a chance, they said. The twenty-year disparity in their ages made it doomed from the start. Their reasoning was wrong; this match, despite its ultimate failure, was far more successful than so many people anticipated. For the first two years at least they were ecstatically happy. Wilding provided the security and tranquility that Elizabeth desperately needed and craved. For the first time she had her own roots. They bought a luxurious house high in the Hollywood hills and developed their own intimate circle of friends.

The Girl Who Had Everything was the title of Elizabeth's latest film, and she did. Her world was complete in January, 1953, when she gave birth to her first child, 7 lb. 3 oz. Michael Howard, born by Caesarian section, as indeed all of her three children would be. Elizabeth, still not quite twenty-one, never looked more radiant; America's florists voted her Mother of the Year. But now came troubles of a different kind—her first extraordinary run of ill health. While she was filming *Elephant Walk* a metal splinter pierced an eye, and after removal it left behind a trace of rust. In June an operation saved her sight. Next, touring Scandinavia in September, she had a nervous breakdown. The overenthusiasm of fans was blamed. Wilding explained, "We are pursued by crazy, film-struck fans wherever we go. They even behave like maniacs, storming over us like wolf packs for autographs, poking pens in our eyes, and tearing our clothes." Then came a knee injury, and in February, after the arrival of her second child, 5 lb. 12 oz. Christopher Edward, born on the mother's twenty-third birthday, Liz was temporarily crippled by spinal trouble—a recurring condition, later aggravated through a crushed spinal disc, that would many times leave her faint with pain. It was the first page of a vast catalog of injuries and illnesses in the life of a star with the world's most widely recorded medical and marital history.

Lastly, the marriage itself began to creak under stress. Wilding was the most gentlemanly and considerate of husbands; he and Elizabeth were always to remain on the friendliest of terms. But the love in their life faded. The disparity in their careers, more than the disparity in ages, was a problem. They faced financial difficulties, and then their work pulled them in opposite directions. While Liz's screen popularity was rising, her husband was decreasingly in demand. His golden years as a cinema box-office idol were waning. It had been a strategic error to leave England, where he had been offered roles more suited to his essentially English style. Elizabeth, in contrast, had again scored a major success under the direction of George Stevens and on loan to another studio. When Warner Brothers failed to get Grace Kelly, they cast Elizabeth in Edna Ferber's *Giant*, with Rock Hudson and the ill-fated James Dean. In this role she had to age from eighteen to fifty, and it won her an Oscar nomination.

In July, 1956, the Wildings separated, and a new male figure, more dynamic than any of his predecessors, stormed into Elizabeth's life. Tough, thickset Mike Todd, née Avrom Hirsch Goldbogen, was the son of an unemployed Jewish rabbi; an ever-dauntless, go-getting wheeler-dealer, who without formal education had become a millionaire at nineteen in the construction business. Since then he had made and lost gigantic fortunes, and now emerged as the latest Hollywood super-showman with his production of the all-star extravaganza *Around the World in Eighty Days*. Never a man to waste seconds, he telephoned Elizabeth the day after her separation was announced and boldly told her that he proposed to marry her. She left for Kentucky to make *Raintree County* with Monty Clift, but there was no escaping this hurricane of a man. He persistently telephoned, sent crateloads of flowers, and finally his private plane to bring her back to New York. Shortly after the premiere of his Jules Verne epic they became engaged, and Wilding journeyed to Mexico to speed the proceedings of what Liz termed a "friendly divorce." Four days later, near Acapulco, she became Mrs. Mike Todd.

This time there was an even greater age disparity, but it mattered not at all. Elizabeth had at last found the perfect love. "Why did I have to wait until I was twenty-five before this happened to me?" she later exclaimed. "Why did it have to come so late?" She had never known a man like Todd—a man who could be masterful and yet tender, who had a zest for living and loving no less than her own, who never ceased to proclaim and demonstrate his adoration, and who, like her, lived in a world where all things were possible. Every Saturday was a wedding anniversary to Todd. In successive weeks he bought her a unique champagne mink, a tiara, a Persian necklace, a Rolls Royce, and two poodles;

he gave her whole theaters. They had stormy, brawling scenes in public, and yet it meant nothing. Elizabeth called it love talk. "We have more fun fighting than most people do when they are expressing their affection." Life was tempestuous, spectacular, glittering, full of tears as well as laughter. And for Elizabeth, rarely bored, rarely neglected, this was near paradise.

The Todds were mobbed around the globe as they toured to publicize *Around the World in Eighty Days*. Then Elizabeth was blessed with the one precious gift that had eluded her—a daughter, Elizabeth Frances. Her third and last child, prematurely born, weighed only 4 lb. 4 oz.; a resuscitator worked for fourteen minutes before the baby took her first breath, and then she spent more than a month in an oxygen tent. But Liza grew strong and darkly beautiful, and her mother adored her. Soon afterward, Liz happily exclaimed: "I am now finished with being a filmstar. From now on, I just want to be Mike Todd's missus." But for the moment she was committed to another film, her twenty-fifth, playing an erotic child bride in *Cat on a Hot Tin Roof*.

On March 22, 1958, the world suddenly became a duller place. Mike Todd, the dynamo with a heart, was dead. It was a Saturday; the perfect marriage was just thirteen months old. Reluctantly, he had left Elizabeth to fly from Hollywood, via Tulsa, Oklahoma, to attend the New York Friars Club dinner in his honor as "Showman of the Year." His private plane, *Lucky Liz*, crashed in the New Mexico desert, and all they found of Mike was his wedding ring, charred and bent. If Elizabeth had not been confined to bed with bronchitis, she would have perished with him. In the ensuing months, as hysteria gave way to blackest despair, she often wished that she had. "If only I had died with him," she cried. "Without Mike now I feel like half a pair of scissors. That's what he used to tell me when he was away from me, and now I understand." Her famed powers of emotional recuperation were not so much in evidence now. The extent of her love was tragically clear; her grief overwhelming.

So often Elizabeth has been publicly censured for her behavior, but never remotely has she acted with the callous disregard for human dignity and feelings that was exhibited by many hundreds of sensation-seekers in her darkest hour. At the Chicago funeral of Mike Todd, it was shown with horrifying realism to what degree a superstar can be tormented by the public. They came in their thousands, not to mourn but to gawk—thoughtless, screaming fans who besieged the young widow, pulled at her veil, even rocked her car. This was the price of her stardom. Long ago she had passed through the celebrity barrier to the point where she was a sensational attraction, not out of personal choice, but because her public wanted it so. Three weeks later, pale and withdrawn, Elizabeth returned to the set of *Cat on a Hot Tin Roof*, to lose her own identity in the part of Maggie, playing opposite Paul Newman. She had no thought of retirement now; Mike had been her only motivation for that. For the moment she was the subject of universal sympathy, and praise for the professional way she soldiered on. The pendulum would soon swing the other way.

Elizabeth, the widow and mother of three, was still only twenty-six years old, her beauty undiminished. It was obvious that she would eventually remarry and so, after the briefest respite that decency allowed, gossip columnists returned to the familiar pastime of linking her with a variety of men. Most notably she became linked with producer Arthur Loew, Jr., millionaire son of the MGM chief. They were old friends and had the wit to laugh at the rumors. At one dinner party, with guests crowded around in the parlor, they could not resist having their little joke. Loew spoke dramatically in a loud whisper: "Will you tell them. . . . Or shall I?"

"You tell them," said Liz coyly as everyone looked toward them.

"Dinner is served," announced Loew.

The vipers struck on September 8, 1958. That day the news broke of a Liz Taylor–Eddie Fisher romance. The floodgates were opened to let loose an almighty cataract of scorn and condemnation that roared on for months and resounded around the world. "Oh, no, not Eddie Fisher," was the first reaction. Not Eddie, the clean-cut "Coca-Cola Kid," the husband of the lovable peaches-and-cream girl, Debbie Reynolds? Not the Eddie Fisher who eight months earlier, on his own television show, had breathlessly told forty million viewers that his second child had been born only minutes before—a boy named Todd Emmanuel, after the late Mike Todd? It was ridiculous. There must be some mistake. But as Eddie and Elizabeth went nightclubbing in New York, it soon became apparent that there was no mistake. And from that point an outraged society turned on Elizabeth with all the bitterness and fury of a woman scorned. It was "the great betrayal," the act of a "heartless witch." She was, voiced one magazine, "selfish and cruel to the point of depravity."

Several factors combined to raise the affair to the proportions of what *McCall's* ultimately described as being "the most turbulent Hollywood scandal of the past decade." First, the Fisher match had been successfully puffed up to the status of the most heavenly of Hollywood marriages. Eddie, the Jewish-American crooner, and Debbie, the darling screen star of *Tammy*, were the great American sweethearts. Second, Eddie had been one of Mike Todd's closest friends, and the Fishers especially had comforted Elizabeth in her time of grief. Third, and most damaging of all, it was popularly put about that Liz had been one of Debbie's greatest friends. Now, it was alleged, she had betrayed that friendship by stealing Debbie's man. In these circumstances it was no wonder that Elizabeth was booed, hissed, smeared, and bombarded with obscene letters. Yet, in truth, she had never been one of Debbie's closest friends. More pertinently, she had not broken up a blissfully happy couple. Though it was not generally known, the Fishers' marriage had been under considerable stress before Elizabeth came along. But it made no difference. The fact remained that she was "the other woman," and with her marital record, she was regarded as fair game for the self-appointed moralists. A few friends stood by her. Richard Brooks, who had directed her last film, was one who spoke up on her behalf, stressing her loyalty and her love of life and talking about "the phony morality" of a society in which men were secretly jealous of Eddie and women were scared of losing their husbands. But otherwise, Liz and Eddie were isolated by public opinion, and ironically all the snide gossip and stone-throwing served only to strengthen the bond between them. They had only one another to lean upon in this crisis, and on April 1, 1959 (Debbie's birthday), they announced their engagement.

Inevitably, as Liz declared her love for Eddie and talked once more about retiring to concentrate on domestic life, the columnists could not resist recalling some of her other statements at her time of marriage:

"I am now Mrs. Hilton. You can take it from me that my romantic life is settled forever. There is no other future for me than as Nicky's wife."

"It is wonderful marrying a man like Michael (Wilding) who is twice my age. He is so mature and that is what I need."

"I have given Mike (Todd) my love. My eternal love."

And now: *"I love Eddie dearly. I'm committed to make a couple of films and after that it is finished for me. I will be Mrs. Eddie Fisher."*

This time, she insisted, it was the real thing, and now it was for keeps. Of course it was, said the cynics, but for how long?

In the midst of that mad scandal, Elizabeth's position looked hopeless. Public opinion was overwhelmingly against her. Almost certainly the mass disapproval of her private life ruined her once excellent chance of winning an Oscar for her part in *Cat on a Hot Tin Roof*. And yet this extraordinary fallen idol would survive the scandal, not merely because of a near-fatal illness that was to bring her universal sympathy, but more because the world was conditioned to expect the girl who had grown up in a private wonderland to lead a life far removed from normal standards of behavior and convention. It had been different when Ingrid Bergman became emotionally involved with Italian director Roberto Rossellini; in this case the woman had had an entirely wholesome image, and because of it she was so much more vulnerable. Partly through an absurd sense of having been betrayed, public opinion reacted that much more intolerantly, and Bergman's career suffered for years. But Elizabeth, cradled and rocked in Hollywood romance, would weather the storm to emerge an even bigger star than before. Fisher was the one whose career would suffer most over the long term, for he had fed the legend of an idyllic home life with Debbie, and the fans were not so prepared to accept an idol with feet of clay. Conversely, riding on a great wave of public sympathy, Debbie would see her earning power soar.

In March, 1959, Miss Taylor was converted to the Jewish faith at Temple Israel in Hollywood and given the Jewish name of Elisheba Rachel. Two months later, in Las Vegas, she married Eddie Fisher, who had Mike Todd, Jr. as his best man. So, seeking to fill the gap that widowhood had made in her bittersweet life, Elizabeth embarked on her fourth honeymoon—sailing in the Mediterranean on a yacht provided by Sam Spiegel, producer of her next film, *Suddenly Last Summer.* For this film her fee had soared to a new high of half a million dollars, and under Joe Mankiewicz's direction, she was to give one of her greatest performances. It brought her third Oscar nomination in three years—and yet another disappointment as the prize went to Simone Signoret for *Room at the Top.*

It was while working in London on *Suddenly Last Summer* that Elizabeth received a telephone call from Walter Wanger. Eddie answered the call, and Wanger explained that he wanted her for his next epic, *Cleopatra.* Liz thought it an absurd idea and told Eddie jokingly: "Tell him I'll do it for a million dollars." She never expected to be taken seriously, but Wanger agreed. Such was Elizabeth's box-office pulling power that she secured the unprecedented deal of $1 million against 10 percent of the gross, plus $1,250 a week "living expenses." Gleefully she accepted. Now only one thing clouded her future: the fact that she had first to complete her MGM contract for one more film called *Butterfield 8.* She complained that Gloria, her call-girl role in this movie, was virtually a prostitute, and that the script was pornographic. But there was no escape. She was compelled to honor this commitment for a fee around $125,000 if she wanted to be released for the million-dollar assignment. Liz hated giving way and made her feelings painfully apparent, but she still turned in a superb performance. Then on August 31, 1960, accompanied by Eddie, she arrived in London to start work on *Cleopatra.* The story of the most bizarre, sensational, and extravagant film production of all time had begun.

For years, Wanger had planned to make a film about the Queen of the Nile. Originally Joan Collins had been suggested for the role; more recently there had been powerful lobbying for Susan Hayward, but Wanger wanted Taylor. He visualized his Cleo as the quintessence of youthful femininity and strength, and who combined these qualities more spectacularly than Elizabeth. Over the years of planning, the budget for *Cleopatra* had leaped from two to five million dollars. Now it was to be filmed in the Todd A-O process with Rouben Mamoulian as director, Peter Finch as Caesar, and Stephen Boyd as Antony. The locations in Italy were written off because of the clash with the Olympic Games in Rome, and 20th Century-Fox proceeded to make Rome in London. Palm trees were flown over from Hollywood and Egypt; the sets covered eight acres of rain-soaked palaces and temples. Trucks lumbered into Pinewood with a cargo of 142 miles of tubular steel, 20,000 cubic feet of timber, 7 tons of nails, and 300 gallons of paint. The monster show-cake was built; the candles were lit. Then the great edifice crumbled.

In October the million-dollar Cleopatra was burning with Malta fever, and after a spell in the London Clinic, she was ordered to take a long rest. Meanwhile, the scene at Pinewood was chaos. There were holdups through a Hairdressers' Union strike and troubles with script, costumes, and weather. "It was sheer lunacy," said Mamoulian. "The insurance people were full of nervous chicken. They said, 'Shoot some film, shoot anything, as long as you can keep the film going.' Well, we tried it. Rain, mud, slush and fog, it was stinking weather. On a good day, whenever a word was spoken, you could see the vapor coming from the actors' mouths. It was like a tobacco commercial. We didn't have one inch of film with Liz in it." By mid-January, 1961, Elizabeth was apparently recovered and ready for work, but now there were new problems. Mamoulian had resigned; Finch and Boyd were committed elsewhere; the script was judged unsatisfactory and had to be drastically rewritten. So recasting was planned, and much to Elizabeth's approval, Joe Mankiewicz was brought in as the new writer-director. The plan was to start shooting in April.

It was on February 26, the eve of her 29th birthday, that Elizabeth Taylor went to bed at the Dorchester with all the symptoms of a common cold or influenza. On March 4, eleven doctors, including Lord Evans, the Queen's physician, were at her bedside. Her condition was critical. She was in a high fever; her breathing had almost stopped completely. As they rushed her to the London Clinic, there were reports that the great star was dying.

The story of Elizabeth's fight to live is now legend, one of the most comprehensively and intimately recorded medical cases of all time. Five times, overcome by the suffocating effects of lobar pneumonia, she stopped breathing. For two suspenseful days she hovered on the brink of death—gasping, rasping labored breath in an iron lung. A tracheotomy was performed on her throat to give her breath. Above her head a cat's cradle of tubes dripped blood into her veins and food into her stomach. *Cleopatra* was forgotten. The haggling behind the scenes stopped. From Hollywood, Spyros Skouras, the supremo of Fox, cabled: "Do anything, anything to make Liz happy. She is the only one who matters, the only one who counts. Forget the picture." Telegrams poured in from all over the world and filled huge laundry baskets at the hospital. Outside, vast crowds waited in silence.

As Elizabeth lay there, the film was shelved again, and at Pinewood the $600,000 sets crashed to the ground. But six days later this extraordinary cinema queen was sitting up in bed, drinking champagne. Two weeks later she came out of the hospital wearing a strip of plaster on her neck the way another woman would wear a string of pearls. "This scar is my badge of life. I wear it with pride, because it reminds me of the time my life was saved." The quotes began to read like an old Bette Davis movie script, but the events were horrifyingly real. One London specialist, Dr. Carl Goldman, was quoted: "Out of every one hundred who have Miss Taylor's type of pneumonia, rarely do two survive. On four occasions Miss Taylor was as near to death as she could be. Her courage and willpower pulled her through."

So once again the great switch was pulled on the public-controlled image of this dark, alluring beauty who had changed from the innocent Lassie-lover to the diabolical *femme fatale*, from the tragic young widow to the callous marriage-wrecker. Suddenly Lady Macbeth was restored as Helen of Troy. The crowds cheered her when she left the London Clinic. They cheered her again shortly afterward at the annual presentation of Motion Picture Academy Awards. Three times in three years she had been rejected there; now, incredibly, they were honoring her with her first Best Actress Oscar—for Gloria of *Butterfield 8*, the role she had never wanted, and a picture which had failed to impress the critics. Of course, it was really a sympathy vote; she recognized that. But she no longer cared. She only felt joy at remaining alive.

Elizabeth explained her feelings that summer at a Los Angeles Medical Fund dinner. Sitting next to Attorney General Robert Kennedy, she said: "Throughout those many critical hours in the operating theater at the London Clinic, wanting to live was so strong within me—so overpowering, so all-consuming—that I remember it, strangely perhaps as an incredible and agonizing pain. As if every nerve, every muscle, my whole physical being, was being strained to the point of torture by this insistence upon life, to the last ounce of my strength, to the last gasp of my breath. But then, gradually and inevitably and finally, that last ounce of strength was drawn. I remember I had focused desperately on the light hanging directly above me. It had become something I needed almost fanatically to continue to see; that light had become my vision of life itself. But yet slowly, as if its course of power were my own fading strength and inability to breathe, it faded and dimmed—ironically enough, like a well-done theatrical effect—to blackness. I have never known, or do I think there can be, a greater loneliness. . . . And then I coughed. I moved. I breathed. And I looked. That hanging lamp—that most beautiful light my world had ever known—began faintly to glow again, to shine again."

Here, with rhetorical excess, was Elizabeth Taylor, the actress of hypersensitive emotions, responding to a dramatic situation and behaving like the all-time Hollywood movie star that she was. It was what her public really wanted; what it had come to expect. She had lived now for nearly thirty years, and for all the love and pain she had experienced, it might as well have been a century. Physically, mentally, and emotionally, she had taken more punishment than any other star who lives in the headlines. Yet ever resilient, here she was back in the center of the limelight, more vibrant, more electrifying and glamorous than ever. It had taken a near-fatal illness to make millions of people aware of how much they cherished the existence of this bright, breathtaking shooting star, whose sudden unpredictable flashes could fill minds and hearts with wonder. Today they praised Elizabeth. Tomorrow they might condemn her. But they would not be without her for anything. She illuminated a world that could be unbearably gray; she made unreality real. She opened a window into private dreams and fantasies.

Scandal in Rome

And so they came to Rome—a new Caesar, Rex Harrison; a new Antony, Richard Burton; a new director, Joe Mankiewicz; a new director of photography, Leon Shamroy. Plus an almost entirely new supporting cast, and a multitude of technicians, secretaries, makeup artists, hairdressers, servants, sycophants, and hangers-on. Only two principal characters had stepped out of the wreckage of Pinewood's *Cleopatra*—producer Walter Wanger and the indestructible Cleo herself, Elizabeth Taylor. Now, just one year since they had shot the first scene with Peter Finch's Caesar and Stephen Boyd's Antony entering the city of Alexandria, this supercolossal saga of misfortune and strife was being started anew with an extravagance and sensationalism worthy of the ancient Roman Games. Cinecittà was the new Circus Maximus. An entire building was converted for the

personal use of Miss Taylor—bathrooms, rooms for her costumes
and wigs, rooms for her private staff, an office for Eddie Fisher—
and when the cigar-stuffed faces showed it to her, even Liz exclaimed that it seemed "a bit much." But nothing was too much.
In case of illness they allowed her to bring over her family physician from Hollywood, with all expenses paid. Money was no object. They were building Rome in Rome, and slightly bigger than
the original. At Anzio they had hired a private beach from Prince
Borghese at a cost of $150,000 to build Alexandria; then they had
to spend another $13,000 to clear the beach of mines.

The weather was beautiful until they started shooting on September 25, 1961. Then it rained. And on *Cleo* it never rained, but
it poured. An elephant went mad and dancing girls went on
strike. There was a teacup storm with the discovery of a call girl
on the payroll. But who could possibly blame the film company?
Thousands of extras were being employed every day. For one
scene they took on six thousand, and at $12 a day, schoolteachers
and lawyers were joining up—so why not the oldest profession?
Such was the confusion of extras that some would come to the
studios, slip into togas, walk across the location, nip over the
fence, change back into city gear, and catch a bus into Rome for a
day's work. In the evening they returned the same way, changed
back into Roman costume, and joined the pay queue. Expendi-
tures soared, and so did fears of repercussions in the boardroom.
Twentieth Century-Fox had lost some $60 million in the past
few years; now, in the face of mounting criticism from share-
holders, the position of President Spyros P. Skouras was perilously balanced. The order went out for vigorous economies, but
still the production burned up dollars at a rate of two million a
month. The economies were mostly ineffectual, and often petty
—like cutting down on paper cups and taking away the trailer
Rex Harrison used as a portable dressing room. When the latter
happened, Rex erupted and threatened to catch the next plane out
of Rome. The trailer was restored. It was especially senseless to
aggravate Harrison. In the early months of filming he was the
outstanding working actor, the complete professional. As Burton
recalls, when this Caesar was roused he had an hilarious habit of

creating Italian expletives by adding "o" to English words, snapping "stupido" and "idioto" at native technicians. But when the film was completed, it would be seen that his strong portrayal dominated the entire first half of the production.

In contrast, Richard all this time was mostly kicking his heels in the wings—gagged until Harrison was eliminated. It was a rare experience for an actor accustomed to nonstop pressure of work. It was also curious. Fox had paid $50,000 to buy him out of *Camelot* ahead of time. He was needed urgently, they said—and no, he couldn't take a restful sea voyage to Italy. Yet, in the first nineteen weeks, he did no more than one full week's work. He filled in the time by reading, visiting night spots, and starting to learn some Russian. Occasionally, he said, he popped his head round a marble column; otherwise he had an interminable wait for the assassination of Caesar. Not until late January, 1962, was he to have the pleasure of working with the legendary Miss Taylor.

Although they were only casually acquainted before *Cleopatra*, Burton already knew more about Elizabeth than could be gleaned from her mountain of publicity. She was always a popular topic for the Hollywood gossips; and Richard had an outstandingly reliable source of information since he shared one of her closest friends, Roddy McDowall. Richard was a malcontent in the Taibach Co-op when the pixie-faced Roddy won child stardom overnight as Huw Morgan in the great Welsh weepie, *How Green Was My Valley*. The same Roddy had co-starred with Elizabeth in her first major picture, *Lassie Come Home*. He had helped her to settle in New York after her disastrous first marriage. It was at a party in his apartment that she had first met Eddie Fisher, then on Army leave. It was at Elizabeth's suggestion that he had been brought into *Cleopatra* to play Octavian. Roddy has always rated among Elizabeth's greatest admirers. A few years ago he told a journalist, "I look at her sometimes and just burst out laughing, she's so beautiful." Richard came to know him well during *Camelot*'s long run, and having been bought out of the show together, they traveled to Rome together and shared the same villa on the Appian Way, along with Sybil, the children, and Roddy's partner in a photography business. Nearby, at $3,000-a-month rental, Liz had taken the Villa Papa, a ranchstyle house with seven bedrooms and six bathrooms that stood on extensive grounds screened by high walls. Here she lived with Eddie, her three children, a collie, a St. Bernard, three terriers, and two Siamese cats. And soon her family was to be increased. On January 15, the Fishers announced that they had adopted Maria Schell, a little German girl who had been found at the age of nine months, covered with abscesses, suffering from malnutrition, and lying in a laundry basket on top of two pillows. Maria, now one year old, had a crippled hip and was entering a Munich clinic for the first of a series of operations.

While Roddy had sung Elizabeth's praises to Richard, Liz had heard plenty of stories about Burton, the prince of Shakespearean players, the brilliant conversationalist, impressionist, and ladykiller. She had been told that he knew the whole script, including everyone else's lines, before he started working; and she rather envied him his Old Vic background and stature as a stage actor. But she also remembered how long ago she had met him at Stewart Granger's house, and thinking him rather brash, had given him "the cold fish eye." In the circumstances, their first meeting in Rome was something of an anticlimax, at least for Elizabeth. As she recalled it, his first words to her were: "Has anybody ever told you that you're a very pretty girl?" ("And I said to myself, 'Oy, gevaldt, here's the great lover, the great wit, the great intellectual of Wales, and he comes out with a line like that.' I couldn't believe it. I couldn't wait to get back to the dressing room where all the girls were and tell them.")*

In mid-October, Elizabeth and Richard were seated next to one another at a dinner dance given by the Kirk Douglases, and two weeks later the Fishers visited the set to watch Burton at work. On New Year's Eve, when the Burtons threw a party, the Fishers were the guests of honor. The friendship of Elizabeth and Richard developed apace as they went out in groups to nightclubs

* Elizabeth Taylor, *Elizabeth Taylor: An Informal Memoir*, (New York, Harper & Row, Publishers, 1964).

and restaurants. Eddie was more or less a teetotaller in those days, and he favored quiet family evenings at home, but Liz liked to unwind with some social life after a day at the studios, and she found nightclubbing far more entertaining and relaxing now that Richard was around. Eddie went along, too, though with less enthusiasm. It had been fun for him in Rome at first, watching his wife play the ruthless, bewitching Queen of the Nile and hosting at smart dinner parties. But he was not directly involved with the filming, and understandably the role of an inactive Prince Consort became a little wearing at times.

So, with the dawn of a new year, the great symphony of scandal began, rising in a few weeks from tinkling whispers to a crescendo of gossip-mongering that reverberated around the world, blazing across every newspaper in every language that could be set up in type. Elizabeth, as the queen of fatal fascination who ensnared, weakened, and destroyed her lovers, and Richard, as her last great paramour, played their first scene on January 22. Immediately the sparks began to fly. The first day Richard was suffering with a king-sized hangover and enough discomfort to arouse the strong mother instinct in Elizabeth. She helped the togaed Welshman to steady his coffee cup. Later, when he stumbled over a line, it endeared him to her a little more. No longer overawed by his reputation as an actor, she decided that he was rather "vulnerable and sweet," and later she recalled: "If it had been a planned strategic campaign, Caesar couldn't have done it better. He was captivating. My heart went out to him."

The next day there was tension between Elizabeth and Eddie, and two days later a leading member of the production team remarked, "Liz and Rich are not just playing the love scenes. This is for real, on and off the set. That I feel for sure." We laughed cynically; how often we had heard that kind of publicity guff. Then, in an interview with Roderick Mann of the London *Sunday Express*, Richard talked for the first time about *Cleopatra*: "They say it will cost over $20 million, but it will still make a fortune. For Liz is absolutely marvelous. They did a breathtaking shot of her the other day lying absolutely nude on a day bed. That ought to be good for around $20 million on its own. I must say Liz fascinates me. What is it about her, I wonder, that makes her so good? Off the screen she's just a nice, charming girl. But on the screen, she is absolutely compelling. She looks at you with those eyes and your blood churns, I tell you."

This was familiar-sounding publicity talk, too. Yet this time there was a difference; Richard meant every word. Meanwhile, his effect on Elizabeth was curious and so profound that she later likened it to the experience of a sleeping princess being awakened by a Prince Charming. Until this time she had been sleeping in the past—still wearing Mike Todd's wedding ring, the one twisted and charred relic of the air crash four years before, and still surrounding herself with pictures of Mike at home. Even Eddie, as Mike's great friend, was a permanent reminder of her idyllic third marriage. But now, breezing into her petrified Eden, came a whirlwind of a man in the Mike Todd tradition, another self-made man with a sufficiently powerful, vivid, and irresistible personality to charm her out of the past and into the present. Once she had fallen in love with Richard, she took off Mike's ring for the first time since his death and began to look forward to each day with a new freshness and nervous excitement. Years later she was to explain that she could never have married a man like Burton if she had not been previously married to Todd, because without that experience she would not have known how to cope with the dynamic, mercurial Welshman.

By the end of January, everyone connected with *Cleopatra* was aware of this powerful mutual attraction, and from then on the story became an unbelievable publicity handout or an impossibly exaggerated film script: a flashbulb glare at life as fleeting looks and touching hands became imprisoned in still, idiotically frozen pictures propped up for inspection and speculation on a billion breakfast tables. What precisely happened has since become lost in the swirling mists of rumor, denial, and counterdenial. So many different versions have emanated from persons involved in the making of *Cleopatra* that truth can best be served by simply recording, amid mounting tension and confusion, how the events unfolded and rocked the world:

February 14. Eddie left Rome on business. Elizabeth visited the set to watch Richard working and went out with him in the evening.

February 16. We learned that Sybil had left for New York to visit Richard's sick foster-father. The whisper went around that Richard had told Liz that he could no longer imperil his marriage.

February 17. Liz was rushed to the hospital by ambulance with sirens screaming. There were wild unfounded rumors of a heart attack and a suicide attempt; to allay them, the studio put out a food poisoning story, attributing the blame to a tin of bully beef. (Long afterward, Walter Wanger, who was at the villa that night, explained that it was a minor incident arising because Miss Taylor had taken "a few Seconals" merely to help her to sleep and someone in the house had panicked.)

February 18. Eddie immediately flew back to Rome from Milan. Richard was flying back from Paris where he had been briefly working on *The Longest Day.*

February 19. Publicity man Chris Hofer put out a statement in Burton's name denying rumors of romance. It was published all over the world: "For the past several days uncontrolled rumors have been growing about Elizabeth and myself. Statements attributed to me have been distorted out of proportion, and a series of coincidences has lent plausibility to a situation which has become damaging to Elizabeth. Mr. Fisher, who has business interests of his own, merely went out of town to attend to them for a few days. My foster-father, Philip Burton, has been quite ill in New York, and my wife, Sybil, flew there to be with him for a time, since my schedule does not permit me to be there. He is very dear to both of us. Elizabeth and I have been close friends for over twelve years. I have known her since she was a child star and would certainly never do anything to hurt her personally or professionally. In answer to these rumors, my normal inclination would be simply to say 'No comment,' but I feel that in this case things should be explained to protect Elizabeth." Meanwhile a Fox official denied the statement was made with Burton's knowledge, and Miss Taylor dismissed the whole business as "nonsense." Eddie had now collected her from the hospital and everyone was insisting they were perfectly happy. A film company spokesman told us: "Mrs. Burton is in Rome with her husband now. All this is typical *Dolce Vita* set rumor. Whenever a good-looking man and a beautiful girl play a love scene, everyone here starts trying to make something out of it."

February 20. Burton said he never issued nor authorized a denial of a romance that never existed. "I have always believed that professional publicity should be kept as far as possible from one's personal life. Now, more than ever before, I believe my reasoning is justified." So it was back to Hofer who explained: "If Richard says he knew nothing about it, I have to go along with him. After all, I work for him. But I think pressure has been put on Richard by the studio, because he did approve the statement before I issued it."

February 27. Eddie threw a big champagne party to celebrate Liz's thirtieth birthday.

March 1. Richard fell asleep on the set, having been out all night on his traditional St. David's Day bender.

March 3. It was revealed that Sybil had returned to New York; that Burton was being seen about with Pat, the twenty-year-old chorus girl from New York's Copacabana whom he had met during *Camelot*; and that Liz was verbally sparring with him on the set.

March 5. Liz and Rich began playing their big *Cleopatra* love scene. Pat watched them filming, but like other visitors, she was discouraged by officials from coming to the set.

March 8. Louella Parsons reported in the Los Angeles *Herald-Examiner* that Liz's marriage was virtually finished, and the Fishers subsequently denied this story through a Hollywood lawyer.

March 13. Liz's parents had arrived in Rome. She was now constantly seen in the company of Eddie again.

March 19. Eddie had to fly to New York for recording sessions.

March 22. In Genoa, Rex Harrison married Rachel Roberts, Sybil's friend since Stratford days together.

March 27. Sybil arrived in London with the children. It was her birthday. The rumors of romance, she said, were nonsense. "I was furious about it. Richard was furious, and so was Elizabeth. You see, Richard and I have known Elizabeth since she was married to Michael Wilding. Naturally, we're all very friendly." In New York, Eddie Fisher went into a hospital for three days' complete rest.

March 29. Fisher left the hospital suddenly, held a large press conference, and denied his marriage was breaking up. "One thing is undeniable. I love Liz, and she loves me. The marriage is fine. Just fine. Even before I married, the wiseacres were saying it would never last. Well, it's lasted this long [three years] and it's going to last a lot longer. . . . The only romance between Burton and Elizabeth is the romance they play as Antony and Cleopatra. . . ."

March 30. A few hours after that statement, Liz and Richard were nightclubbing in Rome until dawn. Arm in arm and smiling, they visited Il Pipistrello (The Bat) and Bricktop's. And, as always, they were pursued by the *paparazzi,* the marauding wolf-packs of opportunist photographers.

April 1. Emlyn Williams, godfather to the Burtons' first daughter, briefly visited Richard in Rome, and left behind an acid letter in which he chastised him and Elizabeth for what he regarded as irresponsible behavior and expressed the opinion that theirs was an infatuation that could not last. He wrote: "April 1, 1962—known as April Fool's Day. Could it be Richard Burton's year to play the part?" (Years later Williams explained to us, "Sybil was bereft at that time. She really did want to know what was happening. She'd just come from Rome herself and was convinced that there was nothing in it. But a great friend of Sybil's had said to me, 'If only you could go over and see what is happening.' I wouldn't have done so otherwise, because it wasn't in my nature to do that sort of thing, and it would never be again. Anyway, it was obvious to me. All I did was to throw them into each other's arms, and Richard told me himself, 'I'm going to marry her.' So I came back with this terribly difficult message—like one of those messengers in a play bringing the bad news. It was a very bad part I had. Very poor." With the best intentions, Mr. Williams had rather overplayed his hand in Rome. He had been reading the riot act to Richard when Elizabeth entered the room and impulsively he said, "Look at her, she's just a third-rate chorus girl." Afterwards, he thought he hadn't really made the right kind of remarks, and when he got home he told his wife what he had said. Molly Williams drew herself up to her full height. "Emlyn," she said haughtily, "when you met me *I* was a third-rate chorus girl.")

April 2. Liz and Richard went out for the evening. Joe Mankiewicz quipped, "As far as I'm concerned, Miss Taylor may fall in love with Mao Tse-tung as long as she finishes her work in the film," and Walter Wanger admitted, "This is a very peculiar situation we have here." Meanwhile anxiety was aroused at the Munich orphanage, where the Fishers had adopted Maria last January. The German Embassy in Rome confirmed that it had been asked to make inquiries into the child's welfare.

April 3. At midnight, in New York, a jointly approved statement by the Fishers was released to the effect that divorce proceedings were to be instituted. In Rome, Liz was besieged by photographers, but despite the domestic crisis she arrived punctually to continue shooting the Nile banquet scene, which publicists proudly described as "one of the greatest debauch scenes in history." A few weeks earlier it had not been unusual for her to arrive late or miss shooting altogether. Now she was never late for a call, and there was fresh hope that the picture might be completed by the end of June. From London we learned that Sybil had collapsed and was now staying at the Hampstead home of her brother-in-law Ivor Jenkins. Emlyn Williams consoled her and explained to the press: "It's not very nice, you know, when you read that your husband is running around with another woman. It has not been nice for Sybil . . . I just cannot imagine that Richard would throw away his life like this. They are exceedingly happy and he adores his daughters."

April 4. An astrologer predicted that Richard and Elizabeth would marry this year and find happiness since he was a Scorpio and his Sun was in conjunction with Miss Taylor's Moon.

April 7. Burton flew to Paris to shoot a scene in *The Longest Day*. He was mobbed by pressmen. Sybil met him, and they dined at Maxim's with Zanuck and Donald Houston. Asked what he was going to do next, he said with mock seriousness, "I think I may kill myself."

April 8. Burton flew back to Rome, Sybil to London. He now flatly denied stories of a romance with Liz.

April 9. Sybil took four-year-old Kate to the London Palladium pantomime and reportedly said, "Liz Taylor? I adore her. She's an old friend of mine."

April 13. Using separate cars, Liz and Richard went nightclubbing in Rome. She said she had no plans to rush into another marriage and was in no hurry to get a divorce. When the film was finished, she would go home to Gstaad for a long rest with the children. Burton talked about his hopes of being clear at the weekend to fly to London to see Sybil. "She says she is not going to Rome because everyone is telling her that is the thing she really ought to do. She is stubborn and so am I. Sybil says, 'Damn it, why should I do what everyone says I ought to do?' " Told that there were many critics, including the Vatican newspaper, of her conduct as a mother, Liz asked, "Could I sue the Vatican?" And Mankiewicz discussed a new silly rumor: "Some people are saying that secretly I am in love with Elizabeth, but I don't see where I get the time. I'm directing the picture all day and writing all night."

April 16. We learned that Liz and Richard had spent a quiet weekend at a small fishing village ninety miles north of Rome.

April 22. With three days free from filming, they spent Easter in the seaside resort of Porto Santo Stefano. It ended with Liz going into the hospital. The trouble: a bruised and bleeding nose caused when her chauffeur suddenly braked and she struck her head against the front seat of her car. Italian newspapers reported that the holiday had ended in a row.

April 23. Sybil arrived in Rome and friends discovered that she was greatly distressed by a situation she recognized as much more than mere rumor.

April 26. Signor Egido Ariosto, Undersecretary of the Ministry of the Interior, said: "Miss Taylor, with her amorous and nonamorous conduct, which, unfortunately, morbidly interests newspapers and magazines, perhaps without her wishing to do so, defies Italian public opinion. But I have the impression that Miss Taylor is exceeding the limits and, in fact, risks destroying herself."

April 27. Sybil and Richard arrived at the Rome airport to meet daughter Kate flying in from London. Then they drove off in separate cars.

April 29. The Burtons were seen in town with daughter Kate. Later Kate was pictured in a playground with four-year-old Liza Todd Fisher.

May 3. Elizabeth's parents, Mr. and Mrs. Francis Taylor, arrived.

May 4. Burton's former Italian housekeeper began telling sensational stories about his romance with Liz in a weekly magazine. Burton later talked about a smear campaign and the possibility of legal action.

May 22. Georgian Congresswoman Iris Blitch said the U.S. Attorney General should "take measures to determine whether or not Miss Taylor and Mr. Burton are ineligible for reentry into the United States on the grounds of undesirability."

June 13. For three weeks, the 400-strong *Cleopatra* team now took over the island of Ischia, neighbor of Capri, moving in with a giant barge of plastic gold, war galleys, and Egyptian reedboats ready to film the huge spectacle of the Battle of Actium. With temperatures soaring into the eighties, Liz spent many of her off-duty hours lounging in a bikini. Richard would join her in sunbathing on the deck of a private yacht anchored far offshore, but even there the long lenses of the *paparazzi* spied on them as they courted.

July 11. They attended the Two Worlds' Festival in Spoleto for an evening of light opera. Soon after, Burton left for Egypt for some final scenes, while Liz spent a week with her four children at Gstaad, Switzerland.

July 28. At last, the final shot of *Cleopatra* in Rome. The fabulous Roman sets in Cinecittà were dismantled; Fox's famous

School for Scandal was breaking up forever. After ten mad months of work and play, Mr. Burton and Mrs. Fisher had packed their bags and gone their separate ways.

Here came a natural break in the continuing saga of the fatally attracted filmstars, and for the next four months their day to day adventures were given a long overdue rest. In September, Elizabeth joined Rex Harrison and Rachel Roberts at Santa Margherita on the Italian Riviera, and Richard was staying with his own family in Switzerland. Supreme optimists now saw a distinct chance that *la grande affaire de coeur* might die a natural death, and this might have been just conceivably possible if their work had kept them continents apart. However, they were not even separated by frontiers. The Burtons had their villa on the west side of Lake Geneva; Elizabeth now returned to hers on the eastern side, an hour's drive away by fast car. It was too convenient.

Public opinion—fashioned on reported facts, but denied firsthand knowledge of the personalities involved—tended to condemn Richard and Elizabeth as two overindulgent hedonists. Yet they were not insensitive to the pain they were causing others, and their relationship was not easily renewed after leaving Rome. Moreover, it was unreasonable throughout the *Cleopatra* scandal that Elizabeth had been the principal target of public approbrium. Not for the first time was she portrayed as the bewitching *femme fatale,* the voluptuous seductress, the queen of marriage-wreckers, and the underlying implication was that it was natural enough for such a virile man as Burton to fall for the irresistible charms of the woman once described (by her then husband Michael Wilding) as "a seething mass of feminine wiles." But this was absurd. The shrewd and worldly Welshman had become involved with his eyes wide open—fully conscious of the perils of the situation, fully aware of Elizabeth's faults as a temperamental, wildly extravagant romantic who had been pampered since babyhood. It changed nothing. He loved the complete woman—for him the perfect cocktail of beauty and fire, of tenderness and passion. In fact it was Elizabeth, toward the end of filming *Cleopatra*, who wrote to Richard saying that they were making too many people unhappy and should separate. But separation only confirmed their feelings for one another. She had her children with her at Gstaad, and her parents were living nearby; still she felt desperately lonely. Meanwhile, across the lake, Richard soon found life too quiet and conventional after the agony and ecstasy of living in Rome. He missed Elizabeth more than he had dreamed possible; he missed the electrifying atmosphere they generated whenever they were together. And finally it was he who telephoned and arranged to meet her at the Château de Chillon on Lake Geneva.

It was a strange reunion. There was no audience now, no *paparazzi* in the trees, no film publicists fussing in the background. For the first time they were simply meeting as two people in love. Richard drove himself eastwards to the Château. Liz came from the opposite direction, driven by her parents. Once they were left alone together, they both felt strangely ill at ease; even Richard the great talker was tongue-tied. There were long awkward silences before they began to unwind. They had lunch together; then he drove her home. The gulf had been breached; thereafter they knew they had to see one another again. Several more times they met for lunch and, late in October, *Cleopatra* brought them together for a longer time as both were called to Paris to help Mankiewicz with some dubbing on the soundtrack. In Paris they learned that Darryl Zanuck, the new working president of Fox, and the company's largest single stockholder, had decided to end "The Mank's" association with the picture and would take over the editing himself. Liz and Richard sent protest cables, but in vain. Mr. Zanuck issued a firm statement: "In exchange for top compensation and a considerable expense account, Joseph Mankiewicz has for two years spent his time, talent, and $35,000,000 of 20th Century-Fox's stockholders' money to direct and complete the first cut of the film *Cleopatra*. He has earned a well-deserved rest." Later Zanuck and Mankiewicz reached a better understanding and left for Spain to do over some battle sequences. Richard and Elizabeth were not needed. They were free from *Cleopatra*'s clutches at last.

There the great love affair might have ended, but they did not choose it to end. In Paris, Anatole de Grunwald, producer of

Burton's first two films, lined him up for the role of an oil tycoon in his film *The V.I.P.s* If she wanted it, there was a suitable role for Miss Taylor as the tycoon's wife who is planning to run off with a gigolo. Elizabeth accepted, and so *le scandale,* as Richard called it, went on. The film was different, the location was different, but the delicate situation remained unchanged. Now they could never return to their positions before *Cleopatra.* The epic had not merely brought them together; it had bonded them together as two campaigners, who side by side had survived a thousand skirmishes. The emotion-charged experiences in Rome had been sometimes exhilarating for them, more often nightmarish, but those experiences were theirs alone, exclusively shared in the face of almost overwhelming opposition. They were isolated by public opinion, just as Elizabeth and Eddie had been in 1958.

The V.I.P.s

On the cold, foggy morning of December 6, 1962, stormy scenes welcomed the arrival at London's Victoria Station of the night ferry express from Paris. Crowds jostled for vantage points around the customs entrance. Strong-arm men roughly forced back a battery of photographers. For the first time in more than two years Burton was back in Britain. He had left quietly and without a care in the world, as the Crown Prince of the Old Vic and the future king of *Camelot.* Now he was returning with his life in emotional confusion and turmoil, and at his side, in a black coat with white fur collar and matching fur hat, was his Dark Lady of the Sonnets, her beauty strikingly luminous against the contrasting gray backcloth of British Rail. Having dutifully worn smiles for the flashbulbs, the two superstars departed in separate cars—she in a blue Mark 10 Jaguar, he in a blue station wagon. But their destinations were the same: the Dorchester Hotel where, whatever evil tongues might say, they occupied separate suites. In the months ahead they were to appear as man and wife in *The V.I.P.s*, Terence Rattigan's elaborate story of assorted celebrities marooned by fog in the VIP lounge of London Airport. In real life they were to enact more nebulous roles in a seemingly interminable romantic drama. The world had cast them as lovers; yet neither was free to play the part with natural abandon. They were, as Richard expressed it, in a period of "suspended animation."

While filming was delayed by technical difficulties, Richard passed the days by introducing Elizabeth to his friends and his old haunts, the pubs and the rugby grounds. At Twickenham, on the day of the Oxford–Cambridge University match, he boldly escorted the dazzling Liz into the male holy of holies, the exclusive International Bar, where for once the presence of a woman was not discouraged. They drank best bitter, joined in a lusty song about O'Reilly's daughter, and automatically attracted a great crowd of ex-internationals. Four days later they were at another rugger match—Aberavon versus London Welsh at Old Deer Park—and again they joined in the ritual afterwards. Richard, who had played for both clubs in his brief life as a wild wing-forward, seemed to be in his element, and he and Liz seemed wonderfully spirited and gay, utterly at ease together. But then, the other side of Richard's life was not paraded in quite the same way.

Christmas, essentially a family time, was drawing near, and Sybil and the children were about to return from Switzerland to stay in Hampstead. Soon Richard would be leaving Liz at the Dorchester several times each week to visit them; he romped with the children, took Sybil out to dinner and the theater. No cameraman captured these discreet outings, and in this sense he had not changed at all. He still belonged to two worlds—the private, cozy world of the family man, and the entirely public, hedonistic world of the showman. The only difference was that for the first time he shared the latter world with a constant companion. In this way, Sybil and Elizabeth were virtually worlds apart. He loved them both in their different ways, and yet he could not lead such a double life indefinitely. In time, he would be compelled to devote his affection to one woman—not merely because social convention demanded it, but more because he could not love one without hurting the other.

In the confusion of his divided emotions and troubled conscience he began drinking so heavily that there were fears that he might become an alcoholic. The criticism of the world he could take, but not the bitter disapproval of his brother Ivor and the rest of the family in Wales. Graham, who was the first to make his peace with Richard, recalls a night in the Dorchester when the three of them were invited out to dinner. "But Richard was missing. I didn't know what the hell had happened to him. Elizabeth, as usual, had taken ages to get ready, and when she finally prepared to leave, Richard turned up as pissed as a newt. He had obviously had a bloody great barney with Ivor and he wouldn't come out with us. He was so upset that he was rude to Elizabeth, and I had to take her to the dinner on my own. At that time Ivor was in Hampstead with the children, and Richard worried more about his opinion than all the rest of the family put together. In fact, at the beginning of *The V.I.P.s* I stood in as Richard's double for a week so that he could go down to Wales and sort things out with relations. But all through that film it was a trying time. Ivor was really forceful and sort of inferred that it was either Elizabeth or him." Or in other words, Elizabeth or Sybil.

Brook Williams, who remained strictly neutral, even though he later offered to marry Sybil, says: "I felt sorry for both of them. But I didn't take any side. I felt too many people took sides. Everybody, it seemed, had to be on one side or the other, and I thought it was none of our business and presumptious for anyone except the immediate family to take sides." For the most part, the Jenkins family took the attitude that the way Richard conducted his life was his own affair. At the same time, they were too deeply attached to Sybil to open their hearts automatically to a rival woman, and at first they viewed Elizabeth with deep suspicion and resentment. Once they met her, however, their feelings began to change. Graham went along fully prepared to dislike her and came away completely captivated by her. It was her simplic- ity, her natural sense of humor and earthiness that surprised him; she had none of the airs and aloofness he had expected. And it was not just the Jenkins men who were won over by her charms. Hilda recalls the first occasion Richard took Elizabeth to meet the family in the little house in Penhydd Street, Pontrhydyfen. "Richard rang me and said, 'Don't prepare anything because we can't be sure when we'll arrive,' and so I thought I'd better not say a word about it and let him come when he comes. But I had reporters here from morning to night, and when they came they brought two cars—the Mini Cooper and the Rolls Royce driven by the chauffeur. And, of course, that drew the crowds straight away. It was impossible. If Richard comes alone, it's all right. I just tell people to leave him alone. But with Elizabeth coming, you couldn't do that. It was her first time here and she really en- joyed it. Oh, she was great. My first impression was, well, all right; and then I got to know her and she was very nice. She en- joyed a meal with us, our way—you know, good plain homecook- ing because Richard doesn't like a lot of fuss—and I had some gooseberry tart and cream, and she said it was fabulous."

Never for a moment, however, was it easy for Richard and Elizabeth to make peace with the Welsh clan, and as Elizabeth has expressed it, they were put through such an ordeal that if their love had not been valid it would have "disintegrated and turned into anything from disgust to shame." What did happen during these crucial months of their "Dorchester Period" was that Rich- ard's attraction toward Elizabeth became stronger and more meaningful. Previously the showman in him had thrived on the excitement generated by having her constantly at his side, but now he admired her all the more for the surprising ease with which she fitted into his own rough way of life, mixing with his riotous friends in the pubs, standing on a windswept touchline to watch rugby, and breaking through the icy resistance of his sterner Welsh relations.

Without Elizabeth, however, Richard made one trip back to Wales that ended unhappily. On a Saturday night in mid-Janu- ary, he was returning from the England–Wales match at Cardiff

Arms Park when a gang of youths fell upon him outside Paddington Station, and he emerged from the fracas with an enormous
black eye. Richard explained, "I got out of the train and searched
for a taxi. The snow was crisp and even and there wasn't a thing
in sight. I started muttering about this marvelous taxi service London had. I found myself talking to ordinary passersby—and surrounded by half a dozen little boys or what these days they call
Teddy Boys. Suddenly somebody started lunging out. Then a
really small boy got me on the ground. And there you're helpless.
They just kicked me all over. One of them put his boot in my
eye—luckily, it wasn't a winklepicker." Next day, when photographed with Liz, he looked a dead ringer for General Dayan.

Life was emotionally uncomfortable for Richard and Liz during their "Dorchester Period," but it was certainly never dull. In
March, as stand-ins for Princess Margaret and Lord Snowdon at
the Paris charity film premiere of *Lawrence of Arabia*, they were
a regal couple dancing till dawn in Dior dress and tiara and white
tie and tails. A week later they were making headlines less ele-
gantly at London Airport where Richard became angry at having
to film with Elizabeth before a crowd of onlookers and photographers. He cursed so ripely that women blushed and retreated out
of earshot, and a policeman warned him to watch his language because one lady had complained. It made him madder still. "It's a
pity you people don't run the airport correctly and keep these
crowds away." Scarcely a day went by without Richard and Elizabeth being in the news, and the outcome was not hard to predict.
On April 2, there at last came formal recognition of a situation
that had seemed apparent for eighteen months. Sybil arrived in
New York with her two children and a nurse, and her American
lawyer Aaron Frosch announced that the Burtons had agreed to a
legal separation. A divorce had not been considered or discussed,
but all financial arrangements for a separation had been concluded.

Sybil's decision to move to New York was not a carefully calculated one; rather it emerged suddenly as being the only clear
avenue ahead in a muddled, marital maze. She had still not abandoned all hope of a reconciliation, but she did feel a desperate

need to escape for a while from familiar faces and surroundings in London. She was never to regret the move. It was a good time to be in New York—spring, when the city with the best and worst of everything has recovered from the harshness of winter and has not yet moved into the oppressive heat of midsummer. There was so much to keep her mind occupied. Sightseeing with the children, setting up a new home, going to nightclubs. The Royal Ballet was in town, and she loved the ballet even more than the theater, and soon she was involved in a social whirl far gayer than anything she had known in London. No longer living in the shadow of a famous husband, she eventually experienced a new kind of freedom. She was never left alone for long periods because she had close old friends around her, like Philip Burton and Roddy McDowall, and new ones like Jeremy Geidt of *The Establishment* satirical group at The Strollers nightclub. You can chew over a dilemma for so long. Finally there comes a point when it is suddenly a colossal bore and pales into minor significance. After some uneasy months in New York, Sybil arrived at that point, where she became too immersed in the present to dwell on the past. And so now did brother Ivor, who finally accepted Elizabeth as part of Richard's future.

The breakup of the Burtons' marriage had divided their friends into three distinct groups—those who were close to Richard, those who sided with Sybil, and those who remained neutral. But almost everyone, whatever their viewpoint, shared one same reaction—astonishment that the separation should have occurred. Stanley Baker says: "To this day—and I don't give a damn what Richard says—it is extraordinary that their marriage ever broke up. In this superficial world that we live in, there is so much nonsense talked, so much pretense, and yet here was one girl who had none of that. She was a genuine person with great humor, wit, intelligence, and warmth. An attractive woman, a very sexy woman. It seemed that they were a perfect bloody match, a perfect foil for each other. Love? I don't know anything about that; it's a purely personal thing. But Elizabeth and Sybil are so diametrically opposed. And by this time, let's face it, Richard knew a lot about life in this business and must have realized how superficial it is, how long certain things can last, and what your values are. Yes, it is extraordinary that that marriage broke up, and it shows how wrong you can be about people. I just thought—and it appeared not only to me, but to everybody—that Richard and Sybil were two peas in a pod, dead right for each other. They had great warmth and they were wonderful company. They used to sing together, and they were like one, they really were. I remember going out to Italy and talking to Richard and putting my head on the chopping block. He said at the time, 'Nothing will change the way I feel about Sybil. Nothing will break our marriage.' And hell, a week later they were split up. So something drastic must have happened—in a week, in a day, in an hour maybe."

Graham Jenkins has expressed the belief, that if it were allowed, Richard's solution would have been to have two wives— Sybil and Elizabeth. And some of Richard's friends share that view. "I think it's absolutely right that he would have loved to have been married to both of them," says Robert Hardy. "Like a nubile emperor. But such is the nature of woman that you can't really do that. It's the hardest thing in the world to keep a mistress whom you love and to be married. I don't believe it's ever going to change—such is woman's need and determination to keep monogamous. Anyway, I'm sure Richard would never go through all that again because it's a very, very tough thing if you're worried about the other person. If the marriage breaks up both ways, then it's different; also if you're in that state where the wives come and go and everybody understands, tra-la-la, tra-la-la. But this was certainly not true of Richard. He was in this vast position where his every move was examined, and yet he behaved, I believe, in exactly the same way he would have behaved if nobody had known about it. The same thing would have happened. He loved Elizabeth; he also loved Sybil."

One person put in an especially awkward position by the breakup was Philip Burton. He was deeply fond of both Richard and Sybil, but now circumstances forced him to be closer to Sybil. He fully sympathized with her, and as a New York resident he could give her much-needed practical help when she came with the children to settle in Manhattan. Unhappily, the

Cleopatra scandal had occurred at a time when he had troubles of his own. In November, 1961, he had brought to London a play which, through no fault of his own, was an unmitigated disaster. The play, *A Wreath for Udomo*, with sets designed by Julie Andrews' husband, Tony Walton, and a mainly African cast, opened at The Lyric, Hammersmith, where Richard had scored his early stage successes. Five minutes before curtain-up, a leading actor was taken ill, and with all the leading critics out front, the opening was delayed for a quarter of an hour. Then the sick player slurred and stumbled through the first act and collapsed on stage during the second. When the curtain came down he was lying half outside and was dragged back by his legs, and Phil Burton had to face the unenviable task of going out front to announce that the show was abandoned. Back in New York, he was directing another play when he himself became ill. A canker appeared on his tongue and for a time there were grave fears of cancer. It proved a false alarm and penicillin worked a cure. Since then Mr. Burton had concentrated on his new role as director of an acting school.

Meanwhile, in London, filming of *The V.I.P.s* was completed, and producer Anatole de Grunwald could breathe an enormous sigh of relief. He had made the picture without sickness insurance for the actress whose illness during *Cleopatra* had resulted in Fox making claims for millions of dollars against the underwriters, and all that Liz had suffered during filming was slight knee trouble that took her very briefly to the London Clinic. Now de Grunwald praised her for never being late and for working with "marvelous professionalism." His picture, with a star-studded cast including Orson Welles, Rod Taylor, Margaret Rutherford, Maggie Smith, and Louis Jordan, had been made at just a tenth of the cost of *Cleopatra*, and for a while it was destined to do even bigger business at the box office than the sumptuous Roman epic.

It was said that the *Cleopatra* affair had been seriously damaging to the reputations of Burton and Taylor and that it had discouraged film companies from seeking their services. Yet they had scarcely suffered financial harm. She had set her million-dollar precedent, and she maintained that fee for her less demanding role in *The V.I.P.s.* Richard, for the first time, was now paid half a million dollars for a picture, thus quadrupling his pre-*Cleopatra* figure of $125,000. As Wanger had remarked during the filming in Rome: "When he came to this picture some months ago he was a well-known star but not famous; his salary was good, but not huge. Suddenly his name has become a household word."

Yet the impression persisted that Burton was somehow plunging lemming-like toward disaster. *Time* magazine now awarded him their cover-page accolade and recalled the words of Mankiewicz: "Show a Welshman one thousand exits, one of which is marked 'Self-Destruction,' and he will go right through that door." According to *Time*, Richard was "chained in taffeta" at the Dorchester.

> The outcome of the Taylor–Burton game must inevitably yield up a loser. If he should ever marry her, he will be the Oxford boy who became the fifth husband of the Wife of Bath. If she loses him, she loses her reputation as a fatal beauty, an all-consuming man-eater, the Cleopatra of the twentieth century.
>
> With or without company, Elizabeth tries to stay close by him twenty-five hours a day, filling poor Richard's almanac with some dull stretches of prose as well as short bursts of poetry. . . . In his less insouciant moments, he tears himself to pieces, maddened with guilt. "Anonymous," he says is the word that describes him, for he has given up everything that truly matters to him. Borrowing Keats' epitaph, he says, again and again, "My name is writ in water." Now that Sybil has gone to New York, he sits quandried in London. Does he want to be the richest actor in the world, the most famous actor in the world, or the best actor in the world—and in what order? Or just a household word?

That Burton was already a household word was clearly demonstrated by the unusual advertising for *Cleopatra*. The New York posters merely presented a giant painting of Elizabeth and Richard in their classical costumes, and the name of the Rivoli Theater. There was no need to name the film or its stars; their universally recognized faces told it all. Eventually the posters had to be changed because Rex Harrison, who dominated the first half of the epic, demanded his right to equal billing. But the fact remained that *le scandale* had provided the main pillar of publicity for *Cleopatra*. Darryl Zanuck, president of Fox, said, "I think the Taylor–Burton association is quite constructive for our organization." And it was certainly constructive for its stars. It was now estimated that if the film simply broke even, Elizabeth would earn at least $7 million—$1,725,000 in salary, plus ten percent of most of the gross; more than double the record $3 million William Holden had picked up from *The Bridge on the River Kwai*, and the largest sum ever paid to an employee for any single project. Richard's pay was a comparative peanut-packet of a quarter of a million dollars. But there were other benefits. As *Time* magazine summed it up: "In the short space of a year or so, his name has become about as well-known as a name can be. Everyone, in short, knows who Richard Burton is, or at least what he is at the moment. He is the demi-Atlas of this earth, the arm and burgonet of men, the fellow who is living with Elizabeth Taylor. Stevedores admire him. Movie idols envy him. He is a kind of folk hero out of nowhere, with an odd name like Richard instead of Tab, Rock, or Rip, who has out-tabbed, outrocked, and outstripped the lot of them. He is the new Mr. Box Office."

Nevertheless, it was too soon to hail Burton's arrival among the superstars. He would not be the most sought-after of actors if the $37 million *Cleopatra* spelled ruin for Fox, as the prophets of doom were loudly predicting. The film, three years in the making, was at last unveiled in June at a four-hour premiere in New York, and the reviews were confusingly mixed. Judith Crist (New York *Herald-Tribune*) reported: "*Cleopatra* is at best a major disappointment, at worst an extravagant exercise in tedium. All is monumental, but the people are not. The Mountain of Notoriety has produced a mouse." Bosley Crowther (*The New York Times*) judged it to be "a surpassing entertainment, one of the great film epics of our day . . . a generally brilliant and satisfying film." Generally, the critics raved about the performance of Harrison and were reasonably impressed with Burton. The acid was reserved for Miss Taylor. Derogatory remarks were made about her voice and looks; one critic thought she often spoke like a fishwife. That morning, after reading some of the worst reviews she had ever received, Elizabeth turned up late for her London pub lunch with Richard. She picked at her food and was silent, and there were tears in her eyes. Richard gently took her hand and argued that the critics had completely missed the point: that this Cleopatra was intended to be a great female politician, not just a great lover girl.

Back at the Dorchester, the reporters were waiting for him. "What do you think of the reviews then, Richard? Sent you up a bit, didn't they? How about Liz? How's she taking it? What you got to say, Dickie? Rex Harrison did all right then." Richard shouldered his way through the crowd in Park Lane and gave one farewell quote: "Rex Harrison is a good actor. I'm pleased for him. It was a great role. He couldn't do wrong in the part; even a haberdasher could play it." Next morning, in America, it was reported, "Richard Burton says Rex Harrison played Caesar like a haberdasher."

When we met Richard for lunch next day, he said, "Isn't that typical. Look, do us a favor, will you? You know what Liz and I really think about Rex. So just for the record, you know, if you could squeeze it in somewhere that Liz and myself think Rex was brilliant. He's an extraordinary craftsman. Great style. There's no sour grapes. I'm just trying to protect Liz. She's got kicked in the teeth by one or two critics. It hurts. I understand it in a way. After all those years and all that money, and all that ballyhoo— the biggest, the greatest, et cetera, et cetera—it's all too human for people to say, 'Right, let's see if they were worth it.' They come with rocks in their hands and there's a big temptation to let fly. *The New York Times* called them 'sceptics predisposed to give *Cleopatra* the needle.' I go along with that. And I go along with their critic who says her portrayal of Cleo is one of force and dignity with all the impressive arrogance and pride of an ancient queen. Of course, I'm protective towards Elizabeth. I love her. And she's a great actress."

A few weeks later *Cleopatra* arrived in London. It had been pruned by twenty-two minutes, but still some critics found it a grueling experience to sit through. And so did Elizabeth, who thought they had cut out her best bits. She had been trapped into seeing it by the Foreign Office, who had asked her to be the hostess to the Bolshoi Ballet. "Afterwards," she said, "I raced back to the Dorchester and just made it to the downstairs lavatory and vomited." At this point, despite huge advance bookings, it remained highly uncertain whether Fox would recover the tens of millions invested in the film. (In fact, the epic would begin making a profit within three years of its release, so preserving Elizabeth's proud claim that she had never starred in a film that lost money.) Meanwhile, Richard the Protector went on talking through dozens of interviews about Elizabeth's great qualities as an actress and as a woman. She was, he said, the best actress he had ever worked with—excepting, of course, Dame Edith Evans —and Liz, in turn, sang his praises to complete a mutual admiration double-act that received extraordinary publicity. Burton recalled: "I think it was Bernard Shaw who talked about the danger of the private or public life of an actor becoming more compelling to him than his work. Then, said Shaw, an artist begins to die a little. That stage has not and never will be reached." By the early summer of 1963, however, he seemed to have come perilously near to the brink. "I have achieved a sort of diabolical fame," he told Peter Evans of the London *Daily Express* in a rare moment of searching self-analysis. "It has nothing to do with my reputation as an actor. That counts for little now. I am the diabolically famous Richard Burton. . . . Happiness? What is that? I have no idea what mythical happiness might be. Contentment? I don't think it is possible for me ever to be content. I am neurotic. Actors are, and people. My father now. A miner. You wouldn't think miners were neurotic—slashing away at that coal face, smashing out their anger and passions and fury. My father was shaking with neurosis. . . . You know what I want most out of life? I'll tell you. Within the tiny confines of my own career to give a great performance. Just once."

Burton's attitude to acting hadn't really changed; the size of the check was still his standard measurement of success. At the same time, his ego as an actor had been seriously undernourished during the long period of marital hiatus. He was rather tired of seeing his work submerged beneath publicity devoted to his private life, and he was especially sick of talk about his "selling out" to Hollywood—"What do they mean? Didn't Olivier humble himself in *Spartacus*? And would they accuse Elizabeth of selling out if she turned from films to the stage?" Professionally, as well as emotionally, it was an uneasy time for him. While he hungered for a solid, worthwhile film role in which to flex his dramatic muscles, there was an unnerving lull in the market as producers cautiously waited to see whether *Cleopatra* would stand or fall. In these circumstances, he was extremely fortunate to receive one outstanding offer, and one that was not merely bait to capture Elizabeth as well. Producer Hal Wallis wanted him for his film of Jean Anouilh's *Becket*. The money was modest on Richard's standards, but for once he had the sense to recognize the dramatic possibilities of such a picture, and not least he was impressed by the distinguished company that Wallis had assembled—Peter O'Toole, Gielgud, Martita Hunt, Sir Donald Wolfit, and Pamela Brown. Here was no *Ice Palace* or *Bramble Bush* to tackle with adequate but uninspired effort. This one would demand a performance of the highest quality if he were not to be overshadowed on the screen.

When he studied *Becket*, he automatically concluded that King Henry II, a bawdy, lusty playboy monarch in Anouilh's freely irreverent version of history, was the role for him. But Liz thought otherwise. "Becket's the part for you," she said positively.

"What!" Richard exclaimed. "After all the scandal you want me to play a saint? Are you crazy?"

"No," said Elizabeth. "But you'd be crazy to play the king. It's the kind of part you're always playing. It's too obvious." And in time he realized she was absolutely right.

Richard confessed that in approaching *Becket* he was making a determined effort to be a genuinely good film actor for only about the fourth time in a career of nineteen movies. So far he regarded *Look Back in Anger* as his only worthwhile film achievement and now, significantly, he was excited by another film project based on a stage play. It was not just the quality of the script and the strength of the cast that fired his ambition. Above all, his serious approach was inspired by Elizabeth. Later, when she achieved new heights in dramatic screen roles, people would remark on how much Richard had improved her as an actress. But Elizabeth had infinitely more film experience than Richard, and in reality, her influence upon his acting was more immediate and no less beneficial. She was responsible for his awakening as a film star. She opened his eyes to subtleties of technique that had previously escaped him; she taught him to exploit his natural stillness more fully before the cameras; she encouraged him to achieve more dramatic effect by pitching his resonant voice more softly. Her greatest contribution, however, was in persuading him to regard moviemaking with the kind of respect he accorded a Shakespearean stage production. Previously, says Richard, it was largely his disrespect for filming as a craft, and a certain arrogance to the whole business that blinded him to many of the subtleties of which Liz made him more aware. Now he openly acknowledged that perhaps he had something to learn from the great filmstars, even those without experience in the tougher school of the stage.

In *Becket*, more than any film before, Burton was working with talents who commanded his deepest respect. Most notably, there was Gielgud, as the King of France. Then there was Peter Glenville, a brilliant actor-turned-director, who had staged Olivier's *Becket* most successfully on Broadway; the same Glenville who had sacked the unknown Burton from a London play some fifteen years before, which was another incentive for Richard to stretch himself to full stature. Third and not least, he was influenced by the presence of a 6 ft. 2 in., part-Irish beanpole called Peter O'Toole. Burton has stressed how the caliber of his acting can be influenced by the inspiration of others around him, and how he must be working opposite players he respects if he is to approach his best. In *Becket* it was therefore essential that he should have a keen rapport with the actor playing King Henry, so interdependent are the two roles, and in this sense the choice of O'Toole could not have been more propitious. Contrasting in physique but finely attuned in mind, Burton and O'Toole were perfect foils for each other—the greatest of friends, yet both gustily trying to act the other off the screen and so spurring the other towards peak performance. For three joyful months in the summer of 1963, life at Shepperton was enlivened and enriched by the rollicking *camaraderie* of the hard-drinking Welshman and the equally hard-drinking son of an Irish bookmaker; two sons of Bacchus who set sparks flying as they dueled with wit and words on the film set and reveled in each other's company at the local hostelry.

The Night of the Long Sausages

When Richard and Elizabeth were starring in *The V.I.P.s* at Elstree, they worked on a closed set. No press was allowed. They were in England and the trees were empty of *paparazzi*. Even the Italian and French photographers, as conspicuous as CIA men with their trench coats bulging with cameras and wearing dark glasses and Brillo-pad hairdos, got negative results as they exhausted their expense accounts and their welcome in the Dorchester cocktail bar and Curzon Street nightspots. The two filmstars were living in uneasy and isolated splendor. A young actor, sometime nightclub comic, and probably the most chitchat Englishman since Samuel Pepys, got a part in the film as a newspaper reporter, and he told the real reporters that they could ask as many questions as they liked about Burton and Taylor, provided that they did not quote him. And then, to every question, crew-cut David Frost answered "No comment." It was not until Richard started shooting *Becket* that the star-crossed lovers descended from their lonely pedestal to find a sanctuary for togetherness and gaiety in an ancient inn set in a village square that seemed to be populated with chapters of characters who somehow had escaped the pens of P. G. Wodehouse and J. P. Donleavy.

Seamus Peter Patrick O'Toole, the Connemara-conceived Yorkshireman who knew every pub in England where the licensing laws had never taken on, introduced Richard to the Shepperton village square, with its church of St. Nicholas bounded on either side by a pub and with five drinking establishments within a pickled onion's throw of one another. The problem was to choose the one in which to eat and drink during lunch hours when Elizabeth was visiting the set. There was The Hovel, jolly amusing for some, but frighteningly eccentric for others, with most things inside at an odd slant, including the landlord Len who displayed his appendix in a bottle on the bar along with a shrunken head and a pickled penis of uncertain age and origin. Richard thought it too gruesome for Elizabeth's tastes, and anyway he didn't care much for Len's sense of humor, which included having a loudspeaker hooked up to the ladies' lavatory and a wind machine that blew up customers' skirts. Moreover, the menu which featured "a chicken feed—sixpence" as the dish of the day didn't exactly please him, since it turned out to be a handful of corn thrown on a plate. One point to commend The Hovel was the fact that Len, who had burned his television set on the Guy Fawkes bonfire in 1953, had not the faintest notion who Burton and O'Toole might be. But this was not enough. As for the pub next door, the Red Lion, it was too small, and the owner didn't care to have filmstars interrupting the lunchtime darts match with orders of food. The Anchor Hotel was judged too large and too formal, and the Warren Lodge never came to life until evening.

But pubmaster O'Toole knew the perfect place—the King's Head, where Archie the landlord greeted Richard with the immortal line: "Now is the winter of our discontent made glorious summer by this leg of pork." The pork indeed was glorious, and

as succulent as other dishes long lost to English menus and prepared by Archie's wife Ruth, a gorgeous Edwardian lady with
breasts like feather pillows and a heart as warm as her delicious
treacle tarts. Richard called Ruth "Mummy," and she gave him
exactly what he fancied most—tripe-and-onions. And Archie, in
Billy Bunter check trousers and colored waistcoat, with face
aflame with brandy and whiskers, called Richard "Master"—"I
say, master," he boomed, "if you want a pint and some sausages,
come any evening. You can meet everyone and then they'll never
bother you again." And Richard, delighted with Archie's jolly
roar and sensing the warm protectiveness of Ruth, agreed to
make an entrance that evening—"with a certain little girl I'd like
you to meet."

It was a day of extraordinary happenings in Shepperton
Square. Raymond Ray, a retired actor who wore a monocle,
blazer, shabby yachting cap, and tatty tennis shoes, and who had
an undying passion for *chemin de fer*, tidied up the tea-stained
cabin of his waterlogged little cruiser on the Thames—"In case,
dear boy, Rich and Liz fancy a game." A village character of ancient vintage, he smoked Player's Perfectos in a long cigarette
holder and was well-known as the erstwhile journalist who once
stole one of Lord Beaverbrook's secretaries, along with a motorbike, and put her into an interesting condition on Beachy Head.
Now his newest and most extravagant ambition was to organize
what he called in *Guys and Dolls* parlance "the biggest floatin'
crap game in the world"; and if his boat wasn't big enough, he
thought he might invite the superstars back to the house of Olive
Oil, a local housewife so named because her husband John, who
had won £8,000 on the football pools, bore a certain resemblance
to Popeye. "I say, Archie," said Ray, "I feel Rich and Liz would
enjoy a game of chemmy, don't you? I'll bring along my shoe."
But Archie wanted no suggestions. As the hour of arrival drew
near he paced the area around his engraved "landlord's stool" like
Laughton on the *Bounty*. Strangers got short shrift. "Bog off,
master. This is a private do for Mr. Burton and a certain little
gal."

A town crier running naked through the village shouting

"Oyez, Oyez" couldn't have gathered a bigger crowd into the low-timbered bar of the King's Head. Pegleg, the local rag-and-bone merchant, who wore a belt containing all the regimental cap badges of Britain round his belly, sank his eighteenth pint and said, "Ar-r-r! I like a nice piece of crackling." And Britannia, a mighty local lady with a bum like a cane chair, sighed as Pegleg grabbed her where she wanted it to hurt. "Oh! What a lovely day. Isn't it all too, too romantic." And two well-known local homosexuals, who spent all day long happily exploring each other in the certain knowledge that they would never find a lady, went off hand in hand to dress up in Indian squawlike gear to impress Richard and Elizabeth.

It was June and hot, and the square was crowded with children at play while their fathers, still wearing bowler hats from the city, were hustled grumbling into the King's Head by wives who wore cocktail dresses after spending the afternoon in curlers and telephoning each other with "Guess who's coming for sausages at Archie's." And to add to the excitement and general sartorial confusion, the local horsey crowd had been celebrating Ladies' Day at nearby Ascot racecourse and were pinned against the walls of the bar like butterflies in their picture hats and gray toppers. No way-out film director could have dreamed up such a scene. It was like the guests of *Quiet Wedding* overflowing into the party of *Breakfast at Tiffany's*, and most everyone was merry with drink when Ray, standing on lookout, threw up a naval salute as Richard and Elizabeth rolled up in a Rolls. Archie, watchchain glistening like a mayor's badge of office and his muttonchop whiskers dewdropped in brandy, waited to welcome the V.I.P.s. But there was slight confusion. Elizabeth couldn't get through the door. Maybe it was because it was Ascot Week, or more probably because she had come direct from the airport after shopping in Paris, but she was wearing an enormous hat that just wouldn't fit sideways or longways through the body-jammed doorway. Richard, always cool, suggested she leave it with one of the small boys outside—"He could always fly it as a kite, love." But instead she bent it a little, and Archie, a mountain of muscle and beef who could cradle a beer barrel like a baby in his barn-

door arms, efficiently cleared the entrance by hauling aside the sa-
luting Ray and sweeping down with the other arm as he bowed
deeply to the queen of celluloid. If there had been a puddle of
beer on the floor, this landlord would surely have dropped Ray in
it so that Elizabeth would not get her feet wet.

Meanwhile, the crowd in the bar had frozen like a film still.
Not a sound. "What will you have, love?" asked Richard.

"A pint like you, of course," said Elizabeth.

"Well, go on. Get them then."

Onlookers listened in wonder and disbelief, and henpecked
husbands trod on their wives' toes as they stepped back and
watched Elizabeth—instantly transformed from elegant duchess
into buxom serving-wench—carry two heavy pots of Director's
best bitter back to the table. In the hangover of tomorrow there
would be no morning cups of tea in bed for the matriarchs of
Shepperton. Elizabeth sipped her pint, and every man in the bar
swallowed hard. It was one thing to say, "Last night I saw Elizabeth Taylor," but something else, something quite extraordinary,
to say, "Last night I had a pint in my local with Liz Taylor and
Richard Burton." And there were still the bangers to come.

John Gregson, the English filmstar who had moved into the
village five years ago so that he would be near Shepperton Studios, and who had since made all his films in Elstree on the other
side of London, remembers it vividly as what he calls "The Night
of the Long Sausages." "Richard had a great thing about Archie's
marvelous sausages and this lunchtime he had told Ruth: 'I'm
bringing a little girl in tonight and I want you to have a sausage
for her.' In the middle of the afternoon, she phoned me and said
she was worried because they didn't usually do sausages in the
evenings, and the place would be crowded and quite different
from lunchtime. She felt it was going to be awful and she wanted
me to give some moral support and show a friendly face. Well,
the news had spread on the grapevine that the mighty Burton and
Elizabeth Taylor were coming to the King's Head. And Archie
was celebrating in no uncertain fashion. He had cordoned off a
corner of the bar, and no local dared set foot over the imaginary
line.

"Now this wasn't the effect Richard wanted to create at all. I think that he seriously wanted to bring her down for a quiet pint of beer and a sausage; to make her feel at home, to be the good Welsh solid pub man, and to get away from all this great movie star sort of thing. It was going to be homely. But life's not quite like that. When Ruth called me to say they had arrived, I went along and found the pub was packed, and there in the corner was Richard and Liz, and Archie said, 'Sit there.' Now the British public is very funny. They can go one of two ways. Either they can go overboard—'Can I have your autograph?' 'Can I have a lock of your hair?' 'Can I stroke your feet?'—or else they take it the other way—'Let's be polite. Good God, the poor fellow has just come in for a drink. After all, he's really just the same as us. Let him enjoy himself if he wants to.'

"So everybody was studiously ignoring the fact that there, sitting in the corner, was your actual Elizabeth Taylor and your actual Richard Burton. But the pub was very full, and everybody was pretending not to look and was making artificial conversation—'How's your swine fever? . . . How's your luck? . . .' Chatting like mad. There was a slight note of hysteria and unreality about the whole thing. Through the leaded windowpanes I could see people streaming from The Anchor across the square, and this was getting weird. In the meantime the order had been given for the sausages, which they don't normally do in the evenings. The barman came with the sausages, which were precariously balanced on little sticks—not these tiny cocktail things, but great big sizzling hot bangers, eight inches long and as wide as silver dollars. Now Elizabeth had on this beautiful white dress. It must have cost a fortune. It looked glorious. She'd got a pint of best bitter in one hand and in the other hand the sausage, and then the sausage eases itself off the stick and falls slap on her lap. At this point, a character standing at the bar, who is actually the brother of Graham Stark the comedian, went potty and fell down on his knees and pulled out a handkerchief and started to wipe the grease stains off Liz's dress. And then, when he looked up and saw those beautiful violet eyes looking down at him, he went into some sort of poetic ecstasy and said, 'You don't want to stay down there at those hotels like the Savoy and the Dorchester and all that—that's not for you. Come home, come home with me and play with my pekes.'

"And she's sitting there, with an empty sausage stick, and Richard is asking, 'What's that he's saying?' And she is saying 'I think he wants me to go home with him and play with his pekes.' At that moment, a lady who was sitting alongside me, being very frozen about the whole thing, suddenly said, 'She's pretty but she's an adulteress.' Now sometimes you can make a remark that you don't intend everyone to hear, but it falls right in the middle of a pause in the general conversation. That's exactly where it fell. Richard turned to me and said, 'What did she say?' And I immediately said, 'Oh, it's all right. She said, "What a pity about her dress."' "

Despite the Night of the Long Sausages, Elizabeth fell in love with the King's Head, and she lunched there every day with Richard and Peter O'Toole. Archie was right. The locals came to accept them by ignoring them. Elizabeth, sometimes wearing jeans, felt so at ease that she would wander into "Ma" Rowley's corner shop and buy ice creams for her sons Michael and Christopher and any other kids who happened to be there. And little Mr. Leslie Rowley, who rarely knew the price of anything, would occasionally knock over a row of canned beans in his excitement, and old Ray, sunning himself on The Anchor steps, would kiss Liz's hand like a French count whenever Archie wasn't looking. Here Richard and Elizabeth were able to relax in amusing anecdotes about the storm of world opinion they had weathered, and one day, over the tripe-and-onions in the backroom bar, they talked for the first time about what it had felt like to live through the crazy year of *Cleopatra*.

"It was mad, mad, mad," Richard told us. "Denials to statements never made. I knew all the jokes. Liz goes for a Burton. Burton-Tailoring. The lot. We had it all, right up to here. It was like a pack of mad Manx cats chasing their tails and all the time we were shooting a film. That was forgotten. The script was about twelve hours ahead of the cameras, and we were filming as much as five pages a day. Joe Mankiewicz was directing and writing the whole thing. Honestly, the rumors were fantastic. There was one marvelous one that I was taking Liz out to cover up the affair that she was really having with Joe. One day on the set we sent that one up. Joe told the publicity department, 'Yes, there's some truth in that. Actually Mr. Burton and I are in love and Liz is being used as a front.' " Richard chuckled. He even laughed as they recalled the nightmare of being hounded by the *paparazzi*, the Roman shutterbugs that descended on them like locusts, pursuing them by night and day on a scale not even paralleled by the hounding of Anita Ekberg during the making of *La Dolce Vita.*

"Remember, Richard," said Elizabeth, "when the two priests came to the door with cameras under their cassocks and that one the kids called Creeper. You can laugh now, but he followed us everywhere. He was a funny little wretch, never a smile. One day I was out with the children picking these beans—you know, the little green ones that grow wild and you eat with cheese. I was just in a pair of old jeans and a shirt, looking a bit of a mess, when one of the kids shouted out: 'There's Creeper!' And sure enough, there he was hiding behind a bush. It was the last straw. I went up to him smiling but swearing through my teeth. He just stood there, the dope. Then I took his camera. And WHAM, I hit him one. But he was back next day. The children, Michael, Christopher, and Liza, were chasing him. I think they became rather fond of Creeper.

"You know, you would never believe what went on with those *paparazzi*. They hung on the trees like bird-pecked apples. They even had a girl on the set walking around with a camera hidden in her top-knot. If you came down in the middle of the night, there would be a blinding flash of light. It got so that you'd sneak around opening every cupboard before you took a bath. They were a bloody nuisance."

"I remember another time," said Burton, "when I was waiting for Liz at the bar of a nightclub. She came in, saw all these photographers, and burst into tears and ran. I did not even see her. Didn't know she was there. I'm sitting there like a muggins while she's being chased by the *paparazzi*. Next day, of course, there are pictures of Liz running, and I'm supposed to have beaten her up again."

"Remember . . . remember. . . ." *Cleopatra* had left them with myriad memories they would never forget. But while they now saw the comedy in the mad antics of the *paparazzi,* they still felt bitterness about the spiteful gossip and downright vicious lies told about them in Rome, and Elizabeth remembered especially the day she had received a black eye and bruised nose. "Everybody said Richard had thumped me. And in a way that all happened through the *paparazzi.* I remember it was Easter. We had gone down to Porto Santo Stefano, and we sat eating a bag of oranges when miles away we saw a *paparazzi* lurking in the rocks. When we saw him we decided to go back to Rome separately. My driver had to brake suddenly, and I was thrown against the plastic ashtray. The result—more rumors."

We suggested that in the final analysis the great Roman scandal had not exactly damaged them financially; that here was a classic case to support the cynical argument that any publicity, however bad, however distorted, could be advantageous. But once we sought to defend the way newsmen probed into the private lives of film stars, Elizabeth started throwing out four-letter words like confetti. "Shush, Mum," said Richard. "You'll be giving a bad impression. Pour out the wine, there's a love. Of course, there's publicity and publicity, good and bad. It's necessary and I don't knock anyone for doing his job. Let's face it. What do I read on a Sunday? What's the first thing I turn to? Bad publicity for the government and fascinating reading for millions. Of course, I read the Profumo affair and every word about Christine Keeler. Who doesn't? And who didn't read all about us? About Liz and myself? You can't be sanctimonious about things until you read them. That's the fun about being sanctimonious; you have to have expert knowledge before you can condemn."

And then quite casually, still sitting in Archie's bar, Richard suddenly said: "I want to marry Elizabeth, and I will marry her. There have been all kinds of rumors, but this is what is going to happen. No ifs, no buts. She wants to marry me. I want to marry her."

Elizabeth, dressed all in turquoise, interrupted, "Yes, that's right. I really love Richard—even in his Welsh darkness. . . ."

"That's enough of that, Taffy Taylor," said Burton. "Anyway, I think we should drink on this. Scotch?"

"No," said Elizabeth. "Champagne. Nothing but champagne will do."

So at last it was confirmed—firmly, officially, exclusively. We broke the news that a Burton–Taylor partnership was positively in prospect once they were free to marry, and the story was flashed around the world. The speculation and conjecture was at an end, and in Shepperton at least the gossiping died down until a few weeks later, when Britannia came into Archie's and said: "Haven't you heard? Haven't you read? Richard Burton's never slept with Elizabeth Taylor. Honest! It's in the papers. And he says she's got short legs, a double chin, and too big a chest."

What she was talking about was the topic of the day for morning coffee parties—the things Richard had said to Ken Tynan in an interview for *Playboy* magazine and now picked up by newspapers all over the world. Most especially the housewives were intrigued by Richard's dogmatic reference to monogamy being absolutely imperative. "It's the one thing we must always abide by. The minute you go against the idea of monogomy, nothing satisfies anymore. Suppose you make love to a woman, which is exciting in itself. Suppose you make love to her twice, thirty times, forty times. It can't be enough just to go to bed with her. There has to be something else. Something more than absolute compulsion of body. . . . Sexually the relationship may cease, but you must never move outside it. If you have an imaginative spouse you may find other solutions, but certainly you mustn't violate the idea of monogamy. If you do, it destroys you. It's a killing process and it shouldn't be encouraged. . . . Love and sex are part of the same thing. Sex alone is utterly unimportant anyway. If you're involved purely sexually with somebody else— whether it's a man or a woman or a swan—and that makes you deviate from your ideas of absolute right and wrong, then there's something intensely wrong with that involvement. That doesn't mean that you should not leave your wife. If you have to go, go.

But don't keep skipping back and forth. You can't use sex as a crutch to get away from her—a kind of moral intellectual psychic crutch. You can't say to her: 'I'm terribly sorry, but I can't sleep in the same bed with you any more because I simply *have* to go off with this infinitely more fascinating girl.' There is no such thing as a more fascinating girl. They are all the same, and our appetites are all the same. Sex is no excuse. There is no excuse for infidelity."

Well! At the studios, dressed as the saintly *Becket,* Richard rubbed his hands over his face and slapped his forehead. "Don't tell me. They've been sending me up all morning. Peter O'Toole has been reading the story out to me and asking what it means. And Elizabeth has been on the phone. Now do me a favor—when she comes down later, no cracks about that double chin and the short legs. Did I say it? You know me. Of course I did. It was in an interview that lasted six hours with Ken Tynan. Tape recorder going the whole time at the Dorchester along with the drinks. I dictated enough to make *Gone With the Wind* look like a slim volume of verse. I'm a confusion of talk. For instance, I heard myself saying on one part of the tape: 'Good writing is for the minority, because the minority are the only ones who can judge.' And then later I heard myself saying: 'Good writing can only be judged by the number of people who read it. The more who read it the better it is.' Anyway, Elizabeth is mock mad at me. I bet when she comes here she'll say, 'What does that bandy little Welsh dwarf mean?'—or words to that effect."

Elizabeth arrived with her three children, Michael, Christopher, and Liza, and what she said to us was: "Honestly, you wouldn't believe it. When I came out of the hotel there was a photographer waiting to see if he could get a shot of Richard and myself having a punchup. Really! I don't know what he expected to see—tears streaming down my face? A black eye? But, of course, I'm not mad with Richard. I love him, and I'm going to marry him. It's just that he suffers from this intoxication of words. It's a Welsh disease, I'm sure. But I'm not going to let him get away with it. When he comes off the set, pretend that I've made some monstrous statement about him."

The children ran laughing up to her and pulled her towards the row of horses that were waiting to be used in the next scene. "Please Mummy, please Mummy," squealed little Liza, dancing with excitement. "The man said we could have a ride on the horse if we gave him sixpence."

"Not until you've had your haircut." And with that Elizabeth produced a pair of scissors from nowhere and started to clip Liza's long raven hair.

Elizabeth glanced across at the outdoor set—a beautiful reproduction of a French village—and she sighed and said, "It reminds me of a village in one of the Greek islands. I said to Richard yesterday, when we were wandering around the set, that I wished it were for real. Oh, I do love him. Old bandy legs."

Little Michael, nine, and always protective toward his mother and his younger brother and sister, looked up and said, "Who do you love, Mummy?"

"Richard, darling. I said I loved Richard."

"And I do too, Mummy. I love him very much."

They had now finished the scene in which O'Toole as King Henry tells Becket that he is going to be Archbishop of Canterbury. Richard came over and tossed Liza into the air. His eyes flickered warily from Elizabeth to us, and Elizabeth looked up at the sky, whistling through her teeth. Very formally, we asked him to comment on a statement by Miss Taylor that he was a bible-black, lying Welsh git. And Richard held up his hand and cocked his head in a crafty schoolboy smile. "It's no good. I can read her face. And hear that so-called whistling coming from herself? That's supposed to be Beethoven's Fifth. It's our special signal and it means all is peace. Doesn't she look lovely, though? Suit you marvelously those pants, girl."

"Yes. I wore them just for you," she replied with a Welsh accent. "Thought they would please you. Show off my short legs to advantage like. And I thought the blouse would emphasize my double chins. Lovely I look, isn't it?"

"Oh yes, my old fatty Taffy," said Richard. And then he clapped a hand to his mouth. "Oh, no. There I go again. I must stop it. Did you see that now poor old Stephen Ward is dead, we've been promoted to the front page again? And have you heard what the locals have been saying about how I've been neglecting poor old you, and how sympathetic they are?"

"They didn't believe all that? Surely not, Richard. It's a wonder that anyone could understand what you were talking about. And by the way, what were you talking about?"

"We won't go into that, love. But they didn't believe it really, did they?"

"Of course not," said Liz, poking out her tongue. "They never believe anything they read in the papers, do they?"

Richard's pronouncement on monogamy didn't puzzle friends who knew him well. Like so many of his arguments, it was Jesuitical and slightly puritanical. Without being at all religious in the conventional sense, he is a man with an acute and profound awareness of sin (which he calls guilt), and he was simply emphasizing that he would find it impossible to be unfaithful to a wife without suffering a terrible sense of guilt. Similarly he feels sinfulness in being a capitalist and guilt about being a socialist only at heart, and because of these conflicts he normally prefers, like the colonel in the mess, not to become involved in discussions about sex, politics, or religion. Partly because of this, too, he prefers the company of colorful and entertaining people who are strictly uncomplicated—intelligent perhaps, but not grimly so. And in Shepperton he found such company in abundance. It was funsville—with good food and good wine, amusing and witty talk, and Archie booming 'Bog off, master,' to anyone likely to sneak in with an embarrassing question.

Every day provided some curious but harmless entertainment for Richard to record in his scrupulously kept diary of a nomad actor. On the film set there was the joyous adventure of working with O'Toole, and in the King's Head there was always the eccentricity of some newly discovered character in a close-knit community that considered itself sane and the rest of the world mad. There was, for example, the day that Richard met Len, the man who was regularly collecting for charity and getting celebrities to sign cricket bats and the like for raffling on behalf of a good cause. "Go on in, master," said Archie, when Len asked if he

could get the signatures of Richard or Elizabeth. And a few minutes later Richard came out from the back bar and asked Archie,
"Who in the name of hell is that? A bloke has just come in and
asked Elizabeth if she would please be good enough and kind
enough to give him her signature. 'You want my autograph?' said
Elizabeth. 'I will be delighted.' Then she was just about to sign a
menu when this bloke said, 'No, no, no. I don't want you to write
it on paper. I want you to sign my balls.' And Elizabeth said,
'That's going to be a bit difficult, isn't it?' Then this fellow says,
'No, no. I've left a bit of space between Bobby Moore and John
Lennon.' Now Archie, tell me. Just what in the name of God is
going on?"

"Oh," said Archie. "He's a nice chap. No harm in him at all.
Just tell Elizabeth to sign with a ballpoint—it's the easiest thing
for signing his balls. By the way, master, he forgot to take them
in with him." Archie reached behind the bar and gave Richard a
couple of soccer balls.

Richard would never forget the warmth and understanding and
general *bonhomie* that welcomed him at the pub of Archie and
"Mummy," nor the unusual army of eccentrics that populated the
square at that particular time. But the character who amused him
most was his co-star O'Toole, blue and twinkling of eye, and all
arms and legs, looking, as he put it, "like a beautiful, emaciated
secretary bird." O'Toole had a wicked sense of fun that immediately appealed to Burton, and like Richard, he never lost his thirst
or dried up with his fund of stories—including an hilarious one
about how he got rid of his stammer and lisp, along with his teeth,
when he was kicked in the mouth while playing fullback for a
Navy rugby team against the Swedish police. Illustrating how an
actor may be influenced in his private life by the character he is
playing on stage or screen, Richard tells the story of how he only
drank heavily with O'Toole when they were shooting the early
debauchery scenes that showed Becket and the King in their
roistering, wenching youth. Once he became Archbishop of Canterbury, so his story goes, he instinctively reformed and found
himself staying in at nights and reading poetry and sipping a
harmless wine. But it was not quite that way. In reality, the two

tipplers only agreed to stay on the wagon until they had come to grips with their roles, and after ten days they felt confident enough to shatter the pledge. On the day King Henry had to place the ring of the Chancellor of England on Becket's finger, they were both nicely stoned, and as Richard remembers it, O'Toole was "like a man threading a needle wearing boxing gloves." But there was no dialogue and the scene was soon successfully done. Indeed, they had an extraordinary ability to switch from the beer-swilling of Archie's at lunchtime to the solemnity of the great plaster reconstruction of twelfth-century Canterbury Cathedral on stage H of Shepperton Studios. When film executives from Hollywood visited the set to see how their investment was developing, they were horrified to see Burton and O'Toole reeling about and slurring their speech just as shooting was about to begin. But it was just their way of fun. At the first call for action they were instantly sober.

Considering that this production brought so many talents together in harmony, the end product might be judged faintly disappointing. *Becket* was a good film, never a great one. It was seen to have some quite magnificent moments and to be beautifully acted, and yet something indefinable was lacking in the entertainment as a whole. Midway it appeared to sag and to lose a pace that was never fully recovered, and certainly in the transfer from the intimacy of the theater to the spectacle of wide-screen Panavision Anouilh's central theme, the conflict between Church and Crown dividing spiritual brothers, somehow became less compelling. But if the total result fell short of expectation, Richard's performance never did. It was relatively simple for him to play a ranting, larger-than-life character, but as Becket he had to convey without words great depths of inner torment and spiritual serenity, and at the same time hold the interest of his audience. This he did supremely well. Never was his gift of stillness used to greater effect. On film, as he had done on the stage, he made "silence garrulous" and "brought his cathedral on with him."

Becket gave just the right kind of boost to Burton's prestige. The critics loved him once more. They welcomed him back to the halls of acting glory and his performance was likened to an iceberg of inspiration, one-seventh to be seen and heard above the surface, but six-sevenths below, all age and experience and understanding. And as Richard triumphed, Elizabeth could purr justifiably with much self-satisfaction. She had been proved absolutely right in her insistence that he should play the saint, because despite O'Toole's arresting king, it was Becket who made the more profound impression. Moreover, the performance showed how much he had learned from her about "economy"—the economy of movement, voice, and expression.

After those three riotous months in Shepperton, Richard wrote in an article for *Life* magazine: "Acting is universally regarded as a craft, and I claim it to be nothing more except in the hands of the odd few men and women who once or twice in a lifetime elevate it into something odd and mystical and deeply disturbing. I believe Peter O'Toole to have this strange quality." In *Becket*, Richard reminded us that he had that same quality too.

The Night of the Iguana

Elizabeth was scared. From her window she could see thousands of people massed behind barriers at Mexico City airport, and the natives looked decidedly restless. At first she refused to leave the airliner. Then she became even more scared as a Mexican film official in gaucho gear climbed aboard, grabbed her by the arm, and shouted, "Follow El Indio. You will be safe with me." The Mexican was toting two six-shooters, and Liz didn't feel safe with him at all. "Get this bloody maniac off the plane before I kill him," yelled Burton. Crew members promptly disarmed Miss Taylor's well-meaning protector and escorted him off.

The "maniac" was Emilio (El Indio) Fernandez, a gun-loving

film director and actor, renowned for having shot and seriously wounded his last producer, and he was now acting as assistant to director John Huston. Officially he was there to give the stars a formal welcome, but the situation was too explosive to have armed civilians at large. Instead, a huge police escort came to the rescue, and the stars finally found sanctuary within their suite at the Maria Isabel Hotel.

So in September, 1963, Burton arrived in Mexico for the filming of Tennessee Williams's *The Night of the Iguana,* and the bold, brassy entrance of Fernandez, with his gun belt and king-sized sombrero, was a fitting fanfare for the gathering of the most extraordinary complex of couples ever to be assembled for the making of one movie. Indeed, Huston had gathered together such a curious mixture of characters that if they had all been written into a film script, it would have been regarded as too farfetched to be true.

While Liz was there to monopolize his nonworking hours, Burton had three contrastingly attractive ladies to occupy his attention on the set—Ava Gardner, the sultry, bosomy brunette, once labeled "the most beautiful animal on earth"; Deborah Kerr, cool, serene, and long since restored to prim and proper parts after her beach frolic with Burt Lancaster in *From Here to Eternity;* and Sue Lyon, the seventeen-year-old, still very much type-cast as the sex nymph after her adventures in *Lolita.* It was a trio of co-stars that suggested endless possibilities to the gossip-writers.

Miss Kerr was accompanied by her husband, screenwriter Peter Viertel, who had once been a frequent escort to Miss Gardner, and who had written an acid novel, *White Hunter, Black Heart,* about a film director who bore more than a sneaking resemblance to Huston. Miss Gardner, who had arrived direct from Madrid and the bullfights with her brother-in-law, two maids, a secretary, and a hairdresser, was not married, but her former husband Artie Shaw was currently married to Evelyn Keyes, former wife of Huston. As for Miss Lyon, she was being energetically courted in Mexico by boyfriend Hampton Francher III, who would later marry her after obtaining a divorce from his first wife, Joanne. And just to add to the confusion, others present included author Budd Schulberg, whose former wife Virginia Ray had once been married to Miss Kerr's husband; and Mike Wilding, second husband of Miss Taylor, who had arrived in his new role as Burton's agent. In fact, of all the leading personalities present, Tennessee Williams was the only one who had never been involved in matrimonial difficulties. He was still unmarried.

Huston, with his wicked sense of humor, was tickled pink at having brought these assorted souls together, and he never doubted that he could get them to work in harmony. He understood his stars. As a bizarre present, he gave gold-plated derringers to his three leading ladies and to Liz, Richard, and producer Ray Stark. Each gunbox contained five gold-plated bullets bearing the names of the other five recipients.

The wild, remote locations chosen by Huston for the film were Puerto Vallarta, a village some four hundred miles from Mexico City on the rugged west coast, and the primitive settlement of Mismaloya, previously inhabited only by an Indian tribe. High up on the Mismaloya peninsula he had forty bungalows built as living quarters; also a replica of a ramshackle hotel, the principal film set. Later, after some vigorous campaigning by Burton, a bar was also set up there. Hundreds of laborers toiled in the scorching sun to make Mismaloya habitable and accessible. Meanwhile, preliminary shooting went ahead across the bay at Puerto Vallarta. There, at $2,000 a month, Liz had rented a splendid white stucco villa on the slope of an area known locally as Gringo Gulch. The four-story house was ideal for her needs. Set amid coconut palms and papaya and banana trees, it had six bedrooms and six bathrooms. She moved in with her three children by marriage, plus her secretary, cook, and chauffeur. Later Burton's secretary, Jim Benton, joined the entourage there.

Wilding had been wonderfully understanding when Liz wanted a divorce so that she could marry Mike Todd, and he had stood by her during the tragedy of Todd's death and the scandal of the Fishers' breakup. Now he was equally helpful, ensuring that she and Richard were comfortably installed in the rented villa. He had remained on friendly terms with all three of his ex-wives, particularly Elizabeth, and his mission in Mexico afforded him the chance to spend time with his two sons, Michael and Christopher. Professionally, this was an uneasy time for the actor who had once been the top romantic star of the British screen. The previous year, when his third marriage to wealthy Susan Nell was breaking up, he had been fired by Universal-International from the set of *If a Man Answers*. Temporarily he had suffered a mental block about learning his lines, and now, at fifty-one, he was bravely attempting to start a new career as a Hollywood agent. Burton and Taylor were among his first clients.

Although more than ten thousand non-Mexican couples each year consummate a "quickie" Mexican divorce, many citizens south of the border took an intolerant view of the collection of divorcees and colorful characters that was building up in their Catholic country for *Iguana*. One publication called *Siempre* went so far as to state that Puerto Vallarta was in danger of corruption and that children were being "introduced to sex, drink, drugs, vice, and carnal bestiality by the garbage of the United States; gangsters, nymphomaniacs, heroin-taking blondes. . . ." As for the gossip columnists, they tried hard to play with intriguing permutations and possible pairings. In reality, however, the filming was tackled with diligence and a minimum of hanky-panky by stars who were professionals to the fingertips. Indeed, the gossip-writers were so starved for sensational stories that the tastiest tidbit was the news of someone who complained of being distracted from acting by the sight of Sue Lyon and Hampton Francher III persistently necking in the background. Huston, a past master at soothing temperamental stars, faced up to this problem squarely. He asked Francher to keep off the set.

There was no real clash of personalities on *Iguana,* and never a hint of another *Cleopatra* situation developing. As a defrocked, whiskey-soaked priest in the film, Burton was lured into Miss Lyon's lair, emotionally involved with Miss Gardner, and comforted by Miss Kerr. Off the set, he only had eyes for Liz, and Miss Taylor was quite an eyeful. With the notable exception of Sue Lyon, called upon to wiggle in a baby doll outfit, the stars were shabbily dressed for their roles. Liz, in contrast, could wear what she pleased, and usually she pleased to wear curvaceous slacks and sweaters or sensational bikinis. When shooting started at Mismaloya, she would set out each day, usually around noon, to join Richard there. Without a harbor at Vallarta, this was an elaborate procedure that involved reaching deep water by dugout canoe, climbing with difficulty into her rented launch named *Taffy,* making a twenty-minute ride across the bay, and then getting ashore by jumping onto a floating pier. After that came the long, hard climb to Huston's film set, three hundred feet above. There Burton would greet her with a variety of cries—"Hi, Luv"; "Ah, Elizabethicus"; or with mock formality, "Good morning, Miss Taylor." Usually she brought him a hot lunch, and sometimes daughter Liza went along for the ride. After lunch they would watch the action, or more often, descend to the beach to swim and sunbathe. Liz had ordered forty bikinis from Paris for this holiday in Mexico.

At first she was prone to fuss over Richard on the set. Once, much to the chagrin of the official hairdresser, she started to make final adjustments to Burton's hair. In an act of defiance, he grabbed a bottle of beer and poured it over his head. "How do I bloody look now?" he asked. Thereafter Liz kept more in the background when shooting was in progress. For the first time in her life she was on location not as a star but as a visitor, and she adjusted to her new subsidiary role surprisingly well. Mismaloya, however, was hardly a paradise for her holiday. The heat could be oppressive. There was dysentery, and the place was infested with all manner of reptiles, insects, and bugs: scorpions, snakes, giant land crabs, poisonous lizards, mosquitoes, flies, and fleas. Sue Lyon was once nipped by a scorpion, and when Liz foolishly ventured out in chic, open sandals, her feet were invaded by chigoes—tropical fleas that burrow into the skin, and left to wander, work their way into the blood stream. Miss Taylor, veteran of so many operations, had them dug out with a knife.

In *The Night of the Iguana*, Burton was playing a broken, disenchanted minister, T. Laurence Shannon, defrocked for being too intimate in dispensing comfort to a female parishioner and now reduced to acting as a travel courier for a busload of matronly American tourists. Once again, women threaten his downfall. The youngest tourist, a chaperoned seductress called Charlotte (Sue Lyon), is discovered in his bedroom, and the frustrated spinsters turn nasty. Desperately seeking time to win back their favor, Shannon causes an engine failure and gets his bus stranded at the crumbling hotel run by his friend Maxine (Ava Gardner). There his faith in human goodness is restored by a sketch artist (Deborah Kerr) and her nonagenarian grandfather (Cyril Delavanti), a penniless poet. The iguana? A giant lizard, pursued, captured, and held on a chain until fat enough to eat. One was tethered at Maxine's hotel—a living symbol of man's own dilemma.

So soon after *Becket,* Richard could count himself lucky to be involved in a project written by a master craftsman, directed by another, and combining many brilliant talents. He was getting handsomely paid—$500,000, compared with Miss Gardner's $400,000 and Miss Kerr's $250,000. Moreover, he was ideally suited to the well-scripted role of a booze-sodden minister, so powerful of voice, so tormented within, and so unwittingly desirable to women. With a proper sense of dedication to his part, Burton bashed the bottle hard and enjoyed long sessions in the Vallarta bars, but more often propped up a stool at the open bar on the Playa D'Oro beach. Mostly he drank *tequila;* sometimes the local *raicilla,* a vicious cactus brandy concoction. But he also kept himself fit with regular exercise, sparring and playing football on the beach and table tennis with ex-prizefighter Bobby LaSalle, whom Huston had picked up while filming *The Misfits* with Monroe and Gable. After *Iguana,* LaSalle would be useful to Richard and Elizabeth as a private bodyguard. He was quick with his feet and fists, and none too slow with his wits. One night at the beach bar, Liz was remarking on the winning way she seemed to have with all kinds of animals. The professional boxer shot a glance towards Burton, "Yeah, maybe," he cracked. "But you're a long way from taming him."

Early in December, *Iguana* was complete in the can and Huston threw a colossal, riotous party that lasted twelve hours and saw most everyone properly stoned. Just as *Cleopatra* had been ill-starred from start to finish, so conversely this one had gone swingingly well throughout. They had finished ahead of schedule, and they had scored a fully deserved hit. Of course, there were isolated mishaps. Two technicians were injured, one seriously, when a balcony collapsed; and there could have been a major tragedy at the start when they shot a sequence with the bus taking hairpin bends on the narrow mountain road above Vallarta. The loaded bus veered too near the cliff edge and earth began to slip as it teetered on the edge. Some of the ladies were terrified as they scrambled clear, but Burton came away grinning and cracking jokes. He didn't laugh, however, when they shot the symbolic scene in which he had to let loose the tethered iguana. The well-fed reptile showed complete disinterest in his release, and not even prodding with broomsticks would persuade him to toddle off into the jungle. Huston, never defeated, arranged for the iguana to be given a sharp but harmless shot of electricity. "That'll make him jump," he said. It did. It also made Burton jump with a yell. He happened to have a hand on the beast as a technician prodded it with a live wire.

For Richard and Liz, those two months of the *Iguana* provided a happy escape from the nightmare of facing endless, often noxious questions about their relationship and future plans. They were still pursued by reporters, but not more than they could handle. Once on the Mismaloya location, they were isolated from telephones and television. Meanwhile, of course, the "civilized" world outside had gone on buzzing with reports and counter-reports about the Taylor–Burton–Fisher triangle. In October, Fisher was quoted as saying that it might be a long time before he and Liz were divorced; that he had telephoned Liz in Mexico to ask whether she wanted him to start Nevada divorce proceedings and that she had replied she was in no hurry. At the same time, Liz was reported to be complaining that he did all his talking to the press and not to her. Publicly the situation remained one of utter and tedious confusion. Then one week after they completed *Iguana,* the situation suddenly became clearer. In Puerto Vallarta, before the Supreme Court of Jalisco, Sybil was granted a divorce on the grounds of "abandonment and cruel and inhuman treatment."

None of the parties had to appear. Everything was handled expertly and discreetly by lawyers. The New York office of the Burtons' lawyer, Mr. Aaron Frosch, released a statement: "The parties had, prior to the divorce, concluded a property settlement which provides a trust for each of the two children and for the establishment of substantial separate funds both for Mrs. Burton and Mr. Burton. The custody of the children, Katharine, aged six, and Jessica, four, will, of course, remain with Mrs. Burton, with provision for totally free visitation rights at all times. At no time was there any difficulty relating to the formation of the property settlement agreement. Mrs. Burton is expected to return to the Burton home in Geneva, Switzerland, possession of which she has retained." (The settlement was believed to be one million dollars, plus half a million to be paid over the next ten years.) In Hollywood, Eddie Fisher reportedly jumped in the air on hearing the news, shouted, "Marvelous! Bravo!"; and then broke into song, clicking his fingers and singing the first two bars of the Mexican number, "Guadalajara." He said that he would help Liz in any way to get a divorce. Sybil, who came through this difficult time with utmost dignity, said nothing. Then after weeks of silence, she explained, "I never thought of myself as a 'sad lady,' but I longed to be anonymous. I survived my troubles because of marvelous friends. Now I can sink back into just being anonymous." In fact, she was destined to achieve less anonymity than ever before.

After a brief visit to Hollywood, Richard and Liz flew back to Mexico in time for Miss Taylor to preside on Christmas Day at the annual gift-giving for children in Puerto Vallarta. But there was another purpose for going back. On January 14, 1964, Elizabeth filed an abandonment petition and the judge gave her husband twenty-one days to reply. Mr. Fisher did not journey to Mexico to contest the petition. He said he was sick of the tawdry affair that had dragged on for so long with angry words, denials, and accusations being bandied across continents. "Now when it suits them, they plant themselves in Mexico and say what they want—and demand it now. Like children asking for a lollipop. I am not going to be part of the slanging match. I'll leave that to Burton—he is famous for making statements."

The situation again seemed hopelessly confusing. There were wildly contradictory reports about the financial claims which Mr. Fisher was allegedly making. There was also a great deal of uncertainty about the validity of the divorce moves in Mexico. *Time* magazine described Richard and Sybil as "one of 10,000-plus non-Mexican couples who each year consummate a Mexican divorce in the not-quite-polygamous marriage ritual that has been called 'serial monogamy.' " Doubts about their divorce were raised because Sybil had not been present when it was granted. The legal position was highly complicated, and Richard, not failing to see the goonish side, remarked outrageously, "If you come down to it, Elizabeth may not even have been legally married to Mike Todd (in Acapulco, Mexico) after the Wilding divorce. So that means no one was ever married to anyone really, and we might just as well all start again and get married and divorced on the Koran." Finally, however, the lawyers established that everything was absolutely legal, and it was just as well; Elizabeth's wedding dress was almost complete at the time she filed for divorce. On March 5, Judge Arcadio Estrada—the same official who had granted a divorce to Sybil—ruled that Liz was divorced, and he judged that Fisher, by failing to present himself in court, had presumably confessed to Miss Taylor's charge of abandonment. Ten days later Elizabeth would become Mrs. Burton.

Hamlet

Despite the joy and triumphs and diamond-studded prosperity that have followed, Richard and Elizabeth can never forget the appalling unpleasantness to which they were subjected in the months immediately prior to their marriage. In the first ten weeks of 1964 they virtually ran the gauntlet to the altar—mobbed in the United States and Canada by violent, hysterical fans, and savagely attacked and abused in public by self-appointed arbiters of individual morality. Their ordeal began at the end of a thirteen-hour flight from Mexico when they were besieged at Los Angeles airport by a thousand screaming fans. Next they were mobbed in Toronto, and outside their hotel the righteous demonstrators shouted insults and paraded banners with such crackpot slogans as "Drink not the wine of adultery." At a charity preview of *Hamlet*, Elizabeth was hissed and given the slow-handclap by a so-called society audience, and across the border, UN Representative Michael Feighan (Democrat, Ohio), chairman of the House immigration subcommittee, was asking the State Department to revoke Richard's visa. Burton's admission, he argued, would be "detrimental to the morals of the youth of our nation." His request was rejected, and Government legal experts properly replied that the actor had not been charged with any moral crime and that he had announced his intention of marrying Miss Taylor as soon as she was free. Yet the outcry from the sanctimonious raged on, and throughout this period of mounting public ridicule, Richard had to apply himself to the challenge of the leading role in Sir John Gielgud's production of *Hamlet*.

Burton's ability to go on with this commitment speaks volumes for the resilience, self-discipline, and sheer professionalism of the man. But far more remarkable is the fact that he resisted the pressures and distractions to achieve a *tour de force*. This *Hamlet* would become his most spectacular stage success, and yet curiously the production that reestablished him as a serious actor was largely an unplanned child of impulse and chance, conceived during the filming of *Becket* when Gielgud was called in as an emergency replacement to play the King of France. They were then shooting on location near Newcastle in the north of England, and it so happened that Gielgud was appearing at Newcastle in an ill-fated play, *The Ides of March*. Richard and Elizabeth went along to see his play, and afterwards, when they met in the bar of the Station Hotel, Sir John asked Burton what he was doing next year for Shakespeare's quadricentennial. "Oh, someone wants me to do Hamlet in New York," said Richard. "I'll do it, if you'll direct it." Afterwards he couldn't imagine why he had said it. He had no compelling urge to play Hamlet again. But Gielgud promptly agreed, and Richard was too proud to back down. "Over supper we made a kind of joke of it and I really never thought anything would come of it," says Sir John. "I rather gathered when we started off that Richard had done it as a kind of dare, and had thought no more about it, and then rather casually got himself involved. But I must say that once he took it on he was extremely enthusiastic and never ran it down or slacked in any way in getting it ready."

Since O'Toole was to play Hamlet at the National Theater in London, it was logical that Burton's Hamlet should be staged in New York. They also agreed that they should break away from traditional period costume. Richard was adamant about not wanting to wear doublet and hose. "In tights my legs look like a pair of stockings idly thrown over a bed rail." And this perfectly suited Sir John, since he had long harbored the notion of doing *Hamlet* as a final rehearsal run-through, without formal costumes or scenery. Often he had observed that the run-through of a Shakespeare production was performed with a pace and naturalness that was somehow lost once the players donned costumes and worked amid formal sets. It was a commonly recognized phenomenon in the theater—hence so many attempts at playing in modern dress and contemporary sets. But this, too, could prove unsatisfactory, as audiences were distracted by the sight of Shakespearean characters taking cocktails and puffing cigars. Therefore Gielgud aimed to capture the essence of the final run-through, keeping props to the barest essentials, and seeking the utmost simplicity so as to place maximum weight on plot and verse. Within reason, players would dress themselves as they would do for ordinary rehearsals, choosing clothes in which they felt comfortable for the characters they were playing.

The combination of Gielgud and Burton was especially intriguing. The former belonged to the old school of acting and was the supreme master of lyrical effect, the euphonic quality; the latter was more the actor of his time, concerned with meanings and impressions, and leaning towards a rather more conversational style of speech. Richard's primary aim was to make the play understood by the widest possible audience; to make people feel they were seeing it for the first time. If necessary, he said, he was prepared to "maul and brutalize" the verse toward that aim. Therein lay the basic difference between their approach. While Burton would sometimes put sense before sensibility, meaning before mellifluence, Gielgud instinctively sought to safeguard the beauty of the poetry and the correctness of the rhythm. But despite this divergence, they remained a formidable team. Neither was so arrogant as to imagine that he knew it all; each had much to offer the other. Burton, after all, was no grunting Brando, whom Gielgud describes as possessing "a kind of neurotic charm." He might seek to capture Hamlet's soul-searching moods in modern style, but he could still speak poetry with a rare sweetness. On the other hand, he was at times the headstrong thoroughbred in need of subtle restraint—being persuaded to slow the pace at one point to make acceleration more effective elsewhere, and to play down one line to lend emphasis to another. Gielgud, ever courteous and self-effacing, provided the discipline and subtlety that Richard rather badly needed after so long a break from the theater.

Theirs was a curious relationship. At the age of eighteen, Richard had been five times in one week to see, or rather hear, Gielgud's *Hamlet*. Now, after hearing Sir John as the Ghost in the first rehearsal, his admiration was no less great: "He's the best bloody verse actor in the world. You can't speak in brutal prose when Sir John is speaking." Yet his deep-rooted respect could not persuade him to follow blindly the master player. His own style was now too sharply defined for that. He readily "took direction" and accorded with Gielgud's wishes, but only where he recognized the validity of them, and where the direction did not interfere with his own personal design. When he disagreed over some minor point of emphasis or inflection, he would not dispute it fiercely; instead, with devious humility and charm, he would convey his agreement and move on. But when they came on the same passage another time it was not unusual to find Richard still going his own sweet way. On the other hand, when he disagreed over a basic piece of interpretation, he unhesitatingly stood his ground and politely but firmly argued his case. And invariably, where they begged to differ, the actor had his way. He could never be a puppet player, and from his Old Vic experience he had learned to his cost that a melodious reading ideal for Gielgud was not necessarily suitable for him. He knew also that it is imperative for the actor to bring something of himself to this particular role if he is to achieve convincing power. Gielgud was as conscious of this as anyone, and so, while he reasoned and explained and debated, he never insisted that the actor should do it his way. Burton, with good cause, called him the best director with whom he had ever worked.

At the Toronto rehearsals Richard seemed to be his usual witty and extrovert self. But his uncertainty in the readings betrayed his taut nerves. He was, in fact, working under a fearful strain. Though the town had only three newspapers, there were always at least fifty reporters hovering in the background, watching his and Elizabeth's every move, even noting the food they ate and the liquor they drank. Photographers were everywhere, and always there were the hordes of fans and demonstrators around the theater and outside the King Edward Hotel, where they sheltered in the closely guarded four rooms of their $65-a-day viceregal suite, which members of the *Hamlet* company called "the zoo." Richard observed: "I've been in the most expensive musical, the most expensive movie. And now I'm in the most pressurized *Hamlet*."

Gielgud cannot recall rehearsing in more bizarre circumstances. "It was extraordinary. They had to exercise their dogs on the roof in Toronto because they couldn't go out on to the street. And it was rather sad to see them in the hotel, holed up in a suite with a man with a machine gun in the corridor. It made it very difficult to get him alone, and even when I went out to lunch with him between rehearsals there'd be four or five of the entourage sitting at adjoining tables, preventing people coming up and talking to him. When I said, 'Please, this is my lunch,' Richard said, 'No, No. They'll pay.' We sailed out and the entourage was left to pay the bill, which rather embarrassed me. I did ask them once to supper in Toronto, and it was the cheapest entertaining I ever did. I invited them to a steak house after the play and we had a marvelous supper with a lot of champagne. We were about ten or fifteen people, but when I asked for the bill the management wouldn't give me one, and when we came out there were two hundred people in the snow, waiting to see them drive away. The next morning I went back to tip the waiters at least, and they said, 'No. No. No. We were paid so much extra by the proprietor last night that we wouldn't dream of taking a penny.' So I was never able to be host to them in a proper way, and, of course, that tremendous princeliness does isolate you in a funny way, and I felt sorry I couldn't get to know them better, in a more intimate way, because of all the hoo-ha that was going on in the newspapers and in every kind of moment that they put their noses outside the door.

"I thought it was a great strain on their relationship and on their relationship with all the company. And I thought that he handled that marvelously. He was very popular with the company. He took great pains to be nice to everybody. But it must have been a great strain for him, and it wasn't my idea of really working as one likes to do at rehearsals—intimately, privately, without the glare of publicity. Of course, the management in some ways rather liked it because it meant this enormous, fantastic business which they did everywhere with the play."

Burton has never been more apprehensive about a return to the stage than he was in Toronto. He was still getting his lines muddled when they came to the "dress" rehearsal on February 24, and the unevenness of his performance suggested that his dramatic muscles had slackened with too much film work and easy living. Yet the following night, resolute and utterly professional, he rose to the urgency of the occasion and came through the first public performance as near word-perfect as anyone could tell. It was a strange evening in the vast and opulent O'Keefe Center. Such was the interest in the arrival of Elizabeth Taylor that the start of the performance was delayed for over forty minutes as hundreds of people remained standing, some perched on their seats like penguins at feeding time and stretching for a glimpse of Hamlet's wife. (Thereafter it was decided that Liz would not sit out front again until they opened in New York.) Then the curtain went up on the plainest of sets—some steps leading to a bare platform—and the players appeared in their self-chosen rehearsal clothes. Polonius (Hume Cronyn) in a conservative pin-striped business suit, with watch and chain and pince-nez; Gertrude (Eileen Herlie) and Ophelia (Linda Marsh) in long white skirts; Claudius (Alfred Drake) in blue blazer and gray trousers. Burton stuck simply to a black V-neck sweater and black trousers.

"The play's the thing," he said, "wherein I'll capture the conscience of the king." But was the play alone, stripped of all extraneous trappings, enough to capture the imagination of the audience? The critics came up with different answers. Nathan Cohen of the *Toronto Star* thought the whole thing to be "an unmitigated disaster" and Burton to be "artistically impotent." Ron Evans of the *Toronto Telegram* wrote: "Burton's performance is a masterpiece. He is the closest we shall come in this generation to the complete Hamlet." And the third Toronto critic, Herbert Whitakker of *The Globe and Mail,* praised Burton in many respects but found his performance disappointing. There was strong criticism of the costumes and sets, and of other players, and the general reaction among the company was one of gloom and despair. Gielgud nobly blamed himself for the poor staging, told the cast not to worry about the reviews, and called a special rehearsal before the next performance. Everyone felt that major improvements were necessary if they were to survive on Broadway.

During those anxious weeks in Toronto, Richard strove as hard as anyone for a more polished performance. He asked for extra rehearsals and cooperated with the rest of the cast in every way. All the time Elizabeth hovered in the background, playing a humble but positive part, helping with makeup and running little errands. On Sunday, March 15, however, they afforded themselves the luxury of one day's rest from the play to attend a rather pressing engagement. By chartered plane they flew to Montreal and were married the same day in the Royal Suite 810 of the Ritz-Carlton Hotel. Only a few close friends, mostly members of the *Hamlet* company, were invited, and Elizabeth did not even tell her parents until twenty-four hours before the wedding. It was the simplest of ceremonies, with Bob Wilson—Richard's valet, barman, and general aide—standing in as best man. The bride looked stunning in a knee-length yellow chiffon dress and with hyacinths and a yellow ribbon in her hair; Richard wore a plain dark suit and red tie. Afterward he said, "I have been so nervous about this and having to play Hamlet eight times a week in Toronto that I have lost twelve pounds. Now I just feel terribly relieved." And his relief was echoed around the world.

It was a strange anticlimax to the most publicized love affair of the decade. For over two years the world had followed the confusing, tortuous course of the great Antony–Cleopatra romance. Now in a flash, the speculation, the scandal, the great global game of sniping at Burton and Taylor was ended. They were the same two people and yet, by the unyielding laws of moral convention, they were not. The Unitarian Church had waved its magic wand and overnight they were somehow more acceptable—man and wife, Mr. and Mrs. Burton. It was all over in fifteen minutes— without pomp and ceremony, without cameramen, reporters, and swarms of fans. There was not even time for a honeymoon. Next day the bridegroom would be back on the Toronto stage telling Ophelia, "I say, we will have no more marriages."

Now that they were married, the Burtons briefly imagined that the excessive interest in their private lives would diminish. This illusion was quickly shattered. As soon as they left the sanctuary of the Ritz-Carlton the great public circus started up all over again. The wedding had served only to stimulate their frenzied following. Disorderly crowds swarmed around them at Montreal Airport, and four days later when *Hamlet* moved on from Toronto the newlyweds experienced the worst public mauling of their lives. Complete chaos greeted their arrival at Boston's Logan Airport. Some five hundred fanatical fans broke through the barriers and surrounded the plane. They peered in windows, screamed and waved, and with the police overwhelmed, the *Hamlet* company was marooned on board for an hour. Finally, after the plane had been towed inside a hangar, the Burtons escaped by sending their staff ahead in a decoy car. But worse lay ahead; at the Sheraton Plaza Hotel they found more than a thousand people compressed into the lobby. Engulfed by an uncontrollable mob, they had to battle their way to the elevator, and from the scrum Richard emerged bleeding from scratches on the face. Elizabeth was reduced to tears, had hair torn from her head, and was bruised on the back. One girl in the crowd ended up with a broken leg.

For the Burtons that day was an unforgettable nightmare, but at least it was the peak of mob madness. Thereafter their treatment in public would progressively improve. Their ordeal was virtually over. Released from the nerve-racking tension of a shadowy relationship, they could now begin to enjoy the advantages of social respectability. And their position was strengthened because all the time *Hamlet* was snowballing into a fantastic success. In Toronto it had grossed over $400,000 in four weeks; Richard, on 15 percent of the gross, picked up $60,000, a remarkable sum for a pre-Broadway warm-up engagement. The opening at Boston's Schubert Theater was even more encouraging. Richard received a standing ovation and excellent notices, and the two weeks there grossed some $140,000, the maximum possible, with all standing room sold. Now came the crucial test, the Broadway opening before the most demanding critics of all, and at Richard's suggestion they gave two previews in New York so as to be well into their stride for the third-night official opening. This was a glittering mink-and-diamond affair, but, despite six curtain calls, it was not immediately apparent whether they had a triumph or failure. "There were so many celebrities out on the other side of the footlights they hardly had time to notice us," said Richard. "They were a chill and indifferent audience, strange, not normal. They did not laugh at the jokes, which is a good indication that something is wrong. They did not pay attention." Afterwards, a lavish party was held in Burton's honor in the Rainbow Room, sixty-five floors up in the Rockefeller Plaza. There was dancing and singing until near dawn, and over 650 guests attended, including Jackie Kennedy's sister, Princess Lee Radziwill, Dorothy and Lillian Gish, Myrna Loy, Van Heflin, Monty Clift, Allan

Jay Lerner, Emlyn Williams, Michael Wilding, and Margaret Leighton. When Richard arrived with Elizabeth and saw such an extravagant and formal gathering, he growled, "Let's get away from this rubbish," but he stayed on to drink cheerfully with the gossip columnists.

This was a spectacular welcome as only New York society could stage, but the welcome that mattered more came the next morning from the critics. The so-called Butchers of Broadway swung their cleavers savagely at the production as a whole, but over Richard's performance they were almost wholly enthusiastic. Howard Taubman of *The New York Times* described it as "a performance of electrical power and sweeping vitality." Norman Nadel of the *World-Telegraph* said it was "so lucid and sensible that people will speak of it for years." Walter Kerr, veteran critic of the *Herald Tribune*, threw bouquets and one hurtful brickbat. He described Burton as "one of the most magnificently equipped actors living [who] places on open display not only all of his reverberating resources . . . but also all of the myriad qualities which the man Hamlet requires. All except one. Mr. Burton is without feeling."

Later came the verdict of *Time*: "As acting, Richard Burton's performance is a technician's marvel. His voice has gem-cutting precision and he can outroar Times Square traffic, though he lacks the liquid melody that Gielgud supplies as the voice of Hamlet's father's unseen ghost. His hands punctuate the speeches with percussive rhythm and instinctive grace. He is virile, yet mannerly, as sweet of temper as he is quick to anger, and his wary eyes dart from foe to friend with the swiftness of the thought. . . . Shakespeare's kingliest crown is English, and as this 400th anniversary year begins, Richard Burton's lips are brushing it with glory."

It was a smash hit unlike any other in three centuries of Shakespearean productions. The success of Burton's plain-clothed *Hamlet* was incredible, unprecedented, and mystifying. He broke the record for the greatest number of *Hamlet* performances on Broadway, reaching 136 compared with the record of 132 previously shared by Gielgud and Maurice Evans. He starred in the most profitable Shakespeare stage production ever presented in New York, playing to 204,000 people who paid $1,718,862 during the seventeen-week run. His *Hamlet* was recorded by Columbia Records, and it was put on celluloid by a new filming process for showing at a thousand movie theaters. By this process it could be filmed during a regular performance without special lighting or inconvenience to the audience, and without extra work by the players. It enabled Burton's stage *Hamlet* to be preserved for posterity, and it boosted the gross takings of the production to a staggering $6,000,000.

Though the entire company could take pride in the success, there was never a glimmer of doubt that Burton was the great box-office attraction responsible for this Broadway bonanza. When he missed two performances because of an abscessed tonsil, roughly forty percent of the ticket holders demanded their money back, and during those seventeen weeks he never played to one empty seat. Of course it could be reasoned that all the *Cleopatra* ballyhoo had freakishly boosted his drawing power, but no one could dispute that he left an indelible mark of his own on this *Hamlet*. The London *Times* New York dramatic critic put it most dogmatically: "Mr. Richard Burton's Hamlet is a success. The Hamlet of his producer, Sir John Gielgud, is, on the whole, a failure." This was an unworthy oversimplification. The Hamlets of player and director can never be fairly judged as totally separate entities; they are interlocked like inseparable Siamese twins, one drawing strength from the other. But certainly, Burton's Hamlet was the dominant twin in this production.

How far did Gielgud feel the production was successful in the light of what he set out to achieve by presenting it as a final run-through? His candid reply enables us to see this overpublicized *Hamlet* in a far truer perspective than was permitted at the time, when it was quite impossible to measure how much of its extravagant success was due to the fascination of the Burtons and the curiosity they inspired.

> I thought it was only successful in that it suited Richard rather well—because he didn't want to wear Eliza-

bethan costume and that was really what it all started
from. I think in a much smaller theater it would have
been more successful. We played in Toronto for more
than a month on this impossible stage at the O'Keefe
Center which holds 2,600 to 2,700 people. Richard
had such authority and power that of course he dominated the play with great ease. But even in New York
it wasn't a very happy theater. I don't think it's good
to play Shakespeare in enormous great barns, although
the flow of the verse allows for it, and the broad style,
of course, carries very well in a big house, and he has a
great star personality. But it couldn't be very subtle or
very elaborately devious. It was rather straightforward
and athletic and vocal, and I don't see how anybody
else can play Hamlet in those sort of theaters in a more
restrained way. I very much admired his ability to
spread himself over the play and dominate it in the
way he did. The company wasn't altogether happy. I
had never worked with most of them, and one had to
find them through auditions in America, which was
very difficult for me, and except for one or two very
good performances like Hume Cronyn's, I don't think
it was awfully happily cast or acted. The New York
actors were all worrying about motivation. I wanted in
the short time we had at our disposal to get a swift,
well-spoken, straight production of the play, and I
didn't think that they responded to that very cleverly.
I didn't feel that the production grew as I would like to
see a Shakespeare production grow. It's always difficult, even in England, in a few weeks to collect a
number of people to play a Shakespeare play; that's
why repertory theaters like the National and the
Shakespeare create some sort of team unity which is
usually more rewarding, and most commercial productions suffer, having been got together too quickly
and having too many actors who don't know how to
work together. However, it was an enormous success,

and it was interesting to work with Richard because I did succeed, I think, in not imposing my own performance on his, and I did, I think, help him over the actual saving of energy. He said to me that I taught him where to relax and where to let the play ride so that he could make his climaxes more effective; and although I didn't give him inflections or line readings or anything like that, I did give him a lot of ideas about how to simplify and save his energy and so on. I know what I suffered trying to play Hamlet eight times a week for three or four months in New York. But Richard has tremendous stamina and he stayed the course very well. He's obviously a very strong physical character; he can go out on the town, you know, and still not be knocked out by it the next day.

Yes, I suppose that he did lack a certain discipline after being away in films. But it didn't seem to affect his performance. He has enormous dash, you see, panache and enthusiasm, and yet a certain brooding thing which is also very beautiful. I call him the "Shropshire Lad Hamlet," no matter. I remember saying to him right at the beginning: "I don't know why you don't play Macbeth or Coriolanus because I think they're more your kind of part." But he felt, I think, that he had had some success in it at the Old Vic and had not quite done himself justice, and that he would like to have another shot at it while he was young enough—which I understand. I mean it's such a great part, and he has so many gifts for it. Of course, he was magnificent in many scenes. It was just that I think he's not an introvert character basically. His most beautiful performances have been simpler characters. He doesn't anyhow, on the stage or on the screen, give me the impression of being a very complicated man. Of course, he is complicated—like everybody; but there's something very free and open about him which is not to my mind the essential thing about Hamlet. Hamlet is rather a mystery.

During that entire Broadway run there was only one disconcerting moment for Burton: on the night of May 6 a man from the balcony began booing loudly during one of the soliloquies. Others cheered to drown the one hostile voice, but the demonstrator would not be silenced. When players appeared individually for curtain calls, he reserved one solitary boo for Burton. At the next call, Richard asked for the curtain to be kept up. Then he approached the footlights and told the audience: "We have been playing this production in public for over eighty performances. Some have liked it, some have not. But I can assure you, we have never been booed." The fans cheered. The mysterious man in the balcony booed as loudly as ever.

Elizabeth had a touch of influenza that night and remained in their Regency suite. When Richard arrived home she was in bed enjoying a television movie in which she was seeing Peter Sellers for the first time.

"I was booed tonight," he growled.

"Really?" said Liz, her violet eyes still glued to the gogglebox.

"Oh, turn that bloody thing off," said Richard, sulkily seeking an audience.

"Shush! I can't hear."

"Don't you understand," he went on. "I was actually booed. On the stage."

"Yes, dear," said Liz. "Never mind."

Richard stalked out of the room and changed into his pajamas. When he returned and found he was still eclipsed by television, he stormed across the room and kicked the set over with a bare foot. It crashed against a wall and one of the knobs fell to the floor. He kicked it again. This time his foot struck the bared metal screw, and as the screw cut deep between his first two toes he let out an almighty yell of anguish. Blood gushed from the wound. Four-letter expletives sliced the air. Elizabeth, remembering his tendency toward hemophilia, automatically fetched the bandage and iodine, but at the same time she dissolved into fits of laughter that literally made Richard hopping mad. Next day he went on stage with a pronounced limp and grumbled: "Some critics have said I play Hamlet like Richard the Third anyway. So what the hell is the difference?"

It was the events outside the theater as much as those inside which made this one of the most extraordinary runs Broadway has ever seen. Every night except Sundays, literally thousands of fans would mass around the corner of Broadway and 46th Street to catch a glimpse of the Burtons entering and leaving the Lunt-Fontanne Theater, and it was an incredible ritual that became a recognized feature of the New York scene. Around 11:30 every night the idols of the show business world would emerge from the theater under a large marquee—Elizabeth always wearing something new, Richard the strong Prince Consort close behind. Teen-agers squealed and screamed, the great crowd pressed more strongly against the police barriers. Seconds later a limousine, flanked by mounted police, pulled away and the great "royal" parade was over for another night. *Time* judged it to be "the fastest, flashiest show around," pushing the Empire State Building, Madison Square Garden, the Statue of Liberty, the Guggenheim Museum, Radio City Music Hall, and Central Park into second place as New York attractions.

One night we shared this extraordinary experience with the Burtons. As we left the theater together, the crowd, hot and sticky and stained in the tropical night, surged forward and made the great canyon of skyscrapers boom and echo with a mighty roar. Police with revolvers swinging bare on their hips cleared a path for us to reach the car. Then the crowd broke through the linked arms of the police and Liz lost her shoe. She smiled but hurried on. Split-second timing was needed to escape the Lunt-Fontanne. As we drove off, Richard pointed out a bar across the street. "It's a good place for a drink, but to reach it we have to drive around four or five blocks and approach it discreetly from the opposite direction."

Curiously, he was still puzzled by the mass adulation. "At first I thought the somewhat illicit quality of our relationship before we were married was bringing them. We assumed that once we married it would stop."

"Nonsense," said Elizabeth. "That doesn't have anything to do with it, darling. You're the Frank Sinatra of Shakespeare."

But Burton was more than that. Sinatra, who stopped the roar of Broadway traffic in his bobby-sox days, called backstage one night and remarked that even he had never seen anything quite like it. This was endorsed by the veteran stage doorman, Mr. Peter Green. "I have never seen anything like this in fifty years of show business. Not even John Barrymore could draw crowds like this every night." It was not merely the passion of the fans that was so extraordinary. The Burtons wondered, too, at the way they were received in social circles, with instant warmth where once had been frosty looks. They were two colorful outlaws, suddenly pardoned and welcomed back to the community as folk heroes. As Elizabeth said, "There's no deodorant like success."

Many old wounds were healing now, and no reconciliation pleased Richard more than his reunion with the man most responsible for his development as an actor, his foster-father Philip Burton. It was not easily achieved, since *le scandale* had driven a deep wedge between the two men. Phil Burton had loathed all the public exposure of Richard's private life, and he had felt compelled to side with Sybil during the *Cleopatra* affair. Moreover, he had been directly embarrassed by the Burton–Taylor romance. On the day after a Congressman proposed that Richard should be banned from the States on moral grounds, his second "father" was facing his examination for American citizenship. The examiner somehow regarded this issue as being relevant to the applicant's fitness to become an American, but happily it did not influence the final decision. The application was passed.

It was Elizabeth, acting on her own initiative, who finally brought Burton senior and junior back together. During rehearsals of *Hamlet*, when Richard was in a highly nervous state, she swallowed her pride and boldly telephoned the man she had never met, the man she knew must feel hostile toward her. "Richard needs you," she said. "Please come." Subsequently Philip Burton spoke to Sybil, and she agreed that he ought to go if Richard needed him. So the father-son relationship was restored, and soon afterward Philip Burton was charmed by Elizabeth, and he came to recognize how well-founded and meaningful the marriage really was.

Another notable reconciliation took place on the eve of the New York opening of *Hamlet*. In his opulent ten-room suite at the Regency on Park Avenue, Richard was reunited with Emlyn and Molly Williams. When he answered the door, he kissed them both and whispered that Elizabeth was terrified about the meeting. But there was no need for nervousness now. All was forgiven. Emlyn told Liz: "The last time we were together, you met Mr. Hyde. This time, Mrs. Burton, it's Doctor Jekyll." They laughed, and a new warm relationship was begun.

"I had been terribly forthright in Rome," recalls Williams. "But when the years passed by and they really did get married and they were going to be together for life as far as one could see, it was quite rightly all made up. I was appearing in *The Deputy*— known as *The Representative* in London—when Elizabeth telephoned. She was sweet and very nervous, and it was very touching that Richard wanted to see us the night before he opened. You can't keep up a nonfriendship indefinitely, and anyway, Sybil was doing very well and it was all working out wonderfully."

In this way, Richard's propitious *Hamlet* period was like the last sentimental scene of a sugary soap opera, with a variety of characters flitting happily across the set after enduring all the trials imposed on them by the plot. Richard was again close to the two guiding stars of his youth. And he was working with the third great influential force, Sir John Gielgud. The Burtons were at last accepted as two people genuinely in love. Elizabeth's ex-husband Michael Wilding was now in New York and finding new happiness with Margaret Leighton. Eddie Fisher was all forgiving and forgetting when he bumped into Liz in a Manhattan hotel. Debbie Reynolds was happily married to shoe millionaire Harry Karl. It was a happier time for Sybil, too.

Sybil Burton's life in New York had changed dramatically. It happened largely through her regular visits to The Strollers club and her friendship with Jeremy Geidt, a member of the English satirical group called The Establishment. He did not give her the usual tea-and-sympathy routine, but kept plugging the line: "Well, what are you going to do next?" Together they conceived the idea of setting up as a production team and taking over the upper floors of the club to open a theater. Sybil had always been attracted by behind-the-scenes theater work, and she had a flair especially for casting. Now, as co-director of The Establishment Theater Company, she found new scope for self-expression. She was responsible for the off-Broadway production of *The Ginger Man*; then came the highly successful staging of *The Knack* and the not-so-popular play, *Square in the Eye*. Later, when The Establishment group left New York, she was to take over The Strollers club and turn it into the top discotheque of the Western world. She invited her wealthy New York friends to invest in the project; Sammy Davis, Jr. was one who chipped in a thousand dollars. She named the night spot Arthur—not after Richard's role in *Camelot*, but after the name given to a haircut style by Beatle George Harrison in the film, *A Hard Day's Night*. Then she hired a sensational, swinging group called The Wild Ones, and almost immediately Arthur's became Manhattan's preferred nightspot, with a host of celebrities paying to endure the crush and the amplified thunder of music. Improbably, Sybil was to become the most celebrated hostess in town, appearing almost daily in the fashion and gossip columns, pictured frugging with Nureyev, hugging Farley Granger, dancing with Lord Snowdon's uncle, and dining with actor Victor Spinetti.

Sybil astonished even old friends with her extraordinary energy, flair, and commercial sense. She had already had one proposal of marriage—from Emlyn Williams's actor-son Brook ("It wasn't all that serious and I was turned down quite rightly. After all, as she said, there would be two Williamses and she would become Sybil Williams Williams")—and eventually, in June, 1965, she was to astonish everyone even more by marrying Jordan Christopher, the young, long-haired leader of The Wild Ones quintet. The alliance of 36-year-old Sybil Burton, the ash-blonde Welsh Methodist and mother of two, and the 24-year-old Macedonian rock 'n' roller from Akron, Ohio, inevitably brought forth a cacophony of caterwauling from the society prudes; they tut-tutted at the age difference and talked about it as a Pal Joey thing. But Christopher, the guitar-thumping pop singer, also had the experience of a broken marriage behind him, and the match proved a success. In this way, to her everlasting credit, Sybil completed her recovery from personal disaster. She prospered and made an entirely new world for herself with such dramatic change that by mid-1965 she would be described as the "white tornado" of New York's jet set.

"I admired her tremendously," says Emlyn Williams. "When she married it was very hard to tell which friends were Richard's and which were hers. But you did realize afterwards that they were not just her friends because Richard was a successful actor. They adored her, too, and people like Roddy McDowall were marvelous. They stuck by her and were permanent friends. My fear was that if she was going to make the break, she would disappear into the Welsh valleys and become just a sad little lady, but not at all. She had always behaved so beautifully, and it is marvelous that she was to become a great personality on her own. It was a happy ending to a very bumpy journey."

But Sybil's success was still in the future. For the moment, this was essentially Richard's golden year. His *Hamlet* was his greatest stage triumph to date. His *Becket* had recently won high praise from the critics. And then, amid more first-night ballyhoo in New York, *The Night of the Iguana* was given tumultuous applause at its celebrity-packed world premiere at the Philharmonic Hall. Ava Gardner, the onetime barefoot girl of Grabtown, North Carolina, stole this picture with possibly the most inspired performance of her career. Richard, in contrast, received a few harsh notices, most notably from Bosley Crowther (*The New York Times*) who wrote: "Burton is spectacularly gross, a figure of wild disarrangement, but without a shred of real sincerity. And in his ridiculous early fumbling with Sue Lyon, whose acting is painfully awkward, he is farcical when he isn't grotesque." But Crowther's opinion belonged to a tiny minority. More typical was the criticism of Judith Crist (New York *Herald Tribune*) who called it "an absorbing film of rare content and even rarer maturity." *The Night of the Iguana* was a veritable blockbuster, a top box-office success and certainly one of the most interesting pictures in which Burton had so far appeared.

Richard at this point was acquiring an unfailing Midas touch that would serve him for years to come. Any enterprise he now cared to tackle seemed certain to produce pure gold; together, he and Elizabeth were endowed with the power to unlock all the treasures of the show-business world. Their rare magnetism was emphasized when they undertook a poetry-reading session at the Lunt-Fontanne Theater to raise funds for Philip Burton's new American Musical and Dramatic Academy. The reading, with seats priced at $50 and $100, was a sellout. Again huge crowds gathered outside the theater, and the fabulous conglomeration of celebrities inside included two sisters of the late President Kennedy, scores of filmstars, leading industrialists, composers, playwrights, and directors. Elizabeth's great friend Monty Clift was there; so were her parents and the Fox president, Walter Wanger.

Elizabeth was terrified beforehand. She had never appeared on stage since she was a child, and she rightly guessed that many people would come in the hope of seeing her fall flat on her face. To prepare for the one session, she spent a month practicing with Phil Burton, three hours a day, five days a week, just as Richard had worked with his tutor so many years before. During the performance her Professor Higgins sat behind her, mouthing every word she said. But his fears were unfounded. Elizabeth, if not inspired, was far better than anyone anticipated. Richard began by reading *To His Coy Mistress* by Andrew Marvell, and Elizabeth responded in a Cockney accent with Thomas Hardy's *The Ruined Maid*. She also read William Butler Yeats' *Three Bushes*, which told of two women who loved the same man, and came across clear and strong with the line: "What could I do but drop down dead if I lost my chastity." Richard's readings included the "death of kings" speech from *Richard II*, the St. Crispin's Day speech from *Henry V*, and one of his favorite poems, D. H. Lawrence's *Snake*. Together they read T. S. Eliot's *Portrait of a Lady* and the twenty-third Psalm, which was especially moving as Elizabeth spoke in English and Richard took alternate lines in Welsh. "I didn't know she was going to be this good," said Richard during the performance. And Liz, who had been sweating at the start, was able to tell the society audience: "See, you did get something for your money."

But the man who benefited most from this slick piece of showmanship was Phil Burton. In 1962 he had become director of an acting school which steadily ran into financial difficulties and which, by March 1964, was virtually bankrupt. He advised closing it down and opening a new academy on a nonprofit basis. Aaron Frosch, who was also Richard's lawyer, arranged for the AMDA to be registered as a charitable institution, and Richard provided $27,000 to get the old school through its final term. Now a further $30,000 was raised by the poetry reading held at Philip Burton's suggestion, and it was this money that enabled the Academy to start its new life.

As New York high society paid homage to the Burtons during that summer of supreme success, it was easy to forget how ridiculed and abused they had been only a few months before. They had journeyed through the heart of the fire and emerged glowing with popularity. Nothing could seriously disturb them after surviving that ordeal. One day, in the lobby of a New York hotel, Elizabeth was handed a writ for $50 million. She smiled graciously and said "Thank you very much," and then regally passed it over to her personal manager Dick Hanley. Richard thought that deliciously polite, and when he saw that Peter Sellers was being sued for only two million dollars he promptly sent off a one-word cable: CHEAPSKATE. They could afford to laugh in the face of adversity now. Life was becoming one long, carefree, extravagant romp.

Toward the end of the *Hamlet* season, Richard was visited backstage by Spyros "Papa" Skouras, now chairman of 20th Century-Fox. The big, ebullient Greek threw his arms around the star and exclaimed, "My dear Richard, you were always my favorite actor."

"In that case," said Burton, "why are you suing me for so much?"

The answer was that Fox alleged various breaches of contract by Elizabeth in the filming of *Cleopatra* and claimed that she and Richard had depreciated the commercial value of the picture by their "conduct and deportment" during and after the filming. But the Burtons shrugged off this staggering demand and let the lawyers worry about the absurd tangle of suits and countersuits which had arisen in *Cleopatra*'s wake. So farcical was the situation that they eventually found that, while being sued for $50 million by Fox, they were also co-defendants with Fox in respect of a $6 million suit brought by film exhibitors.

But even *Cleopatra* would eventually pay its way, such was the Burtons' golden touch. From this point the Welsh miner's son could calculate his fortune in millions. Yet he would never accept that *le scandale* had been chiefly responsible for his suddenly increasing wealth. He argued that other stars had landed good parts because of notoriety, but had then failed through lack of ability. He also claimed with some justification that his price as an actor did not really soar spectacularly until he had triumphed as *Hamlet* in New York. *Becket* and *Night of the Iguana* then added to his stature. Thereafter he was able to demand and get half a million dollars for each film, plus a percentage of the profits.

The Burtons were now firmly established as the top-earning man-and-wife team in the business, and they intended to capitalize on their popularity before it should fade. For six months it had been planned that they should co-star in *Sands of Kalahari*, a film drama of five men and a woman stranded in the Kalahari Desert. They liked the script, and it was to be produced by their old friend, Stanley Baker, but they could not agree to terms. Baker explained: "Liz wanted a million dollars and he wanted half a million, and we would have given it to them. But they also asked for a higher percentage of the gross profits than we could afford." He was deeply disappointed, but there was no ill-feeling between the two film tycoons from Wales. "You can't let friendship interfere with business," says Baker.

In this way, after four months in New York, the rehabilitation of Burton the Great Actor was complete. He had left as King of *Camelot* and had returned as Prince of Denmark. Now his fame, wealth, and professional stature stood higher than ever before. On August 18, he and Liz flew off for Los Angeles en route to Mexico for a holiday. They feared another mauling by locustlike swarms of fans on the way. At San Francisco Airport nearly ten thousand shrieking girls were held back by a wire enclosure five feet high, and the Burtons passed by them almost unnoticed. These fans had eyes only for four long-haired youths about to begin an American tour. Cried Richard: "Thank God for the Beatles."

Winning Streak

Every once in a while," said Burton, "you have to make a pot-boiler." He spoke with an air of resignation, but there was no hint of bitterness. After all, the world's most publicized lovers were now being paid a record $1,750,000 for making whoopee on a sandy sun-kissed shore in Vincente Minnelli's *The Sandpiper*. Frocked in *Becket*, defrocked in *Iguana*, the Rev. Richard Burton would this time strip off his dog collar to surrender to the charms of a nature-loving unmarried mother. "When you are on a winning streak," he explained, "you play it until it turns sour."

It was totally predictable that the Hollywood money-men would aim to cash in on the profusion of free publicity in recent years by projecting Richard and Elizabeth as illicit lovers on the screen. A remake of *Lady Chatterley's Lover* was the first suggestion, but this was rejected because Burton's oratorical powers could hardly be squandered on a mere lecherous gamekeeper. Something more subtle was needed. So producer Marty Ransohoff, a film executive as renowned for his shrewdness as Old Brer Fox (his Filmways Company gave the world such super-light television trifles as *The Beverly Hillbillies, Petticoat Junction, Green Acres*, and *The Addams Family*), dreamed up a story calculated to show off to maximum advantage the obvious assets of the highest paid husband-and-wife team in history.

In theory, *The Sandpiper* could not fail. Liz would look deliciously seductive as a bohemian artist who lives above a beach in Monterey and has her free-loving, free-living routine disturbed when a juvenile court sends her illegitimate son to a boys' school. Richard's stillness and vocal range would be fully utilized in the role of the Reverend Dr. Ed Hewitt, a minister-headmaster who wrestles with his conscience as he betrays his conventional wife (Eva Marie Saint) for the permissive, progressive parent. Again, we could have those agonizing close-ups of Burton going into his now familiar long-suffering, soul-searching routine, and finally announcing his resignation from the pulpit and disappearing to start life anew. All filmed in spectacular Panovision-Metrocolor, it was the sex-and-sermon formula as before, and the ending was precisely where we came in for *The Night of the Iguana*. Only one powerful ingredient for the making of another smash-hit was missing: a convincing script.

Unlike Richard, Elizabeth liked the script, and she acted as if she believed in every word, and consequently gave the film a semblance of sincerity. From her own viewpoint, her judgment was sound enough. It was, in fact, just her kind of old-fashioned romantic movie—pure escapism that a decade earlier would have been the pride of all Odeons, lightly treated, and ending with Audrey Hepburn and William Holden, hand in hand on a golden shore, walking away barefoot toward a fried-egg sunset. Minnelli, maker of such dreamy musicals as *Meet Me in St. Louis* and *An American in Paris*, was a past master at sending filmgoers home with a warm glow in their hearts. But *Sandpiper* belonged to a different era, and in the swinging sixties a more sophisticated treatment was sought. Pure sentiment was not enough; it had to be taken seriously—given social and moral undertones, and a sad, almost cynical ending. Unfortunately the script, with its platitudes and "true romance" situations, was not up to this task.

Burton seized the few worthwhile acting opportunities he was given, and contributed more by occasionally challenging the logic of the script. For example, would a minister of the Church automatically kiss a woman after confessing his illicit love for her? He thought not. So Liz kissed him, and it was much more effective. No amount of subtle interpretation, however, could disguise the basic phoniness of the dialogue, and one could only wonder at Richard's self-control as Liz looked up into his eyes and said, "Men have been staring at me and rubbing up against me since I was twelve years old"; or as he looked into her eyes and whispered, "You should always have a man's footprints behind you, Laura." The result was a pop-movie that made healthy noises at the box office. Richard, however, was rather put in the shade as Elizabeth, her bosom never visibly more ample, dominated the wide-screen in her own aesthetic and inimitable fashion. And the critics did not like it. Not exceptional was the view of Leonard Mosley (London *Daily Express*) who wrote: "It is one of those films which I thought were buried with Louis B. Mayer. . . . But how, how, could such blooming beauty and such vintage brains have allowed themselves—with all that money, all that time to think, all those opportunities to pick and choose—to get mixed up in a phony like this film . . . ? Richard Burton keeps his clothes on for most of the film. So far as I am concerned, however, he emerged temporarily divested of his reputation as an actor."

Although *The Sandpiper* had little artistic merit, it was at least an agreeable exercise for its honeymooning stars, working together on an idyllic location in the Big Sur area of Northern California, and then in Paris. It was essentially a happy film unit. Liz had worked with Minnelli before when she was eighteen, still to be married, playing Spencer Tracy's ecstatic daughter in *Father of the Bride*. Now fourteen years and five husbands later, she was as gay and vivacious as she had been as a screen bride-to-be. A French technician on the Paris set described the Burtons as behaving "more like lovers than any lovers I have seen." Constantly they were poking fun at one another. When Richard missed a line, Liz started giggling. "I'm so henpecked," he sighed. "I don't know why I bother to act."

"You don't," teased Liz.

"I can get a divorce on the grounds of that," he rallied.

When Richard unveiled a controversial nude statue of Liz, he kissed the forehead and said, "The breasts are exactly alike. So are the belly and the buttocks. The only thing that isn't right are the arms—hers aren't so slim." But the wisecracks were never malicious, simply an integral part of their newly-developed double act. Richard, determined never to be stuck with the Mr. Elizabeth Taylor label, was playing Rhett Butler, the masterly, independent male. Elizabeth was Scarlett O'Hara, the dark, sensitive spitfire who needed a man to dominate her but who could never be completely submissive. They gave an entertaining performance, but the smart repartee fooled no one. Even Philip Burton, once opposed to the match, observed: "I think that Richard is really in love for the first time. He is now giving as well as taking. Even after their two and a half years together it's a mutual, blissful relationship. They're like two teen-agers. They can't stand being apart from each other."

While the oral sparring served as a shield to sentiment, they were not averse to lowering it and openly discussing and analyzing their relationship with the sort of frankness more usually reserved for the psychiatrist's couch. In Paris, Richard said: "Elizabeth is a combination of a sphinx, a seductress, and a woman who holds drawing-room parties for writers. It is not her physical beauty which made me fall in love with her (I'm not going to give you a list of her defects) but her loyalty. What I love in Liz is this: She is an extraordinary mother. She would never sacrifice her children for anything or for any man. . . . I feel that I now have the last word with Elizabeth. She still struggles a bit but it cuts no ice with me. Her tears leave me cold. When she throws a fit of temper I remain like marble. In the end she surrenders unconditionally and lets me make the decisions. For she is a good and generous woman." Similarly, Liz explained: "Richard has to be the boss. I know that. It's important for both of us. I need a man strong enough to rule me, and that is not easy. I have been a star since I was twelve, and I have been spoiled terribly."

The world's press lapped up every word. Godfrey Winn was

inspired to compose a popular thesis on his belief that women "secretly long to be dominated not intellectually but emotionally." And this was just an appetizer. With remarkable flair, unaided by the publicity quote-merchants, the Burtons were to maintain over the next few years a steady output of personal observations about sex, death, love, marriage, money, and each other; and their words were so widely and solemnly recorded that they might have emanated from the Oracle at Delphi or have been gleaned from the inner thoughts of Mao.

Richard: "Falling in love isn't an instant thing. It is an accumulation of detail. A slow storing up of knowledge about someone. That's how it was with Elizabeth, anyway. I knew it would cause havoc in my private life. With my wife and children and sisters. But there it was, finally, painfully, unavoidable.

"I have to feel very deeply about someone before I can become emotionally or sexually involved. I've played opposite some ladies who would have welcomed an affair. One, in particular, never stopped chasing. But I could hardly bear to touch her. You'd be surprised at the morals of many women stars who are regarded by the public as goody-two-shoes. They leap into bed with any male in grabbing distance. That's what makes me mad when I read stuff hinting that Liz is a scarlet woman because she's been married five times. She's only had five men in her life whereas those goody-two-shoes have lost count.

"All this stuff about Elizabeth being the most beautiful woman in the world is absolute nonsense. She's a pretty girl, of course. She has wonderful eyes and a double chin. She has the shape of a Welsh village girl. Her legs are really quite stumpy.

"Elizabeth has splendid breasts. I don't like to see them trussed up.

"She is the only woman I know who can, at thirty-five, wake in the morning and look as lovely as though she'd just made up. She certainly has the most beautiful skin in the world, whereas I look as though I'm to be interred at midday.

"Elizabeth tries to be a shrew, wants to be an autocrat, and unsuccessfully attempts tyranny in little things. But we never had any question of who was the boss. She always realized I was to run the show. I do this by talking, talking, talking. My little shrew is invariably tamed after a bit of talking.

"I cannot see life without Elizabeth. She is my everything— my breath, my blood, my mind, and my imagination. If anything happened to her, I would wither and die."

And Liz: "I think sex is absolutely gorgeous. I'm not a sex queen or a sex symbol. I don't think I want to be one. Maybe Richard and I are sex symbols together because we suggest love. At first, illicit love. It seems curious that our society today finds illicit love more attractive than married love. Our love is married love now. But there is still a suggestion, I suppose, of rampant sex on the wild.

"I used to belt him and he hated it. Finally he belted me one back and my eardrum did not function correctly for some time. With Richard, I don't get away with nuttin'. I need strength in a man more than any other quality. I rely on him totally now.

"Terrible fights we have. Sometimes they're in public and we hear whispers of 'That marriage won't last long.' But we know better. Even if we're in the middle of a flamer, suddenly I'll catch his eye and we give a knowing wink because we both know that once we are cuddled up in bed it will be forgotten.

"Shall I tell you how happy I am? I even enjoy lying awake at nights. Yes, I enjoy insomnia—not that I have it that much. But when I do, I lie there with a sense of joy because I love every moment of my life. Sometimes I get nervous and wonder if I am not going to have to pay for all this happiness. I wonder what would happen to me if I lost Richard.

"I am pretty enough, but I am not a great beauty. I don't have a complex about my looks, but I'm too short of leg, too big in the arms, one too many chins, big feet, big hands, too fat.

"Richard is a very sexy man. He's got that sort of jungle essence that one can sense. It's not the way he combs his hair, nor the things he wears; he doesn't think about having muscles. It's what he says and thinks.

"I love Richard and wouldn't dream of looking at another man. I don't want anybody else. But if it should happen in ten years, when I go through menopause, I think I would kill myself—because that's what the act would amount to."

While filming *The Sandpiper*, Richard had his first short story published—a deeply moving, semi-autobiographical piece about a childhood Christmas in Wales. Immediately it was discussed for the possible bearing it might have on his relationship with Elizabeth, for he wrote cryptically: "When my mother died, she, my sister, had become my mother, and more mother to me than any mother could ever have been. I was immensely proud of her. I shone in the reflection of her green-eyed, black-haired, Gypsy beauty. . . . She was innocent and guileless and infinitely protectable. She was naïve to the point of saintliness and wept a lot at the misery of others. She felt all tragedies except her own. I had read of the Knights of Chivalry and I knew that I had a bounden duty to protect her above all other creatures. It wasn't until thirty years later, when I saw her in another woman, that I realized I had been searching for her all my life." Who was this other woman? The columnists drew the inescapable conclusion. But, happily, the literary merit of Richard's *A Christmas Story* was not overlooked. His short story was published as a hardback book, and the reviews meant more to him than any rave notices for a stage or screen performance. They stoked the bright glowing embers of a writing talent that had the potential to set the literary world ablaze.

The year 1964 was almost over now, and for Burton what an extraordinary year of fulfillment it had been. As he celebrated Christmas in the Swiss resort of Gstaad—a Christmas not remotely related to his storybook memories of death and deprivation in Wales—he could reflect how the past twelve months had seen his elevation to the position where the popular press was referring to him as "the most envied man in the world." Fame and fortune . . . Elizabeth for a wife . . . threefold triumphs as filmstar, Shakespearean actor, and writer. Now he had just about everything he could have wished himself. Yet he still viewed the future with his inborn Celtic suspicion and caution, still took nothing for granted. While the year had seen him climb into tenth place in the Hollywood Motion Picture Herald's Poll of the leading box-office favorites, he knew full well that he would never consolidate that position with potboilers like *The Sandpiper.* His winning streak of fornicating clerics was at an end. He needed a new kind of role, one with originality and dramatic scope. Providentially, just such a part awaited him. As Alec Leamas, the seedy, shiftless secret agent of John Le Carré's best-selling novel *The Spy Who Came in From the Cold,* Burton now faced a film role quite unlike anything he had done before. He found it comparatively easy to launch into speeches of power and passion that somehow released his inner tensions, but in this essay on loneliness the dialogue was tight and reduced mainly to monosyllables, and his task was made all the more difficult because he had so little to say. "The others do all the acting," he explained. "As Leamas, I just react." It contrasted harshly with his work on *The Sandpiper.* From the coziness and comfort of filming in Californian sunshine and then briefly in Paris, he was plunged into gray Spartan locations that matched the cheerlessness of a story to be filmed in black and white. For Christmas, Elizabeth had bought him thirty-seven tailor-made suits at a cost of nearly $15,000, but for the next four months he was compelled to wear a crumpled, ill-fitting, 12-guinea ($35) suit, and a shabby raincoat. He worked in the cold and rain outside the main gates of Wormwood Scrubs, in drab back streets of Dublin, in the snows of Bavaria. The work was challenging and rewarding, and some critics would judge this to be his greatest screen performance. Yet it was a disturbing time for Richard, now in his fortieth year. In keeping with the miserable Leamas, he drank more heavily, and as he became immersed in the role, some of the character's extreme gloom rubbed off on him. And he recalled how somebody had once written that the Welsh were among the most brilliantly intelligent tribes in the world with a talent for everything except being middle-aged.

During a brief stay in London he took Elizabeth on a sentimental journey back to Wales. They went to Port Talbot and saw Aberavon beat Rosslyn Park, and at Cardiff Arms Park Elizabeth wore a red bowler, and they joined the jostling Welsh crowd in the traditional chorus of *Cwm Rhondda* as Wales beat England 14–3. "It was without doubt one of the worst experiences of lack of crowd control that I have ever known," says Graham Jenkins, recalling the scenes in the Queen's Hotel after the match. Even without the presence of the Burtons, the Queen's on a Saturday night after a rugby international is the most jam-packed spot on earth. "But this time it was worse. The crowd just wouldn't let us get out. We failed miserably a few times and if Haydn Mainwaring, that great Welsh tackler, hadn't barged a way through the kitchens, we would have been in serious trouble. Gaston was waiting with the car out the back in Westgage Street and we escaped back to Cwmavon. Elizabeth especially wanted to go to the Copper House to meet Will Dai because Richard had told her so many funny stories about him."

Richard now took perverse delight in showing Liz off in the village pub where the miners looked on like farmers at a cattle auction admiring prime beef. And as they entered, Will Dai looked up and growled: "Ah, it's the l-love b-b-birds. D-d-douglas F-f-fairbanks and M-m-mary P-p-pickford." His mates chuckled, and then the whole pub roared with laughter as Will, who was over eighty, looked closely at Liz and said in Welsh: "It's a f-f-funny th-thing, b-but if I had a n-new b-b-bloody engine, I w-wouldn't mind having a wr-wr-wrestle with her myself." Richard translated and Elizabeth laughed, but her laughter ended in a sudden yelp as a miner put a hand on the shapely seat of her ski pants. She swung round and gave him a clip on the jaw, and Richard roared as the miner grinned and said, "Ooh, look at her, Rich. Dom, she's a high-spirited one."

The visit so filled Richard with nostalgia that he talked loosely about buying a house in Kent and paying British taxes again. The mood would pass, but for the moment he was sick of living out of suitcases, of setting up home in a succession of luxury suites—the St. Regis or Regency in New York, the Dorchester in London, the Lancaster in Paris. Usually their entourage was comprised of Liz's four children, a tutor, two secretaries and a chauffeur, and a variety of pets, and always the traveling created new problems and difficulties.

When filming moved on to Dublin, Richard faced more nostalgia. In *The Spy* he had been working with Robert Hardy for the first time since their Stratford days, and now on the set he thought he recognized another ghost from his far-distant Oxford and Air Force days. He sent over a second assistant who said, "Excuse me, sir, but somebody thinks they know you, but they're not sure. Did you used to be known as Old Mick Misell?" The short balding man grinned through his teeth and said that he did indeed, and that evening Elizabeth poured the drinks while the two former RAF cadets spent hours reminiscing. It was their first meeting since 1947. Richard had then offered to help Misell get work in the theater, but the Jewish boy had proudly chosen to make his own way. His attitude was still much the same. He did not want to trade on their friendship and now, having what he describes as "a cough and spit part" in the film, he had not felt justified in approaching the star. For Mick Misell, alias Warren Mitchell, success had not come easily, but in another three years he would be the most talked-about actor on British television.

For two months the Burtons occupied the penthouse suite in Dublin's Gresham Hotel, and it was an uneasy time for both of them. Liz had over $50,000 worth of jewels stolen. Daughter Maria went down with measles. And since *Cleopatra* was currently running at the cinema facing their sixth-floor suite, they were pursued more than usual by hordes of fans. When Richard was being filmed in exterior night scenes, crash barriers were needed to hold back the crowds. But it was Elizabeth, though not working, who faced the greatest strain. In February she flew to Paris to console her chauffeur, Gaston Sanz, whose sixteen-year-old son had been killed in a shooting-gallery accident. Gaston, a powerful, square-built Basque, much decorated for wartime service in the Free French Commandos, had been with Miss Taylor for twelve years, and now she shared in his grief, accompanying him to the inquest and to the funeral. Only her compassion and support, he says, saved him from breaking down completely—"I wouldn't be here now if it wasn't for her." Elizabeth had been only a few days back in Dublin when she had to fly off again, following news that her father had had a stroke in Los Angeles. For days, as he hovered between life and death, she held the family together. Mr. Taylor survived. The words of Richard's *Christmas Story* came back to mind: "She felt all tragedies except her own. . . ."

After the final East German scenes for *The Spy* had been shot near the Bavarian sports resort of Garmisch, the Burtons took an isolated villa in the Antibes and enjoyed an idyllic family holiday away from the maddening crowd. During the holiday Richard heard that Sybil had remarried. He sent her his best wishes and commented, "Good luck to her. I hope she will be very happy. She is a woman of very good taste—except when it came to me." He was tired. In seeking to capture the moral and physical disintegration of the hard-drinking Leamas, he had drained himself emotionally. But the result more than justified those uncomfortable months of endeavor. In the summer, when the Burtons were working in Hollywood, the release of *The Sandpiper* brought them blistering criticism, but several months later the damage was completely repaired by the rapturous reception given to *The Spy Who Came in From the Cold*. The film faithfully followed the book except in one trivial detail: the name of Leamas's girl friend (Claire Bloom) had for obvious reasons been changed from Liz to Nan. Alexander Walker (London *Evening Standard*) wrote: "Richard Burton's performance completely rehabilitates him as an actor to respect. Playing this most difficult part of a character who can only react to things that are done to him, he succeeds in giving Leamas the impressiveness of a burned-out volcano." Cecil Wilson (London *Daily Mail*) judged that Burton had succeeded in "outshining anything he has done on the screen before." Leonard Mosley (London *Daily Express*) went further: "His performance makes you forgive him for every bad part he has ever played, every good part he has ever messed up, and every indiscretion he has ever committed off screen or on. If he doesn't win an Oscar for it this year there is not only no justice left in Hollywood, but no judgment either."

After reaching this summit, it seemed improbable that Burton could sustain such a prestigious position, simply because such meaty roles as Leamas the spy are all too few and far between.

But remarkably, he was now to follow one outstanding film performance with another of equal if not greater merit. It was while riding across America in the famous Superchief express train that he was introduced to Edward Albee's hit play, *Who's Afraid of Virginia Woolf?* Elizabeth was reading the role of Martha, the foul-mouthed, vindictive shrew, and late in the evening she passed the script to Richard and then fell asleep. He flipped through a few pages and became so excited by the raw dialogue that he read the whole thing through twice. At dawn he woke his wife and told her, "I don't think you're old enough to be Martha. And I'm sure you haven't the passion or the power. Anyway, you'd better play it to stop anyone else from doing it and causing a sensation." Richard's judgment was wrong; his advice was sound.

There was an overwhelming weight of argument as to why Miss Taylor should *not* accept this unlikely part. Martha in the play was fifty-two, a spreading, profanely vicious bitch; Liz was thirty-two, and had never played a woman so ugly in body and mind. Moreover, the wiseacres said it was impossible to make a worthwhile movie out of a play so expertly designed for the stage, and when Elizabeth finally did accept the offer they automatically presumed that Albee's savage study of a married couple would be grossly debased to accommodate an actress renowned for her physical charms. They seriously underrated Miss Taylor's range as a dramatic actress. As the slatternly Martha, she was to give the most devastating performance of her career; more astoundingly, she would play the role without any concession to looks, appearing as never before with fattened face, double chin, graying wig, bags under eyes, mascara running, slip-strap showing. This was the new Elizabeth Taylor—a beauty queen who, under Richard's influence, would willingly throw all vanity to the winds in the cause of true acting.

The major casting problem now was the role of the vulture-pecked husband, George. Arthur Hill, so magnificent in the stage production, was the obvious choice, but the play-it-safe film promotors were insisting on a star of international repute. After long debate, Richard was offered the lead. His initial reaction was that he could never play so weak and ineffectual a character, but he soon rose to the bait when Liz astutely accused him of lacking sufficient confidence to tackle the role. That, for the cussed Burton, was an irresistible challenge. Once they were officially cast as combatants in this marital cockfight, Richard and Elizabeth received telegrams from Shelley Winters and many others familiar with the play—messages begging them not to do it. "No marriage can withstand the corrosive hatred of those lines," said the prophets of doom. "It'll break you up as sure as anything. You'll end up fighting like cats and dogs at home after doing it day after day on the set." But it never worked out that way. The only fights they had at home were domestic duels staged for the benefit of the children, who demanded to see what mum and dad had been doing at the studio all day. Fascinated by the cut-and-thrust over the kitchen table, the kids persuaded them to do it again and again, and in this way the love-hate relationship of George and Martha was never allowed to become anything more than a game for two players.

Much to the Burtons' approval, the director was Mike Nichols, who had been a close friend of Richard since the days of *Camelot* when he was acting in the adjacent theater. But it was a controversial choice because Nichols, for all the brilliance of his Broadway farces, had never directed a film before, and this was certainly no farce. Yet he took to film direction as naturally as Orson Welles took to it in *Citizen Kane*, and later *The Graduate* would confirm his position as America's most successful movie director. Nichols can be quite a ruthless seeker of realism. When filming *Catch-22*, he took drastic action to get the right kind of squeal out of Paula Prentiss as she played a love scene in which Alan Arkin had to slide a hand up her skirt. Ordering a take for sound only, he stood behind the actress, and as Arkin made his move, he smothered her breasts with his hands. She yelped perfectly. Nichols was not so unorthodox in directing Elizabeth, but his touch was no less deft. Liz completely lost her own identity as she became immersed in the character of the spitting, screaming, spiteful harridan.

In *Who's Afraid of Virginia Woolf?* the Burtons scored their greatest double triumph, and by a master stroke of planning their next film involved them in another battle of the sexes, in Franco Zeffirelli's film version of *The Taming of the Shrew*. The protracted conflict on the screen dovetailed neatly with their playful sparring in public, and it offered enormous scope for more entertaining publicity about the "world's most exciting marriage." Before tackling *The Shrew*, however, they had a three-year-old promise to fulfill. In May, 1963, when having lunch in Merton College, Oxford, with Richard's old English tutor, Professor Nevill Coghill, they had offered to appear in an OUDS fund-raising production of *Dr. Faustus*. All the profits would go towards the scheme for building a new Oxford center for the arts, with a theater, library, and scenery workshop. The Burtons had kept three weeks free to return to Oxford, and such was their fantastic earning power that Richard calculated they were theoretically losing two million dollars by doing the play. But it was not entirely an act of self-sacrifice on his part. Since schooldays he had been in love with the great majestic speeches of *Faustus*, and now he had the chance to declaim them, without having to face the drudgery of a long run. His appearance would be for one week only.

While the undergraduates had already rehearsed for two months, the Burtons arrived in Oxford with just ten days to prepare their roles. It was no strain on Elizabeth, required only to be devastatingly alluring as the silent vision of Helen of Troy, but it was absurd to expect any actor to master the all-embracing part of Faustus in that time. Richard, however, in the estimation of his former tutor, came remarkably close to perfection. Coghill recalls, "I went through the play alone with Richard, and we perfectly agreed on all points of interpretation and balance. But I never interfered with his performance during rehearsals, except at his request and to teach him the necessary movements to fit in with the existing production. I would sometimes go up and make a quiet suggestion, which he would take at once, or say 'that'll be coming in later.' Very gradually he began putting in certain effects that he had studied, effects of voice that were sudden and overwhelming. I remember the shock of thrill that went through the entire cast when for the first time he let us hear the voice and see the gesture of his 'Earth, GAPE!' in the last act. So the performance grew gradually through a fortnight to something tremendous (in the old sense of that word—something that makes you tremble). So far from being disappointed with the result, it was unspeakably better than anything I had foreseen."

Honorary critics shared Coghill's enthusiasm. Edmund Blunden, Professor of Poetry at Oxford, wrote in the undergraduate newspaper *Cherwell*: "To praise most cordially all whom we watched would be just. The gusto and swiftness of the performance was one of the finest efforts that an amateur company, even assisted by two actors of genius, could ever make." How utterly different was the reaction of the professional critics. *The Times* drama critic judged it to be "a sad example of university drama at its worst. . . . The cast themselves—notably below the OUDS standard of the previous years—are largely to blame. But their inadequacy is needlessly exposed by Nevill Coghill's direction which aims at stateliness and achieves only lethargy. . . . Mr. Burton seems to be walking through the part and his contribution to the stiff high jinks in the Vatican are almost as embarrassing as those of the undergraduate actors." There were other notices no less severe. Indeed, for a charity production with a predominantly amateur cast and a professional star given only ten days to rehearse, this *Faustus* received an unnecessarily savage panning.

At the time, a disappointed Nevill Coghill tersely remarked: "What do you expect from a pig but a grunt?" Today he reflects with wry humor: "We made a great mistake over the critics. I ought to have known better. Because we wanted to sell every seat at top prices and throw none away, we decided to allow each critic one ticket only. As it was, this numbered thirty or more seats, but it meant that no critic could bring wife or mistress; which annoyed their womenfolk and deprived them of sex. Secondly, we had no drinks-party for them to meet the cast before the play, so they had nothing to cheer them for their visit to Oxford, and to two actors (Richard and Elizabeth) who have the worst newspaper-image (deliberately and wickedly fostered) of any famous actors in the world. So I ought not to have been surprised when they told me the press had come down with thunder and slaughter on our production. But I confess I was; because it was among the best work I ever did as a production, and my part in it was topped by two inconceivably wonderful stars. I cannot describe the breathless silence of Helen's slow walk round the entire stage, an unbelievable beauty; and the awed moment when Richard (again, almost without motion, yet with an extreme anguish communicated) counted the strokes of the clock in the final scene."

Despite the scathing reviews, Richard was moderately pleased with his performance, and it improved through the week. And what mattered most to Coghill was that this *Faustus* raised more than $22,000 toward his dream of a "cultural laboratory" for Oxford. Moreover, it did much to stimulate interest in drama among undergraduates. The audiences were enthusiastic; students queued all night in freezing weather to obtain tickets. It was the farewell production of Professor Coghill, an Oxford figure so deeply loved that former students and friends contributed to a book* of collected reflections to mark his retirement as Merton Professor of English Literature. But it was not the end of his working association with the Burtons. Six months later they would meet again in Rome as Richard daringly produced a film version of their *Faustus.*

The Taming of the Shrew

O n March 15, 1966, the Burtons spent their second wedding anniversary squabbling under Zeffirelli's direction in *The Taming of the Shrew,* just as six months before they had convincingly fought like wildcats in *Virginia Woolf.* Off set, however,

---

* *To Nevill Coghill from Friends,* collected by John Lawler and W. H. Auden, (London, Faber and Faber), 1966.

there was no viciousness in their puppylike snapping, and they went on to celebrate at an Italian nightclub, where they smooched around the dance floor like a couple of honeymooners. "After two years our marriage seems to be surviving very well," said Richard. They had both been tamed. And how much their life together had changed was signified by their presence in Rome, along with the children, dogs, cats, goldfish, tortoises, a rabbit and a bird. After the persecutions and indignities of *Cleopatra*, they had sworn they would never work in the Eternal City again, but here they were, back in a luxury villa on the Appian Way where once they were clay pigeons for the Vatican, the press, and the swarms of *paparazzi* who came disguised as priests with cameras in their cassocks and as plumbers with ladders to reach bathroom windows. The Italian press still had an irritating habit of referring to them as "Miss Taylor and Mr. Taylor No. 5." But their privacy was no longer invaded, and they had an eight-man bodyguard if anyone tried.

The Burtons agreed to work in Rome because this was Zeffirelli's first film as a full director. He was a pale, soft-spoken Italian of immense personal charm, with a fame previously confined to spectacular opera and Shakespearean stage productions. For years he had wanted to film *The Taming of the Shrew*, and he had resisted suggestions that Sophia Loren and Mastroianni would be perfect casting in order to have Elizabeth as Katharina and Richard as Petruchio. Under his direction, a bold and exciting production was assured. Never one to be restricted by convention or orthodoxy, he had once directed a modern-dress *Hamlet* in which the Prince said, "To be or not to be, what the Hell." He was unknown in England until 1958, when he came over to direct Joan Sutherland in *Lucia di Lammermoor* at Covent Garden. On meeting the singer, then heavily clothed against the cold, his first question was: "Where are the bosoms?" His production was a smash. Now, with the same boldness and flair, he exploited all the bawdy, outrageous, and rollicking angles of *The Shrew*. He persuaded Liz to show a near-maximum of décolletage as she flounced through scenes as the cursing, cussing "Kate the Crust"; he had Richard fumbling through his clothes for a wedding ring that was finally unearthed in his codpiece. Though the words were strictly Shakespeare's, something like two-fifths of the original dialogue was cut. The accent was on action and color, and he predicted the film would go over well with a Walt Disney audience. "We intend to make Shakespeare as successful a screenwriter as Abby Mann."

In one unbroken sequence, Zeffirelli had a bearded Burton chasing a clawing, biting, spitting Elizabeth all over and round a barn, upstairs and down, onto the rooftops, and finally plunging together through the tiles onto bales of hay. "It would have been very difficult to do it with another actress," said Richard. "You can throw your wife about, but it's difficult to throw, say, Sophia Loren around. And with Elizabeth I was permitted to do extreme physical things that wouldn't have been allowed with another actress. Anyway, there wouldn't have been the same *joie de vivre* with someone else." Certainly with Liz rolling barrels and throwing apples, and Richard swinging Tarzan-like by a rope, the chase had all the gay abandon of a fast-moving Disney scene. But *Bambi*-lovers were never exposed to such spicy language and daring frolics as this. Eight days were spent shooting that one scenic romp. The twenty-foot drop through the roof was done by stunt players. Richard, who was always prone to vertigo ("I get dizzy just standing on a brick"), would not even stay to watch.

The Burtons, filming together for the fifth time and now paying themselves as co-producers, reveled in their work. And later Zeffirelli recalled: "Elizabeth and I came from different planets—her world of the movies and mine of the theater—and Richard was the great leveler. He was the bridge. Elizabeth was very shy to play Shakespeare to begin with, but she brought a marvelous devotion. On the first day, I remember, she was like a girl coming to her marriage too young; she had extreme concern and humility. That day she was really enchanting. . . . I consider that Elizabeth, with no Shakespearean background, gave the more interesting performance because she invented the part from scratch. To some extent Richard was affected by his knowledge of the classics, as are all established actors—except Olivier."

While they were filming in Rome, Hollywood was preparing

for the annual Oscar awards, and at last Richard seemed to have an outstanding chance of winning the one big prize that still eluded him. He was nominated for *The Spy Who Came in From the Cold,* and some judged that his only serious rival was Olivier with *Othello.* But the prophets were wrong. Instead, the Best Actor Oscar went to Lee Marvin for his cowardly cowboy of *Cat Ballou,* while Julie Christie took the Best Actress award for *Darling.* But there were plenty of consolations for Richard. In June, he was named the best foreign actor by leaders of the Italian film industry, and two weeks later *Who's Afraid of Virginia Woolf?,* the most controversial film Hollywood had produced in decades, exploded onto the screen in New York and was hailed with ecstatic acclaim by the critics. Stanley Kauffman (*The New York Times*) judged it to be "one of the most scathingly honest American films ever made. . . . Miss Taylor does the best work of her career, sustained and urgent. . . . Burton is utterly convincing." The New York *Daily News* gave the film top four-star rating and declaimed, "Miss Taylor is nothing less than brilliant as the shrewish, slovenly, blasphemous, frustrated, slightly wacky, alcoholic wife of a meek, unambitious assistant professor of history. The Albee vehicle has also given Burton a chance to display his disciplined art in the role of the victim of a wife's vituperative tongue."

This was much more than just another triumph for the Burtons. As Leonard Mosley (London *Daily Express*) put it: "If Elizabeth Taylor and Richard Burton died tomorrow, at least they could die happy. For tonight, they changed the shape of the cinema as Hollywood has always known it, and it will never be the same again. The film is the most savage study of a marital relationship which has ever been made. And it would never have been shown—at least in the form in which we saw it tonight— had not Burton and Taylor been its stars. They acted as standard-bearers in a revolution against the American system of film censorship—and they won."

Here was no watered-down version of Albee's vitriolic dialogue. Liberally laced with foul abuse and oral obscenities, it defied the taboos of the U.S. film industry, and Warner Brothers made only one concession—that no one under eighteen should see the film unless accompanied by an adult. It was a breakthrough for adult entertainment—the first film for general release in America to be so heavily spiced with swearwords. The story is told that Hermione Gingold was repeating some of the Woolf-isms on her way home from the Manhattan premiere when her business manager said, "Please, Hermione, not in front of a cab driver." A New York judge commented that he would give thirty days to anyone who used those words in his courtroom, the film was banned in Nova Scotia because of its "obscenity and blasphemy," and a cinema manager in Nashville, Tennessee, was arrested for showing "profanity" on the screen. But the world at large recognized it as a genuine work of art. It was showered with honors, and Liz was generally expected to walk off with her second Oscar.

The release of that film was beautifully timed. It was now suggested that the Burtons could become as great an acting partnership as the Oliviers had once been, and except for publicity about Miss Taylor falling in love with Zeffirelli, nothing could have been better geared to promote interest in *The Taming of the Shrew*. Meanwhile in Rome, the stars fully exploited the battle-of-the-sexes publicity angle. Elizabeth, as spitfire Kate, had her dressing room plastered with privately printed posters declaring: "Now on location in Rome—Elizabeth Taylor in *The Taming of the Shrew* and introducing Richard Burton." And when Richard replied with his own special posters, she went back to the drawing board and came out with: "Elizabeth Taylor, Academy Award-Winning Actress and Shakespearean Coach to Richard Burton." How these joyful days contrasted with their previous experience in Rome. This time filming was never interrupted or delayed, and the worst that happened to accident-prone Elizabeth was a minor bump on the head when Charlie Brown, her Abyssinian cat, fell on her head as a butter-fingered butler tried to rescue it from a fir tree.

One event, however, did cast a dark shadow over those otherwise carefree days: the news that Montgomery Clift had died of heart disease in New York. Elizabeth was shattered, and outside of her own family, no death could have shocked her more. Monty was like a brother to her—one of her closest friends since she was seventeen and starring opposite him in *A Place in the Sun*. Now her mind went back to another day of horror when she was told he was dead. It had happened when she was married to Michael Wilding and they were giving a dinner party for Monty, Rock Hudson, Kevin McCarthy, and others. Afterward Monty crashed in his car on the vicious corkscrew bend descending from her home overlooking Beverly Hills. The car smashed into a telegraph pole, and when Liz reached him and crawled inside to lift his head from the wheel, she found herself covered with blood. His jaw was broken in four places, his face terribly mutilated and needing extensive plastic surgery. Now, at forty-six, the life of this quietly dedicated actor was ended. Liz had been due to co-star with him in *Reflections in a Golden Eye*.

After *The Taming of the Shrew*, Richard and Elizabeth stayed on in Rome to work on a project that had film producers chewing their cigars in Groucho Marx disbelief. Burton was putting up a million dollars of his own money to film *Dr. Faustus* on behalf of the Oxford University Theater Fund, and with the exception of himself and Elizabeth, all the cast would be amateurs—some forty students, plus a couple of dons. The risk was colossal. Mention of Marlowe was enough to make the most speculative of producers take to the hills, and even with the world's biggest box-office couple involved, there were no financiers eager to back such an offbeat project. After all, the stage production by the same team had been despised by the critics. And however brilliantly they exploited the extra advantages of wide screen and color, the fact remained that they were still working with a windbag of a play that sags into mediocrity in its middle with tedious conjuring tricks and acutely embarrassing attempts at comedy. Yet Richard went ahead, indulging his film-making fancies as never before.

All the actors, including the millionaire Burtons, agreed to work on the union minimum of $45 a week, and Richard co-directed with his old tutor, Nevill Coghill. Working from Marlowe's 1604 text, they began by cutting some of the comic scenes that Coghill describes as absolutely hopeless ("even the Crazy

Gang couldn't have made them work") and providing the play with its desperately needed middle by looting material from other Marlowe works. "We did it by expanding the notion present in the original of *The Seven Deadly Sins,*" says Coghill. "As this expansion needed dialogue, we chose avarice from *The Jew of Malta,* and so on. We did not think it proper to write sham-Marlowe, but thought he would not mind if we borrowed from his other works. I dare say the script we finished with was not as good as we had hoped, and in production it was—and had to be on grounds of economy—modified here and there. I do not say it was perfect, but it at least offered a viable solution to the main purpose—of making a great vehicle out of Marlowe for Richard."

Richard, so passionately in love with the poetry of *Faustus,* spared nothing of himself in striving to make this film a success. With only two months allowed for filming, he gave it all his time, from six in the morning to late at night. He gathered around him such outstanding technicians as Gabriel Pogany, director of photography, and John De Cuir, production designer. He exploited Elizabeth's box-office value by giving her many more entrancing entrances, and he encouraged the introduction of a dazzling array of special effects. The result was a film version infinitely more exciting and convincing than the stage production. Indeed, the early shots were impressive enough to persuade Columbia to take over the financing and distribution and so relieving Richard of huge responsibility. When the film was given its world premiere in Oxford one year later, Alexander Walker, the London *Evening Standard* critic, properly observed: "It is an act of piety on Burton's part. The only profit it is likely to bring him is the satisfaction of preserving a performance that proves him still to be one of his generation's great classical actors. . . . Ultimately, however, Dr. Faustus stands or falls by the stature of its star, and here, Burton is magnificent. Ably supported by the Oxford players—much better rehearsed than before, and with Andreas Teuber an outstanding Mephistopheles—his performance swells to fill the screen more movingly than it did the stage. His voice takes all the trumpet calls of pride, and fearful flutes of remorse, in the damnation story, without missing a note."

This *Faustus* appealed to the eye with its resplendence of color photography and arrested the ear with its grandeur of poetry. But inevitably it held little attraction for the great mass of moviegoers, who were left feeling hopelessly deprived without a story-line clearly defined and developed. It was, in short, a collector's piece. "As a single performance by Richard, I think it is a classic film," says Coghill. "Who else can speak poetry like that and make it part of the living story he is enacting? Almost no one. But it was not a financial success because there are not many who care for these things." Indeed not. Among those who did not care for it were a number of prominent critics who judged it too theatrical and boring. Later, when it was seen in America, the *Time* reviewer wrote caustically, "When she (Liz) welcomes Burton to an eternity of damnation, her eyeballs and teeth are dripping pink in what seems to be a hellish combination of conjunctivitis and trench mouth. Mercifully mute throughout, she merely moves in and out of camera range, breasting the waves of candle smoke, dry-ice vapor and vulgarity that swirls through the sets." Elizabeth thought that notice so distasteful and malicious that she resolved never to subscribe to the magazine again.

After making *Faustus*, Richard went briefly to flooded Florence to give his services as narrator for Zeffirelli's documentary on behalf of the Italian Art Rescue Fund; then he and Elizabeth visited London to contribute to a television show in aid of the Aberfan Disaster Fund. There was no lack of film offers for them now; they were being overwhelmed with scripts, though all too often the stories were unnecessarily designed to provide parts for both of them. Richard told one Italian producer, "I do wish you chaps could get it into your heads that although we've done five films together, that doesn't make us Laurel and Hardy." The Burtons were committed to one more picture together after the Christmas holidays. Then they had separate projects. Their next film, begun in January, 1967, was Graham Green's *The Comedians*, a complex story set to a background of brutality and corruption in the police state of Haiti. Once again they were to be involved in an illicit love affair—Elizabeth as the unfaithful wife of a lovable but unloved South American ambassador (Peter Ustinov);

Richard as a self-disgusted, guilt-ridden hotelier who professes his belief in nothing but ends up leading a guerrilla revolt. Elizabeth's role was a comparatively small one and Richard originally advised her against accepting it. "In my experience," he said, "people who play small parts tend to be thought of as small-part players." But then it was artfully suggested that Sophia Loren was itching for the part and would be great in the love scenes with Burton, and that settled it for Elizabeth. She grabbed the part, and Richard gallantly insisted that he was delighted because he could no longer do love scenes with any other actress. "I just don't enjoy kissing other ladies anymore."

Under Glenville's direction, they went on location to the West Nigerian state of Dahomey, where they enjoyed the rare experience of moving about in public without being instantly recognized and mobbed. One night when Richard was out late on a tour of the bars, Elizabeth got chauffeur Gaston to telephone around for him. At one hotel the receptionist answered: "Richard Burton? Is he black or white?" This refreshing anonymity lasted just six weeks. Then from darkest Africa the Burtons moved on to the glitter of the Royal Command Performance of *The Taming of the Shrew*. They were about to step back into the limelight in a style that was spectacular even by their superextravagant standards.

It was an occasion unlike any other in their lives, and they planned to savor every satisfying second of it. Four years earlier they had moved into separate suites at the Dorchester to begin an uneasy existence as the odd couple held in "suspended animation." Now they were returning in open triumph, to be honored by royalty, hailed by the fans, and most of all to be welcomed by the entire Jenkins clan. This time they did not discreetly move into the Dorchester; they practically took over the place as they turned their long weekend visit into a monumental family celebration. Richard had hired fourteen suites to accommodate his family, and on the train from Port Talbot to London old Tom looked sternly at the family group and said: "Now look, just because you're having something for nothing, you're not to spend your brother's money like a load of banshees." He was absolutely amazed when he saw the service at the Dorchester. "Would you believe it?" he told his brothers. "All I did was go downstairs and ask for the television room and they sent four electricians up to my room just to plug in a set."

"As a get-together we hadn't had anything like it before in our entire lives," says Hilda. "All first class from Port Talbot and our eldest brother Tom in charge and telling us not to behave like millionaires, and we felt just like that with Rolls Royces driving us from Paddington station to the Dorchester. It was too beautiful. I just can't tell you. In every room there were gorgeous flowers. I never saw such beautiful arrangements—with cards saying 'Hope your stay will be a happy one—Richard and Elizabeth.' We were only sad for one thing. My father would have been tickled pink to have been there. Richard told us to order what we liked and not to pay for a blessed thing. And we didn't. When we eventually went back in the train my brother Verdun said 'Now I know what it feels like to be a bankrupt millionaire.' "

Never has such a family invasion disturbed the dignity of the Dorchester in such delightful style. Richard's six brothers and five sisters, plus husbands and wives, children, aunts and uncles, brought spring to Park Lane with their uninhibited happiness. "What's this on the menu?" said Verdun, squinting at the French. And when a nephew translated, he exclaimed, "Chicken! Duw! With such bloody fancy words I thought it was turkey at least." It was the beginning of a weekend of glorious extravagance and nostalgia—the last full flourish of the wide-spreading family tree that had taken firm root in the black earth of Pontrhydyfen. At 6 A.M. on Sunday morning, Elizabeth finally retired to snatch two hours' sleep. Richard never got to bed. All through the night he went on yarning and drinking with his brothers. Then, bleary-eyed, he accompanied Liz to the rehearsal of the Royal presentation. The following day was Elizabeth's thirty-fifth birthday. He gave her a £160,000 diamond and emerald bracelet—and for all his relatives and close friends he provided 150 circle seats at the Command Performance. That night of regal splendor he faced the formalities with rare ebullience. He told Princess Margaret that he was nervous, but it never showed. On the stage of the Odeon Theater, Leicester Square, Wales' most celebrated son brashly told the audience: "My real name, of course, is Richard Jenkins and therefore my wife is Lizzie Jenkins. And up there in the circle is a young lady whose real name is Maggie Jones. When we took over the Dorchester it was only a desperate attempt to try to keep up with the Joneses."

So the great Jenkins junket went on. Back at the Dorchester, the Welsh relatives mingled with some two hundred celebrities at Elizabeth's birthday ball, and afterward the serious drinking began. At the piano Christopher Plummer played and sang a selection from *The Sound of Music,* and when the family asked Verdun to sing he yelled across the ballroom floor: "As soon as that bloody Baron Von Trapp shuts his trap I'll conduct the Jenkins hundred-voice choir, brought at enormous expense from South Wales, in a selection of hymns." Towering Welsh songs flooded out of the ballroom windows into the night air and across the way a Swansea-bred policeman kicked imaginary goals on his Hyde Park beat.

In the plush and perfumed Dorchester urinals a whole row of Jenkinses lined up against the marble wall, including Tom the Fullback, Will Waistcoat (so named because of his dress when he was a company sergeant major), and Dai Plus Fours, who wore such fancy pants when he was a sergeant in the police. Standing in the middle was the great Welsh international fly-half Cliff Morgan, and when he called out "Hey Jenks," heads on either side turned towards him. "Hey Jenks," he said, addressing young Graham on the right wing, "doesn't it make your cock look shabby in here." Later, old Tom Jenkins nudged Richard and the two of them rounded up the footsore waiters in their tired penguin suits and sat them down at the tables while Hilda and her sisters waited on them. Doyen members of the Dorchester staff could scarcely believe their eyes. Elizabeth Taylor was dancing with waiters in their braces and other famous stars were behind the bar serving the kitchen staff while millionaire guests were washing glasses. Next evening Richard was still holding court. The luggage was packed, the cars were waiting, and the plane was booked. He kept stalling and talked about later planes, and all the time the drinks and anecdotes flowed. Finally, a day behind schedule, the Burtons abdicated from the Dorchester. For Richard there would be many more lavish and riotous nights. For most of his sisters, brothers, nephews, and nieces, it was *the* night of a lifetime.

For Elizabeth, unfortunately, the joyful abandon of that weekend was lost through a tragedy on her birthday—the death of Mr. Frank Flannagan, a lifelong American friend and a member of her staff. He died of a heart attack shortly after midnight, and Elizabeth had to leave her own party to comfort his widow Agnes, who was also her personal hairdresser. But otherwise the Burtons' visit to London as Royal Command stars was more successful than they had dreamed possible, and most important of all *The Taming of the Shrew,* the first film Richard had produced, was reasonably well-received. There were a few harsh notices, but mostly the critics praised the gusto and rollicking sport of the film, and in box-office terms it proved a surefire blockbuster. Three weeks later, to add to their pleasure, the Burtons were both nominated for British Film Academy awards for their work on *Who's Afraid of Virginia Woolf?* But the awards which interested them most were those shortly to be presented by the Motion Picture Academy. Could they become the first husband-and-wife team to win Oscars simultaneously?

In April, 1967, as they continued work on *The Comedians* in the south of France, this seemed a real possibility. Altogether *Virginia Woolf* had thirteen nominations—more than any other picture—and Burton had still to win his first Oscar. "I'm sure he'll win it," said Liz. "Of course, it would be a giggle if we both got it, but it's not necessary. I've got one already—for my tracheotomy." But Richard was the one who judged right; a week before the ceremony he remarked that he seemed "destined to be always the bridesmaid." And so it happened. Both he and his wife had had five Oscar nominations over the years. Now Elizabeth collected the Best Actress award for the second time while he missed out again. The irony, however, was that the Best Actor award went deservedly to one Shakespearean actor, who had concentrated, unlike Richard, more on the stage than the screen—Paul Scofield, picked for his playing of Sir Thomas More in *Man for All Seasons,* and now busy rehearsing *Macbeth* at Stratford. "I had made up my mind that Richard Burton would get it," said the quiet, unassuming Best Actor. Instead, his Oscar was just one of six that went to the low-budget *Man for All Seasons,* and these included the Best Picture award.

But this was a fleabite of a disappointment for Richard at a time when he and Liz enjoyed unrivaled success. Never before had life been so sweet for them. They visited London where Liz, dripping with a million dollars' worth of jewels, collected her Oscar at a Grosvenor House ceremony. Then they cleaned up the British Film Academy Awards. Liz took the Best Actress prize, Richard the top British actor award. *Virginia Woolf* was voted the best film from any source and *The Spy Who Came in From the Cold* was the best British film of the year. Together, those two pictures won seven out of twenty awards. The real prize for the Burtons, however, could be counted in millions. *Virginia Woolf* had already grossed eighteen million dollars and Liz's percentage was believed to be the highest in movie-making history. It was estimated that she could pick up four million dollars for that work alone. *The Spy* and *The Shrew* were also reaping huge profits. Elizabeth had *Reflections in a Golden Eye* coming out that year, and then there was still *Dr. Faustus* which they were holding back from general release to avoid overexposure.

The Burtons' unfailing Midas touch was by no means confined to films. Richard and partners had recently bought 500 acres of real estate in Tenerife for about $250,000; now it was valued at a cool million. Even on holiday in the Mediterranean they were pursued by success. In Monte Carlo, in June, they learned that the Harlech Consortium—headed by Lord Harlech, former British Ambassador in Washington—had won the Independent Television contract for Wales and South West England. Between them the Burtons held 158,400 shares and Richard, along with his boyhood understudy Stanley Baker, was to become a director of the company governing the western commercial station. "A TV station. That's all we need," Liz gaily quipped as she went off on a huge shopping spree. Back in Britain, doubts were being raised as to whether Burton could lawfully become a director of such a national concern while paying taxes in Switzerland. "How much will Burton sacrifice in taxes for the land of his fathers?" asked Robert Pitman in the London *Daily Express*. "With Liz, will he now come home again to Wales? Or will Richard IV swiftly abdicate like Richard II?" But Richard did get a directorship. And for all the ensuing criticism about his inadequate contribution to the Welsh television programs, it was undeniable that his interest in Harlech TV was more emotional than financial, since he could easily have invested his money in enterprises far more likely to reap fat dividends.

At this stage one could only reflect in wonder at how radically the Burtons' image had changed. Could it be just four years ago that savagely criticized Dick and Liz were living in their uncomfortable state of marital limbo in the Dorchester Hotel? How odd to recall those words of *Time* magazine: "The outcome of the Taylor–Burton game must inevitably yield up a loser." Where was the loser now? Once ostracized and scorned, they were rehabilitated to a degree that seemed impossible a few years before. In London and New York they were feted by The Establishment. In Paris they dined with the Windsors. In Rome they were accepted as solid citizens who did invaluable work for charity. They had been honored co-stars of a Royal Film Performance. Richard was Britain's newest television tycoon. And now, as they celebrated their third wedding anniversary, written tributes were paid to them by a host of celebrities, including Sammy Davis, Jr., Julie Andrews, Peter Ustinov, and Sir John Gielgud. Philip Burton, once so horrified by their liaison, expressed his feelings for them in glowing terms. Emlyn Williams, who had castigated them on April Fool's Day, 1962, wrote: "This time it's me that's the Fool. But I'm quite happy about it."

Of course, there were limits even to the success of the Burtons. Wolf Mankowitz, who had worked on the *Faustus* film script, wrote in a letter to *The Guardian* that their work on that film was "the largest individual act of philanthropy made towards either the amateur or the professional theater in this country. . . . If the

Beatles are worth a medal, Mr. Burton is due for a Life Peerage."
Similarly, American newspapers became absurdly imaginative in
predicting that the Queen would give Richard a knighthood in
the 1967 Birthday Honors List. There was not even a C.B.E. for
his many charity-raising efforts. Nevertheless, he and Elizabeth
had unquestionably reached the zenith of their box-office power
and prestige. When they started a three-month holiday in the
spring it was said that Hollywood almost had a nervous breakdown, since nearly half of the U.S. film industry's income for
movies in theatrical distribution came from pictures starring one
or both of them. This was an exaggeration, but the credibility of
the story illustrated well how they had become far and away the
biggest money-makers in moviedom. Their signatures on a contract were sufficient to secure a guarantee of virtually any amount
of money, and they were capitalizing on the situation by working
together as often as possible. "People hinted that if we kept on
doing films together it would destroy us," said Burton, "but that
is rubbish. We only really enjoy working together. It's total comfort for both of us. And there is something else—we can tell just
by looking at each other's eyes if we are at all off-key. We don't
have to say a word."

Boom Time

The luxury yacht *Odysseia* slapped through Mediterranean
waters with a priceless cargo of jewels that had graced the
necks and fingers of royalty and precious paintings brushed by
the genius of French Impressionists. For a quarter of a million
dollars the Burtons had acquired a floating Edwardian palace of
walnut and chrome that afforded complete privacy for them-

selves, the children, two pekes, two Yorkshire terriers, and an Abyssinian cat. They were Sardinia-bound to make their eighth picture together. The movie, originally called *Goforth,* then *Sunburst,* and finally *Boom,* was the most aptly named film since Liz's *The Girl Who Had Everything.* For this was Boom-time for the Burtons. On the screen Elizabeth was playing Mrs. Flora Goforth, the richest woman in the world. Off the screen Richard was making their name a more familiar synonym for wealth than Rockefeller.

The new image of the Burtons as superspenders was launched by the purchase of the yacht, which had seven bedrooms and three bathrooms and a huge organ installed by a former eccentric owner, who liked to take her out in heavy storms to get the right atmosphere for playing Bach. Elizabeth had fallen in love with the *Odysseia* when they had chartered her in the south of France. Richard bought the yacht, renamed her *Kalizma* after Kate, Liza and little Maria, and had the organ ripped out and replaced with a bar. Later he casually spent another £100,000 on a face-lift that included installation of radar equipment, deep freeze, hand-painted furniture, Chippendale mirrors, Louis XIV chairs, Regency sofas and Super Peerless Wilton carpeting that was quickly messed by untrained cats and dogs. It was only the beginning. Just as they arrived in Sardinia like royalty, with their yacht and their own private household, like royalty they would leave—flying in a privately rented $850,000 Hawker Siddeley 125 Executive jet with all modern conveniences and stereo and videotape screen. Not for them were the fuss and formality of a scheduled arrival at London Airport. A Customs official had to make a special journey to Abingdon RAF airfield to check their privileged entry into the country.

The power and the wealth of the Burtons were constantly in evidence at this time. During the making of *Boom* in the summer of 1967, they fixed their own working hours and surrounded themselves with a private establishment of secretaries and dressers as difficult to penetrate as any royal court. The location was in a desolate spot, but the Burtons could always sail off for weekend trips around Corsica and to Venice where they were feted at gala balls. The following year Richard was starring in *Where Eagles Dare,* and after his location work near Salzburg, he and Elizabeth made another spectacular entry into Britain—one so bizarre that it had columnists exploring their Rogets for appropriate words of supreme extravagance. The *Kalizma* was now in dry dock for refitting, and because they couldn't otherwise return to Britain without putting the dogs into quarantine, they had hired the 200-ton diesel yacht *Beatriz of Bolivia* from the Patino tin family at the modest rental of $2,500 a week. They sailed up the Thames to the Tower of London, dropped anchor, and then Rolls Royced off to their Dorchester suite, leaving their four-legged friends behind them. So, throughout the spring of 1968, guides on the river pleasure-steamers gave the Beefeaters of the Tower earaches with their "and on the left, ladies and gentlemen, we have the Burtons' yacht—the most expensive floating dog kennel in the world."

Arthur Kattendyke Strange David Archibald Gore, the eighth Earl of Arran, known as "Boofy Gore," or sometimes "Goofy Bore," to his colleagues on the London *Evening News,* wrote in his weekly tittle-tattle column about the ridiculous dog-boat and pampered stars, and how tiresome it was all becoming. Robert Hardy, long-time friend of both Boofy and Richard, disapproved of the article so much that he threw a dinner party for the Burtons at Bucks Club and invited Lord Arran and a few others including Robert Morley and his wife Joan. "I told Boofy that he really ought not to write about people in those terms unless he had met them. I thought 'you've only got to meet Richard, hold your horses for a bit, and listen, and you'll find an extraordinary creature.' Anyway, it was all arranged. But the party didn't go well; they were just so opposite to each other. Unfortunately, when we got up and moved around, Richard and Arran were left together. Then, suddenly, Richard turned his sardonic eye on Arran and said, 'You bore me.' The next thing I knew Elizabeth was coming over to me. 'We've got to get Richard out,' she said. 'He's been ghastly. Did you hear what he said?' It was an extraordinary scene. Anyway, the 'carriage' was summoned, and the horses which had been white when they arrived were changed for black. It was that kind of party."

Afterward, Lord Arran revealed his side of the incident. "I was having a frightfully interesting conversation with Liz Taylor. We were talking about quarantine regulations. Earlier we had let Mr. Burton hold the floor. I realized I was in the presence of the great, so I let him get on with it. I knew my place and I kept it. There was this marvelous spread of oysters and champagne and the party was going really well. Then, halfway through my discussion with Miss Taylor, Mr. Burton suddenly said, 'I'm bored.' I said 'You mustn't be bored. We're all frightfully nice people and trying our best, you know.' He then said that he found me boring too. I replied immediately—what I said wasn't very polite, so I can't repeat it. Anyway, then we all got up and went home. I could see that Miss Taylor was very cross about it indeed. I personally didn't care two hoots, but I did mind about these nice Hardys. When you give a party like that it must be heartbreaking for it to go wrong. They must have cried. I don't think Mr. Burton was drunk anymore than I was—I had my usual quota for the night. No, I just think he didn't like the cut of my jib, as my father used to say. What irritated me was that I hadn't really said much that evening. I had deliberately left the conversation to him. I think he's accustomed to getting everything his own way, that's all. He might even dislike lords for all I know. Anyway, he was very rude. And it came like a thunderclap out of the blue."

Hardy blames himself for the mess. "I think Richard was tired, and he was bored. I shouldn't have given the party. Richard shouldn't have accepted. It doesn't matter which way it goes. It was very much my fault really. I think he felt a bit hedged in and that I'd thrown a journalist at him, one who was also a peer, in a sort of privilegey club. I remember him turning to me at one point and saying: 'You're a cunt. I hate all this fucking privilege —all the people going round saying, you sit here and so on.' If I were a trained host I would have had the nuance to know that this party couldn't have worked."

The incident illustrated that Richard, for all his superwealth and his acknowledged place in high society, had not changed in his basic characteristics. The wild, rebellious Welshman was still no great respecter of conventions or personages, still had an instinctive distaste for unnecessary pomp and formality. But only those who knew and understood him well could appreciate that there was no calculated malice or indeed any significance when he exploded into a bout of such sudden snarling hostility. It was typical, too, that the following day the errant guest should send out lengthy telegrams apologizing to everyone at the party. Hardy not only received a telegraphed apology, but also copies of cables sent to all the other guests. "He was packing the post office with apologetic telegrams, and each was about five pages long." Shortly afterward, Burton invited both Hardy and Lord Arran to a private showing of *Boom,* followed by a supper party.

The purpose of the Burtons' stay in London was film-making. Elizabeth was starring with Bob Mitchum and Mia Farrow in *Secret Ceremony;* Richard was doing more scenes for *Where Eagles Dare* and then he was to star in *Laughter in the Dark,* directed by Tony Richardson and produced by Neil Hartley, the team recently responsible for *The Charge of the Light Brigade.* Yet it was always their social activities that received the greatest publicity, and from this point the transformation of Burton the actor into Burton the supercelebrity could be judged complete. His purple patch as an actor had come between 1963 and 1967 with his stage triumph as *Hamlet* and such worthy films as *Becket, The Night of the Iguana, The Spy Who Came in From the Cold,* and *Who's Afraid of Virginia Woolf?* Thereafter, as he indulged his own film-making whims and reveled in globe-trotting work and play with Elizabeth, his celebrity image became more and more dominant. The kind of publicity that he helped to create by actions and words maintained worldwide interest in the seemingly enviable life of Burton the husband, the big spender and socialite. His work, in comparison, took on lesser significance.

For example, shortly after the making of *Boom,* Richard's previous film, *The Comedians,* opened in New York to unenthusiastic reviews. Critics called it "sketchy . . . no great shakes . . . conventional . . . obvious." Yet the public still flocked to see the Burtons on the screen and mobbed them whenever they made a public appearance. Curiously, after near four years of legality, the Liz–Richard relationship had lost none of its strange fascination.

They were not just another middle-aged married couple; they were seen as two volcanic personalities living side by side in unexpected harmony but periodically giving off enough sparks to maintain the element of danger and excitement. The social columnists dwelled lovingly on their pyrotechnic displays of affection, and significantly the critics paid special attention to their lovemaking on the screen.

Ian Christie, the London *Daily Express* critic, wrote: "The Burtons seem to revel in togetherness as they earn their daily crust. *The Comedians* is the seventh film in which they have appeared together, and they both give faultless performances. . . . Burton kisses Taylor with such passion and devotion that it is easy to imagine a less contented wife complaining that she doesn't get that sort of treatment at home. . . . I'd say these two had something very special going for them to have such a successful life both in public and privately." Conversely, Alexander Walker (London *Evening Standard*) wrote: "Amazing how a couple like the Burtons seldom manage to generate a spark of credible passion when together on the screen—principally, I think, because Miss Taylor's power to play strong-willed women precludes her from making a successful pitch for our sympathy."

It was only natural that critics should take diametrically opposed views of the Burtons in love scenes. Public opinion was no less divided about their compatibility in real life. Was theirs really a perfect match as all the evidence suggested? Could Elizabeth, with three broken marriages behind her, settle down forever with one man? Where would it end? Such questions were the subject of endless chitchat, and the Burtons only stimulated the public's enormous appetite for such trifles by their occasional outbursts, their little displays of temperament, and their more extravagant displays of affection. In the meantime, the critics could savage their films as they pleased. The Burtons' status as social celebrities, if not as superstars, remained unimpaired.

In February, 1968, the film of *Dr. Faustus* was given its delayed showing in New York and Richard received one of the worst drubbings of his career. Renata Adler of *The New York Times* judged: "*Dr. Faustus* is of an awfulness that bends the mind. The Burtons . . . are clearly having a lovely time; at moments one has the feeling that *Faustus* was shot mainly as a home movie for them to enjoy at home." *Women's Wear Daily* called it "not a movie but a self-produced opportunity for exhibitionism, widescreen art style." The film was not a financial success. But still the Burtons' superstar charisma was unchanged. At the New York premiere of *Dr. Faustus* they were almost overwhelmed by a thousand fans outside the Rendezvous Cinema; the crowd burst through police barriers and photographers were thrown to their knees. After the premiere the stars were feted by hundreds of celebrities at a glittering ball in aid of Philip Burton's American Musical and Dramatic Academy. Among those who paid $200 to attend were Senator and Mrs. Robert Kennedy, Lord Harlech, Perle Mesta, Peter Lawford, Spyros Skouras, and the then Linda Bird Johnson. They toasted Richard and Liz until the early hours.

Later that year, *Boom* hit the American screens and was hailed there as "outright junk." The main defect was that not even skillful revision of the script by Tennessee Williams could disguise the fact that the leading parts were originally intended for a woman much older than Liz and a man younger than Burton. But Richard promptly sent a letter to director Joseph Losey saying, "Dear Joe, I don't care a tu'penny bugger what the critics say; it is a magical combination of words and vision." And later Losey commented, "I feel that the film was ahead of its time. It perplexed the British and American critics, but it had a different reception from the Continental critics, and we firmly believe it to be a remarkable picture." Maybe *Boom* was underestimated. Nevertheless, it was undeniable that Richard was currently moving into a fairly undistinguished period in his career. Of course it could be argued that *Faustus*, though blatantly noncommercial, was at least a project nobly conceived and tackled. But not even that could be said about his next picture to be shown. This was *Candy*, the bizarre adventures of a teen-age nymphomaniac; a movie overpublicized as a teasing sex odyssey, a glorious pornographic spoof, and the ultimate in sexual frankness on the screen.

A remarkable number of distinguished actors lent their talents to this frivolous and extravagant exercise in eroticism. Christian

Marquand, who had once played Brigitte Bardot's lover in *And God Created Woman*, was the director, and he also happened to be a great friend of Marlon Brando. When Brando was working with Elizabeth on *Reflections in a Golden Eye*, Marquand persuaded him to take a cameo role in *Candy*. Brando, in turn, roped in his good friend Burton, and thereafter it was relatively easy to attract other big names—Walter Matthau, Ringo Starr, James Coburn, Charles Aznavour, John Huston. To play Zero, his chauffeur, Richard brought in another old friend, former world middleweight champion Sugar Ray Robinson. For most of them it was simply a lighthearted romp, an escape from serious acting, and Richard especially was in his element as McPhisto, a caricature of a drunken, long-haired Welsh poet who, during a lecture tour, has the first nibble of Candy in his mirror-plated Mercedes Benz and persuades her that she should give herself to any man who needs her. This silly film had Candy constantly losing her knickers as she was seduced in a succession of improbable places—on top of a grand piano, on a billiards table, in a hospital bed, in a police patrol car—and in one scene, with Liz looking on, Richard was called upon to lose his trousers. At that point in the filming he roared across the set: "Elizabeth, this is the man you married!"

It was essentially a fun performance on his part and not to be taken seriously. In rather the same vein he tackled *Where Eagles Dare*. ("I'm just doing this one for the kids. I want them to be able to enjoy one of my pictures and not associate me solely with the highbrow stuff.") Ostensibly a taut adventure drama, this one was greeted with derisive laughter at the London press showing. The story of a commando-type raid on the "impregnable" mountaintop headquarters of the German Secret Service was totally implausible and riddled with clichés. Yet it mattered not at all. The action and spectacle were everything, and such was the popular appeal of an Alistair Maclean yarn, with its breathtaking cable-car scenes and James Bondish situations, that the film proved a colossal financial success.

Richard had no illusions about *Where Eagles Dare*. In a picture that was ninety percent action, his role demanded a minimum of acting ability and was never artistically stimulating. The great master of the spoken word ("I have this pyrotechnic ability with my voice") exploded only firecrackers and blanks. After one non-speaking gunfight, he remarked, "This is what Elizabeth calls money for old rope." The strain on him was strictly physical as he worked long hours on back-projection filming and rediscovered long-forgotten muscles in toiling in bitter winter weather on a 5000-foot mountain in Austria. But even the physical challenge was not all that great. Stuntmen tackled the athletic scenes and those that were impossible for a star shaking with chronic acrophobia. Though Richard found it exhausting, actress Mary Ure, taking a working holiday from her home and looking after the children and her husband, actor-writer Robert Shaw, insisted that it was all a damned sight easier than housework. And co-star Clint Eastwood quipped: "They ought to change the title to *Where Doubles Dare.*"

At the time he completed *Where Eagles Dare*, Burton had not the faintest notion of the staggering financial return he was to receive from his profit-sharing interest in a picture destined to be a box-office smash all over the world. Yet his style of living and expenditure continued to rise to such a high peak of opulence and ostentation that the phrase, "Who do you think you are, bloody Richard Burton?" became virtually a cliché for anyone buying a round of drinks out of turn. In May, 1968, he bought Elizabeth the 33-carat Krupp diamond for $305,000—her "ping-pong perfect gem" which she had won by taking ten points off him at table tennis "when he was pissed." Two months later, at Sotheby's auction, he picked up a Picasso drawing for a mere $21,600 while his wife, attending the same sale with Princess Elizabeth of Yugoslavia, snapped up a Monet for $120,000. Almost daily now the Burtons were projected in headlines as the most enviable couple in the world, the man and wife who had "his" and "hers" of everything that money could buy. Their world seemed cozy, utterly secure, and nearly idyllic. In reality, it was quite the reverse.

Though Richard never let it show, that English summer was the unhappiest and most disturbing time in his whole life—a time fraught with appalling anxiety, grief, and despair. The first indication that all was not right with his world came early in July with the shock announcement that after two weeks of work, Woodfall Film Productions was replacing him with Nicol Williamson and starting anew on the picture *Laughter in the Dark*. According to the film company, he was "fired" for being "unpunctual and unprofessional." Richard sent a good-luck telegram to his replacement but refused to comment. The only unsolicited statement for his defense came from actor Robert Beatty who argued: "Woodfall is behaving like an immature bride with a brilliant husband who divorces him because he arrived a bit late for dinner. Having worked with him for five months (on *Where Eagles Dare*) I can say that Richard is a professional to his fingertips. You cannot work in the theater as long as he has and not be. If he has been unpunctual then it is because he was unhappy with the film."

It was suggested that Burton was relieved, and happy to quit the film, because he had been in England since February, and after six months' residence he could be taxed on all his income for the year. This belief was totally unfounded. He had his program more subtly planned than that. His part in *Laughter in the Dark* had been scheduled for completion by the end of August and the last month's shooting was to be done on location abroad. So it was in his interest to be punctual. The truth of the matter was that he was working under too great a nervous strain. In the past year film commitments had taken the Burtons to Africa and London, France, London again, Italy, Sardinia, New York, Austria, and several more times back to England. This nomadic life, with a nonstop social whirl and the whole artificial business of film-making, was becoming wearisome. And there was another unpublicized factor: his extreme and growing concern about Elizabeth's health.

Richard was about to face a series of harrowing incidents more dreadful in their buildup than anything he had known before. It started with Elizabeth complaining of a dragging discomfort deep inside her, an ache more persistent and dull than the stabbing pain she often experienced as a legacy of chronic back injuries. As a child she had injured her back in a riding accident; then, just before her marriage to Mike Todd, she had fallen down the stairway on a houseboat. Three discs were gone. Surgeons cut away dead bone down to the nerve center and took bone from her hip and pelvis to build up the lower vertebrae of her spinal column. Soon afterwards the injury was aggravated when she was carrying Liza. Elizabeth had learned to live with the recurring pains. But this new dull and nagging ache was something else.

At this time, Elizabeth was capable of bearing a child of Richard's, and she wanted this more than anything else, even though the risks were extreme for a woman of thirty-six who was unable to give birth in the natural way. All three of her children had been delivered by Caesarean section, and Richard told us that the prospect of her undergoing such an operation a fourth time would involve a fifty-fifty life and death chance. "A baby could be born, but Elizabeth could die. As far as I am concerned that risk is not on. I cannot see life without Elizabeth. She is my everything—my breath, my blood, my mind, and my imagination. If anything happened to her I would wither and die. You ask me why we don't come out and adopt a baby now. As a brawny, mining-type Welshman I have always believed in my own flesh and blood. I have been completely wrong. A child is a child and the accident of procreation is a gift that is abused by too many parents. All this I have discovered through Elizabeth. . . . Children can belong to anybody—it makes no difference to one's love and responsibility. But to adopt a child requires more thought and more preparation than the probable accident of conception. We have the money to indulge ourselves with pets, but we can take no risk at all with a child that is going to bear our name."

It was while they were vaguely contemplating adopting a baby that Elizabeth's condition worsened. She hoped that she was pregnant, but she did not really believe it. And after filming *Secret Ceremony* with Mia Farrow, she told Richard that she feared something was seriously wrong. Doctors agreed. She was sent into the Fitzroy Nuffield nursing home where an exploratory operation proved inconclusive. Cancer was the fearful question mark that could not be completely dismissed, but the gynecologists were certain of one thing: she should immediately undergo major surgery for the removal of the womb. They explained to her that the risks were minimal and that contrary to ill-informed popular belief, this type of hysterectomy did not result in the patient losing her femininity, because while the womb was removed, the ovaries would be left intact. After a three-hour operation, Elizabeth's executive administrator Dick Hanley told reporters that it had been successful—"and, thank God, it is not cancer." The "partial hysterectomy" made only one vital difference to Elizabeth. She would never be able to have another child.

Meanwhile, the *Laughter in the Dark* affair was dragging on. There were reported threats of legal action from both sides, and Nicol Williamson, who had forgotten to reply to Richard's good-luck telegram, told a reporter: "I'm thoroughly convinced I'm better than him." And just to add to Richard's discomfort, there were snide newspaper reports about his Welsh nationalism—"He flies his Red Dragon flag, but he doesn't pay British taxes." With Elizabeth recovering fast, Richard took all the personal attacks in his stride. But then came another depressing blow—news from Switzerland that his old, long-serving gardener had hanged himself in the garage of the villa at Celigny. Over the years Richard had become very fond of the old man, and now he decided to fly to his funeral, with his daughter Kate, Liza, brother Ivor and his wife Gwen, and Emlyn Williams's son Brook. Just as Emlyn had become a "theatrical godfather" to Richard, so Richard had become something of a godfather to Emlyn's son. He had given the boy his first pair of roller skates, had visited him when he was at school at Stowe, and had later invited him to spend holidays with various girl friends at the Celigny villa. Like Ivor, Brook had known the old gardener well.

After the funeral in Geneva, Richard agreed that they should drive back to Celigny and visit the villa that had become something of a ghost house since his separation from Sybil. Liza had never seen the villa where Kate had spent her early childhood, and Brook especially looked forward to seeing the place again. "We had such wonderful times there," he said. "About two hundred yards from the house and over a railway bridge is the Café de la Gare. Once, after an enormous lunch, we were stranded there in the pouring rain and stayed on drinking all day. And there was another place on the lake where we celebrated my birthday. We were drinking there from about five in the afternoon until three in the morning and four of us consumed thirty-seven demi-litres of white wine. Then everyone started arguing and disappeared in different directions. Richard went for a swim fully clothed in the lake. And Ivor crept into his bedroom where his wife was asleep, took all his clothes off, and then put on his best midnight blue suit, socks, shoes and tie, and climbed into bed. I fell asleep on the terrace."

The car from Geneva now pulled in at the Café de la Gare, and, because it was getting late and Richard disliked flying at night, they decided to stay at the house overnight. While they were finishing their meal, Ivor went on ahead to open up the villa. "It was empty, of course," says Brook, "because the gardener had looked after the place alone. Anyway, Ivor had such a wonderful memory that although he hadn't been there for years, he knew exactly where the light switches were. The idea was that he could go in and find the sheets so that Gwen could make up the beds. It was the last time Ivor ever walked. We worked out later what happened. You have to go up three steps and across a little porch to turn on the outside light so that you can get in through the French windows. Well, Ivor got up the steps, but he must have caught his foot in the grill that lets air into the basement. He fell to the right and broke his neck on the windowsill. This is how we think it happened. He literally missed his footing in the dark. And it left him completely paralyzed."

The accident shattered Richard more than anything else in his life. Ivor was his strength and his idol. He absolutely worshipped him. As a babe he had laughed in the winds as Ivor ran piggyback with him over the hills. As a child he had learned to punch his own weight against Ivor in the outhouse of Dan-y-bont. As a schoolboy he had cheered as his big brother ploughed through heavy seas in the great Mumbles to Aberavon swimming race and scrummed down with the giants of Welsh rugby in the Neath power pack. Ivor was his hero, brother, father, confessor, and best friend. Even when Richard was a star in Hollywood, he was still looking on with awe and respect as Ivor, strong of body and will, grabbed Humphrey Bogart by the lapels, lifted him clean off the floor, and shook him for saying something of which he didn't approve. And during the *Cleopatra* scandal in Rome, Ivor had shaken Richard more than all the critics in the Vatican and the Italian Government by walking out on him in protest at his treatment of Sybil. Richard feared and respected Ivor more than any other man on earth. Now this colossus, this enormous independent spirit, was trapped in a useless body and confined to a wheelchair for the rest of his days. Richard had become his brother's keeper. He was too heartbroken to go into long explanations of what had happened. To the rest of the world it was simply dismissed as a skiing accident. It was no business of theirs. This was the family's own private grief.

"I was going to see Elizabeth in the hospital at this time," says Robert Hardy, "and I have never seen Richard so terribly reduced by circumstances. He was so conciliating between his worry about Elizabeth, and his desperate concern for Ivor, the life center of the family." Ivor was now flown by the Burtons' private plane to England's famous Stoke Mandeville Hospital near Aylesbury, Bucks, and Richard insisted that Elizabeth should have a complete rest before starting work on her next film. In mid-August he booked a cruise to New York on the *Queen Elizabeth*, and they sailed with the children, plus Stanley Baker's fifteen-year-old daughter, Sally.

The following month the Burtons were in Paris—Richard, unbelievably, playing Rex Harrison's lover in *Staircase*, while Elizabeth settled for a more conventional relationship with Warren Beatty in *The Only Game in Town*. Five months before, Richard had impulsively signed for this part as a queer barber, and Elizabeth had encouraged him. But now, as filming time approached, both he and Harrison were beginning to have grave doubts. "Is it wise, what we're doing?" asked Rex.

"Listen, love," said Richard. "We're too old, too rich, and too famous to do it. So—let's do it."

This was mock bravado on Burton's part. Secretly, the whole project alarmed him. The role of Harry, the fat, balding, mild-mannered "wife," was absolutely alien to the Welshman who had once dismissed Romeo as too prissy a part to play. It entailed the abandonment of his two cherished assets—robust masculinity and a firm, virile voice; it meant horrifying his adoring female fans as he presented himself as a pathetic-looking "pregnant pelican" with head swathed in bandages to conceal his total alopecia. Only stubborn pride prevented Richard from ducking out of this challenge. Neither he nor Rex would have had a moment's regret if the whole project had been cancelled.

Inevitably these improbable bedfellows found themselves the butt of merciless ragging. Elizabeth was very wicked. She proposed that Richard and Rex should move into the Plaza Athenée Hotel together while she went to live with Rex's wife, Rachel Roberts. And Stanley Donen, one of Liz's former boyfriends, now both producer and director of *Staircase*, suggested that Burton might pull off the Best Actress Oscar for his performance. Richard took it all in good humor. "You must establish your credentials as a man pretty thoroughly before you can afford to take the risk of playing a poof. I've been in training for this role most of my life."

Richard also pointed out how his own behavior was so often influenced by the roles he was playing. Now, as he portrayed a frumpish and flabby homosexual, he said he was drinking less, and becoming more sympathetic and meek.

"Yeah," cracked Liz. "But the influence stops right there, buster."

On the surface, Elizabeth was as bright and lively as ever. When it was observed that she and Richard had both pushed their fees up to an all-time high of $1,250,000 each, she cracked, "Sure, the price of food is going up. And diamonds, too." But, in fact, she was constantly in pain during the filming in Paris. The bone that long ago was used to fuse together three vertebrae was powdering, and at times she worked with an ugly corset-brace to bind the spine. "When we wake up in the morning," said Richard, "I marvel at the beauty of this exquisite creature lying beside me.

Then she gets up and takes those first tiny hesitant steps with her terrible, hurting back. Suddenly she is an old lady."

In February, 1969, as soon as the Paris filming was completed, Elizabeth went into the Cedars of Lebanon Hospital, Los Angeles, for a week-long series of tests and X rays of the degenerating disc in her spine. Afterward, under doctors' orders, she went with Richard to their villa in Mexico for a long rest. "I feel completely happy," she said. "Although life is not all enjoyment, I have with Richard the strength and love I longed for. And now, with my children in Puerto Vallarta, I feel like the happiest woman in the world, even though my back trouble does not let me enjoy this happiness totally."

Elizabeth was now to have her longest break from film-making in a quarter of a century while Richard, padded and bearded, had to masquerade as Henry VIII in *Anne of the Thousand Days.* So in mid-May the Burtons were back in Britain, along with their floating dog kennel and entourage of secretaries and servants. Across Offa's Dyke, bomb outrages by Welsh nationalists were signaling the forthcoming investiture of a new Prince of Wales at Caernarvon Castle, and Burton made appropriately patriotic noises, crying out for *y iaith* (the preservation of the Welsh tongue), flying the Welsh flag, and displaying the Red Dragon on his car and dressing room doors. But while he recorded a television narration for the ceremony, he passed up the chance of attending the investiture and staying as the guest of Princess Margaret on Lord Snowdon's yacht. Filming took precedence, as he was now intent on striving for a powerful screen performance. As with *Becket,* he was working at Shepperton Studios on a project planned by the veteran American producer, Hal B. Wallis. And once again it was a production that seemed to have all the necessary ingredients for a huge box-office success.

The Court Without a Country

I owe my performance to Richard Burton," said the French-Canadian actress Genevieve Bujold. "He was generous, kind, helpful, and witty. And generosity was the one great quality." The elfin-faced star of *Anne of the Thousand Days* had just collected Hollywood's coveted Golden Globe award for the best dramatic actress of the year. The same film won awards for the best director and best script. But Richard, whose loud and lustful monarch dominated this highly commercial Panavision-Technicolor production, went without a prize. Again, two months later, when the three thousand members of the Motion Picture Academy cast their votes, there were high hopes that he would win an honor. But once more his Oscar nomination failed. The Best Actor award went to 63-year-old John Wayne for his hard-drinking patch-eyed marshal of *True Grit*—the crowning moment in his forty years of film-making. Wayne had been nominated for an Oscar only once before in his life.

During the ceremonies, Richard sat slumped in the audience, busy scrutinizing a piece of paper and seemingly disinterested in the stage proceedings. Even Elizabeth, radiant as she presented the best film award for *Midnight Cowboy*, appeared unusually subdued. The next day commentators remarked that Richard couldn't conceal his disappointment at being a two-time loser to a drunken cowboy. (His King had been trumped by the Duke's one-eyed knave, and previously he had lost out as *The Spy Who Came in From the Cold* to Lee Marvin's hot *Cat Ballou*.) But those Hollywood eyes that thought Richard was glumly crossing off the ten Oscar nominations of *Anne of the Thousand Days* were mistaken. He was, in fact, muttering to himself because he was cramming a list of Spanish irregular verbs.

There is no doubt, however, that another Oscar in the family at this particular time would have been a valuable boost to the Burtons' prestige as the greatest husband-and-wife team in show business, and it might possibly have helped to cool the mounting criticism that they and other superstars were directly responsible for the financial chaos in the film industry. Mr. John Terry, managing director of Britain's National Film Finance Corporation, declared: "I would think that no actor, actress or director is worth fees of more than $50,000. One hears reports that the Burtons' fees for a film are a million dollars. This is not just ridiculous. It's monstrous." And after another year of spectacular losses (five of the seven major studios had between them lost more than $85 million), there were many people in the industry who agreed with him.

The Hollywood "toy town" that had dazzled Burton two decades ago was now lying in ruins. Early in 1970, eight films were shooting in the film factories that once churned out three thousand movies a year. MGM was putting its props from three thousand pictures under the hammer—everything from Tarzan's loincloth to poor Judy Garland's Wizard of Oz gear. Twentieth Century-Fox was cutting back its worldwide staff by forty percent and reducing its advertising expenditure by nearly $5 million. On Sunset Boulevard there were more out-of-work actors than yippies. That year, three out of four of the Screen Actors Guild's 33,000 members earned less in Hollywood than a pit-face worker from Pontrhydyfen; and by May, 1970, more than 46 percent of the 24,580 film craftsmen were unemployed. It was the same sad story in Britain—eight out of every ten actors out of work, plus some 2,000 of the 3,000 members of the Association of Cinematograph, Television and Allied Technicians.

Approximately seventy percent of films, large and small, were financial failures, and since a movie needs to gross two and a half times its cost to break even, it was clear that only a suicidal maniac, or a near-genius like David Lean, could contemplate a big-budget *Cleopatra* in the seventies. As Darryl Zanuck, last of the

Hollywood titans, growled: "Once you're over the four-million-dollar category, you're sticking your chin out." At this point everyone was talking about the staggering success of such low-budget movies as *The Graduate*, *Midnight Cowboy*, *Bonnie and Clyde*, and *Easy Rider*, and automatically producers were encouraged to aim at the under-thirties and project younger people in star roles. Taking an extreme view of the so-called trend, James Aubrey, new president of MGM, stated: "The older stars are going to have to play older roles if they want to work with us. We can't make a picture with Burt Lancaster and Deborah Kerr groping with each other any more. That's obscene. It's like watching a couple of grandparents pawing each other." He included Liz (thirty-six) and Richard (forty-four) in this. But since the Burtons indulged in screen clawing, rather than pawing, this observation was scarcely relevant.

The huge misconception during this film crisis, however, was the popular belief that the Burtons' Million-Dollar Bubble had burst at last. *Cleopatra* had been the extraordinary turning point in Richard's fortunes, and it was calculated that the seven pictures he and Elizabeth made together or separately between 1962 and 1966 had grossed over $200 million. Now show business writers were suggesting they were on the downward path, and superficially it did seem that they had passed their peak earning years. In 1970, Richard took his longest rest ever from filming and did not even leave the Mexican sunshine to be presented to the Queen at the Royal Film Performance of *Anne of the Thousand Days*. Meanwhile, Elizabeth was still dogged by ill health and twice went into the hospital for minor operations. And when the Burtons had a few public tiffs, the gossip columnists were further encouraged to suggest that their idyllic, fortune-making partnership was beginning to disintegrate.

Again and again it was stressed in newspapers and magazines: "The million-dollar era for the fabulous Burtons is over. No longer can they command a million-dollar fee before going before the cameras." And when Richard arrived in England to film *Villain*, he played up to this myth by riding with Elizabeth in the London Airport bus instead of her white Rolls Royce. But the conclusion that they were having to face up to harsh economic realities was totally false. True, they were not taking million-dollar guarantees—though they would surely have gained them if they had insisted upon it. What was really happening was that their financial dealings were being conducted on a more subtle level. After ten years of having their cake and eating it, they were simply gaining a bigger slice by taking a percentage of the total gross profits of all their productions. Long before the film industry announced a revolutionary agreement to cut out wild and wasteful extravagances and colossal salaries for superstars, Richard and Elizabeth had drawn up new contracts that made them partners rather than employees of the producers. It meant that a film could be set up at a comparatively low budget, and the smaller the Burtons' salary, the higher was their percentage of the box-office returns. It was said that they were having to gamble where once they were guaranteed a million dollars each. But, in truth, it was a gamble they couldn't lose. Even if a film failed to pay its way at the box office—an extremely remote possibility in view of the powerful drawing power of their names—they could recoup the difference from the sale of the television rights.

The so-called death of the star system was partly an illusion. Despite what Hollywood moguls were saying, the superstar appeal of the Burtons remained. And while companies might get away with paying peanuts to a brand-new star, like Dustin Hoffman in *The Graduate*, they were still left with the irritating problem of paying him his worth for the next film. It was a simple marketplace transaction based on supply and demand. The only difference between the thirties and forties and the sixties and seventies was that the slave market of contracts had become a free market of talent. The wheeler-dealers paid their money and they took their choice.

Richard had received a trivial sum (by his standards) for starring in *Where Eagles Dare* and had settled for a percentage of the returns. We asked him whether this meant gross or net. He whistled. And then replied: "It's too fantastic. I dare not tell you how much I get each week while that film is running. It's quite indecent. My deal—just say it's ten percent which it's not—means that when you pay a dollar or a pound over the box office, I get ten cents or ten new pence on every ticket. And this film, don't forget, old love, was in the top ten of world movies in its first year and came third in the British pop poll. I haven't taken a penny in advance for *Villain*, but if the equivalent of a Rolls Royce doesn't turn up each week from Bombay or Hong Kong in a couple of years' time, I'll be rather surprised."

Richard now claims that he outspends Onassis—"When I went from the Air Force into the theater my ambition was to make a million, but after I had made it I felt the need to make two million, then three, and then four. And then I found to my surprise that money is not all that interesting. It's only important if you haven't got any." He talks about it as "Monopoly money." Yet, for all his apparent extravagance, he has never lost his terror of being reduced to poverty, and he shrewdly recognizes that diamonds, like Liz's old masters, are a man's best friend in an inflationary world of shrinking paper pounds and dollars. "We went over to diamonds when gold began wobbling. We reckoned they were as good a bet as any—and easily portable, you know."

Like royalty, he never actually handles money. We were with him on the way home from the studios one day when he pulled into a London pub for a pint. Chauffeur Gaston, his carrier of ready cash, was not with us, so when it came to Richard's turn to buy a round, he asked his temporary driver for a small loan. The driver was broke, and so were we. The landlord was not at home, and Richard, faintly panic-stricken, didn't like to confuse the young Irish barman by trying to explain that he was your actual Richard Burton, without a penny to bless himself. Suddenly, he shot out of the door and returned seconds later with a cupped handful of loose change. "Where did you get that?" we asked. "Bloody hell," he said. "Good job I remembered. I know the old bloke who sells newspapers outside on the corner and my credit's okay with him." Eventually we climbed back into the Rolls and the rascally paper-seller leaned through the window and cracked: "Don't forget your *Evening Standard*, Rich. And here's a couple of bob to keep you going 'til the old woman gives you your pocket money."

What are the Burtons really worth? He is impossibly and perhaps deliberately vague on the subject. He mumbles in terms of
$30 million, but he doesn't really know. "No, that's not including
things like the land in Tenerife. I've no idea exactly what that's
worth." And to confuse any calculations, they are accumulating
more material wealth all the time. Producers and directors, for
example, are liable to give Liz a bauble or two at the end of a
film—though sometimes stories of gifts are exaggerated. (John
Heyman for one would like it known that he did *not* give her a
£25,000 brooch after producing *Boom*—a report that almost
queered him with the taxman.) Then again, so many of their possessions, like jewels and works of art, are increasing in value at an
inestimable rate. For the Burtons it is very much a case of money
attracting more money. Even their cars—the green Rolls Royce
is one of only twelve ever made—appreciate in value.

The great bulk of their material wealth lies in property, jewels,
and paintings. As the daughter of an art dealer, Elizabeth has a
shrewd eye for bargains, and the Burtons' collection of paintings
is certainly worth several million dollars. As for jewelry, no other
filmstar has a more fabulous array than Elizabeth. When the
Royal Family's financial "plight" was being widely headlined a
few years ago, one suggested solution was that the Queen should
"flog" the Crown Jewels to the Burtons. Elizabeth's jewelbox is
worth at least $4 million and probably much more, since Mike
Todd first developed her taste in emeralds, diamonds, and rubies.
Gifts to her from Richard include the 69-carat million-dollar
"Cartier" Diamond, as big as a pigeon's egg, and the $305,000
Krupp diamond, and the $37,000 Peregrina Pearl which King
Philip of Spain gave to Henry VIII's daughter, Mary Tudor, in
1554. Besides land in Tenerife and Ireland and property in Mexico and Switzerland, they also have interests in a variety of busi-
ness enterprises, including a Paris boutique and a company providing private jets and helicopters for business executives.

Richard estimates their income as varying from $2 million to
$4 million a year and expenditure at $700,000 upwards. His annual insurance payments to Lloyds of London for Elizabeth's jewels alone are more than a hundred times what his brother Tom

draws per year as an old-age pensioner in Cwmavon, and after he bought the *Kalizma* yacht for Elizabeth, he swapped it with her for a Van Gogh—as casually as he once swapped cigarette cards with Dilly Dummer on The Side in Taibach. With such infinite wealth and power, one might imagine that Richard has changed out of all recognition from the rugger-playing Prince of Denmark of Old Vic days. Yet, to his closest friends, the truly remarkable thing is how little the man within has changed.

"I remember being interviewed on the radio about him," says Robert Hardy. "A whole lot of people were talking about him, and the questions were really angled to get one to say that the man had changed, that this great grandeur and pomp that surrounds him is a far cry from the days when I first knew him. Well, in a way, it is a far cry, because then he hadn't got two pennies to rub together. Yet basically I don't think anything has changed. The only major difference is that it's difficult to get hold of him because he is surrounded by so many people and needs so much protection in his position.

"I was absolutely fascinated when I met him at the Dorchester after the showing of *Staircase*. I went to lunch with him and about fifty-five people were there. I wrote to him afterwards that it was like a minor German court of the eighteenth or seventeenth century—where those admitted were given the most marvelous entertainment, caviar and champagne, and then, at a certain time, groups of people were shown the door. This would leave a kind of inner circle, and then they were shown the door, leaving a nucleus of three or four. It was marvelous. No one actually came in and bowed, but it was quite clear what status one had. I think this is so wise, since otherwise everybody would hang around for hours. Years before, when we were stuck together in the same RAF station, we became inseparable at times. But even then you could never be regarded as Richard's best friend because of the court of people surrounding him. I am saying really that he had all that attention then, and the fact that he hadn't got any money didn't seem to make any difference at all. He always had what he wanted."

Today it is even more difficult to judge who Richard's best

friends really are. Inevitably, the sheer bigness of his celebrity image has drastically affected many of his personal relationships, even with his own relatives. Hardy remembers the time Richard casually offered him his private jet plane when he learned that he was going on holiday to Greece. "He gave me the jet—just like that. It was marvelous. Irresistible. The difficulty, of course, is to what degree do you maintain a friendship with somebody who can do this sort of thing? To what degree does one try to keep the friendship going with somebody who, after all, doesn't need your friendship because he has so much power and wealth? It's very difficult and one only hopes that one maintains such a friendship for nobler reasons."

Warren Mitchell was inhibited in this way when he worked on *The Spy Who Came in From the Cold* and found that his old Air Force pal was the star. "Neither of us felt inclined to set our next meeting because we were just in different worlds. Luckily, I'm accepted walking down the street. But Richard—when you get to be a super superstar like that, people want to touch and grab. He told me that with Liz he couldn't go out for a meal in a restaurant. It was just impossible. So you're condemned to a kind of weird existence in a hotel room or in your own place around your own pool with a small quota of friends. And at that level you do tend to attract a lot of yes-men."

Dozens of friends and relatives regret the splendid isolation of the Burtons and bemoan the difficulty they have in making contact with Richard now. "One trouble," says Donald Houston, "is that he has such a phobia about telephones. I read a play written by Gwyn Thomas about Aneurin Bevan and then I tried to get hold of Richard at the Dorchester. But when I phoned I could never get through. Eventually I told him that I wasn't going to ring again and try to get through the entourage. Yet at other times Richard might say, 'You've been a fine old bugger—not getting in touch with me for so long.' It can be really frustrating if you're an old chum. He sent the most marvelous presents when I was in hospital at Christmas after *Where Eagles Dare*. They kept sending things, and my wife wrote to them to thank them. But I don't think they ever got the letters. At other times, when he is filming, his dressing room will be full of people. But some friends just don't want to be part of a queue, and they wish the approach would come from the other side sometimes."

Says Stanley Baker: "I have constant arguments with people who call themselves his friends but who get a little upset because he doesn't either write or telephone. That's their problem. He's got a life to lead. And you don't have to see a friend constantly; you don't have to be regularly in touch. The test of friendship is when you meet. Without saying a word you know you are still friends. But still there are petty ones who call themselves his friends and then behind his back—because of jealousy or envy or whatever—knock him. I have more fights about this than anything else."

As Professor Coghill expresses it: "Richard gives me the impression of being protected by secretaries who are themselves protected by other secretaries; and none of them answer letters. A wise provision. Many ancient emperors were guarded by deaf mutes." Brook Williams agrees. "Lots of people who should get through to him don't—and sometimes vice versa. But they can't be too careful. There are so many cranks and con-men about."

This is absolutely true. And it can be dangerous for the Burtons to lower the protective screen around them for a second. For example, when they were filming *Sandpiper* in Paris and staying at the Lancaster Hotel, two people from a French magazine came along with the parents of Maria, Liz's adopted daughter. They had brought these simple country folk from Germany on the pretext that the Burtons wanted them to see Maria, and then, as they confronted Elizabeth with them in the hotel lounge, the flashbulbs popped to capture pictures of the humble parents in wealthy surroundings. The need for top security was never more strikingly apparent than in the autumn of 1970. Ostensibly it was a propitious time for the Burtons. They attended the Caxton Hall wedding of Liz's eighteen-year-old son Michael Wilding and nineteen-year-old Beth Clutter, daughter of an American oceanologist. The following month, on his forty-fifth birthday, Richard went to Buckingham Palace, and watched by Elizabeth and sister Cissie, he received the C.B.E. from the Queen. But behind the scenes it was a time of alarming tension and hysteria. Police were keeping a close watch on the Dorchester after an anonymous telephone call threatening to kidnap Elizabeth. Then came an irresponsible newspaper report that the Burtons—along with Sinatra, Tom Jones, and Steve McQueen—were marked down for death by the Charles Manson "family" on trial for the Sharon Tate murders.

Bravely, but rather unwisely, the Burtons still kept their promise to appear on stage at the Round House's Cinema City Exhibition for their first-ever open public discussion of their work. Between showings of the films *Virginia Woolf* and *Boom*, they came on to answer questions from a predominantly young, long-haired and vociferous audience. Plainclothesmen hovered nervously in the background; in the auditorium the atmosphere was disturbingly tense. "Shut your mouth, woman," Richard snarled when Liz interrupted a story he was telling. It was their bit of fun. But it encouraged a too-familiar relationship with the fans, and there followed an impertinent question about how the fantasy of *Boom* might be compared with the fantasy in their real life, then a totally improper reference to the Manson "death list," and finally threats by members of the audience to strip because Burton had attacked the increasing nudity in the cinema. The evening left behind a nasty taste, and it was a timely reminder of how necessary it had become for the Burtons to keep themselves aloof and inaccessible. This they normally do with a superefficiency that defies all but a handful of friends to contact them directly.

In the Burtons' entourage, the man closest to Richard is Bob Wilson, a tall, slim, charming, soft-spoken American Negro. Long before *Camelot* days, he was Richard's right-hand man— valet, barman, and general aide. Today he is virtually one of the family, so close that he was best man at the Burtons' wedding, and having such an understanding with Richard that he then told his boss that he would kill him if he ever played around with another woman. Now that brother Ivor is no longer on the scene, there is no other member of the entourage who can talk to Burton in such man-to-man style. Another constant companion of the Burtons is first secretary Jim Benton, a dark, laconic, and inscrutable American who is the most formidable obstacle to those trying to get through to his employers. His is the least enviable duty, and inevitably he is seen as "the heavy" by those frustrated in attempts to contact Richard or Elizabeth. But he is only seeking to protect them, and with the aid of another secretary, George Davis, he does so remarkably well.

Two others who often travel with the Burtons are Monsieur Raymond, the major-domo, who describes himself as "chief steward, chief purser and chief interpreter" on the yacht, and Gaston Sanz, their principal chauffeur. At one time, they also had a regular personal bodyguard in Bobby LaSalle, an ex-prizefighter who went to Hollywood in 1932, the year Elizabeth was born, as technical adviser on *The Prizefighter and the Lady*, starring Max Baer and Myrna Loy. It was insane to tangle with him. He wore clip-on bow ties so that no opponent could throttle him with his own necktie, and high-heeled pointed shoes to sink into anyone who wanted to play rough. But LaSalle left the payroll some years ago, and until recently they relied primarily for day-to-day protection on Gaston, a short, beefy Basque, holder of the Medaille Militaire and the Croix de Guerre for wartime heroics in the Free French Commandos. Nicknamed Oddjob by Oxford students, he is proficient in judo, has tossed aside many a snatch photographer in his time, and would not hesitate to lay down his life for Richard and Elizabeth. He worships them, and his unswerving loyalty has been reciprocated. When he accidentally wrecked their brand new £7,000 Cadillac in England a few years ago, they automatically accepted his explanation and stood by him.

But it is the Burtons' way of life, more than the protection of the staff, that isolates them so much from friends and relatives. When they are filming, often on studio call at dawn and studying their scripts by evening, they have little time or energy left for social outings, and when they are not working, they are usually far away from old acquaintances in Switzerland or Mexico. In a sense they are rulers of a court without a country, jetting and yachting around the globe with their private household, and having Puerto Vallarta as their Balmoral and Gstaad as their Sandringham. At Gstaad, they can enjoy the peace and privacy and low taxation that has attracted so many other celebrities to the shores of Lac Léman—Charles Chaplin, Peter Ustinov, Audrey Hepburn, James Mason, Noel Coward, Jackie Stewart, Alistair Maclean, Vladimir Nabokov, Prince Napoleon. But more and more they have come to regard the villa in Mexico as their principal base—the same big white house that they first rented when Richard was filming *Iguana*, and which they now own.

Casa Kimberley stands high up at the back of the town, about half a mile inland from the bay and on an ancient cobbled street without a name. A narrow arched bridge spans the street and connects the main house with their small "playhouse." Here they have everything they need—luxury, comfort, and privacy behind a huge, locked wrought-iron gate and walls topped with barbed wire. Inside the gate, pink steps lead up to "Burton's Bar," which stretches along one side of a luxurious forty-foot living room, and this leads off to a square courtyard and the children's quarters. Over the bridge and in the annex is the swimming pool. Richard thrashes about the pool every day, and very occasionally goes horseback riding in the jungle as part of his ritual for shedding the rolls of fat he rapidly accumulates on his vodka-swilling excursions to London, Paris, New York, Rome, or Los Angeles.

"Why they want to live there I cannot imagine," says Mead Roberts. "It is one of the hellholes of the world. There was a pigsty literally across the way before they bought the land and built the annex with the Bridge of Sighs. Right next door was a grocery store. There is a view of the sea, but the weather is terrible. It is so humid you would die, except for two or three months of the year when the weather is nice. There is no place to go; nothing to do. It is neither rustic in a picturesque way, nor is it Acapulco-like."

In fact, for those who like sunshine, the weather is magnificent for around seven months of the year, and both the Burtons and secretary Benton, who has his own house there, call it paradise. True, it is not Montego Bay. Their view of the sea takes in the shanty quarters of Puerto Vallarta's poorest citizens. But then they never wished to isolate themselves completely from the harsh realities of life. They take an interest in the town's affairs and have made large unpublicized donations to local charities, especially children's welfare. They do not go out much at night, but Liz will shop at the general store on the corner, and though tourists can sometimes be a nuisance, the local residents respect their privacy. Within the walls of Casa Kimberley they are so safe from prying eyes that they can sunbathe in the nude without fear of the most enterprising of *paparazzi*.

Following the Burtons around, seeing the enormous emotional pressures of life in the public eye, and listening to the regrets of many friends, it is easy to become sentimental about the past and to sympathize with Burton's loss of freedom and contact—the freedom to walk down a busy street, to travel anonymously, and spend more time with his old cronies. But such sympathy is misplaced. In reality, Richard does not miss this freedom so greatly. "The advantages far outweigh the disadvantages," he argues, and though money is so much Monopoly paper to him and fairy dust to Elizabeth, he would not be without it and all the comforts it can bring for himself and the family. He likes mixing with old pals in a plain British pub. He dislikes stuffy formal occasions and is perfectly happy to stop at a fish-and-chip shop and eat his supper out of a newspaper in the back of the Rolls. At the same time, he likes the VIP treatment; prefers traveling first-class and getting the best table and best service when he visits a restaurant. As he said years ago, "It seems to me that coming from where I came from, from the very depths of the working class, if I'm going anywhere I must go as high as I possibly can."

His heroes are Alexander the Great, Napoleon, Wellington, Julius Caesar, Churchill—men of strength and purpose. He likes power, and wealth represents power. Not only the power to indulge one's own fancies, but also the power to do good for others. While their self-indulgent extravagances command massive publicity, both Richard and Elizabeth make huge philanthropic gestures that are often unrevealed—donations for research into paraplegia (Ivor is a paraplegic), hemophilia (Richard and three of his brothers are mild sufferers of the blood defect that causes prolonged bleeding from even a small cut), cancer, leukemia, and heart disease; support for theater funds and lost causes like Biafra.

And many, many times, Richard, and more especially Elizabeth, have concerned themselves with individual cases of suffering. During the filming of *Iguana*, Richard had his shoes shined by a boy bootblack who suffered from an advanced cataract in one eye. They sent him to an eye specialist in Guadalajara, and though nothing could be done for him, the boy at least enjoyed a free holiday in the town. Similarly in 1969, when Liz heard that polio victim David Ryder was walking on crutches from John O'Groats to Land's End to raise funds for research, she turned out to join him on the last lap. Cynics sneered that it was a publicity stunt. But Elizabeth needs free publicity like she needs fake pearls. The truth is that she is genuinely and spontaneously moved to compassion at the slightest touch to her heartstrings. And almost too easily, sometimes, she becomes involved.

The future? In his cups Richard occasionally talks of the middle forties as though he were in his sixties, and he pictures himself as a querulous old grandfather with children sitting at his feet and listening to his stories; an old man with gray hair, fat, and suffering from gout. Like grandpappy William Jenkins in 1899, careening down from The Miner's in his wheelchair, he sees himself going out with a bang. But Elizabeth will be there forever, indestructible, vibrant, and except for a third chin, as mysteriously glamorous as ever. He talks sometimes of ending his days back in the Afan valley; but then, he loves romancing. One cannot really see him living amid the slag heaps of Pontrhydyfen. The world of his roots is too wet and too damp; it still has mortality rates higher than in any other parts of Britain, with heart disease, cancer, pneumonia, and bronchitis all considerably above the national average.

It is not uncommon for Welshmen to become more acutely aware of their heritage with the passing of time in other lands. Only by living outside *Cymru* do they fully realize how different are traditions and attitudes elsewhere, and then their Welsh influence becomes accentuated. But Richard is different. He has spent more than two-thirds of his life away from Wales, and though he loves to go back for a visit, there is little to hold him there now. Many of his childhood friends and acquaintances remain in the Port Talbot area—Dennis Burgess, Dilly Dummer, and his school sweetheart Susie Preece; the lovely ladies at No. 6 Connaught Street; Charlie Hockin, back as a teacher at Eastern school where little Hubert Davies, who once fought in the playground for Phil Burton's production of *How Green Was My Valley*, is now the headmaster; Alderman Heycock, once a loco driver on the old Dyffryn railway and now Lord Heycock of Taibach ("Someone should have told him," says Richard wickedly, "that Taibach means 'little shithouses.' "); and Tom and Verdun and Hilda, and little brother Graham, who never went down the mine, but rose to become general manager of the Aberavon Lido, the biggest municipal sports and entertainment complex in Wales.

This, however, is not the world for the supermillionaire. A gray and vigorous but vulgar valley dominated by the awesome conglomeration of the blast furnaces, rolling mills, and strip mills of the ever-growing Steel Company of Wales. It is strictly a soul-stirring spot to revisit—a forcible reminder of the past that helps Richard to beware of becoming smug, or as Daddy Ni used to say, "a bit fancy." He can always make a sentimental journey around by The Side, past the *Cach* (now a bingo hall), looking into the Youth Club (where once he arrived unheralded from Hollywood and brought near hysteria to the hall), and into Eastern school (where the kids have color TV provided by Richie), driving up to the Copper House and on to Hilda's at Pontrhydyfen, and walking by Dan-y-bont (finally sold to a couple who topped a $5,000 plus offer made by Graham on Richard's behalf). But there can be no permanent going back. The world of Richie Jenkins and Richard Burton are universes apart.

Burton—The Man and the Myth

T ruth, as Meredith Jones used to say, is a shadowy wing-three-quarter running forever down a ghostly touchline and nobody will ever catch him. Richard Burton, the most gifted of his pupils, has since given a near-perfect demonstration of that elusive run—careering through life as an ever-untouchable, jinking figure who confuses all truth-seekers with contradictory attitudes and actions and exquisitely woven stories that constitute a web of truths, half-truths, and outright lies. He does so because he has his own conception of truth, which he tackles in a style so individual and subtle that it defies others to do the same. His perception of detail is razor-sharp, but he has an artistic contempt for precise facts, dates, and figures. In recalling and capturing places, faces, and events, he favors the colorful splodge of the impressionist painter rather than the dark-room precision of the photographer. And who is to say that in doing so, he does not come closer to laying that ghost-runner called truth?

All this, however, is no aid to the pursuit of the truth about Burton, since the pursuer must by necessity pick his way through the minefield of half-truths and inventions laid by a genius of a storyteller whose principal aim is to entertain and never to inform. After working with him in *The Robe*, Dawn Adams observed: "Richard is a remarkable actor on the stage and in films. But in private life he is an even better one. When you're with him, you believe him, but afterwards—you wonder." Dennis Burgess, who has known him intimately for a generation, says, "There is that terrible phrase someone once employed—'legitimate hyperbole.' This is Rich. I used to say to him, 'That's not the story you told six weeks ago.' So often he contradicts himself and it's impossible to pin him down to hard facts. Sometimes his stories are out-and-out lies." Yet, in reality, to call Richard a liar has no more application than to label Shakespeare one for being unfaithful to history. In his conduct of everyday life, he is blazingly honest. In conversation he is the perpetual actor. Given an audience, be it in theater pit or pub, he instinctively seeks to command it and not to be upstaged. In the former, he is rehearsed and restricted by his script; in the latter he is undisciplined, though no less inspired as he unlocks his astonishing treasure trove of tales. In both cases, however, it remains essentially a performance. Stories may be falsely presented as historical fact, but they are not calculated lies, only the embroidery of a masterweaver seeking to dazzle and delight. Burton the storyteller has never been one to let concern for accuracy outweigh his concern for effect.

Though his memory of events is strangely erratic and may be bolstered by instant flashes and fancies of his imagination, he is such a lucid and powerful raconteur that the most skeptical of listeners could be excused for taking his words as gospel. A few years ago actor William Redfield (playing Guildenstern) wrote his book *Letters From an Actor* (Cassell & Co., Ltd., 1967), in which he recorded the daily happenings and his own impressions during the three months of preparing the 1964 Gielgud–Burton *Hamlet*. Painstakingly he included some of Richard's fascinating tales of the theater, and he was especially delighted by anecdotes about Olivier's ingenuity in playing Titus Andronicus. At great length and in infinite detail, Burton described how Olivier, required to chop off his own left hand with a hatchet, delivered a long speech with special pauses so that he could perform the conjuring trick of releasing an artificial hand secured beneath his sleeve. But when Redfield checked with the play he found that Titus has no long speech at this point, and moreover he does not chop off the hand himself! Less happily, Redfield faithfully repeated an entertaining story that Burton told about Sir Ralph Richardson and director Basil Dean. Both men strongly denied there was any truth in it, and after the printing Redfield had to add a note to his book stating that the story had no foundation in fact.

Richard's unreliable memory of certain events is curious. He has a mind like a sponge that soaks up most everything he reads, and yet he does get facts wrong, even when telling stories from firsthand experience. On the David Frost Show, for example, his longest and funniest and most elaborate anecdote recalled the time he was playing Prince Hal at Stratford and how he had drunk steadily through St. David's Day, as was his wont, before going on stage in chain mail and armor. Eloquently and discreetly he described his cross-legged agony during a play lasting three and a quarter hours—"with a vein standing out on my forehead, and just hoping and waiting for the curtain to come down"; how the floodgates finally burst open and in his discomfiture he went after Redgrave so ferociously that he snapped a sword in half and then threw Sir Michael across the stage. In fact, the St. David's Day angle, of which he made so much play, was entirely false, since the production did not open until a month after the day of the patron saint of Wales. But in essence his "once more into the breeches" story was true, and after all it was only the spirit of the incident that really mattered.

Burton tells and retells so many stories that they grow or become confused, but so marginally that he does not realize it and sincerely he believes he is reproducing the original. Similarly, too, his stories overlap with versions told by others. He has given a colorful account of how snoopers took the Dorchester suite below his and Elizabeth's and stood on a ladder with a listening device pressed against the ceiling in the hope of hearing them having a fearful row. Elizabeth, sharing his adventures, has set a similar incident in New York's Regency Hotel, where eavesdroppers stood on chairs and put empty glasses to the ceiling. Stanley Baker claims that Burton has actually "pinched" stories about his own father, a one-legged coal miner in the Rhondda Valley. "My father had a job as a night watchman in Tylerstown. He adored kids, and when they gathered round his fire he used to frighten the life out of them by saying he could mesmerize them. 'Just look into my eyes for three seconds,' he would say, 'and you'll be out like a light.' And they would all hide their eyes or look away. He was also the chairman for concerts in the main pub, and whenever a fight broke out he would be up there on the window-sill swinging his crutches. Anyway, when Richard and I were in Anzio together, I heard him telling these stories to an American journalist. And I said, 'Eh, hold on a second. That's my father you're talking about, you cunt.' "

With Richard, it is all a matter of values. His memory is so extraordinary that he can accurately recite enormous portions of the Bible and Shakespeare that he learned by heart when he was ten. But lighthearted anecdotes, told while swigging pints with cronies in the local, are hardly to be treated with the same solemn application. This, for the actor, is the perfect relaxation—flexing the dramatic muscles in a spontaneous performance without restraint by script or direction. No actor relaxes more excitingly than Burton. Once embarked on a story, he is incapable of letting it die mid-flight while delving into his memory bank for some half-forgotten detail. The playing is the thing, and so he sweeps onwards, sometimes recalling what he thinks may have happened, or more often, telling a version he has told so many times before that he earnestly believes it to be true. His stories, never dull and invariably enlivened with dramatic dialogue, roll off his facile Welsh tongue, seemingly without effort as he moves from one person's lines to another, from one accent to another. And in the final analysis, he doesn't really care a damn about anecdotal truth. As an actor, his great obsession is that he should never cease to entertain.

A rare gift for mimicry is one of Richard's great assets as a storyteller. Ralph Richardson, Redgrave, Gielgud, Robert Newton, Hugh Griffith, Brando, Martita Hunt—their voices and dozens more are within his range. He can do an hilarious impression of a Welshman and an Englishman discussing a rugby match in a pub, and many years ago, at a New York party, he was so effective as Olivier that the late Vivien Leigh turned around in astonishment because she had thought her husband was in London. He prides himself on being able to surpass Lord Olivier in this one department, and to emphasize the point he tells the story, probably apocryphal, of how Olivier prepared for the role of a Birmingham insurance man in the play *Semi-Detached* by staying in the Midlands to perfect his local accent. "Finally, he tried out his splendid accent in a tobacconist's. The shopkeeper looked oddly at him for a moment. Then he asked, 'Been in the country long, sir?' Larry was absolutely shattered." But on one occasion it was Richard's turn to be deflated after trying out a voice impression. As a young actor he was standing in a hallway entertaining friends with an imitation of Gielgud. "Suddenly I observed that my audience had fallen strangely silent. Then I turned round to find the awesome figure of Sir John directly behind me. In a supremely haughty tone, he declared: 'My dear boy, generally speaking, very good impersonators do not make very good actors.' "

Richard readily admits that he is often putting on an act when not on stage or screen; that this has become an instinctive reaction whenever faced with an audience of one or more—just as a man doing a crossword puzzle on a train might boldly fill in answers because he senses people are watching him. "I suppose most actors never really stop acting. After all, what is life if not one long, desperate struggle to hold the center of the stage? Certainly, I like to be the center of attention, to dominate conversations if I can." Philip Burton has recalled that Richard, even in schooldays, had this compulsive urge to keep on acting, whether off stage or on— "The most outstanding thing was, quite simply, that he never, ever, bored me." And inevitably his tendency to exaggerate, color, and invent grew stronger as his audience became more demanding.

After his first year as a Hollywood filmstar, Richard became bored with trotting out the same answers to the same tedious questions by interviewers, and for light relief he would recourse to making up variations. "What are your secret fears?" he was asked when filming *The Robe*. He invented a few mundane fears but they made no impression, and so the next time the question arose he snapped: "I fear nothing. But I have a mild apprehension of death." The subsequent story was headlined: RICHARD BURTON FEARS DEATH. He had scored, and he quickly became highly adept at throwing out the quotable quote for publicity. And he came to care less and less what was written about him, provided it was not hurtful to others he held dear.

Burton's cavalier attitude to facts is not, however, all that it seems. Just as he has a phobia about being touched physically, so he is shy of being probed too deeply by casual trespassers of the mind. Superficially he appears to be a man of extraordinary candidness. But this gift of expressing himself with perspicuity and acrobatic word imagery, which makes him such a great entertainer, also allows him to suffer fools kindly and to hide his true feelings from inquiring minds. Thus, it is possible to spend hours in animated conversation with him and to discover on leaving that you have left more of yourself behind than you have taken away of him.

Richard has always admitted to the Welsh trait of deviousness, and these days, after so much exposure in the press, he is far more vulnerable and lacking in self-confidence than first impressions suggest. Religion and politics are two subjects to which he will not readily yield, for in neither case are his beliefs and actions easily reconciled. Politically, he is a socialist at heart, and a left-wing socialist at that. He feels a certain nostalgia for politicians in the Aneurin Bevan mold because he likes his heroes to be larger than life and clearly defined in color, not a compromising shade of gray like the Wykehamist Socialists of the first Wilson Administration in Britain. Yet, in practice, while donating money generously, he cannot bring himself to pay British taxes to help subsidize the welfare state, and he is very much the personification of private enterprise. In defense, he can only argue that his concept of socialism is equal opportunity for all but not featherbedding for the indolent. He is reasonably consistent about this in private life, for while he provides fixed allowances for several of his relations and has made substantial gifts to others, he has never supported those who can stand on their own two feet to such an extent that they are deprived of the need and will to think and strive for themselves.

Casual acquaintances of the Jenkins family do not always appreciate this. Some automatically presume that any relations of Burton must be "loaded with dough." It is not so. Brother Graham illustrates this by telling of the time the family clubbed together to send him as a representative to Elizabeth's father's funeral a few years ago. Graham arrived so short of money that he had to take a bus to the Beverly Hills Hotel—probably the first guest in the hotel's history unable to afford the cab fare. When Richard saw him sweating in his heavy black overcoat and clerical gray suit he said, "Good God, Graham, you look like a bloody undertaker. Go into town and buy yourself some lightweight gear." Graham came back wearing an open-necked shirt and trousers held up by a bright-colored tie. "That's better," said Richard. But Graham didn't tell him that he had refused to put a new lightweight suit on Richard's bill because he thought the price absurdly high by Port Talbot standards.

Most of the Jenkins family have a built-in canniness as well as pride that prevents them spending Richard's money too freely. Thus, when Dan-y-bont came onto the market and Richard wanted to buy it for sentimental reasons, Graham acted on his behalf but failed with his bid because he refused to go up to $9,000, judging it to be far more than the dilapidated house was worth. All the immediate relations, plus Ciss and Elfed James's daughters, Marion and Rhianon, have received an equal, five-figure sum of money (before tax) from Richard, and he has either given each brother and sister a car or has helped them to buy their own home, and all of those of retiring age are given a life pension. But the brothers who are young enough to work still need to do so.

Understandably, of course, Burton does provide extravagantly for the children. There is a trust for both of his daughters, and one for each of Elizabeth's children, including her adopted Maria. Liza Todd Burton is already a dollar millionairess, and the financial security of all of them is firmly assured. After all, by the very nature of their situation, the children have become accustomed to a certain privileged style of living, and it is only natural that their parents should wish to safeguard their future. Yet, even in this respect, Richard is not entirely happy. From his own experience as a self-made man, he knows the advantages of being a "hungry fighter," and he recognizes the enormous satisfaction to be derived from money enterprisingly earned and from success independently achieved. He therefore strives to instill a proper sense of values into the children and to see that they are not harmfully pampered and spoiled. In common with most extremely rich parents, he is not altogether successful in this. But he tries, and he cares. There was, for example, the time when young Michael upset the management by throwing a series of wild teen-age parties at the Dorchester. Richard was furious—not especially because of the list of complaints but because he felt that Michael had taken advantage of his privileged position and was winning popularity or notoriety by squandering thousands of dollars. He read him the riot act in a style worthy of the blistering tongue of Meredith Jones himself.

On the subject of religion, as with politics, Richard finds himself in a somewhat ambivalent position and without a drum to beat. While he was taken regularly to chapel as a boy and used to read aloud from Aunt Margaret Ann's huge Welsh Bible with the brass lock, he never became deeply religious; always tugging the opposite way was the wayward influence of Daddy Ni, bitterly scorning and condemning all teetotal chapelgoers. Today Richard is not at all religious in the conventional sense, and yet of the seven cardinal virtues, only the natural virtue of temperance and the theological virtue of faith are denied him. Of all the virtues, the greatest is charity, and to this he subscribes generously and privately. Part cynic, part romantic, he is essentially a kind and simple man with an extraordinary mind and personality.

Truth? Nietzsche argued: "There are no facts; everything is in flux, incomprehensible, elusive; what is relatively most enduring is—our opinions." At least, in the case of Burton, it is rewarding to find how so many opinions of the man independently concur, whether expressed by acquaintances of his youth or of middle-age. As Dennis Burgess says: "The basic fundamental characteristics and traits remain. He has not really changed. And if you don't see Rich for ten years and then suddenly bump into him, it is as though one had met him only the day before. We would carry on just where we had left off. He's got this marvelous warming thing about him. Children who are too young to know of Richard Burton meet him and are fascinated by him—as a person, not as a celebrity. He has this tremendous physical presence which fills a room. And he always had it."

"Forget the filmstar bit," says Robert Hardy. "It's not like saying you have met Gregory Peck or Rock Hudson or whoever. This is something quite out of the ordinary—unique. When you meet Richard, you meet a great man who just happens to have become an actor." And this opinion is echoed again and again.

Donald Houston, who shares Burton's Welsh background: "Besides this magnetism which is just part of the man, Richard has one of the best brains I have ever encountered. He is a mass of facts and information and knowledge, and with his gifts and brains he could have been just as famous in any field he had chosen to take up. He might not have been so well-known because he might not have gained so much publicity in another field. But if he had taken up politics, for instance, I would have expected him to end up as Prime Minister."

Paul Daneman, who worked with him at the Old Vic and the Lyric: "Richard is one of the genuine personalities of our time; not an exhibitionist putting it on. He is one of nature's leaders, one of those people who—whatever he did in life—would have got to the top. In a way, I rather suspect that he may have secretly regretted becoming an actor because it is not a profession to keep one's intellectual powers at full stretch. But at the time he started, I suppose that he felt that he had nothing to lose and everything to gain. The theater was very middle-class then, and he entered it as a kind of regal peasant."

John Neville: "Richard has one of the best minds in an actor that I've ever met—a brilliant, extraordinary mind. I remember we worked fantastically hard when we were at the Old Vic, alternating as Iago and Othello, and at the end of a thirteen hour day we would go out and have drinks together. One night we had been to a number of bars and it was getting late. We had to be at rehearsals at ten next morning. But that morning, just as we were about to start work, Richard said to me, 'I read the most marvelous book last night.' I said, 'Oh yes, what was that?' He replied, *'The History of Mathematics.'* Well, apart from the title, I thought when the hell did he get time to read it. But he really did, you see."

Emlyn Williams: "Richard is tremendously cultivated; much more than I am really because he knows poems and books by heart—the kind of works which one thinks one knows but doesn't really. In the end you believe you've read them. But Richard really has. He is incredibly well-read. And yet he makes light of it all. He is so unpretentious; in himself he is a completely real person."

The bright, darting mind and the commanding presence that once prompted an Oxford don to write, "this boy is a genius," has impressed most everyone who has come to know Burton. But that is not to say that everyone is completely enamored with the man or that everyone speaks favorably of him. It is difficult to imagine anyone rising remotely near his peak of wealth and power without making enemies along the way. Richard is no exception. Yet, such is the straightforward, unchanging earthiness and honesty of the man, that his enemies are remarkably few and hard to find in a profession renowned for bitchiness and jealousy and cutthroat business deals. Who does have unfavorable opinions of Burton? There are a few producers still bitter over abortive plans to make films with him; an actor friend of many years ago who will not even speak his name; a famous director over whom Richard accidentally vomited in the Dorchester; cooled ex-girl friends, and one or two others who have never forgiven his desertion of Sybil. In addition, of course, there are multitudes of other people who do not really *know* Richard and yet will speak ill of him without any real foundation; those who have based their judgment on fleeting impressions. "Don't talk to me about Richard Burton," one well-known lady of the peerage said to us. "I met him once at a gala reception. I told him how much I enjoyed his latest film and then asked him what he thought about a certain romantic actress. And, do you know, he completely ignored me! He just growled, 'Excuse me,' and wandered off to get another drink. Such a rude man!"

Burton is certainly capable of arousing hostility among the Colonel Blimps and those who strictly abide by Auntie Agatha's *Nineteenth Century Guide to Etiquette and Social Graces.* He has never been one to stand on ceremony or indulge in petty gossip, and though he can mix easily with the highest and lowest in social status, he does so only on his own terms, never affected, never artificial. Robert Hardy remembers meeting Richard in 1968 at the big society wedding of Simon Hornby and Sheran Cazalet, daughter of the Queen Mother's racehorse trainer, Peter Cazalet. "The champagne had finished and people were shifting about from table to table in this dazzling, beautiful country house. Sitting around one table there were, in order, the Queen Mother, Richard, Noel Coward, an empty chair, myself, Elizabeth, and then some others. Being a well brought-up little fellow and a devoted royalist, I was being frightfully Ps and Qs, and Richard was talking to the Queen Mother about the first time he had met Princess Margaret. At that moment Princess Margaret arrived and sat down in the vacant chair. Richard turned round and said, 'Ah, I was just telling your er . . . um . . . er . . . er. . . .' The Princess rescued him. 'I believe the phrase you're searching for is Her Majesty the Queen Mother.' That is the absolute bare truth, but by the time the party was an hour older, Noel Coward was going round telling a ghastly, inflated version of the story in which he had Richard snapping his fingers in the Queen Mum's face as he searched for the right words—'Your mother . . . um (snap) . . . er (snap) . . . er (snap).' "

Like most men, of course, Burton can become progressively more outrageous as he drinks, and Burton drinks a lot. Ever since his Oxford days he has fondly fostered his image as the prodigious, hard-drinking hellraiser— "You know, I used to fight people all the time. Hit them, I mean. If anyone made fun of my Welsh accent or started calling me 'Taff' I'd slug them. I once nearly killed a sergeant in the RAF." Now, though not so fierce and quickly short of breath, he remains altogether worthy of his bacchanalian reputation. Stories of his enormous alcoholic consumption are legion. And many of them emanate from himself. He has told how during the filming of *The Spy Who Came in*

From the Cold he had to knock back a whisky—"and it was the last shot of the day and so I decided to use the real hard stuff. We did forty-seven takes. Imagine it—forty-seven whiskies." He has recalled how he was once challenged to a drinking contest by an entire fifteen-strong rugby team, all Welsh miners—"I got through nineteen boilermakers—whisky chased by a pint of beer —but next day I was in no state to remember who won." And in Mexico there is a joke about a recipe for the Richard Burton Cocktail that begins, "first take twenty-one tequilas. . . ." It derives from the day he drank twenty-one straight tequilas and then dived fully clothed into the sea to investigate a companion's belief that he had spotted a shark.

Richard, who includes among his heroes a Lancastrian he met in a Westminster pub and who could down twelve pints of beer while Big Ben was tolling midnight, doubtless exaggerates some tales of his drinking. But not that much. For example, in February, 1967, Richard was to be Brook Williams's best man, but as he was abroad filming *The Comedians,* he sent a telegram saying it was impossible to get to London in time. The wedding was at the Chelsea Registry Office, and shortly before the ceremony actor Terence Longden (the replacement best man) and witness Donald Houston discovered that Brook and his bride planned to stay on in Sean Tracey's pub in the Fulham Road after the reception. They thought this a bit too ordinary for a wedding night, and so they booked a suite at Claridges. After celebrations in the pub, the wedding party moved into the suite for more drinking in the afternoon.

"Eventually the guests drifted away," says Brook. "But later on that night, at about 10:30, Richard, Elizabeth, and Ivor arrived out of the blue. More booze was ordered and finally the hotel ran out of bottles of Dom Perignon, and so we made do with magnums of champagne and then brandies. It all went down on the bill, and next morning the manager said, 'There's been some serious error here because what I've got down is 15 guineas ($38) for your apartment and £189.4s.3d. ($453.65) for wines and spirits. Quite clearly it must be wrong. I'll have it checked for you.' Well, he came back with a whole pile of dockets and he looked through and said, 'Ah, yes, I see what has happened. You've been charged for 36 bottles of Dom Perignon and 14 magnums of champagne. Now you couldn't have had all that.' But we had. And I didn't even have enough money to tip the porter. I had to ring Terry to bring me some cash."

Houston remembers Brook ringing him at eight o'clock in the morning after the alcoholic wedding night. "He was as bright as a button, for he has a fantastic ability to hold his drink, and he was saying, 'You'll never guess what happened last night after you left!' And I heard stories about Ivor falling down and cracking his head on the bathroom floor. And I believe Elizabeth was down on her hands and knees cleaning up the blood when she dropped one of her diamond earrings down the lavatory bowl. At about four in the morning they sent Ivor home in a car and Richard was saying, 'When I finish this drink we'll be off.' But it wasn't a glass he was holding in his hand; it was a bottle of brandy. At noon next day Brook met me at Sean's pub and he was shattered. He had this enormous bill and he said he didn't know what to do because he couldn't pay it. There was talk about clubbing together, since we had talked him into staying at Claridges in the first place. Then it was suggested that he send the bill to Rich. But Brook said he couldn't do that because they had already given him a round-the-world ticket to visit them and have a honeymoon in Mexico. I think Emlyn paid the bill in the end."

Richard is now mainly a vodka-and-tonic man, with the occasional Bloody Mary for starters. Away from the public gaze, in Switzerland and Mexico, he cuts down drastically on his drinking. He never drinks alone. But on the London-Paris-Rome-New York-Los Angeles circuit, when he is continually meeting people, he chooses to drink a lot. Why? He once explained that he only drank when he was working—"to burn up the flatness; the stale, empty, dull deadness that one feels when one goes offstage." More recently he has answered: "To cure you from the agony, the idiocy of this strange world we all live in. I drink because there is no other possible way to escape the attention of the world." In simplest terms, however, he drinks because he genuinely enjoys it. For him drinking is a progressive pastime to be practiced in good company that becomes warmer, more animated, uninhibited, and entertaining with each glass. A spontaneous act of companionship and togetherness. "There's no more lasting pleasure than sitting at a bar and drinking and swapping yarns with your mates," he says. "But I can't understand those people who go home at night and mix themselves a martini."

Richard's ability to entertain and pour out stories gives passing acquaintances the impression of a huge extrovert, but this merely disguises the retiring introvert who needs a couple of drinks to swing into his most scintillating social style. When filming *Under Milk Wood,* he remarked: "Dylan Thomas was several different men—like most of us are. Caught in the early morning he was gentle, sweet, differential, and shy. About opening time he would start to warm up, and between noon and six he was angelic, a marvelous storyteller. After six it was best to head for the hills. He became nasty. I suppose we all do that." It takes an awful lot of vodka to make Burton turn nasty, and let slip the reins on those native traits of "unsure arrogance, mock belligerence, cosmic wit, and large gestures," and even when strangers take to the hills, friends tolerate this explosion of inner rage that is directed against others as a kind of condemnation of his own inadequacy. Elizabeth simply recognizes it as the time signal to put on her hospital matron's voice and snap: "Richard, it's time you had a little nap."

Being fully aware of his own weaknesses and personal failings, Richard can easily accept them in other people. "One of the extraordinary things I have found about him," says Hardy, "is that where he has given his affection profoundly, as he gave it to me, and as he has given it to others, you are automatically forgiven for everything. I have no other friend who is like that at all. When he gave his friendship, it was complete. There was never any question of resentment if you behaved badly according to any code; if you were disloyal, evil, foul-tempered, anything. I don't think he knows what a grudge is. In this way he's so unlike other people, because at the same time he's got this plainly unyielding drive to get power which in most other people is a kind of canalizing, narrowing thing." Once, when Richard threw a party at the Dorchester, one of his guests, a Scotch-wild Welsh-Irishman, behaved absolutely outrageously, insulted Mia Farrow, and finally collapsed in a drunken stupor. Next morning, Richard bore him not the slightest malice and chuckled when he received a telegram of apology: "Sorry, old love, the soldiers were on the lawn and the drums were beating in the poor old head."

Physically, Burton is the antithesis of the spirit, for he is solid and very square. A large head squats low on broad shoulders that are carried stiff with arthritis on a barrel of a 45-inch chest. The eyes are green, wide-spaced, and half-blind to near objects. The pepper-and-salt hair is untidy to hide too much new forehead and runs as thick and white as snow down his pockmarked cheeks. The lips are thin, but the mouth is generous and the teeth surprisingly attractive. He has a faint scar on the chin and wears a punch-twist in the nose. When he first met Elizabeth his head had a common circumference with her waist, but this is no longer true. "Because of fat," he says wickedly. "In the head," she adds laconically. Sitting down he looks taller than when he is standing up on his bandy legs. "This worries him," said *Time* magazine eight years ago. "His imagination takes hold and he sees himself as the world's most conspicuous dwarf. Hence he has a short man's height complex, although he is well above the average height of men." Actually he stands 5 ft. 10 in. in his socks and weighs 175 pounds when stripped of vodka, beer, and buttery chip sandwiches. But he has no filmstar's fancy illusions about his appearance. Recalling a time he went swimming on location, he said: "When I took my clothes off strong men laughed and strangers kissed each other. Stripped, I am monstrous." Dressed, he's no Beau Brummel. Yet his appeal to women is legendary. Philip Burton has confirmed that the girls used to "hang around Richie like cats after cream" when he was only fifteen. And when Richard went to Hollywood, Fredric March was saying, "He has a terrific way with women. I don't think he has missed more than half a dozen."

At times Richard has mischievously encouraged the great lover legend. He once joked that Julie Andrews was his only leading lady he had not slept with, to which she reportedly replied, "How dare he say such an awful thing about me." At other times this

Don Juan image becomes so trivial and tedious that he dismisses it as the ridiculous product of so much film publicity. The truth is, before he fell in love with Elizabeth, his reputation as a ladykiller was not entirely unmerited. Now he describes his adoration of Liz as complete love. He explained to us: "I was very bad. But I started a clean sheet roughly ten years ago. Since then I have never touched, never looked, never smiled at, never done anything with another woman." To which Elizabeth retorted: "You're so full of rubbish. You can't help but flirt with other women. Just flirting, mind you. Anything beyond that, buster, and you'd be singing soprano by now." And when one sees them relaxed in private together, one cannot doubt him for an instant when he swears that he has not seriously looked at another woman since he met Elizabeth. They are mercurial love birds singing with a bittersweet mutual mocking that emerges as perfect harmony. There are no secrets between them. She even knows of his past affairs and accepts them with a witty, bitchy grace ("I must say, Richard, that you have at least shown great taste in the women you marry").

A few years ago a well-known actress whispered to Richard: "Does Elizabeth know about us—what we were?" He replied, just loud enough for Elizabeth to hear: "Not only about us, sweetheart, but about two hundred others." Exaggeration or not, Elizabeth does know about every woman in Richard's life, and although she can be very droll about some of the prettier ones who have become plain and starched, she admits to being jealous of the past. "When I see a woman he knew before me something happens to me inside. But I know intellectually that it's irrational and stupid and my problem. Since I first met Richard he has never given me a single jealous moment." But Elizabeth has given some of Richard's old girl friends a hard time. Like when she walked into a powder room and surprised a beautiful world-known actress at the mirror. Over lunch she made Richard squirm to our roar of laughter with a description of the scene. "I just walked in and she was peeling off her eyelashes and I said, 'Do you wear false eyelashes? Aren't they marvelous! So terribly clever! I've never seen any before, may I see them please?' I put one up to my own eyelashes and said, 'My God, how ever can you stand to wear them? Aren't they terribly, terribly heavy? But they do make one look terribly glamorous. They're terrific, aren't they? But I don't think I could possibly wear them! Don't they make your eyes so terribly heavy at the end of the day if you have to wear them all the time?" For these occasions Elizabeth assumes a little-girl voice of such sweet innocence that sleeping dogs cock up their ears and begin to whimper in distress.

Elizabeth sometimes calls Richard "Charlie Charm," and there is no mystery about his appeal to women. Matronly ladies have set off to interview him with their corsets steeled with skepticism and have come away in maiden form, purring about his piercing green eyes, his rugged manliness, his magnetic voice, his melancholy looks, his sudden darting smiles, his flashes of wit; above all, they are disarmed by his attentiveness and interest. He is a great talker, but he is also a good listener, possessing a gift for making other people feel that they really matter and that he really cares. And unlike so many actors whose favorite topic is themselves, he does care. Women can go into raptures in singing his praises, and none has been more expressive than Tammy Grimes who once eulogized: "He called me 'shining' and I was madly in love with him for at least four days. Strictly an infatuation. He makes women feel beautiful. He is a genius. His acting has such a tragic quality. It comes from a completely unsentimental nature, a pure wonderment, and a deep loneliness. His life is a kaleidoscope. Turn him and you see fifty different patterns. Every time you meet him, you see a million different colors. He is a vodka man with a quicksilver mind and a violent temper. He's moody, completely unpredictable, always fascinating, very frugal, extremely shrewd, a tremendous snob, and a beautiful man."

Conversely, some women find him to be a far less attractive man because, since giving his affection totally to Elizabeth, he has displayed less charm to them. No actress, for example, has worked with Burton more often than Claire Bloom and yet, when approached, she firmly declined to speak to us about him at all. But earlier, in her book *Scratch an Actor* (William Morrow & Co., Inc., 1969) Hollywood columnist Sheilah Graham quoted

Miss Bloom as saying: "He hadn't changed at all, except physically, but that was natural as he was older. He was still drinking, he was still boasting, he was still late, he was still reciting the same poems, and telling the same stories as when he was twenty-three. They were both rather aloof to me. In all the month's shooting (of *The Spy Who Came in From the Cold*) in Ireland, I was never asked to dinner by the Burtons. He was interesting years ago, but now I found him rather boring, as people sometimes are when they get what they have always wanted."

And what did he want? "A beautiful wife, money, and a great career. In the early days he would have included a wish to be the best actor in the world. It was obvious he was going to be a huge star, which is not quite the same as being a great actor. He has confused them. He thinks they are the same."

An interviewer later confronted Richard with these quotes and asked for his comments. "I can tell you in just four words," said Burton. "Hell—hath—no—fury."

A few years ago, Sybil was quoted: "He is always craving admiration. Perhaps that explains his need to go from woman to woman, seeking change and excitement like a frustrated, unhappy child." But all that is past now. The Burtons' love for each other is all-consuming, totally possessive. Robert Hardy says: "A woman's unfaithfulness to Richard would be utterly intolerable. He doesn't give a bugger if one of us who knows him well says that he's a shit. But as far as women go, he could never bear disloyalty. His relationship with a woman must be absolute, because the tribe from which he's bred demands complete loyalty from its womenfolk." Elizabeth expects complete loyalty, too, and Richard gives it to her, even though he jokes that she never gives him a chance to do otherwise. Their togetherness after the seven year itch of marriage dries up the flow of inky-fingered Cassandras. No great lovers in history or fiction, and few suburban lovers have spent so many minutes of each other together. Day in, night out, they never tire of loving each other by pleasing each other. Elizabeth has put it beautifully: "We are so aware that our responsibility is not just to us, but to all the people we have ever hurt."

Stanley Baker, who started in the theater as a boy with Richard, is able to tell any anecdote drawn from the past in front of Elizabeth without embarrassment. It is not that Richard has made any sort of solemn confession to Elizabeth; it is just that she has accepted him exactly as he stands. Their lives are empty of the complication of lies. "When they are together," says Baker, "Richard and Elizabeth really spark. It is a fantastic relationship. They are both immensely kind. They took my daughter to America with them for a holiday and then on to Paris. She adores both of them, particularly Elizabeth, who has very winning ways. What most people don't realize is how honest and generous a person she really is. She needs emotion, she needs warmth, and she is prepared to give it. My daughter is a very sensitive little girl and she gets very upset if she reads anything unfavorable about Elizabeth in the papers. She won't hear a word against Elizabeth. She adores her—and that for me is the yardstick. As for Richard, he has always been extraordinarily generous. He really cares about people. And I don't believe any of the stupid things that have been talked about him and Elizabeth. It's the sensational stories that always make the headlines. If Richard Burton and Elizabeth Taylor happen to have a shouting match in a café in Hollywood, it's in the press next day. If Dai Evans and Lucy Jones do it in Cardiff, who gives a fuck? Nobody cares. No marriage is without these things. My wife and myself are the most frightful rowers. We're careful not to do it in public; maybe we're just careful by nature. But I know that underlying it all, Richard and Elizabeth are genuine people in spite of the lives they are leading."

Elizabeth is a grandmother now. Yet the extraordinary beauty remains, and surprisingly—considering that she has known no other life but the goldfish-bowl existence of the supercelebrity— she is completely without any kind of vanity. Those who know her well automatically describe her as a "mother earth figure," much to the chagrin of those who expect a vision of Aphrodite. She is essentially down-to-earth and has stressed that she needs strength in a man more than any other quality. She found this in Mike Todd. She has found it in Burton. And this strength in itself is a quality hard to define. She likes a man to lead, but not to dominate; to decide, but not to be afraid to go back on a decision. She puts bravery above masculinity and trusts herself to the heart rather than the mind. She eschews all bourgeois definitions and when she says that Richard has got that "sort of jungle essence that one can sense," she is really admiring a princely peasant who has never lost the common touch, but who, like Shakespeare's Owen Glendower, can boast: "All the courses of my life do show I am not in the role of common men."

"I remember," says Hardy, "that Richard and I were once having a long conversation about morality, about what is right and what is wrong, and how you can judge the destruction of a marriage. And he said to me, 'We are the myth-makers.' In any generation and in any system of life there are myth-makers, and this is why he is pursued by the papers and cauterized by public attitudes. He had to become a myth from the moment he was born. Whatever he did, he was destined to do greatly. He did become a myth and then he had the wit and wisdom to say, 'We are the myth-makers.' He meant, 'I am a myth-maker,' and he was right."

Burton the Actor

The legend of the diabolically famous Richard Burton now rests securely on a fortune too colossal ever to be destroyed by artistic failure. Yet, in the final analysis, will his talents as an actor gain him space on the playbill of posterity? It is a game for critics which amuses him greatly, because the man himself cares not a jot what they might say. He did once. Not any more. Now he regards the valhalla of actors as a purgatory of boredom, a second-hand perch for the parrots of first-class minds. If he should be remembered, he would prefer it to be for words written rather than for words repeated aloud and forgotten. Standing as he does, one of the greatest actors in the world, he has neither the dedication nor the true vocation for a profession that he ignores completely offstage. "If I were a bank clerk in Scunthorpe, for instance, or a steel worker in Port Talbot, you wouldn't catch me joining the local dramatic society just for the pleasure of playing Richard III. In the same way, I have no yearning to go to the theater when I'm not working." It is a feeling shared, but seldom expressed, by many great actors who are rarely to be seen on the public side of the footlights.

"Years ago," says Robert Hardy, "we corresponded at great length about Shakespeare, about the nature of acting, the nature of love, and so on. I remember saying, such was my immaturity at the time, that I profoundly believed that an actor was capable of greatness just as was Beethoven or anyone else, and that anyone seeking to be a great actor had to cut everything else out of their lives. They had to be as smooth as a rocket, straight through. I learned later that this was absolute nonsense. That's exactly what Richard never has been. He's like a piece of encrusted something under the ocean, trailing seaweed, a whole mass of little hammerfish and all the rest of it. I don't think he's ever been a dedicated actor. I think you only need to be a dedicated actor, a dedicated priest, a dedicated librarian, or whatever, if you don't exist in the round from the beginning. But in an extraordinary way, Richard did."

Fortune, rather than fame as an actor, has been Burton's spur. In the beginning, with the humility of a novice, he deeply cared what the critics might say about him. They were, supposedly, the judges of the supreme court and the real experts. But his respect for acting quickly diminished, and like the child who saw that the emperor wasn't wearing any clothes, he soon came to realize that many critics were naked of everything but their own ingrown egos. He made this discovery in his Old Vic days when he looked up old newspaper files and found that while he had been compared unfavorably with Olivier, the great Olivier had also suffered by earlier comparison. It was, and is, a case of crabbed age and youth never going together, and just as sportswriters argue pointlessly about the respective merits of past and present quarterbacks and center-forwards, so drama critics compare their Hamlets and Hals. By their invidious comparisons, however, it is our personal belief that Burton has been seriously underestimated by theater historians. A small minority of critics, such as Tynan, have had the ears and the eyes to recognize his unique talent, his extraordinary inborn facility for acting, and to realize, as Coleridge said about Kean, that "to see him act is like reading Shakespeare by flashes of lightning." But the vast majority, with or without pen, have somehow felt cheated by an actor who has achieved rare prominence on the stage without blinding them, year after year, with his genius. They cannot bring themselves to welcome to the halls of theatrical fame an actor who has not wholly and respectfully dedicated himself to his art.

Burton has been made fully aware of their frustration. Shortly after *Cleopatra* and his soaring prosperity, *Time* magazine quoted his onetime agent Harvey Orkin as saying: "This is a man who has sold out. He is trying to get recognition on a trick. He could have been the greatest actor on this planet." To such criticism Richard replies: "I'm never a great actor, always a potential great actor. You never get to be a great actor until you're dead, I suppose." One supposes he supposes correctly, for it is impossible to tell what prestige he might have won if he had remained in Britain and devoted the greater part of his work to the stage. Olivier, Richardson, and Guinness had all received knighthoods by the age of forty-five; Burton on that birthday was at the Palace to collect a modest C.B.E. If he had remained in the theatrical establishment and dutifully conformed with traditions, he most probably would have achieved the accolade of approval by now, rising as Sir Richard to join the lofty names that critics use to discipline unruly players who refuse to play up and play the game of Shakespeare.

Even actors without any sort of classical ambition are deeply disappointed at Burton's seemingly willful refusal to pull on a hair shirt at the National Theater in London. "When I knew him," says Warren Mitchell, "Richard was a very serious and academic

person. He loved literature. He was very intellectual. This is why
I regret his departure from the theater; after all, he must have
made enough money in films to forget his fears of insecurity. You
see, one hopes, one thinks that he must play Lear. But I don't
think he'd have the stamina now. He'd have to go back into training for that. I agree that he could have been anything he wanted.
But he sees himself in this tragic role. He has this Morgan Evans
complex—this self-destructive thing. Because there is no doubt
there were once two up-and-coming giants—Scofield and Burton. They were the same age. They were friends. And there was
no doubt the theater was in their hands. Like it was with Olivier
and Gielgud, say. And Burton has disappointed me. But then, I
should talk of dedication. We've all sold out some way or other. I
swore I'd never do a television commercial, but eventually the
price was so good I couldn't refuse. I like the comforts of life
too."

Has Burton sold out? "I don't think that Richard has any less
regard for the stage or places it on a lesser plane than I do," says
John Neville. "But he followed this path into films, and it's a very
difficult path to kick once you've chosen it." Emlyn Williams
agrees. "I think Richard misses the theater very much. I think he
wants it both ways. He wants to be top of the polls in the films
and also Olivier. And you can't do both. You see, John Gielgud
has to play small parts in films; so do a lot of great actors, including Olivier. But you must devote yourself pretty exclusively to
one or the other in order to become a John Wayne, for what it's
worth in films, or an Olivier in the theater."

Gielgud, the stage idol of Richard's youth, does not altogether
agree. "In a way Richard is in the sort of Errol Flynn–John Barrymore tradition. But I think he has much more discipline than
either of those men. And I can't ever see him letting things slide
the way they did. No, I don't think acting for the cinema is detrimental to one's stage craft. On the contrary, I think it's good for
it because you learn not to cross your Ts and dot your Is too
much. The subtlety of the movies is marvelous. But there again, I
think that if you do films all the time there is a danger for very
fine stage actors. Herbert Marshall, for example, was the most

beautiful and subtle stage actor, but when he had been in films for a few years he became tired and careless. They photographed the same profile; he did the same little tricks of eyebrow, the mouth, or expression. It's awfully easy to acquire a sort of trick personality for films, especially if you're not playing leading parts as Richard does. In supporting parts you can so easily become like Aubrey Smith, those men who went to Hollywood and became a typical English butler, or father, or diplomat, or professor of whatever. You become typed and do the same thing in every film, but I don't think Richard has done that. He has played a lot of parts out of character. He has an enormous variety in his playing, and I think that in *The Spy Who Came in From the Cold* he was marvelous. On the other hand, many of the films—like *The Robe*, I imagine, which I never saw, and *Cleopatra*—didn't really stretch him very much. When you become a sort of sex-appeal figure in an enormous epic, then I don't think much is called upon you, except to come on and show your face and wear your clothes and walk about.

"But I have a feeling that now Richard is anxious to go back to the theater. He's mentioned several plays. He wanted to do the Sartre play with me, *The Devil and the Good God*, which I don't think myself is very good. But it's a wonderful part for him. And I would love to see him play Peer Gynt, for instance. But, of course, it's a terrible difficulty to get back again, though whatever he did would be an enormous draw. He's as skilled as he ever was, and I think he could do many, many things. I don't think, however, that he ought to play princes. He should play warriors or sort of tough heroes. I don't think he has the delicacy or the inbred patrician thing that makes those sort of princely characters in Shakespeare. I'm always so disappointed that I didn't see his Iago, and when I played Othello I would have given my back teeth to have had him as Iago. I think perhaps I wouldn't have made such a failure if I had had him because I'm sure he was absolutely excellent as Iago. Also I wish he had played *The Battle of Schrivings* with me. It was written for Olivier, but when Olivier became unavailable it never occurred to me to send the play to Richard and ask if he would do it. I think if he had played it the play might have been a success. I don't know how stagestruck Richard is today and how much the luxury of filming and the boredom mixture has got hold of him. But in some ways there is some balance between him and Elizabeth—like there was between Vivien and Laurence Olivier. There is a tiny bit of rivalry, as there must be in a marriage. And I would suspect that he knows what a marvelously good film actress she is, and I think she rather longs to act on the stage; and he certainly, I feel, longs to act on the stage to show that he acts better than she does. That's my suspicion anyhow."

What are Burton's greatest qualities as an actor? He himself says that most of his capacity lies in his voice, that extraordinary ability to "suit the action to the word, the word to the action," while letting the magic of his tongue-music "o'erstep not the modesty of nature." But this prodigious power of voice production is the one great technical asset he has acquired and developed by sheer dint of effort. In Taibach days his natural voice needed drastic change; then, long after he had left the disciplined tutorship of Philip Burton, he would spend fifteen to twenty minutes in the shower each morning—shouting, crying out, screaming; mouthing complex poetry, attempting maximum speed without loss of clarity, and especially aiming to keep the power low but penetrating—what he called "convoluted sort of poetry." But Richard also has one quality of voice that is a Celtic gift and not an acquired art. "It is what in Wales we call *hwyl*," says Viv Allen. "A strange quality of voice displayed by professional preachers—a kind of supernatural tone, a minor cadence. Many of the soliloquies in Hamlet mirror it." With this quality, Burton is able to bring to great speeches all the depth and power of a hymn, gently rising to a crescendo of feeling and intensity, as in the excommunication scene of *Becket* in which he achieved such impact that one of the "monks," emotionally stunned, accidentally set fire to himself with his candle.

Burton's second outstanding virtue as an actor is a presence and repose so remarkable that he can, as Tynan said, "make silence garrulous." Neville explains: "Richard has this quite incredible gift of stillness. And in a sense, this is a paradox because he is very athletic as a man and as Coriolanus, for example, he was an extremely athletic actor. But the moving, telling things that Richard can do are done with his stillness. One classic example of his using it is that famous moment in the tavern scene of *Henry IV* when Falstaff says to Prince Hal, 'When you are king don't banish me from your company.' And Richard, as Hal, says, 'I *do*, I *will*.' He does this sort of thing beautifully. He has this quite remarkable physical presence and those eyes which are very wide apart indeed. He can come on stage and just fix an audience with those eyes. This is something that is God-given and which he can use to phenomenal advantage."

From the first moment he walked onto a professional stage, Richard was admired for his extraordinarily natural repose, his faculty for fixing the audience with unblinking eyes and commanding their attention while involved in the most insignificant and inactive roles. Philip Burton had impressed upon him that if he remained still, attention would flow in his direction; also that a finely pitched whisper could be every bit as effective as the most thundering roar. And this combination—"stillness" for want of any precise word—was used with particularly stunning and arresting effect, again in *Becket,* when we saw technicians moved near to tears as Richard knelt and prayed with so convincing an air of sanctity that one felt he was really in the cathedral of Canterbury and not on plastic steps in Shepperton Studios. Yet there are critics who would argue that he has taken too much advantage of his gift for stillness, that it all came too easily to him, and that he would have been a greater actor if he had served a longer, more disciplined and conventional apprenticeship in the theater.

"I think his stillness is a kind of trick," says Hugh Griffith. "One of those tricks which came from his amateur upbringing and which was instilled into him from the beginning. It was thought that these trickeries would carry him into the professional theater, but I am not sure that they did. I believe it was Hazlitt who said in defense of Edmund Kean, when he was being criticized by all sorts of people about his performances, that there is no such thing as trick in matters of genius. It is a very good truism. I think Richard tried to get away with tricks. They were very impressive when used with his face, his personality, his whole presence on a stage, but I tried to persuade him not to use them so much, not to depend on them. However, he couldn't get himself to take advice from somebody who had been in the professional theater for some time.

"What kind of tricks? Well, for example, if you are clever, you will keep your eyes on the edge of the balcony and keep them there if you don't know what else to do. You just stare at a certain spot, a spotlamp or something on the edge of the circle, and then you can't be wrong because everybody will be looking at you. Well, Richard did this with me when we were playing father and son in New York in Anouilh's *Eurydice* which the Americans called *Legend of Lovers*. I was talking to him as father to son, and suddenly I noticed he wasn't listening to me at all. He was just staring at a spot somewhere on the edge of the circle. I stopped. And then I went up to his face and looked along the line that his gaze was taking and said, 'What, what, what . . . are you looking at? *I'm* talking to you.' I don't think he used the same trick afterwards—not with me anyhow. But there's no doubt that he was doing it because he had been told that it was something he ought to do.

"Every actor has to make a start somewhere and there are plenty of tricks he can pick up on the way. But you don't want to start off with them; you are up against a brick wall in that case. And yet I don't think it has stinted him in any kind of fashion, at least not in films. I think he took to filming like a duck to water because a lot of these tricks were more useful to him in the films than in the theater. He has worked terribly hard at everything, and the tricks paid off very soon—though they haven't paid off so much in the theater. In the films you've only to be clever in judging what focus you are in and knowing where to look, which becomes a mechanical thing. My opinion, however, is that he should have been a much better actor with all the qualities, vocal and physical that he's got, and that certain trickeries would have been better washed out of him in a strict school of acting. On the other hand, he's proved his own point—that it doesn't really matter. He's made his money and there it is."

It was Charles Lamb who wrote in praise of Bensley: "He was totally destitute of trick and artifice . . . betrayed none of that *cleverness* which is the bane of serious acting." But virtually all actors, great and small, employ certain tricks of style, and the greater the actor the more subtle they are and more difficult to perceive. We asked Sir John Gielgud how far he thought Burton employed tricks and was guilty of a certain "laziness" in style. He replied: "Well, I think he is a bit inclined to use a trick that Ainley used—which is to gaze over the audience with those very beautiful sex-appeal eyes and dream a bit on stage. And that's the Welshness, you know. It's awfully facile, his beauty of voice. He knows he can have an audience in the hollow of his hand, and that's always a danger. He has never had to fight for the sympathy or the sex appeal of the theater, and that is something which, of course, can be rather dangerous because you find it too easy. I found that a little bit when I saw the Eurovision *Hamlet;* after two hundred performances I did think he was having his own way too much. I would be rather interested to see him in a play that wasn't a success, and see how he would cope with that. It would be very interesting, because in a way my fear is that things have been too easily successful for him. To have to fight his way through a play that was a failure and have his say in it might be a very interesting experience, both for him and the audience."

On this point, producer Frank Hauser says: "What one felt he needed sometimes was rather more all-out attack. Normally he would find his way round parts far more than plunge at them head-on. The two times I saw him act with tremendous attack were in a very good production of *Coriolanus* by Michael Benthall and in his last performance of Othello when he was certainly in liquor. Then he was sensationally good. When I worked with him I certainly treated him differently than other actors. Richard is a great blarnier and he tries on a lot of the old Welsh charm. But if like me, you have grown up among thousands and thousands of boys who also had great Welsh charm, it doesn't work very well. One was able to see when he was trying to get something too easily and told him, 'We'll have a little less of that.' "

Though Burton says he could never be dedicated to the theater

in the way Olivier and Gielgud and Scofield are, he does genuinely enjoy acting. His handicap is his extremely low boredom
boiling point. "I did many of those Shakespearean roles as a kind
of duty," he explained. "I enjoyed them sometimes, but I found
the stage a bit of drudgery for the most part; the terrifying thing
of playing the same part eight times a week, for say a year, is en-
ervating." As a consequence of his restless disposition, he lacks a
certain discipline as a stage actor, and during the course of a long
run he can become somewhat unorthodox and cavalier. During
his New York *Hamlet,* for example, when he knew that German
adoption officials were visiting the theater, he began his "To be or
not to be" soliloquy in German. And brother Graham recalls the
night he went to see *Camelot.* "There was the heaviest snowfall I
have ever seen, and towards the end of the performance many
people were slipping out to grab the first taxis. Richard came to
the front of the stage and called out, 'Hey, book a cab for me, too,
will you?' " Burton agrees that he is rather undisciplined, but such
is his nature that he would not have it any other way. He has no
desire to go on stage and reproduce an identical performance
night after night. Variation helps him to combat boredom.

It is Burton's misfortune as an actor that comparatively few
people have seen how supremely well he can command a stage,
and that for untold millions his professional reputation rests on his
films, only a handful of which do justice to his rare talents. His
undistinguished record in early films is largely due to his involvement with inferior scripts, sometimes through his own misjudgment, often because as a contract star he had to accept whatever
they gave him. In addition, however, it was due to his failure in
the early years to master all the subtleties of the craft. He was
disdainful about acting for the cinema, rating it far below acting
in the theater, and he frequently made disparaging remarks about
film stardom. Illustrating that films did not demand great acting
ability, he used to recall how he had heard a director briefing Victor Mature. " 'Look, Vic,' said the director, 'you've just found
your wife scalped by Red Indians and your children lying dead.
Now let's see that written on your face.' And Vic looked back at
him steadily and said, 'Listen, I got three expressions—looking

right, looking left, and looking straight ahead. Which one do you want?' " Another favorite example of his was Rock Hudson. "You know, when he first started in films he had a scene to do in which he had to shake hands and say, 'How do you do?' Believe it or not, he found it quite impossible to do the two things together. But eventually, after dozens of takes, he got it right. The public didn't know the difference. Now Rock's a big, big star. So who needs actors?"

Burton only began thinking really seriously about filming as a craft after meeting Elizabeth Taylor. During the filming of *Cleopatra*, he was talking far more respectfully about Rock Hudson. "In some of those light comedies he's proved himself a second Cary Grant. But can you tell me what he's got? What is it he does that rivets your attention?" Similarly, he posed the same questions about Elizabeth. In Rome, he told Roderick Mann of the London *Sunday Express:* "I asked her the other day: 'Come on, love, what is it you do? I'm an old hand at this business and I'd like to know.' She just smiled. She doesn't really know; that's the truth. She doesn't know what it is she does. Technically, I suppose, as a stage actor, I can fault her now and again. But I can't do what she does, whatever it is. We stage actors are an arrogant lot, I know, but I must say I'd love to know what it is that makes someone like Liz a star. Bogart was the same. What was it he had? Of course, the real testing ground for acting talent is still the stage. . . . On the stage, you've got to act. Only talent will save you. There's no great big close-up waiting to help you when you falter. If you choose a bad film, well, you do it and take the money and then forget it. But choose a bad play, and you're faced with the nightly indignity of having to act in it. Perhaps that's why so many good actors do good plays but bad films. Look at John Barrymore, for instance. A not inconsiderable stage actor, you'll agree. But his films were mostly dreadful. Oddly enough, though, an actor possibly learns more from his bad films than his good ones. For if a film is bad you've just got to try to rise above the mediocre lines. You've got to work at it. And that's how you learn."

It was not how Burton learned. He couldn't learn from his bad films because until recently, when he became a co-producer, he never troubled to see them. He hated to see himself on the screen. But he did learn a great deal from Elizabeth about ways to exploit his gifts more effectively for the screen, and with the advantage of her experience and advice he has since made fewer inferior movies—"her judgment of scripts has proved absolutely correct about seventy-five percent of the time, which is extraordinarily good."

Most of Burton's best work for the cinema lies in his post-*Cleopatra* period, and yet it is curious that even now, after more than a quarter of a century as a leading man, he remains essentially a film actor as opposed to a movie star. He has never been typecast; priest and saint, villain and homosexual, hero and romantic, coward and whiner, bully and braggart—he has played them all. Not so the conventional movie stars. Gable was forever the rugged and forceful male taking two stairs at a time as he carried Scarlett O'Hara off to his bed; Tracy was the eternal father figure. John Wayne could never play the homosexual, nor James Stewart the sadistic bully, so clearly are their cinema images defined. Burton, in contrast, has continued to run the whole gamut of film roles, bringing to the cinema the range of the true stage actor's craft. Yet, in his own peculiar way, he is no less true to type because he maintains his own indelible style; whether turbaned in *Staircase* or blacked-up in *The Rains of Ranchipur,* whether bearded as Petruchio or Henry VIII, he is instantly identifiable. Such is his strange gift of "stillness"—his technique of projecting power from within, while remaining immobile—that he comes across most strikingly when playing the soul-searching, guilt-ridden personality in his quiet moments, with the fixed look and minimum movement of the head. Just as Wayne was born to fight and to ride, just as Cooper was born to personify modesty and honor, just as Gable was born to project masculinity, so in his own way Burton was born to brood on the screen. But this ability to brood —applied to best advantage in the role of "the flawed and vulnerable man"—is scarcely the stuff of which screen immortals are made, and so he has remained the film actor without an image.

What of the future? In 1968, Richard told us: "My interest in the cinema is moving from acting to production. We have our own company, and both Elizabeth and myself will retire from acting within the next two years. I think Elizabeth will go first, and then I will back out after I have gone through commitments that are inked into my diary. Every morning I write one thousand words in that diary. I don't do any push-ups. My exercises are mental rather than physical, and when I retire I will concentrate on writing. Let's face it, I have not been a dedicated actor. It's all bloody marvelous luck. I had the right sort of clock and the right sort of coal-black bobbin Welsh voice. I also had the amazing luck of being adopted by Phil Burton and streaking away to Oxford and other places from my large Jenkins family." The following year, Richard was still talking of retiring at the age of forty-five. "Look at my contemporaries—Olivier, Gielgud, Scofield, Richardson. They love acting. Me, I'm different. Much of the time it's just tedium for me. Last year I had a few months off in Mexico, the first holiday I'd had in fifteen years, and I suddenly realized that doing nothing was marvelous. What I'd like to do now is appear in two plays—Jean Paul Sartre's *The Devil and the Good God* and *King Lear*—and then just disappear from view."

Since then, Richard has had an even longer rest from acting, and during the months of lazing in Mexico he learned more about the mental and physical hazards of inertia and premature semiretirement. He is physically lazy, but with a mind too tightly sprung to remain inactive for long. At the same time he regards it as rather childish for a man in his late forties to be spending his time learning lines and masquerading as somebody else. It is a fairly common attitude. Sir Alec Guinness has expressed it even more strongly, calling acting an "adolescent craft" and saying that he thought no actor over fifty with the exception of Gielgud was "frightfully interested" in acting. Years earlier the late John Barrymore was saying much the same thing, stressing how trivial it all was if he could carry through a performance when half-drunk and still win the plaudits of the critics.

Richard has remarked about actors— "They're poor, abject,

agreeable, perverse, ill-minded, slightly malicious creatures. They must have the center of the stage or at least the second center. They'd like to stop but they can't. And of that august company of idiots, I'm afraid I'm a member." But unlike most actors, he does have the will and the wealth and the intelligence to stop when he wishes. In advancing years, he will continue to make films, though with decreasing regularity ("the only real purpose of it all is to make money"), and perhaps make a rare appearance on stage out of sheer masochistic cussedness and an urge to prove to himself that he can still do it. Never, however, will he return indefinitely to the theater; he is too easily bored to bother with it for long.

Professor Coghill says cryptically, "Richard's life is by no means over, and I hope he will live many years more to startle and delight us. But I foresee notable changes to come in its general pattern. No one—not even he, I think—knows what surprises may be in store. After all, he is a man of genius."

Surprises? With his accumulated weight and maturity, Richard could return briefly to the stage and shake those who underestimate his talents by giving some brilliant portrayal, say an earth-shattering Lear. And he possesses one other ace-up-the-sleeve to play—the ability, if not the self-discipline, to make a startling contribution to literature. He is a voracious reader—of anything from whodunits to metaphysical poets—and his rare ability as a writer was first revealed with the publication of his Welsh *Christmas Story,* the reviews of which delighted him more than the notices he received for his first *Hamlet,* simply because he stands in greater awe of inspired writers than he does of inspired actors. Since then he has contributed articles to many leading American magazines, mostly pieces too lightweight in subject matter to stretch him fully, but all prepared with meticulous scholarship. Richard really cares what the critics think of his writing. He will go over an essay again and again, reluctant to let it go lest there should be one loose word, one unbalanced phrase, one hint of a cliché that has escaped his attention. As he puts it; "The only thing in life is language—not love, not anything else." And such is his obsessive love affair with language that he truly hates to see it misused. No other activity does he tackle with such grim seriousness and painstaking attention to detail.

In common with many Celtic writers, he has a strange poetic quality and a beautiful sense of onomatopoeia. His prose is melodious and dramatic and always deeply veined with humor. The article about rugby which he contributed to *Touchdown,* a glossyback launched in 1970 to commemorate the centenary of the Rugby Football Union, was a little masterpiece which must inevitably reappear in any great anthologies of writing on the sport. With astonishing word power, magical imagery, and subtle similes, he told about his involvement in the game, about the weird and wonderful characters he had met, about coal dust, beer, blasphemy, unroofed urinals, and unshaved prop-forwards. Professional sports writers read it with an amazement and delight that in some turned to gloom and despair as they realized their own inadequacies and comparative mediocrity.

Emlyn Williams, who has so successfully combined writing with acting, says, "Richard has a great talent as a writer. He rarely writes letters, but when my book *George* (his first volume of autobiography) was published, he sent me the most marvelous letter from Rome where he was filming *Cleopatra*. I could tell then that he was longing to write, and indeed he said, 'I do hope that one day I shall be able to do the same sort of thing.' The ability is very much there. He's so tremendously cultivated." Robert Hardy, one of the few people with whom Richard has corresponded at length, agrees. "I cannot wait for the time when he writes so much that he will discipline that Dylan Thomas bug and really write with absolute freedom."

St. David's Day

Richard Burton flourished a vodka bottle and cried: "It's St. David's Day, and you all know I'm not responsible for anything that happens today. Now let everybody drink. This is the greatest day for Welshmen. My day." There was not another Welshman in sight, and it was not his day. It was Elizabeth's day. On this last day of her work on *X, Y, and Zee* all the crew at South London's Shepperton Studios—electricians, carpenters, painters, sweepers-up—were waiting to take their favorite star for a meal of fish-and-chips and a bit of a knees-up* in the saloon bar of the Barley Mow pub.

"I've got another reason for celebrating at this time," said the Welshman. "Elizabeth is in perfect health again for the first time in two years. She's had a difficult time, but it's all over now. It's absolutely marvelous to see her so happy in her work." Elizabeth was not in perfect health. She was coughing with a common cold that prevented her from doing the final day's dubbing. Nonetheless, she did look stunning and incredibly young for a grandmother-to-be.

"Come on then, love," said Richard, "show us your bum." Liz flipped her derrière with all the gay naughtiness of a Moulin Rouge cancan dancer. Burton grinned. "Good Gawd, isn't she beautiful? You should see her in hot pants."

The dressing room began to fill up. Co-stars Susannah York and Michael Caine, director Brian Hutton, studio workers, and thirteen-year-old Liza Todd Burton, glad of a day off from her

* Cockney for dancing

nearby Ascot boarding school. Richard kept the glasses filled. "Drink up, or by this leek, I will most horribly revenge. On this St. David's Day I drink and drink, I swear."

"Now then, no swearing, Richard," said Elizabeth, deaf to parodies of the Bard. "This is *our* party. If you *must* come, we can probably fit you in a corner out of the way, but you must behave."

"Bloody 'ell," he moaned. "How that woman bosses me about! But, my God, she is beautiful."

"Not 'arf," said an electrician. "But look, we'd better be slippery mate, or else the fish 'n' chips'll be cold."

There was further delay as co-producer Alan Ladd, Jr. delivered to his leading lady a square parcel tied with pink ribbon. Elizabeth squealed with delight as she unwrapped a century-old music box. She pressed the catch and a birdie popped up and tweeted a tune.

Richard groaned. "What a woman! Now she's giving me the bird."

Then the group set off for an unprecedented luncheon, given by ordinary studio floor workers for a star of forty movies who had completely won their hearts. "You know, mate, I've never known anything like this," said an electrician. "Mrs. Burton was bloody marvelous on that film. I've seen 'em all, and I tell you I've never known a happier unit. She was the real electrician. No kiddin', she lit up the set each day. The lads couldn't let 'er go without showing how they felt. She's a cracker."

The cracker patted a seat in the back of the black Rolls Royce, and the electrician and his West Indian mate climbed in beside her. We shared the less luxurious white Rolls with Richard. Then the cavalcade moved off to jam the narrow street outside the Barley Mow with $70,000 worth of streamlined chrome and steel.

The pub was small and neat, gleaming with horse brasses beside an open fire and smelling of strong vinegar from the plates of cod-and-chips that steamed the windows. Cloth-capped Charlie, sixty-five, and full of spicy stories and tunes on the accordion, provided the one-man cabaret. Everyone sang. Richard and Elizabeth chanted a Welsh ditty. Michael Caine told a clean story. Sylphlike Susannah danced a jig.

beth chanted a Welsh ditty. Michael Caine told a clean story. Sylphlike Susannah danced a jig.

"Come on, Elizabeth. Let's see yer knees then." And, while Richard stood up and thumped a tambourine with hairy fist, Liz joined hands with Charlie and gaily swung into a *paso doble*, moving like Ava Gardner in *The Barefoot Contessa*.

The bar clapped. Old ladies lifted their skirts and whirled. Michael Caine became Mike; Susannah, Susie; Elizabeth, Liz. And Richard went to the rescue of the young ones who sat around munching soggy straws in Coca-Cola or else stood in the doorway, looking rather lost and bewildered by the pell-mell screech of so many adults suddenly gone mad. "Right then," he called out. "Who's for a ride in the car?" Then, like some pie-eyed piper, he led them skipping into the back of the Bible-black Rolls, where the volume control of the stereo and television became marked with grubby fingerprints as chauffeur Gaston Sanz, inscrutable behind dark shades, drove them round and round the block to the blare of pop music and a children's TV cartoon called *Magic Roundabout*. "Yer a right sweetheart," said a silver-haired grandmother named Hilda, holding Richard's face in her hands and giving him a juicy kiss that Cockneys know as "tongue sandwich."

In the background Richard saw Elizabeth with tear traces in her eyes. "It's nothing, love," she whispered. "It's just that I went into the 'ladies' and found this man." Richard eyed the young man whom Elizabeth was gently supporting by the arm, and then he observed a pair of crutches against the wall. Then he ordered him a drink, and the landlady explained that the man used the women's toilet because he couldn't easily reach the men's outside loo. Elizabeth stayed with him for a while, listening with deep sympathy to his case history and wondering how she might help. So much, she knew, could be done in modern medicine, especially if you could get the best specialists. But then she was called to one side, and it was quietly explained to her that the man had terminal cancer. There was nothing to be done.

Richard put a comforting arm around her, and Charlie the electrician softly serenaded them on his squeeze-box. More children were gathering around them now—older ones fresh out of school and jealous of their baby brothers guzzling free Cokes and riding high-hat in a Rolls. One little boy called Jason sat on Richard's knee and was treated to a brief and powerful résumé of the story of *Jason and the Golden Fleece*. He didn't even know who Richard Burton was, and he couldn't understand why a soppy girl from his school was going around inviting boys to "kiss the lips that kissed the lips that kissed Elizabeth Taylor." But he liked the steady flow of Cokes-and-crisps that went unchecked until adults started to harmonize in the chorus of "The Party's Over" and then drove off to the studios for more vodka and brandy in "Burton's Bar."

Hours later, beautifully anesthetized, we groped our way in darkness down the unlit steps of the studio fire escape. Elizabeth, ever alert, showed the way, and everyone safely reached the car —everyone, that is, except Richard. At the top of the fire-escape steps, like an anthracite statue, he stood poised to make one last great speech on St. David's Day.

"Quiet now," he cried. "Listen, will you? You are about to hear something quite extraordinary."

We never did hear. On the first syllable of his unidentifiable soliloquy, Elizabeth held her hand on the horn of the black Rolls. Honnnnnnnnnk! Honnnnnnnnnk! Honnnnnnnnnk! The hooting was deafening and unanswerable except by startled owls. Every time the din stopped and Richard drew fresh breath, the hooting resumed, again and again, filling the night with wild spiraling pigeons and horribly vulgar sounds. The actor was on center stage and for once was rendered totally impotent. He got mad and waved his arms. He refused to quit his stand.

After an eternity of hooting and honking, Elizabeth screamed out long, loud, and clear: "Richarrrrrd!" At last he yielded and joined us in the car. The Rolls purred into the night with Richard, Elizabeth, Liza, and Gaston at the wheel, sporting as ever his navy-blue blazer with a breast-pocket badge gilded with Prince of Wales feathers and the legend "Ich Dien Wales."

Richard, nicely warmed for poetry and pugnacious prose and game for all-night revelry, squirmed with frustration as Elizabeth and Liza mocked his passion for the great day of Wales. Their day was over. It had been a huge success, and now they just wanted to snuggle down in bed and watch color television. But not Richard. "It's St. David's Day," he rasped again and again. "Can't you women understand? Oh sweet day, so cool, so calm, so bright. . . ." They giggled in the back like schoolgirls.

"Shut your mouths, will you?" he snarled. Mother and daughter snuggled up to one another, helpless with laughter.

"Christ almighty!" Richard exclaimed. "Here I am, a Welshman on St. David's Day, isolated in a car with a ruddy Irishman, an Englishman, a Frenchman, and two whacky, hysterical American dames."

Gaston grinned. Liza screeched. And Richard growled, "Shut up, Liza Wilding Burton!"

"You're so pixilated," said Elizabeth, "that you're getting my husbands mixed up." The girls laughed louder than ever.

The Rolls pulled up in a narrow north London street on the verge of Hampstead Heath, alongside a Georgian house fresh with bright paint but modest in setting and size. A few paces took us from the pavement, through a tiny hallway, and straight into the lounge. The room was comfortably contemporary and unremarkable except for one shattering, overwhelming detail. The walls were a breathtaking kaleidoscope of Tate and Guggenheim. Wherever the eye fell it stumbled in wonder on originals—classic works instantly familiar but previously unseen except as cheap reproductions. A Van Gogh here, a Monet there. Upstairs and downstairs. A huge Modigliani in the lounge. Utrillos in the hall.

Elizabeth led us around the Aladdin's cave of art treasures. "I gave Richard the Van Gogh and the Monet. And do you see that Utrillo? It's a painting of the Chateau de Chillon by Lake Geneva where Richard and I used to meet after *Cleopatra*. We managed to pick it up at an auction. And that little one there, that's a Noel Coward, and. . . ." In a corner of one of the bedrooms more framed paintings and sketches were piled up on the floor. Elizabeth sorted them out. "Now here we have our own work—that one's by Liza, this one by Michael, and here's an original Elizabeth Burton."

Mother and daughter kissed Richard good night and left him to part with St. David's Day in sweet sorrow. The master of the house stretched out in an armchair, relaxed and mellow. A month before he had completed his first criminal role in *Villain*, and he had filled in the remaining weeks by making a film of *Under Milk Wood*, with Peter O'Toole as Captain Cat and Elizabeth as Rosie Probert. "A wicked devil that O'Toole. *Villain*'s my second time in the part of a queer and he said to me, 'It looks as though you've cornered the limp-wrist market, duckie.' "

We complimented him on his charming "family album" of old masters and suggested that he hadn't done too badly since the days he was working in the Co-op as a thirty-bob-a-week outfitter's apprentice. He smiled. "No, love, not too badly. We have our bad years and good years. One year we got something quite extraordinary, like £4 million, nontaxable. But last year we got nothing because we took the year off. This year? I don't know. I've got my Tito and Trotsky to do. Anyway, we must be out of the country by next week or it will cost us a million or two in taxes."

He filled our glasses once again and slotted a tape recording of *Under Milk Wood* into his stereo cassette player. "Just listen to this," he whispered. "It's quite remarkable how Elizabeth has got the Welsh accent. And O'Toole is absolutely marvelous." But it was only Richard, as the First Narrator, that we heard. Out into the semidarkness tumbled a mighty avalanche of melodious words that bombarded and stunned the senses. "To begin at the beginning: It is a spring, moonless night in the small town, starless and Bible-black, the cobblestreets silent and the hunched, courters'-and-rabbits' wood limping invisible down to the sloeblack, slow, black, crowblack, fishingboat-bobbing sea. The houses are as blind as moles. . . ." All consciousness of time and reality vanished in the spell of enchantment cast by the magic of cascading tu-wit-tu-woo sounds, and when it ended, all was still and silent.

Dylan Thomas of the wild Welsh genius had originally written that inspired narration for the tympanic resonance and tremulous sweetness of Richard's tongue, and now great waves of nostalgia swept over the richest and most famous son of Wales. He looked broodingly into his tall vodka glass. His mind was back in the valleys, back in the far-removed world of his childhood.

"There's nobody like us, I tell you. And by the way, you haven't included in the book that story about my father. Beautiful he was, sitting outside the Miner's Arms on a Saturday night. After he'd had a few jars, he would fix his stupendously stoned eyes on his fellow miners and say in Welsh: *'Pwy sy'n fel ni?'*

"And they would answer, *'Neb.'*

" *'Pwy sy'n fel fi?'*

" *'Neb.'*

" 'Who is like us?'

" 'Nobody.'

" 'Who is like me?'

" 'Nobody.' "